# PERCEPTION AND COMMUNICATION

# PERCEPTION
# AND
# COMMUNICATION

## D. E. BROADBENT

*Applied Psychology Research Unit of the Medical Research Council, Cambridge*

## PERGAMON PRESS

OXFORD · LONDON · NEW YORK · PARIS

PERGAMON PRESS LTD.
*Headington Hill Hall, Oxford*
*4 & 5 Fitzroy Square, London, W.1*
PERGAMON PRESS INC.
*122 East 55th Street, New York 22, N.Y.*
GAUTHIER-VILLARS ED.
*55 Quai des Grands-Augustins, Paris 6*
PERGAMON PRESS G.m.b.H.
*Kaiserstrasse 75, Frankfurt am Main*


Distributed in the Western Hemisphere by
THE MACMILLAN COMPANY · NEW YORK
pursuant to a special arrangement with
Pergamon Press Limited

First published 1958

Reprinted 1964

Library of Congress Card Number 58–11832

Reprinted in Poland

# CONTENTS

CHAPTER                                                     PAGE

1. Introduction: Hearing and Behaviour . . . 1

2. Selective Listening to Speech. . . . . 11

3. Verbal and Bodily Response . . . . . 36

4. The Assessment of Communications Channels for Ease of Listening . . . . . . 68

5. The Effects of Noise on Behaviour . . . . 81

6. The General Nature of Vigilance . . . . 108

7. Some Data on Individual Differences . . . 140

8. The Nature of Extinction . . . . . 174

9. Immediate Memory and the Shifting of Attention . 210

10. The Selective Nature of Learning . . . . 244

11. Recent Views on Skill . . . . . . 268

12. Retrospect and Prospect . . . . . 297

References . . . . . . . 317

Name Index . . . . . . . 333

Subject Index . . . . . . . 337

# CHAPTER 1

# INTRODUCTION: HEARING AND BEHAVIOUR

THE recent appearance in a new version of a justly celebrated work on visual perception (Vernon 1952) makes only too clear how far the study of hearing by psychologists has lagged behind that of vision. The following pages are in no way an attempt to carry out for hearing the task which Vernon has performed for vision: even if the writer felt himself capable of such a task, the corresponding material for the ear is simply not available. We have a great deal of data on the sensory mechanisms and psychophysics of the ear (Stevens and Davis 1938; Wever 1949); yet this type of information is excluded by Vernon, and she is interested rather in the organization of patterns of stimulation into the final experience and response. It is at this level that such classic visual problems of psychology as apparent movement, the constancies, or reversible figures, all arise. A multitude of experiments have been performed on them and provide a sound basis for a broad review; but no corresponding classic problems have arisen from hearing. The nearest approach to equivalent work using the ear rather than the eye is provided by the excellent and detailed studies which have been made of the cues necessary for speech sounds to be intelligible, particularly through a background of noise. Much of this work deals with perception proper, but it has already been most adequately reviewed (Fletcher 1953; Miller 1951), and a further survey would be redundant.

Besides the work on masking and intelligibility of speech, there are a number of isolated aspects of auditory perception which have received attention: for example, the work of Deutsch (1951) on an after-effect of auditory stimulation, which Deutsch suggests may be parallel to the figural after-effects in vision. There are not yet sufficient of these researches in hearing to form the basis of a book comparable to Vernon's; but they provide the hope of such a book in the future. During the past few years the writer has been engaged in research on one such limited aspect, and has investigated it in some detail. Certain of the individual experiments have been published by themselves, but the nature of the

1

problem is such that the purpose and results of each experiment can only be fully appreciated in the light of all the others. The present book is therefore an attempt to provide a general view of the whole line of research, and so to render more easy the task of some future writer who may synthesize the whole field of auditory perception. If an eminent example is to be taken, it would be, not Vernon's book, but rather that of Michotte (1946) which deals with a group of varied experiments centred upon the problem of visually perceived causality. The example is, of course, too eminent: in the ultimate text book of auditory perception the work recounted here will be fortunate if it receives a paragraph. But the target aimed at is to resemble Michotte's work rather than that of Vernon.

## The Value of Auditory Studies

It might well be urged at this point that the reason for the relative neglect of hearing is simply that this sense is comparatively unimportant in man: vision is the most highly developed sense, and therefore the most likely to yield information of psychological importance. Although such an objection would probably never be pushed to the extreme of neglecting hearing altogether, answering it will lead us conveniently to the statement of the writer's particular field of interest, and it may therefore be worth considering. There is no doubt that vision is truly a more important sense for some purposes than hearing is: if we adopt the distinction drawn by Sherrington (1906) between consummatory and precurrent functions, we may interest ourselves in the role of the great cranial receptors as allowing detection and reaction at a distance to environmental events which would otherwise receive no response. Thus food is grasped by a primitive organism only after physical contact, while an animal with vision will see and pursue food from a distance. Sherrington's view, which is closely related to distinctions made by modern students of animal behaviour such as Tinbergen (1951), expresses a true difference between higher and lower forms of life, and on this view vision is clearly important. The precision with which distant events can be located in vision is greater than that possible through hearing. But this development of vision takes place at an evolutionary level below that of man: questions concerning the innate character of, for instance, depth perception, are frequently and legitimately answered from animal experiments. Hearing, on the other hand, is used for a function which is much more highly developed in man than even in the primates: notably communication. Although a brain which can listen to speech can usually also read it, it is the ear which is primary in the development of language and written alphabets are secondary.

The distinction between communication and appetitive (or precurrent) behaviour seems as great as that between the latter and consummatory acts. Many writers have emphasized the importance of language to man: we may take Kubie (in von Foerster 1952) as a recent example. And even though some S–R theorists, such as Seward (1948), have contended that no function is involved in speech which does not also appear in animals; yet there is clearly a quantitative difference between the incidence of such symbolic functions in man and that in other species. Hull (1952) makes it clear that he considers some of the inadequacies of S–R theory when applied to man to be due to the complications produced by language: for example, he appeals to language to explain the importance of latent learning in man as compared with animals. By studying, therefore, the sense with which language is most closely linked we may help to attack some of the most complex human functions. In fact many of the experiments to be described involve the perception of speech, and shed some light on the differences between verbal and bodily responses. These differences are left as a problem for further research by Hull (1952).

There is, however, a second and more compelling reason for studying hearing. In the eye, peripheral processes of sensory adjustment play a great role. A complex stimulus is perceived far more accurately when it falls on the fovea than on the periphery. In the ear sensory adjustment is clearly less important: there are of course two known adjustments, that of the tensor tympani muscle which tightens and slackens the drum, and that of turning the head to give the least obstructed incidence to a particular sound. It would also have been unwise to assume too confidently that no other sensory adjustments are present simply because none are known: but evidence will be presented (in Chapter 9) to show that any such adjustments are not of great importance in the situations used in this work. This greater freedom from peripheral complication is chiefly of importance when more than one stimulus is involved. If we wish to study the visual perception of a shape it is fairly easy to arrange that the shape appears at the point which the subject is fixating. But if we present two shapes at once in different places, any effect on the subject's perception is obviously complicated by the relative distance of the shape from the fovea, the possibility of eye movements, and so on. In another type of situation, it is of little interest if we find that a task is performed equally well in the presence or absence of some visual stimulus: since sensory adjustment may ensure that the latter never affects the worker's nervous system. But a high intensity noise is not to be shut out in this way, and must produce (or fail to produce) its effect by interaction within the nervous system. Hearing is especially suited to studies of interaction between two or more stimuli.

Such studies are at the moment of great potential importance. To appeal again to Sherrington (1906), one of the most powerful tools in the examination of spinal reflexes has been the interaction between reflexes elicited simultaneously or successively. For example, a scratch reflex following stimulation of the left shoulder appears at first sight to involve only the left side of the body: but when both shoulders are stimulated at once it is found that only one scratch reflex can be elicited. In fact the full response involves not only rhythmic motion of the legs on the same side as the stimulus, but also (and less detectably) extension of the opposite leg. The latter component of the reflex is incompatible with a scratch reflex on the opposite side. Much of Sherrington's analysis involves arguing from such facts of interference and alliance between reflexes, to the nervous mechanisms necessary for such interaction. As Konorski (1948) has well pointed out, similar argument is possible in more complex behaviour and has been surprisingly neglected. Konorski considers some of the possibilities in classical conditioned reflexes: the writer has been occupied in studying effects on perception. Such a development is in accordance with Sherrington's own thinking: his last chapter is devoted to topics of binocular rivalry and fusion, and earlier in the book he makes the striking statement that ' the interference of unlike reflexes and the alliance of like reflexes in their action upon their common paths seem to lie at the very root of the great psychical forces of attention '.

There are two reasons why this line of approach is particularly topical at the present day. The first of them is a theoretical one: the current popularity of language, derived from communication theory, for the statement of psychological problems. Owing perhaps to the accident that psychologists working on hearing are naturally those in closest contact with telephone engineers, this popularity has been at its greatest in the auditory field. It may well be that too much has been expected from a purely linguistic device, which by itself will not provide the answer to the problems of psychology—Gregory (1953) has rightly pointed out that considering the brain as a computing machine produces the old problem of ' atomism or Gestalt ? ' in the new language of ' digital or analogue ?'. But new vocabularies do involve some shift in basic assumptions, and perhaps the point of permanent value which will remain in psychology if the fashion for communication theory wanes, will be the emphasis on problems of *capacity.* The latter, in communication theory, is a term representing the limiting quantity of information which can be transmitted through a given channel in a given time: if we send Morse code with a buzzer we cannot send a dot and a dash at the same time but must send them successively. An array of $x$ buzzers would allow us to send $x$ dots and dashes at once, provided we had a listener who could distinguish them.* The fact that any given channel has a limit is a matter of central importance to communication engineers, and it is correspondingly forced on the attention of psychologists who use their terms. Any hypothetical account of brain function must in future consider on the one hand the size of the brain (how many buzzers there are) and on the other hand the rate at which that brain will make reactions to a given set of incoming stimuli (the number of dots and dashes per second).

---

* We will give an amplified account of capacity in Chapter 3, but still in non-technical and therefore inexact terms. For precise definitions of this and other terms in communication theory, reference should be made to the excellent glossary given by MacKay (in von Foerster 1952). All such terms are used in this book with MacKay's definitions, though they are introduced in popular language.

This possibility, that one chain of events physically excludes another, has been somewhat neglected in physiology and psychology, though not of course completely. Sherrington is a striking instance to the contrary, since his account of competition between different reflexes for common paths is essentially based on questions of capacity. But any account in which completely separate neural areas or pathways are postulated for different activities, neglects the possible use of the concept of capacity to explain the interference of these activities: and these types of account are common. Pavlovian theory, for instance, seems to take this path. As will be seen shortly, behaviour theory has similarly neglected the possibilities of incompatibility between different activities.

The second reason for taking the effects of simultaneous stimulation as a topical problem is an empirical one. There has recently been a considerable increase in the study of human performance in situations more life-like than those of classical psychology. This has caused Hull (1952), for example, to include amongst his theorems a derivation of skilled movement from his theoretical postulates. Yet, desirable though it is that scientific psychology should form a unity, the problem which Hull attacks is not one which most workers on skill regard as important. He shows that a particular stimulus will, on his postulates, tend to produce an exact and quantitatively graded response. But the feature of skill which impresses itself most strongly on its investigators is that the skilled worker has available at the same time a whole family of different possible responses. The relationships between the members of this family are, on the observational level, distinct from the accuracy or other qualities of each member. For instance, Bartlett (in Floyd and Welford 1953) points out that continued performance or ' fatigue ' alters the succession or integration of responses rather than their individual qualities. A number of experimental findings of this sort will be referred to later: and their combined effect is to establish the interaction of simultaneous activities as a considerable factual problem.

Hull would, no doubt, have hoped at a later stage to deduce these principles of interaction from his postulates. Equally theorists of nervous mechanism may hope to produce a model of brain function which will explain them. Yet the writer cannot feel that satisfactory explanations can be produced until the facts to be explained are established. This is a view of scientific method which differs sharply from that of many behaviour theorists, and will need further justification; it is noted at this stage merely to introduce the general plan of this book, in which accounts of experiments will usually precede their discussion theoretically. Theorists of nervous mechanisms are perhaps less likely to complain of such an arrangement than behaviour theorists are: it is not unusual to find them saying like Adrian (1954) that ' we must find out what human behaviour is like before we try to explain how it is produced '.

We thus reach the position that studies of multiple stimulation are interesting both because they have recently emerged from various investigations of skill as a factual problem: and because theories must now consider them more than in the past. They are readily carried out through the ear, and this book contains a number of experiments on this topic. It also contains some views on the theoretical implications of these findings, and on the peculiar nature of language: and before turning to the first experimental results we should perhaps indicate the general direction in which such results will afterwards be used for theory.

## Perception and Behaviour Theory

The topic of perception has recently become far more closely related to the rest of behaviour than it used to be. This tendency was implicit in such work as that of Bartlett (1932) or of Sherif (1936), but similar experiments on the effects of motives or social pressures upon perception are now more numerous. With this development the writer is strongly in agreement. From a biological point of view we can hardly consider the structure of experience without its function: yet none the less there are reasons for questioning whether we should study the effects of other functions on perception rather than the effects of perception on other functions.

The classical type of perception experiment is eminently suitable for fields in which all subjects behave similarly, in which the subjects possess an accurate vocabulary for describing their experience, and in which a fairly brief experience is followed by an interval in which it may be described. But these are severe limitations, particularly the last: the closer we come to the problems of everyday life the harder it is to stay within them. It then becomes necessary to set the subject some objectively scorable task, and to find how performance on this task is affected by various stimulus situations: and this is in fact the method used in all the experiments to be described.

Such a technique, in which the behaviour of a subject may be recorded for hours at a time, and in which his own account of his performance does not take a central place in the results, resembles the methods of animal psychologists rather than those of, say, the Gestaltists in perception. It remains true of such writers as Hull, as Bartlett said of the behaviourists in 1932, that they have on the whole been more faithful to the functional point of view than their competitors: and to those who hold that the performance of tasks is a more normal feature of human activity than disembodied experience or judgment are, the work of behaviour theorists must be of great interest. It is therefore to this work that our experiments on auditory perception will be related. The line pursued will sometimes again be one once suggested by Bartlett: that of giving a functional statement (acceptable to behaviour theorists) of problems which they now ignore.

What possible contribution, however, can studies of simultaneous stimulation make to behaviour theory? They are in fact a vital preliminary to any such theory. On Hull's view and certain others, for example, it is asserted that every time a stimulus is followed by a response and the combination is then followed by a reduction in drive, the response will in future be more likely to appear following that stimulus (the ' reinforcement postulate '). This assertion is contrary to a number of experiments, of which we may take one from Pavlov (1927) as a typical example. A dog is presented with a touch and a heat stimulus, and then with food. Eventually it develops a conditioned salivary response appearing even in the absence of food: this response will appear to touch and heat together or to touch alone, but not to heat alone. Yet if heat and food were paired, without the presence of touch, a conditioned response could quite well be established to heat. Clearly in the first part of the experiment, repeated presentation of heat plus salivation plus food, had not established salivation to the heat stimulus, and a simple interpretation of the reinforce-ment postulate is therefore false. Hull was of course perfectly well aware of this difficulty, and therefore also asserted that when two stimuli act together the consequences may be different from the sum of those following each stimulus alone (the postulate of ' afferent stimulus interaction '). But as no conditions were specified under which this interaction would or would not take place, and as there are always far more than two stimuli acting on any actual organism, this extra postulate immediately made it impossible to disprove any part of Hull's theory.

Afferent interaction has frequently been criticized previously: see, for instance, Hilgard (1948). Such criticism has usually been directed against the inadequacy of the postulate to deal with the complexity of perception, and against the fallacy of assigning a neural name to a psychological problem. It was to meet this latter class of objection that Hull (1952) changed the name of the concept to stimulus interaction instead of neural interaction. But the further objection, that afferent interaction makes the entire system untestable, has not perhaps been urged so strenuously: since Hull himself did not in fact make great use of the concept as an escape from experimental testing. When experiments were reported in which simple reinforcement theory seemed inadequate, he was more likely to appeal either to ' secondary reinforcement ' (the transfer of reinforcing power from innately drive reducing situations to stimuli which happen to have been present during such situations) or else to internal and unobservable reactions, which are common to the act now performed and to one which had been reinforced. Afferent interaction seems genuinely to have been used only in cases in which the stimulus was a Gestalt, such as a musical scale, and it was not brought in as an escape clause in other difficulties.

Yet logically it might have been so used. The problem of learning may be stated in simple terms as this: why does an organism learn one reaction rather than another? Hull's answer was, that reactions followed by reinforcement are learned but others are not. Other answers have been given by other theorists, but on the experimental level all are agreed that consummatory acts have some strong connexion with learning. On closer analysis, however, it is found that a reward acts on learning, primarily through its role as a stimulus rather than by satisfying biological need. Thus for example Sheffield and Roby (1950) have shown that a response can be learned if it is rewarded by saccharin solution, and Sheffield, Wolff and Backer (1951) that copulation without ejaculation is an effective reward. An interesting reconsideration of motivation in the light of this and further similar evidence has been given by Deutsch (1953).

But if we must now hold that reward acts as a certain kind of stimulus, then the principles governing afferent stimulus interaction (or simultaneous stimulation, or whatever name we choose for these phenomena) become critically important. For example, we might put forward the view that all stimuli compete to enter a learning mechanism of limited capacity, that reward stimuli are especially likely to win in this competition, and therefore that situations involving reward are most likely to be learned. In such a type of theory afferent stimulus interaction would by itself account for the fact that rewarded responses are learned more readily than unrewarded ones. A similar view has in fact long been advanced by Tolman (see, for instance, Tolman and Postman in Stone 1954), though without making use of a concept of capacity: the special role of reward is referred to as ' perceptual emphasis ', which is probably an unacceptable phrase to many S–R theorists.

Studies of simultaneous stimulation, then, must be carried out before any truly testable theory of behaviour can be formulated. No theory can be adequately tied to observation if it is imprecise about the rules governing stimulus reception. Our present line of enquiry is therefore of distinct relevance to behaviour theory; and although the fact that human subjects are used throughout may seem to introduce an extra complication, the peculiarities of human beings and the advantages of using them may be illuminated by these experiments.

Let us now turn to more factual matters, having prepared the mind of the reader to perceive some aspects of the experiments rather than others; and let us first consider some experiments on the importance of such preparation.

# CHAPTER 2

# SELECTIVE LISTENING TO SPEECH

THE experiments which we will consider first in this chapter are intended to show that listening to two messages does in fact reveal effects which are not purely sensory, and which therefore may be of general interest. After establishing this, we will review the existing literature on selective listening. Many of the results are not yet related to any theoretical interpretation, but will be given for the sake of completeness. As a result parts of the chapter may be more useful for reference than for straightforward reading. Some attempt will however be made to classify the results in a meaningful fashion: but the reader whose interest is primarily theoretical will find the essence of the chapter in the final section on ' Conclusions '.

## *Experiments showing Central Effects*

Broadly speaking, there are two possible ways in which experiments on listening to speech may be carried out. One of these is to require the listener to say or write the message which he has heard. The other way is to put the message in the form of a question and to require an answer. These techniques are not always regarded as differing in any important way; but there are some reasons for thinking that the difference should be kept in mind. The reasons will be examined in the next chapter. For the moment, we may note that experiments on listening to two or more speech channels at the same time have been carried out by both methods. The first ones to be considered here, however, used the question-and-answer technique; they are described in papers by Broadbent (1952b, c).

A set of questions may be devised by showing the listener a piece of paper divided into numbered sections, each bearing some familiar geometrical symbol such as a circle or a cross. Questions of the type ' Is there a cross in section two ?' may then be answered unambiguously ' Yes ' or ' No '. Scoring the answers thus presents no difficulties, and when questions are asked in a normal fashion most listeners can rapidly reach perfect performance on the task. If, however, two questions are asked simultaneously, great difficulty will be met.

While this is a matter of common observation, it is not clear from everyday experience where the difficulty appears. We know that any sound reaching the ear may be ' masked ' by another sound and so fail to be heard. This masking appears in the auditory nerve response (Galambos and Davis 1944; Rosenblith 1950), and is very slight when one sound is in one ear and the other sound in the other ear. That is, masking takes place in the sense-organ itself. It might have been the cause of the difficulty of answering two questions at once; and if so, experiments on selective listening would offer little of interest for general psychology.

But two experiments show that this is not so: the difficulty is not a sensory one. The first of these experiments is to consider the effect of various instructions on performance. To do this, the two voices which ask the questions are given names, and the listener is told that when two questions are asked at once he is only to answer one of them. The experimenter announces, for each pair of questions, which voice is to be answered (using a visual indication): and he does so either before or after the two questions are asked. The former condition produces better results than the latter; indeed, listeners who get the visual signal after the questions have been asked, don't perform significantly better than listeners who have no visual signal at all.

It follows from these results that some mechanism within the listener discards part of the information reaching the ear. If this were not so, then a visual signal after the question would be as good as one before. On the other hand, the information discarded must vary with the experience of the listener, in this case, the visual signal. If this were not so, there would be no effect of the signal at all. But the peripheral masking mechanism does not fit these requirements. It certainly discards part of the incoming information, but the part discarded is determined by the intensities and frequencies of the sounds present. Consequently a visual signal could only influence masking by some adjustment of the sense-organ which would alter these parameters. As was noted in the last chapter, the two principal known adjustments consist of rotation of the head and tightening of the ear-drum. The former is excluded by presenting both the messages through a single loudspeaker: the latter is unlikely to affect one voice and not another arriving simultaneously.  Such an effect is perhaps just conceivable even if unlikely, and there might be some other unknown sensory adjustment.  The following experiment is therefore necessary as a check on the first one.

The reason for suspecting masking when two questions are heard at once, is that the two sets of sounds reach the ear at the same time.  But if we stretch out each question, the gaps between words may be made longer, and it becomes possible to fit each word of one question into a gap between two words of the other question.  The listener would then hear a series of words rather of the following kind: is is the my cat aunt on in the the mat garden? It is harder to answer the question ' Is the cat on the mat? ' when it forms part of such a jumble of words.  Yet no masking can be taking place.  The difficulty is therefore clearly one within the central nervous system.

A number of variations on this experiment are possible: thus the listener may be required to answer both questions or only to answer one, the voices used may be the same or different, and so on.  The results will be described later, but one point of procedure should perhaps be noted at once.  This is that the original experiments did not use ordinary English.  The illustrative phrase ' Is the cat on the mat? ' contains words of widely differing importance, and there are transition probabilities between words which would clearly be upset by inserting other words.  For example, in ordinary English the probability of hearing the word ' the ' twice running is almost negligible. Similar considerations apply to the sequence ' the my '.  Now it has been established experimentally that the probability of a listener hearing a word correctly varies with the probability of that word occurring in the particular situation.  Thus Miller, Heise and Lichten (1951) showed that, under fixed conditions of signal and noise, a listener was less likely to hear a word correctly if he knew it was one of a large number of alternatives, as compared with his performance when he knew the word must have been one of a small number of alternatives.  Similarly, it has long been known that ordinary sentences (which, as stated above, exclude certain sequences of words) are more often heard correctly than a meaningless series of words: see, for instance, Fletcher (1953).

Consequently the experiment of alternating words from two messages would disrupt established speech habits if ordinary language was used, and therefore a code was used in which the transition probabilities were not altered when alternation was introduced. The code was also unfamiliar, so that neither condition was favoured by past experience. Full details are given by Broadbent (1952c).

There are various other experiments which show the importance of factors beyond simple sensory ones. For example Poulton (1953a) has shown that calls over radio channels are more likely to be missed if they are preceded and followed by other irrelevant signals. Again, Cherry (1953) has shown that a listener can, after repeated presentations, separate out two different speech passages recorded by the same voice on the same tape; but that this is not possible if the passages consist merely of streams of clichés. The listener is apparently making use of the transition probabilities between words and phrases, a factor which is clearly not sensory.

We see, then, that the suggestion put forward in the last chapter is being partially fulfilled: experiments on listening to more than one stimulus do reveal difficulties which are central in origin, and may, therefore, apply to senses other than the ear. The next step is to examine the results of experiments on selective listening. Any classification of the situations which have been studied is somewhat arbitrary, but to some extent three kinds of situation can be distinguished. The first of these covers experiments on listening and replying to both of two messages; the second concerns experiments on listening to one message while ignoring other irrelevant sounds. The third case is that in which a jumble of relevant and irrelevant messages arrive, and the listener must monitor them all in order to pick out and answer the relevant ones.

*Listening to two messages at once.*—The results from all the selective listening experiments include, as has been said, many items of isolated interest. But there are two general trends in the results. One of these is the question of the effect on the listener of varying the amount of information presented. To some extent this is equivalent to increasing or decreasing the amount of simultaneous stimulation, but not altogether so.

Modern communication theory regards information as increasing not only with the number of messages received but also with decrease in the probability of each message: that is, with increase in the number of the messages that might have been sent. To revert to the example given in the first chapter, of the buzzer sending dots and dashes, a given dash will convey one unit of information (known as a ' bit ') when the alternative is only a dot. But if we may send out at any moment a dash or a dot, either high-pitched or low-pitched, then a given dash conveys two bits. This is of the first importance, because as will be seen, the performance of selective listeners seems to vary with information as defined by communication theory, rather than with amount of stimulation in the conventional sense.

The second general theme of the results concerns the physical means by which messages are presented. When some of the information is to be discarded, as in the first experiment we considered, it usually seems desirable for that information to reach the listener by a different sensory channel. By ' channel ' we may mean ' sense-organ ', but not always so, since some of the best illustrations of the effect come from the role of auditory localization. Sounds reaching the two ears are of course often perceived as coming from different directions, although the sense-organs affected are the same: and such sounds we shall regard as arriving by different ' channels '.

Let us turn now to the particular situation of listening to two messages at once. All workers appear to agree that increase in the amount of information presented causes a relative decline in efficiency. That is, a smaller proportion of the incoming messages is handled adequately. This does not of course imply that the absolute number of correct answers in a given time declines: if a man works at exactly the same rate in two situations, he will do relatively worse in the situation which demands more.

Thus Webster and Thompson (1953, 1954) found that the greater the amount of overlap between two messages the lower the relative efficiency. But they also analysed the absolute amount of information passing through the listener, and this analysis gave rather different results. Their messages consisted of a call-sign section followed by three English words to be repeated. The call-sign could only be one of a small number of possibilities, while the words were chosen from a large vocabulary and so were less predictable. Thus each call-sign conveyed only little information (fifteen bits) while the words conveyed much (forty bits). Now when messages overlapped, the number of words repeated in a given time was the same as with messages that did not overlap: the output of information was the same although the input was increased. But the number of call-signs correctly identified did increase with overlapping messages. The increase was not as large as the increase in information presented, but it seems to imply that messages conveying little information may be dealt with simultaneously, while those containing much information may not. This point is very relevant to the idea of a limited capacity for the nervous system, which was touched on in the last chapter; and the question will be raised again. For the moment, we may note that the statement ' one cannot do two tasks at once ' must depend on what is meant by the word ' task '.

Poulton (1956) also found a drop in relative efficiency when two relevant messages arrived simultaneously, as compared with isolated messages or with the simultaneous arrival of relevant and irrelevant messages. He used a message consisting of a simple call-sign (two bits) which distinguished the relevant from the irrelevant messages, followed by three digits to be written down. It is interesting to note that the effect of overlapping as opposed to synchronous messages was in his results slight, ' though in the expected direction '; this might be because the overlap condition meant only that the call-sign of one message had to be received at the same time as the digits of the other. As the call-sign carried little information this would put little extra load on the listener.

Poulton distinguishes mishearings from omissions, in scoring all his experiments, the former being influenced more by sensory factors and the latter by central ones. But mishearings were significantly more frequent when answering two messages at once than when listening to one relevant and one irrelevant call. This applied even when the messages were overlapping rather than synchronous. The chief source of error was mixing up of digits from one message with those from the other, which is of course a rather different error from any due to sensory masking. Both types of error appeared as often in the first message of an overlapping pair as in the second. Webster and Thompson found more errors in the second message, but this may be because they were scoring only call-signs in that part of their work. Naturally the call-sign of the second message is more affected than that of the first. But this may not be the only factor operative.

The writer has used the alternate word technique, mentioned at the beginning of the chapter, with the instructions to answer both the interleaved messages. Efficiency is less than when answering only one of them. In another condition two successive messages, not interleaved, were presented and the subject allowed to answer only after both the questions had finished. Performance when answering both messages was again worse than when answering only one of them. Once again, increasing the amount of information reaching the listener in a given time appears to reduce his efficiency. But it should be noted that the interleaved messages were harder than the successive messages even when both were to be answered. In this case the information passed through the listener is the same under either condition, but it will be shown in the next chapter that the successive messages case requires a smaller capacity.

All these experiments, then, agree in general that an increase in the amount of information presented will not produce a corresponding increase in the amount of information assimilated. To some extent, two messages may be dealt with simultaneously if they convey little information. But there is a limit to the amount of information which a listener can absorb in a certain time, that is, he has a limited capacity.

If we now turn to the physical conditions, we find that Poulton varied the spatial arrangement of the loudspeakers which delivered his messages. He compared the use of two loudspeakers one above the other, two loudspeakers on the listener's right front and left front at about 90° separation, and four speakers arranged equidistantly between the right and left front positions. In the latter condition only two speakers could be active at once, but the combination varied. There were no differences between any of these conditions.

Webster and Thompson similarly found little effect of spatial arrangement. They compared a system in which all messages passed through one loudspeaker, and a system in which six separate speakers were used. Both were used with and without ' pull-down ', which is an arrangement whereby one channel is brought to a head-phone or small loudspeaker close to one of the listener's ears. Without pull-down the two spatial arrangements did not differ. But when the simultaneous messages differed markedly in loudness it was found that pull-down was helpful with either one or six other speakers. When the two messages were of markedly different loudness, the best arrangement was the single speaker with pull-down.

This topic of spatial arrangement will also appear repeatedly, since it usually produces more marked effects than it does in the case of listening to both of two messages. It should also be noted that Webster and Thompson found that the louder of two unequal messages was more likely to be heard correctly.*

*Listening to one message against irrelevant background.*—This situation is similar to that used in ordinary masking experiments, and in the numerous studies of intelligibility in noise which have already been mentioned. As we are interested only in the central processes involved in listening, we may confine ourselves to noting some of these which have dealt with the spatial arrangement of sound sources. It is often argued that auditory localization must be carried out centrally since it requires the collating of information from the two ears. This argument is not quite conclusive, since there is some evidence for a direct pathway from one ear to the other (Galambos, Rosenblith and Rosenzweig 1950). Nevertheless it is plausible and is strongly supported by the results given in Chapter 9.

Experiments on the masking of pure tones show that the interaction of the two ears gives curious and at first sight paradoxical effects. For example, it is normally true to say that two ears are better than one: that the binaural threshold is lower than the monaural threshold, or that ' binaural summation ' occurs. But if one listens for a pure tone against a background of noise, the background being heard in both ears, it may be easier to hear the pure tone when it is only in one ear than when it is in both

---

* Tolhurst and Peters (1956) have confirmed this effect for the case in which one message is on one ear and the other on the second ear.

(Hirsh 1948a). This effect has often been called ' binaural in-hibition ', but the name is perhaps unfortunate. It is greatest at low frequencies and high noise intensities.

A related effect may be shown by presenting both the tone and the noise to both ears, but altering the phase relations between the ears. Thus one can arrange the connexions to a pair of head-phones so that when the tone appears, the diaphragms on the two ears move in together towards the head, and out again together: whereas when the noise is applied to the head-phones one dia-phragm moves in while the other moves out and vice versa. We would then speak of the tone being ' in phase ' and the noise ' out of phase '. The binaural threshold for hearing the tone is lower when one sound is in phase and the other out than when both are in the same relationship (Hirsh 1948b). Once again the effect is greatest at fairly low frequencies. Licklider (1948) examined the intelligibility of speech in noise, both being pre-sented through head-phones, and found results comparable to those of Hirsh. Speech was more intelligible when it was in phase at the two ears and noise was out of phase, or when these conditions were reversed, than when both sounds had the same phase relation.

These findings all suggest that a difference in the apparent localization of the speech and noise sources makes understanding of the speech more easy. Hirsh (1950) tested this suggestion directly by delivering speech and noise through two loudspeakers instead of head-phones. The experiment was done in a special room free of echoes as well as in an ordinary room, and the positions of the speakers were varied. When two ears were used separated speakers were better than adjacent ones, or than an arrangement with one speaker in front of the head and one behind. The latter two positions are of course very likely to be confused with one another when fairly low-pitched sounds are used, since the only cue available for distinguishing front from back is the shadow of the external ear. This shadow is less definite with the low-pitched sound. Given that the localization of the loudspeakers was different, the best arrangements tended to be those in which the speech source was directly opposite one ear while the noise source was not: this arrangement gives a better signal-noise ratio, and would be expected to be best from ordinary masking principles. Allowing the head to move increased the effect of position; and replacing the head by a dummy carrying two microphones instead of ears, transmitting to a listener in the next room, gave an even smaller effect of position than on an unmoving live head. When only one ear was used the dummy head gave results largely determined by the signal-noise ratio alone, but the human head still showed a slight effect of separation.

The general conclusion, that a message can most easily be heard in noise when the sounds come from different places, is also supported by results given by Kock (1950). These include the interesting fact that intelligibility is low when the speech and noise come from places which are physically separated but which give the same difference in the time of arrival of the sound at the two ears. These are the positions which give front-back confusions in experiments on localization.

Spatial position is not the only physical variable which has been shown to affect the central process of picking out one set of sounds for response. Egan, Carterette and Thwing (1954) examined the effect of band-pass filtering when listening to one voice in the presence of another. They found that a definite advantage appeared if a high-pass filter set at 500–1000 c/s was put in one of the two channels, preferably the one which was to be ignored. (One might expect this last point as filtering naturally removes some information.) Lower cut-off frequencies, which allowed more of the natural components of the voice to pass, seemed less advantageous. These results were obtained by the ' repeating back ' type of experiment; when subjects were asked to adjust the level of the relevant speech to that at which they ' could with effort understand the meaning of almost every sentence and phrase of the connected discourse ', slightly different results were found. In this case, the level had to be increased if the relevant speech was filtered either high-pass or low-pass, and an advantage was only obtained if the irrelevant speech was filtered. It is likely that this method is not as sensitive as the ' reporting back ' or ' answering questions ' techniques: the advantages of filtering are supported by results which will be given in the next section.

These authors also applied the two messages, both unfiltered, to the same ear, and gave intelligibility tests of the ' repeating back ' type at various intensities of the relevant speech. A curve was found which would be abnormal for speech in noise. Intelligibility did not vary as the intensity of the relevant speech was decreased for 5–10 db below the point at which the relevant and irrelevant speech were equally intense. But when speech is heard in noise its intelligibility declines more or less smoothly with its intensity. It seems reasonable to interpret this discrepancy as the authors did, as owing to the fact that differences in loudness, as well as spatial position and pitch, may be used by the listener to separate the wanted and unwanted speech. Thus it is particularly hard to listen to one of two equally loud voices, and becomes easier when the relevant one is fainter: this effect opposes the normal effect of signal-noise ratio.

Characteristics of the message, as well as of the channel by which it is received, may affect accuracy. Peters (1954a, 1954b) has shown that unwanted speech which is similar in content to the wanted message produces greater difficulty than does a dissimilar background. He also found that if a message is delivered immediately before or after an unwanted one, it is less likely to be correctly heard. It is more damaging for the irrelevant information to follow the wanted message than to precede it.

In the experiments of Egan, Carterette and Thwing and of Peters the wanted and unwanted speech were both recorded on tape by the same individual so as to make more clear the effects of the other variables. The alternate word technique has been used (Broadbent 1952c) to examine the effects of different voices on picking out one sound from a babel.

The method was to instruct the subject to answer the message formed by the alternate words in a series, ignoring the intervening words. In one condition all words were spoken by the same person, while in the other condition one voice was used for the relevant words and another different voice for the irrelevant ones. The latter condition was easier. Again, therefore, a physical difference between the wanted and unwanted sounds assists the central process: the difference between two different voices will be primarily in their spectrum, though there may be slight differences of timing.

An important point is that the usefulness of the contrast between the voices does not depend on learning the pattern of one voice and sticking to it: if one is trying to listen to a voice calling itself G.D.O. and to ignore one which calls itself Turret, one can listen just as well if the two voices change their names over, so that the listener is in fact now ignoring the voice that was formerly relevant. But this applies only with moderately unfamiliar voices, and there is certainly some effect of learning the voice. This point is of particular interest because Spieth, Curtis and Webster (1954) compare the importance of physical factors in picking out a voice to Cherry's experiment on the separation of two streams of speech by the transition probabilities between words and phrases. The transition probability between two words in the same voice is greater than that between two words in different voices: but a change of voice between the end of one message and the beginning of another is also quite probable. Although there is much in this comparison, a caution should be given. This is that Cherry's subjects listened to their tape recordings over and over again, while the experiments on listening to different voices and places presented the sounds only once. Different functions are likely to appear in the two cases.

A last point is also to be learned from the alternate-word experiments: it is harder to listen to one message with irrelevant words interspersed between the relevant ones, even when the two voices differ to some extent. There seems in fact to be some sort of ' distraction ' effect. But spatial separation is more effective than simple differences of voice. Cherry (1953) in one of his experiments required subjects to repeat back continuously speech heard on one ear alone, and found that they could ignore other irrelevant words on the other ear. There may be some distractive effect from irrelevant sounds on the other ear, but it did not produce any obvious disturbance. Egan, Carterette and Thwing have given similar results in more quantitative form. Cherry's results also include a finding which is unique in this section on listening to one of two sounds: it is the only finding about the listener's awareness of the irrelevant signals. During the experiment he changed the nature of the stimulus on the ear which was to be ignored. Although that ear was first stimulated with ordinary speech, it was then given reversed speech having the same spectrum as normal speech but no words or meaning. Other subjects heard a woman's voice follow that of the man who had started the passage, others heard German words instead of English ones, and still others heard a pure tone. These changes were all reversed before the end of the session, so that the subject was only exposed to the changed stimulus during the middle of the period while he was steadily repeating the speech on the other ear. After the experiment all subjects were interrogated about the speech they had to ignore. They could say nothing about its content or even what language it was in: a few noticed ' something queer ' about reversed speech, but others did not. But the change from one voice to another was nearly always noticed, and the change to a pure tone was always noticed.

As has been said, these results of Cherry cannot be classed with those on presenting identical sounds by different means and observing the effects on efficiency. But they are clearly related to our other interest, the amount of information which a listener can absorb. Once again we cannot say simply ' a man cannot listen to two things at once '. On the contrary, he receives some information even from the rejected ear: but there is a limit to the amount, and details of the stimulus on the rejected ear are not recorded. It is especially interesting to note that the features of the rejected voice which are observed are those which are useful in picking out relevant from irrelevant words in the other experiments. Differences in voice are useful when one wants to ignore some words: equally, differences in voice are noticed even when the words are ignored.

But we must beware of supposing that the details of the rejected message can never affect behaviour. Cherry carried out some experiments in which the rejected voice was saying the same as the accepted voice, but after a considerable time delay. As the time delay was progressively reduced, a point was reached at which the listener realized that the two messages were the same. This occurred when the delay was still quite considerable: in general, between 2 and 6 sec. Thus the details of the accepted message must still be producing an effect in the nervous system after such an interval. This finding may be related to the results given in Chapter 9, or to the subject's control of his own speech by auditory feed-back (Lee 1950).

*Monitoring of several channels with response to one at a time.*— The situation which we will now consider is much closer to real life than those which have gone before. In the present case the listener hears speech from a number of different sources, but ignores any messages which are not for him. He is therefore carrying out a combination of the two simpler tasks: he may listen to two call-signs simultaneously, but then can ignore one message and deal only with the other. As before, we are interested largely in central processes which may apply to psychology in general rather than to hearing alone. It is more difficult to be sure of the relative roles of sensory and central processes in this case than it was in the simpler ones, but some such distinction can be made by considering the types of score and the effect of instructions. There are comparatively few results from this type of situation on the effect of varying the amount of information presented to the subject. Many data are to be found, however, on the familiar question of the physical methods used to present the messages: and in addition there are results on the effectiveness of certain types of message in securing response.

The spatial arrangement of the sound sources is again important. It will be remembered that spatial separation is highly beneficial when only one message is to be answered, but not when both are to receive a response. In the monitoring situation, which combines both the other tasks, separation is on the whole desirable but not altogether so. Webster and Thompson found that six channels were handled better when fed through six loudspeakers rather than one, and also that provision of ' pull-down ' facilities was helpful. Spieth, Curtis and Webster found that three loudspeakers were better than one. This was not because of differences in the quality of the sound produced by different echoes in different places, because separation was still useful when the channels were made artificially different in quality by putting different band-pass filters in the circuits. Increasing the angle of separation from 10° to 90° between neighbouring speakers was also helpful. Poulton found that when two loudspeakers were operating fairly continuously, separation was helpful if only one speaker was to be monitored but if both were to be monitored the effects were more equivocal. Fewer messages were misheard with separated speakers, but no fewer were completely missed.

He also noticed that the effects of separation were most useful when a good deal of information was being presented for acceptance or rejection: when one or both of his two loudspeakers gave only occasional calls instead of continuous conversation the advantage of separated speakers became insignificant.

Broadbent (1954b) presented pairs of messages simultaneously, only one of each pair requiring an answer.   Spatial separation of loudspeakers was a help and so also was stereophonic separation. In the latter case the two speakers were always kept apart, and both messages came from both speakers.   Under the stereophonic condition one message was delayed by about 2 msec in one speaker and the other message correspondingly delayed in the other speaker.   This gave an illusion of separated voices without the speakers actually being moved: the fact that such an effect increased efficiency affords another control against changes in quality produced by actually moving speakers, and also a control against moving the head nearer to one speaker.   Stereophonic reproduction through head-phones was also superior to a conventional mixture of voices in head-phones.   A split head-phone with one ear on each channel was inferior to a pair of loudspeakers: this difference would no doubt depend on the particular equipment used, but the point of interest is that a combination of one loudspeaker and one head-phone was as good as a pair of loudspeakers.   Thus it seems plausible that it is the possibility of head movement which is important, as it was in Hirsh's experiments: and certainly it is the relation between the two channels which matters rather than the absolute nature of either.*

Thus the conclusion about spatial separation seems to be that it is more helpful, the more nearly the situation approaches that of the listener ignoring one channel and responding to another. The effect may be less marked when the situation approaches that

* Webster and Solomon (1955) presented groups of up to four simultaneous messages, with instructions to some subjects only to answer one of them: while other subjects had to answer two.   A split head-phone was superior to the conventional type, even when filtering was introduced.   Splitting was even useful when two messages both had to be answered: but in this case there was always at least one irrelevant message as well.

of the listener dealing with two channels simultaneously. But in general it is unlikely to be positively harmful. An unpublished experiment of the writer's should be mentioned because it is the only one known to him in which a harmful effect did appear. The situation in that case was that pairs of call-signs were presented together, one of the call-signs always being the same, and the subject being instructed to answer the other one. When 2 sec were allowed between pairs, spatial separation was helpful; when only 1 sec was allowed it was not. It was positively harmful when 1 sec was allowed and the relevant call-sign had just changed channel. The interpretation of this result will be clearer when the results of Chapter 9 are considered: to anticipate, it will be argued that small quantities of information may arrive simultaneously provided enough time is allowed for the listener to respond to them successively. Thus two call-signs may be dealt with by listening to one, then shifting attention to the other call-sign and listening to that. The shift of attention takes longer when the two calls come from separate spatial positions, and if time is short this may cancel out the other advantage of spatial separation.

Other physical conditions have also been studied: thus Spieth, Curtis and Webster (1954) found that if one of the competing channels was passed through a high or low-pass filter set at 1600 c/s, there was an improvement in performance. It made no difference whether high or low-pass filtering was used, but a condition of high-pass filter in one channel together with a low-pass in the other gave the best results. These authors also found that a visual signal helped identification of the relevant messages, though not understanding of them, once identified. If 'pull-down' was provided, however, understanding also was improved when a visual signal was added. The present writer's own experiment, showing an advantage when a visual signal was provided, has already been mentioned.*

Results on the effect of varying the amount of information handled are given by Poulton (1953a, 1956). He varied the amount of irrelevant information present in his situation by inserting under some conditions a continuous irrelevant con-

---

* More details on the effect of various degrees of filtering are given by Spieth and Webster (1955).

versation as well as the calls which were to be answered. In another condition both the channels were occupied by irrelevant conversation as well as by relevant calls. As the amount of irrelevant material increased efficiency decreased. The amount of relevant information to be handled was also varied in this same experiment by requiring the listener to deal with calls either on one or both channels. There was little difference between the latter conditions except when the largest amount of irrelevant material was present; in which case more calls were completely missed under the conditions of monitoring both channels.

In another experiment the subjects were required to listen for calls amongst a continuous conversation; more calls were missed when the listener had to follow the conversation by moving counters representing aircraft round a board, than when they could ignore the conversation. These results of Poulton's agree with the generalization already advanced that there is some limit to the listener's capacity, but that up to that limit several speech channels may be handled adequately. It is interesting to note, however, that irrelevant information also appears to have some effect: admittedly the decrease in efficiency as the amount of irrelevant material increased could possibly be attributed to masking, but this would not explain the fact that listening to two channels is only worse than listening to one when large amounts of irrelevant information are present. This point will arise again in Chapter 4.*

Finally we may survey the results obtained in monitoring situations on the manner in which arrangement and nature of material can decide whether or not response appears. Spieth, Curtis and Webster (1954) noted that the correct message of a pair stood a better chance of producing a response if the pair of messages was not exactly synchronous. They took a dividing line of 0·2 sec interval between the beginning of the two messages, and found that if the interval was less than this value, efficiency was less than if the interval was between 0·2 and 0·4 sec. Poulton also

* Webster and Solomon (1955) found that their subjects with instructions to answer two messages (out of a jumble of up to four) did relatively worse than those answering only one. Instructions which required the subject to decode each message as well as write it down also impaired performance.

found that synchronous rather than overlapping calls accounted for most failures in one of his experiments. The process of discarding a call as irrelevant appears therefore to be fairly rapid.

A curious point which has appeared in two experiments is that repeating twice the call-sign placed in front of each message does not give any extra advantage to the listener. This was found both by Spieth, Curtis and Webster, and by Broadbent. In the case of the present writer, it was thought before the experiment that it would be useful for the listener to have an opportunity to check any call of which he might be doubtful, but this did not seem to be so. The writer also made call-signs more distinctive by decreasing the phonetic components they had in common, but found no advantage: this line was not, however, pursued very far and might give better results if tried more carefully.

Similarity of relevant and irrelevant material was varied by Poulton, and by Webster and Thompson, both finding that greater similarity decreased efficiency. Poulton used the situation of listening for calls through a background of irrelevant conversation: when the conversation contained references to the control tower whose name would prefix any relevant call, there were more failures to notice calls. There were also more calls reported when no call had occurred.

Webster and Thompson compared meaningless noise and irrelevant speech as background to the relevant material, and found that the latter produced lower efficiency: this result is of course connected with the results from the alternate-word technique, cited in the section above on listening to one channel and ignoring another.

The distribution of material over the various channels used, also affects results. Poulton arranged one loudspeaker to produce an irrelevant conversation as well as relevant calls, while others were producing only relevant calls. The quiet speakers more often received a correct response. They seemed to be unaffected when calls overlapped, while the busy speaker suffered severely. This result is connected with that of Poulton already cited, that calls surrounded by other material on the same channel were more likely to be missed. The sudden appearance of a message in a previously quiet channel seems to favour response. Webster and Thompson, in a rather different variation, concentrated most of their relevant messages on one or two channels and compared this with a situation in which the messages were evenly divided amongst the available channels. The former arrangement was better. It appeared that the greater amount of shifting of response between the different channels caused difficulty in the other case. Shifting was also studied by Broadbent (1952b, c). In this case the channels were distinguished only by the voices heard, not only by spatial position, and the condition of listening steadily to one voice was compared with that of shifting from voice to voice in obedience to a visual cue. In the earlier of the two experiments, which was fairly short, no difference was found: but in the later one it appeared that this was only true for the first dozen or so messages, after which the steady condition was better than that of shifting. As Webster and Thompson point out, analysis by the methods of information theory would describe the more evenly balanced arrangement of messages as conveying more information, so it may be that these results should be classed with those indicating a limit to the listener's capacity. On the other hand, the results of Chapter 9 suggest that shifting between channels requires time; and that therefore listeners adopt special techniques for material on several channels. These techniques reduce the amount of shifting while preserving the relation between any heard item and the channel of its arrival.*

## Some Miscellaneous Results

There are some experiments which do not fit into the three classes already dealt with, but which nevertheless provide points of interest. The main point of connexion with the results already met lies in the question of the quantity of information handled by the listener. In one group of experiments, for example (Broadbent 1952a), only one message at a time was presented to the

* Webster and Sharpe (1955) showed that this monitoring task can be improved by allowing the listener to control the time at which each message is delivered to him; he spreads them evenly so that no undue peaks of information input occur. This is the same principle shown in visual performance by Conrad and Hille (1955) and which will be discussed in Chapter 11. Bertsch, Webster, Klumpp and Thompson (1956) evaluated a tape-recording device which would allow this in the practical situation.

listener, so that selective listening as we have so far considered it was not required. When the rate of presenting messages went up, however, the efficiency of response went down. This seemed to be an effect of too much information in too short a time rather than a result of overlapping stimulus and response, because it was unaffected by changes in the type of response required. Furthermore, in a series of high-speed questions the listener appeared to fall behind and do worse at the end of the series than at the beginning. The concept of limited capacity applies to this situation as well as to that in which two stimuli are actually simultaneous.

It should be noted also that the overlapping of stimulus and response does produce an additional effect independent of the rate of arrival of information. Thus if two relatively isolated questions are presented one after the other, so that response to the first overlaps the second, performance on the second is improved by altering the instructions so that all inessential words are omitted from the response. The stimulus remains the same, so that the rate at which information was handled was the same in either condition; but presumably the longer response required to be controlled in some way by a mechanism which was also needed for listening. (Masking is unlikely, and in any case a similar effect has been shown by Poulton (1953b) by overlapping visual stimuli and manual responses, where masking could not occur.) Many modern views of response organization (e.g. Gibbs 1954) hold that accurate response is obtained by the continual correction of observed discrepancies between the actual and desired responses—a process which is known as negative feed-back in servo and electronic systems.

A last point from this experiment is that, when non-essential words were removed both from the answers and the questions, the situation of overlapping stimulus and response became harder. This removal did of course involve a higher rate of transmission of information, although the amount of stimulation delivered in a given time was the same or rather less. Another group of experiments has a similar moral. In this latter case, there were again two channels, but speech was involved on only one of them (Broadbent 1956a). While questions were being answered, the listener was occasionally presented with a buzzer sound. There were three conditions: in one the listener could ignore the buzzer, in a second he had to make a simple key-pressing response to it, and in the third he had to make the key-pressing response unless another (visual) stimulus also appeared, in which case he had to stamp his foot. The last of these conditions produced the most interference with the simultaneously heard speech, and the first condition produced least. This order of difficulty corresponds with the amount of information which the listener was extracting from the buzzer, and not to the amount of stimulation, which was the same in all cases. (In the last condition the buzzer alone gave no less interference than the buzzer plus the visual signal.) The difference between a description of the results in terms of stimulus and response, and a description in information theory terms becomes most marked when the two-choice task is compared with the simple reaction. In these two cases stimulus and response are exactly the same, and yet the interference with another task varies.* One could no doubt develop an adequate description of the results in S–R terms, probably by speaking of generalized inhibition from the foot-stamping response which was not being made: but such a description is clumsy compared with the information theory description. We have already found repeated evidence that a listener can deal only with a limited amount of information in a given time; it is a simple extension of this result to find that when one task requires the reception of more information another simultaneous task suffers.

Another and rather different line of interest is opened up by this same group of experiments on the effect of a buzzer presented while listening to speech. This is the question of effects of practice. If one can only receive information at a limited rate, some advantage might be gained by doing any particular task in such a way as to take in as little as possible consistent with efficiency; there would then be less interference with other

---

* Another experiment in which the same is true is provided by Webster and Solomon (1955). Some of their subjects were instructed only to answer messages for, say, Miramar: others had to answer both those messages for Miramar and those for Burbank. When presented with simultaneous messages, one for Miramar and one for North Island Tower, the latter group of subjects did worse than the former. There was interference from the stimulus which might have been present but was not.

tasks. Such a way of doing tasks would in this case be likely to appear with practice, if we adopt the common view that behaviour changes in a biologically useful way after experience. Poulton (1952b) has in fact shown this in a task which used visual signals. His subjects had to follow a pointer which oscillated in a regular way; after training they could follow with some accuracy even if their sight of the target was momentarily cut off. They were not completely dependent on incoming information to perform the task.

A similar change in behaviour appeared in subjects who were carrying out the two-choice reaction while listening to speech (Broadbent 1956a). With practice they began to treat the reaction as one-choice, always starting to make one of the two possible reactions and correcting themselves if it proved incorrect. Adopting this kind of performance reduced the interference with the understanding of speech down to the level of a simple reaction. But practice did not abolish the interference altogether, nor reduce the interference due to the simple reaction below the unpractised level. We would hardly suppose that it could do so, as long as the task needs some information to be gathered from the outside world.

There is another effect of practice besides that of changing performance to reduce the amount of information required. When subjects were listening to speech while occasionally reacting to a buzzer, they had difficulty in answering the speech, not only when the buzzer sounded but also between presentations of the buzzer. After practice on the buzzer reaction, this second type of difficulty disappeared, and the speech task was unduly hard only when the buzzer sounded. The theoretical reason for this is not certain, though a suggestion will be made in the next chapter. It is clear, however, that this result of practice means that two tasks can when familiar be carried on at the same time, as long as essential information for the two tasks does not arrive simultaneously. The classical way of describing this was to say that ' rapid alternation of attention ' may appear between two practised tasks.

We can therefore summarize the effects of practice as twofold: it makes performance less dependent on incoming information and it increases the possibility of receiving information for one task during the intervals between the arrival of information for the other.  But there is no sign in existing data of any improvement in dealing with excessive amounts of information arriving truly simultaneously.

A final group of experiments may now be mentioned.  They are by Mowbray (1952, 1953, 1954) and deal with the question of listening while also receiving visual information.  In his first set of results Mowbray required subjects to detect missing items either from the alphabet or from the series of the first twenty numbers.  When one sequence was presented visually and another simultaneously to the ear, there was an increase in the number of errors both of omission and of commission.  The numerals were easier than the alphabets, and when a numeral sequence was given with an alphabet the latter was less affected than the former.  This applied whichever sense received the particular type of material.  Mowbray's second experiment used prose passages of various levels of difficulty as assessed by a Flesch count (Flesch 1948).  After passages were presented comprehension tests were given: once again the easier passages were the most affected when given with more difficult ones.  In this case, however, hearing was more affected than vision whereas in the previous work the two senses were equally affected.  This may be because the visual presentation was a less natural one, being paced mechanically, while the earlier experiment had allowed the subject to read at his own rate.  A striking result from this experiment was that the mean of the scores on the less well comprehended passage of each pair was only at the chance level.  That is, one passage seemed to have been ignored while some information was gathered from the other.  There was one exception to this rule.  When two easy passages were paired, the scores on the less well understood passage were significantly above the chance level.  This finding harmonizes with those already cited, to show that one cannot say ' Two tasks at once are impossible '.  The important variable in the earlier results was the rate at which information must be handled in each task: two tasks at once are to some extent possible if the rate of arrival of information for each is low.  Easy prose by the Flesch criterion is not perhaps to be directly assimilated to a low information content, but it is certainly related to it.

In Mowbray's last experiment he gave his subjects problems,

whose solution required items of information presented either visually or by ear.   He delivered such items always in pairs, one to each sense.   This technique makes the alternation of attention even more difficult than it was in the prose passages experiment, and he could find no evidence that the subjects perceived both items in any pair.   It should be noted that the relevant items were embedded in a stream of irrelevant material: certain results, to appear in Chapter 9, suggest that this was important in securing the result actually found.   Deliberately instructing the subjects that the items were paired gave no better results than leaving them naïve, and Mowbray concluded that successful division of attention did not occur.   It seems that once again the material on one sensory channel was assimilated while that on the other channel was discarded.

## CONCLUSIONS

We see, then, that results of selective listening experiments lead us to three main conclusions.   First, some central, rather than sensory, factors are involved when two messages are presented to the ears at the same time.   Secondly, the effects vary with the number of possible messages that might have arrived and from which the actual ones are chosen.   That is, the rate at which information is arriving is important.   Two messages which convey little information stand a better chance of being dealt with simultaneously than two messages which each convey much information. Thirdly, when some information must be discarded, it is not discarded at random.   Thus if some of the material is irrelevant it is better for it to come from a different place from the relevant material, or to be louder or softer, or to have different frequency characteristics: or to be on the eye instead of the ear.   When no material is to be discarded there is comparatively little advantage in using two or more sensory channels for presenting information.

How are these conclusions related to the everyday belief that ' two tasks at once are impossible ' ?   Or, for that matter, to the everyday habit shared by many people of listening to the radio and reading a book simultaneously ?   Clearly it is not absolutely impossible to do two things at once.   What seems to be impossible, on the basis of the considerable body of evidence we have examined, is to handle more than a critical amount of information in a given time. This may apply even if one task is speeded up, as well as in the case when two tasks are being carried on at the same time. But what in everyday life we call two tasks may very often require the analysis of only a little information. As we said early in the chapter, ordinary English excludes certain sequences of words. Even more so, ordinary novels or radio broadcasts exclude certain sequences of ideas which are theoretically possible. A practised individual can well listen to a play, read a novel, or drive a car without continually taking in large quantities of information. And with practice, as we have seen, two tasks cease to interfere except at the moments when information arrives for both at once. Thus we may well agree that two tasks can be done during the same period without admitting that the human nervous system has more than a limited capacity. There is no doubt that it is limited.

Yet the origin of the emphasis which ordinary speech places on ' doing two things at once ' is also clear. Given that messages contain more than the limiting quantity of information, it will be the words spoken in one voice or from one place which will be understood. Once the limit is reached, one task fails while the other is still adequately performed. So the impression may well be given to the casual observer that ' doing one thing is possible while doing two things is not '. This point is more important than it may seem at first sight. Not only does it bring the results of these experiments into line with common sense, but also it indicates an error which S–R psychology is prone to make. A ' stimulus ', such as a human voice, has many qualities— intensity, pitch, position, and a number of others. To regard two stimuli as different because they differ in one of these, such as pitch, ignores the qualities they have in common. On the other hand, to regard two stimuli as the same when one is chosen from two possibilities and another from a set of fifty, is equally unjustifiable; even when the two are physically identical in every way. The word ' stimulus ' is as vague as the word ' thing ' in the phrase ' doing two things at once ', and for the same reason: it contains enough truth for its unsatisfactory character to be overlooked. In the next chapter we will begin to state a fresh language, which may show up some of the weaknesses of S–R terms in psychology.

# CHAPTER 3

# VERBAL AND BODILY RESPONSE

*General Development of Terms*

IN one sense a new set of descriptive terms can add nothing to a science, as it provides no new experimental results. It is therefore undesirable to multiply sets of terms without special justification; but there are times when the use of one set obscures important relations, and reasons were given, at the end of the last chapter, for thinking that the language of stimulus-response psychology does do this. The present chapter will attempt to set out the consequences of describing behaviour in the terms originally developed for telephone engineering. In particular, we may hope to come on some distinctive features of human verbal behaviour.

To start with a simple case, consider a man performing a psycho-physical experiment. Two pure tones are being used as stimuli, their frequencies being different: and he is asked to say ' high ' when the sound seems to him high-pitched and ' low ' when it does not. If the frequencies are sufficiently different he will say one word consistently when one tone is presented, and the other word when the other tone is presented. The causal lines connecting the tones with the words are partly known to us. We know that, at least for fairly high frequencies, the two different tones will give two different patterns of activity on the basilar membrane in the ear. We also know that the activity in the auditory nerve will be different in the two cases, and that the point of greatest response in the auditory cortex will be different. But beyond this last point we can follow no further; our physiological knowledge becomes inadequate. Yet we do know something about the later points in the chain connecting stimulus to response: we do know that whatever the neural mechanism involved it must have at least two possible states, one corresponding to each of the two tones.

This knowledge is of course used in the study of the special senses. If a person can make distinctive reactions to each of two stimuli, then his sense-organs must take up different states, depending on which of the two stimuli is presented. No physiological mechanism can therefore be postulated for that sense which does not provide such possible states. It is often tempting to make the opposite inference, that when two stimuli do not give different responses the sense-organ must be at fault; but this is clearly a fallacy. There may quite well be two possible states of the neural mechanism up to a point quite close to response, and yet only one in the final stages. Particularly clear examples are given by Tinbergen (1951) in discussing the stimuli which release instinctive behaviour. Many of the characteristics of the parent herring-gull are discriminable by the sense-organs of the chick, and yet produce no distinctive reaction; it is only a limited class of stimuli such as the red patch on the beak of the parent which elicit the response. Another example, which we will be con- ⨍ sidering in some detail later, is the extinction of conditioned responses. In that case a stimulus which is normally followed by a conditioned response is presented many times and ceases to produce a response. The ability of the sense-organs to distinguish the conditioned stimulus from the background is shown by the success of the original conditioning. But after the extinction procedure has been applied there is no longer any difference in response when the stimulus is applied. At some point in the chain of events between stimulus and response the consequences of presenting the conditioned stimulus cease to appear: yet the sense-organ is intact.

⨍ Our interest, then, is purely in the number of states possible at each point in the stimulus-response chain. Broadly speaking, the ability of any mechanism to take up different states depends on the size of the mechanism: the larger it is, the more different states it can assume. But any physically realizable mechanism must have some limit to the possible number of states; and this limitation will affect even the large human brain. Difficulties in performance are likely to appear when the brain is required to take up one of a very large number of states: in other words, if the number of stimuli likely to appear in a situation is extremely large. In ordinary psycho-physical experiments, of course, this does not arise. The number of different cells in the brain is large, and the number of different alternative stimuli presented for subjective judgement small.   When the subject of the experiment ceases to distinguish one stimulus from another it is often because of sensory limitations: but the reader will by now see that, quite apart from sensory limits, situations in which there are a large number of different possible stimuli may well fail to produce different possible responses.   Some later stage in the brain may have too few states which it can assume, and so there will be fewer responses than there are stimuli.   But it may seem difficult for the sense-organs to pass so many different stimuli, as the number of sensory fibres is not of a different order to the number of cells in the brain.   It will now be shown that this is perfectly possible.

Let us consider some very simple quantitative aspects of speech. In the first place, each word is chosen from a vocabulary of fairly definite size.   Basic English contains 850 words; other languages have considerably more, but Basic will do for our purpose, both because it is a definite number and also because it obviously has less than the maximum vocabulary a man can use.   If a man can make a different response to any word of Basic which he hears, he must have at least 850 possible states of each part of the neural mechanism between stimulus and response.   Now suppose that he hears a two-word sentence.   Again, if he makes a response dependent on the sentence, he must have a certain number of possible states: but the number is now the square of 850, namely 732,500.   A three-word sentence requires over 60,000,000 states of any mechanism which will produce an appropriate response to the sentence.   In general, if we make up a kind of vocabulary containing sentences rather than words, this vocabulary will contain $n^t$ sentences if $n$ is the number of possible words and there are $t$ words in each sentence.   (In practice the number of sentences is a little less than this because grammatical usage excludes certain sequences of words: for example, repeating the same word.   This reduction does not affect the argument.)   So the size of the vocabulary from which any sentence is drawn increases sharply with the length of the sentence.

By this point the reader will have realized that it is not fair to ask him to absorb the extremely lengthy series of stimuli which make up this book, and afterwards to produce an appropriate response.   As the length of a speech message goes up there is

bound to come a point at which it is drawn from a set of possibilities larger than the number of states the nervous system can
take up.  Regrettably, it is likely that the reader would make
much the same critical comments about this book even if it had
been written in a slightly different way.  Yet it is obvious that
to some extent the reader will react differently to different books,
and in view of the number of possibilities between which he is
discriminating this must mean that a considerable neural mechanism is coming into play.  This applies to all reading or listening
to speech.  It is therefore extremely unlikely that a listener
should be able to deal with two speech messages simultaneously,
as this would involve doubling the mechanism required.  At this
point we have made contact with the experimental findings of the
last chapter; for they demonstrate that speech messages do
interfere with one another.  Before going further into a theoretical
discussion of the experiments, let us simplify the terms we have
been using.

The process we have been considering, in which one of a set
of possible signals enters a system and one of another set emerges
at the far end, is analogous to that of telephone or radio communication.  The ' number of possible states ' or the ' vocabulary ' which we have considered so far is usually called the
' ensemble ' of signals by communications engineers.  They
speak of the ' information ' conveyed by a signal as increasing
with the size of the ensemble from which it is drawn.  If there
are *n* possibilities, all equally probable, the information is usually
defined as the logarithm of *n*.  (The appearance of the logarithm
should not worry non-mathematical readers: it is merely used to
ensure that information has on this definition a property which is
intuitively reasonable, namely that two signals convey twice as
much information as one.  As we have seen, the ensemble of
two-word sentences is not twice as large as that of single words,
so the information cannot be taken as numerically equal to the
size of the ensemble.)  But information also considers probability
as well as the size of the ensemble, and so is more general than the
latter term.  The reasons for this may be given as follows.

If we return to our psycho-physical experiment, we remember
that the subject says ' high ' to one tone and ' low ' to another.
Suppose we introduce two new tones, but still only allow him an

ensemble of two responses. Given sufficient time he can still indicate that he has heard perfectly a tone drawn from the new ensemble of four. He does this by making a sequence of two responses, saying ' high high ' for the highest note, ' high low ' for the next, ' low high ' for the next, and ' low low ' for the lowest. So our simple account of the situation was inadequate: the limited size of the listener's brain will only decide the size of the ensemble of stimuli which he can deal with *in a given time*. It will not necessarily limit his performance given indefinite time. But suppose that one tone, say the second highest, was presented on nine trials out of ten. An astute listener might then say simply ' high ' to that stimulus, while keeping double responses for the others: and so would be able to deal with more signals in a given time. The probability thus clearly affects the rate at which signals can be handled, and must be taken into account in a measure of information. In practice the average rate of transmission of information through a system is measured as $\sum_{1}^{n} -p_i \log p_i$, where $p_i$ is the probability of the $i$th signal from an ensemble of $n$ signals. The average rate of transmission of any system has an upper limit which we call its ' capacity ', and this capacity cannot be exceeded by any arrangement of the signals corresponding to the various inputs arriving at the system. Such a rearrangement (and particularly a change of the type in which the four tones were represented by sequences of the two words), is known as a change of ' coding '.

These new terms were introduced casually in earlier chapters. They have now become more exact, and allow us to say that the rate of arrival of information in one speech message is so high that it is likely to equal the capacity of the relevant part of the listener's brain. This statement is both more brief than the earlier ones, and also more inclusive since it takes into account the points of probability and of the possible effect of coding changes. The other advantages of this language will perhaps appear in the rest of this book.

## Multi-channel Listening and These Terms

In the last chapter we arrived at three general conclusions about multi-channel listening. First, that some central interference appeared when two messages arrived simultaneously. This we have since seen to be highly reasonable if we consider the information transmitted through the man, since the latter will ultimately be limited by the size of his nervous system. Secondly, we found much evidence that increase in the amount of information per message made listening more difficult; in particular, when messages were chosen from a larger ensemble they interfered more even though they might be physically the same. This finding also has a reasonable interpretation in view of the definition of information we have since considered. (It may be appropriate here to add the caution that raising the amount of information in one of two competing messages does not necessarily cause difficulty in response to that message, but rather to the other one. Thus in the last chapter we note that Webster and Thompson showed worse overall performance when the same ensemble of messages were distributed with unequal probability over various channels, while Poulton found that the messages on the least used channels were the best reported. Equally Mowbray found that interference between two difficult prose passages was greater than that between two easier ones, but that when the competing passages were of unequal difficulty it was the easiest which suffered.)

The third conclusion of the last chapter, however, seems to be less obviously connected with questions of capacity. Why should the listener prefer to listen to one ear and to ignore the other rather than to receive mixed relevant and irrelevant sounds in one ear? Why does a difference in sensory channel help multi-channel listening? The answer, in the terms we have now adopted, is that the sensory channel by which a word arrives conveys little information. Little mechanism is required to decide which sensory channel a particular word has arrived by, to reject words from one channel, and to pass those from another channel on to a further mechanism for the analysis of the remaining information they convey. Such a system is therefore an economical way of keeping down the amount of information passed through the main part of the mechanism.

For those who find abstract terms uncongenial, a practical analogy may be found in a radio receiver designed to eliminate impulse interference, and so present the signal to the listener free from such interference. Such a receiver may make use of the fact that the interference possesses frequency components not present in the desired signal: when an incoming signal has such components it is therefore rejected, and only signals without these frequencies are passed to the later stages of the receiver. This means that the early stages of the receiver must be capable of passing a band-width greater than that of the desired signal, but this extra capacity is justified by the interference-free signal which it permits. This analogy makes another point more noticeable: in one sense, the receiver ' knows ' something about the interference, namely that it possessed frequency components which were not desired. In the same way we will remember from the last chapter that a listener who is repeating one series of words does know that another voice was on the other ear; and he can tell whether this voice was that of a man or a woman. Both the relation between the two ears, and that between the spectra of the incoming voices, were found in other experiments to be cues assisting the hearing of one voice in the presence of another. As we have just been urging, each sound is first analysed for pitch, localization, or other similar qualities, and only sounds possessing certain qualities are passed on for further analysis.

We may call this general point of view the Filter Theory, since it supposes a filter at the entrance to the nervous system which will pass some classes of stimuli but not others. The main alternative explanation for the results given in Chapter 2 would be some sort of bundle theory. By this we mean that the sounds are gathered into classes or bundles by common physical characteristics, that this prevents errors of confusion between two messages, and that this reduction in confusions is responsible for the improvement in performance produced by physical cues. A bundle theory might be based on a view, such as that of Spieth, Curtis and Webster (1954), that the transition probabilities between words sharing common physical cues are higher than those between words not sharing them; if we hear the first half of a sentence the second half usually comes from the same place in the same voice. From the results given in the last chapter it is clear that the results predicted by a bundle theory do occur: there are less confusions when spatial separation is present and both messages are to be answered. But the main advantage of spatial separation comes in the case when one or more irrelevant messages have to be ignored; and this can only be explained by supposing that it is easier to pass one bundle and reject another than to reject stimuli within a bundle that also contains relevant items. This is effectively a filter theory. Indeed, the various results reviewed in the last chapter seem to entail some form of filter theory, as the effect of physical cues varies so much with the task required of the listener.

Before we leave multi-channel listening for more general

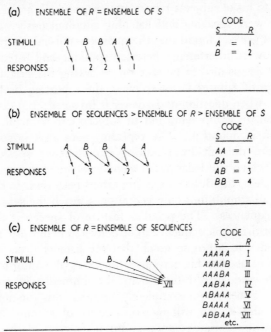

Fig. 1. Three modes of response to a sequence of stimuli.

questions of verbal and bodily response, two other important points should be noticed. The first of them is the difference of technique, noted in the last chapter, between repeating continuously a stream of speech as it was heard, and answering questions. Whichever task the listener is asked to do, he can clearly only perform it correctly if his response preserves all the information in the stimulus. But there is an important difference between the tasks. A listener who is saying what he hears must produce a word for each word that reaches him. Having said it, he can forget it completely while he deals with the next. In other words, at each instant his nervous system need handle only the information conveyed by one word. (Fig. 1A.) The listener who is answering questions, however, must handle all the information in the whole question. (Fig. 1c.) The latter is clearly a task which requires a far greater ensemble of possible states of the nervous system, and should therefore be more likely to cause difficulty in multi-channel tasks. Indeed, Cherry (1953) was able to make subjects repeat a message which arrived so fast that they were speaking and listening simultaneously: although Broadbent (1952a) found that the question-and-answer technique would show an interference between speaking and listening. In general it seems also to be true on reviewing the literature that percentage of failures is lower when the repeating back task is used than when question-and-answer is involved; but differences in material, in equipment, and in subjects are so great that the conclusion is doubtful. The repeating-back task is sometimes made more difficult by requiring simultaneous speaking and listening, which will balance out any advantage of that technique. None the less, the difference is important because it is of course true that all stimuli, not only verbal ones, reach the sense-organs in long sequences. The peculiar feature of speech is that it is normal for the whole sequence to be delivered before any response is required. It is not so much that the listener deals with the information, as that his response preserves the information in the whole sequence rather than the immediately preceding stimulus. Speech is not completely unique in this—in non-verbal situations also a man will receive a series of stimuli and then produce an appropriate response. But it is a particularly common and striking feature of speech that the coding adopted between stimulus and response should be of the type shown in Fig. 1c.

The second point that should be made is in some ways a similar one. It is a false antithesis to suppose that a response must contain either the whole of the information in a stream of stimuli, or else simply that in the last stimulus. To take a mundane example, suppose the reader had read the first sentence in this book, and decided ' That's nonsense '. He can then forget the details of the sentence and remember only that it was nonsense. The same procedure is applied to the next sentence, and so on throughout the book: when the reader can say on being asked for his opinion ' It was *all* nonsense '. This response does not preserve all the information in the book—other books might produce the same response. Yet it is clearly determined by the book as a whole and not by the last word in it. And at each stage during the reading it demands only that the reader's capacity should be sufficient for the sentence in hand plus the fact that all previous sentences were nonsense.

Clearly this is a potent device for allowing a limited capacity system to deal with a sequence of signals, and in fact it is employed by human beings. Take, for example, the results of the word interleaving experiments (Broadbent 1952c) which were mentioned in the last chapter. One of the comparisons given was that between two orders of presentation of the same messages eight words long. The eight words formed two questions each four words long and each chosen from an ensemble of 250 questions. When all four words had arrived the listener could compare the question with a visual picture, and choose his answer from an ensemble of four. The questions were in fact of the type described at the beginning of the last chapter, in which a fairly complex question was asked about a picture but could be answered ' Yes ' or ' No '. Now in the experiment described both questions had to be answered, but it was much easier to do so when all four words from one question were presented before any words from the other question. Great difficulty was produced by interleaving the two questions so that neither was complete before the last two words of the eight presented. The difference between these two orders of presentation lies simply in the fact that one of them allows the listener to forget most of the first question, and remember only which of the four answers was appropriate. He can then deal with the other question while storing rather little information. Other examples of this mechanism will be given later: it is illustrated in Fig 1B. The three modes of response illustrated in that figure are of fundamental importance, and will be mentioned again.

## Verbal and Bodily Response

The use of speech has long been regarded as one of the most distinctive features of man. Those who analyse the functions required of the nervous system have, however, usually found that all those necessary for speech are possessed by lower animals. Heard speech, for example, acts as a ' sign ': it produces a reaction which may be that appropriate to some object which is not now present.   But animals can of course be trained to react to sounds in this way.   Many domestic dogs will respond appropriately to such words as ' walkies ' or ' bone ', and formal experiments on the subject are supplied by conditioning.   More subtle is the function of speech as a ' symbol ', that is a process, generated by the organism itself, which stands for a sign as the sign stands for a physical object.   But Seward (1948), acting on these definitions, has shown that some animal experiments demonstrate the presence of symbols in animals.   We need not follow his argument in detail: the experiments are formal demonstrations of the behaviour of a domestic dog when given a plate. If he responds by going to fetch a bone to put on the plate, some symbolic process must be present in his nervous system.   The experiments quoted by Seward are, of course, better controlled than this example.   His conclusions may be accepted as proving symbolization in animals; but it remains doubtful whether the significant property of language is its most unique one.

The analysis we have made in this chapter suggests rather that language is peculiar in the large quantity of information it requires the listener to handle at any one time; and especially in the emphasis it places on sequences of stimulation.   A large nervous system is clearly a prerequisite for performing this task, in addition to all the others needed for life.   This in itself suggests that we have here a more important aspect of language than its significant function, since it is clearly one in which men have an advantage over animals of other species.

If this point of view is correct, it should follow that species which do not possess language should also be deficient at dealing with stimulus sequences of any kind: whereas our own species should be able to cope with sequences not only of words but also of other stimuli.   There is some evidence that this is true.   For example, one of the tasks which all animals find most difficult is the temporal maze of Hunter (1920).   This is a maze shaped like a T with the two side-arms led back to the foot of the stem, so that the animal returns repeatedly to the same choice-point.   For successful performance right and left turns should be made at the choice-point in a definite sequence—say RRLL. But as the point is always the same there are no different external stimuli to which the right and left responses can be attached: the whole of the information contained in the sequence must be stored within the animal if it is to be successful. It rarely is. (In an ordinary maze, even if the animal is required to learn a sequence of right and left turns in double alternation, each choice-point provides some unique stimuli. The sequence of choices thus places little load on the animal, as in Fig. 1A.)

Another example is that monkeys can learn quite complex locks and catches which bar their way to food: but that a sequence of locks to be opened in a particular order is a very difficult problem (Kinnaman 1902). In both these examples, human beings can do well. Usually their success is ascribed to the use of language, as they may often say aloud the sequence which they adopt. From the present point of view this is putting the cart before the horse: they can use language because they can deal with sequences, and this in turn they can do because of their large nervous system.

The reason, therefore, for the appearance of results which demand a filter theory in speech tasks, rather than in tasks involving other stimuli, is simply that speech is the most obvious case of stimuli being dealt with in sequences. Classic laboratory experiments on the ' unity of attention ' or the ability to do two tasks simultaneously, have been unsatisfactory. Usually their stimuli are selected from a small ensemble, and often it has not been clear at what instant the crucial information arrived from each task. The classic way of putting this difficulty is that attention appears to alternate between the two tasks. The use of speech as a laboratory task allows large quantities of information to be delivered to the subject: the sentences mentioned earlier with their ensemble of 250 possibilities clearly make greater demands on the listener than ordinary choice-reaction and similar tasks. In addition the use of speech allows us to be sure of the instant at which crucial information is delivered; it was mentioned in the last chapter that practised subjects only have difficulty in answering questions at the instant when a buzzer sounds on another channel. They can deal with questions satisfactorily between soundings of the buzzer. This is an objective version of the classical ' alternation of attention ' and shows the importance of precise timing of the incoming stimuli. So multi-channel listening has clear advantages for demonstrating the limited capacity of the human perceptual system, and the existence of a filter mechanism for making economical use of that capacity: but these findings may also apply to other non-verbal tasks. In the next chapter an extension will be made to such tasks involving vision. The present chapter has at this point completed all the argument that is needed for the main theme of the book. The difficulties of multi-channel listening have been ascribed to limited capacity, and the necessity of supposing a filter mechanism indicated. What follows is a diversion from the main argument and the reader may reject it without affecting the validity of the rest of the book. Nevertheless the analysis of verbal behaviour in the language of information theory, which we have just attempted, raises several rather general points about psychology which are worth making.

In the first place, suppose we ask a subject to perform a complex task. He receives a series of stimuli and makes a number of responses during the series: his behaviour is in fact of the types shown in Figs. 1A and B. Now suppose we ask him to speak to us about the task at its conclusion. This is performance of the type shown in Fig. 1c: it requires a considerably greater capacity of the mechanism which can perform it. There is therefore no good reason for supposing that a person-who can do the task will necessarily be able to give an accurate account of his performance. The two types of response require different mechanisms, and it is highly likely that the verbal response will be unrelated to the bodily performance. Most contemporary psychologists know this only too well, and therefore treat with great suspicion verbal reports by human beings about the way they perform tasks. While such reports should not be neglected, they should not be trusted. The information they provide may be valuable evidence of the state of some mechanism within the man, but not necessarily of the mechanism which is producing his bodily responses. The importance of making this clear is that some people (especially non-psychologists) still hold the view that verbal reports provide an extra insight into human behaviour which is not available for animal behaviour: they represent an internal view of the behaviour.

This is too simple an account of introspection. Verbal responses certainly provide additional evidence, but this is because they require an additional mechanism. There is probably no great advantage in having extra evidence if one only gets it by having an extra problem.

It is interesting to examine various experiments in which disagreement between verbal and bodily response has been found, keeping the general informational approach in mind. There are four groups of such experiments, of which the first two are of less importance than the last two. In the first, it is shown that a response may be learned and performed although the person can give no verbal account of the process. An example is the experiment of Maier (1931), in which the problem facing the subject was to tie together two ropes which hung too far apart for one to be reached while holding the other. If the experimenter walked into one rope and set it swinging, the correct solution was more often achieved; it was to swing one rope pendulum-wise so that the other rope could be held and the swinging rope caught on its return by the free hand. But the subjects did not say that they had seen the experimenter walk into the rope: the hint produced solutions but did not appear in introspection.

Now it is clear that in this case both verbal and bodily response preserve the same amount of information. If the experimenter does not walk into the rope the subject will not tie the ropes together, and will say that he cannot do so: if the hint is given the ropes will be tied together and also the subject will say that he knows how to tie them together. To expect him to distinguish in his speech between this particular hint, and any other way of helping the subject to achieve correct solution, is to demand extra information from the verbal response. *A priori* there is no reason to suppose that this is available. A similar experiment is that of Hull (1920) in which complex figures are shown successively to the subject. Certain figures have some feature in common, and the subject must say which figures possess this feature. It is found that he can pick out the correct figures at above-chance level before he has learned the feature sufficiently well to describe it verbally. Here again, he may pick out the figures by hand or he may say ' Yes ' or ' No ': the verbal response preserves as much information as the bodily one. An exact definition would represent extra information, and there is no reason to suppose that this should be available. In brief, in this first group of experiments both verbal and bodily responses appear to the same stimulus, but the subject cannot give an accurate introspective account of the process producing the response. If he could, this would mean that the verbal response was transmitting more information than the bodily one: and if the task is sufficiently complex this is an unreasonable requirement in view of the man's limited capacity.

The second category of experiments is chiefly interesting because it is so small. It is the category in which the verbal response to a stimulus is present but bodily response is not. Almost the only example is the familiar ergometer experiment in which a subject responds by flexing a finger against a resisting force, whenever he sees a light flash. After a brisk series of responses, the subject will reach a point at which he will be unable to flex his finger again despite his verbal report that the light has flashed. It is usually supposed that the bodily response has ' fatigued ' in some sense of that vague term. But other experiments showing disappearance of bodily response while verbal response is still present are extremely rare. This agrees with everyday experience. A driver may say that he sees a red light and brake, or he may regrettably fail to brake and afterwards say that he did not see the red light. Sometimes he may brake ' without thinking ' and only report seeing the red light after a delay or even not at all: but it is very rare for him to say that he saw the light and yet did not brake. If verbal response is present then bodily response is also likely to be found.

Unfortunately for simplicity, two objections to this rule must be considered. The first is that a novice or a man who has been long out of practice may be able to describe the bodily movement appropriate to some skilled performance and yet be unable to perform that movement. This objection is easily met. It does not mean that the bodily response does not preserve the information present in the verbal response, but merely that the coding is inappropriate from the point of view of the observer. The frequency-transposed speech described in the next chapter contains all the information present in ordinary speech, but in an

inappropriate coding.   Similarly if the novice batsman can say
that stroke $A$ is required rather than stroke $B$, he will make an
attempt which is different from the attempt he would make at $B$.
He may not hit the ball, but his bodily responses are different in
the two cases, and thus preserve as much information as his
verbal responses.

The second objection is more subtle.   A man who is trained
and who normally makes an appropriate movement may sometimes make a careless mistake, and yet be aware of his error
before its consequences could be perceived.   This is difficult to
show experimentally, because most situations include the possibility of some sort of knowledge of results.   The subject may say
that he is aware of his error for the same reason that he corrects
it by bodily movement, because he now sees and feels his hand to
be in the wrong place.   But an experiment by Bates (reported in
Hick and Bates 1950, p. 22) shows a more important point than
this.   In this experiment the subject was asked to press a key
which would stop a clock pointer, so that the pointer should stop
at a certain mark.   He was not to press the key if the experimenter
stopped the pointer before it reached the mark.   The results
showed, as might be expected, that if the experimenter stopped
the pointer well in advance the subject refrained from response,
but if the pointer was stopped at the last moment the subject
responded and thought that he had stopped the pointer himself.
There was an intermediate range, the one of chief interest to us,
where the subject pressed the key and yet knew that he should
not have done so.   This cannot have been due to knowledge of
results, and so seems to be a case of an appropriate verbal response
with an inappropriate bodily one.

The crucial point in answering this objection is the time at
which the response appears.   The key is pressed long before the
subject says that he should not have pressed it.   As we said
earlier, the time taken for transmission of information must always
be considered as well as the amount concerned.   A delay before
a particular response appears will allow more information to pass
into the decision-taking mechanism, and so there may sometimes
be cases in which a man may make a rapid but mistaken response
of one kind and a slower correct response of another kind.

The bodily response need not always be the more rapid one: it would be quite possible for a man to take later bodily action to correct a mistaken verbal order.   If these answers are regarded as adequate we may stick to our generalization that a man who can tell us about a situation can usually do something about it. He may do the wrong thing, but some bodily response is likely to appear conveying as much information as the verbal one.

The converse is not true, and is responsible for the last two groups of experiments on discrepancy between verbal and bodily response.   A man may well act on a stimulus and be unable to report it verbally.   The cases in which this happens include those of faint and barely noticeable stimulation, and those of highly practised ' automatic ' skills.   An example of the first of these is the experiment of Lazarus and McCleary (1951). They showed subjects a number of nonsense words, and gave them electric shocks with certain words.   Soon the subjects were conditioned to those words and showed a lowered skin resistance when the words appeared.   (Skin resistance is an inverse measure of emotional response.)   If now the exposure is reduced there comes a point at which the subjects make mistakes and cannot say which word has been presented.   But in this experiment even when the subjects said the wrong word, they still gave a skin response to the words previously paired with shock.   Bodily response was appearing when verbal response was not.

From our point of view, this is not surprising.   The presence or absence of shock with a word gives only two possible inputs. The information contributed by this input was preserved in response, with words of this degree of visibility.   But the response of identifying the correct word would have preserved considerably more information: there were ten possibilities.   So in this case a ' correct ' bodily response could be made by a mechanism of smaller capacity than that needed for a ' correct ' verbal response, and we have throughout insisted that this may often occur and that when it does the verbal response may be inappropriate. Bricker and Chapanis (1953) have put such a point of view by asking subjects in a similar situation to go on guessing after failing to say the correct word.   The series of guesses before the correct word was reached was shorter than would be expected by chance, and shorter than in a control experiment in which none of the stimulus words was in fact presented.   So by using suitable means it is possible to show the small amount of information contributed by a briefly exposed stimulus, even in verbal response.

This type of study therefore harmonizes well with our distinction between speech and other forms of response: they show different forms of coding, speech normally requiring a greater capacity from the mechanism which produces it. If adequate capacity is available for a verbal response, it is very likely that bodily response will also be present if the situation is one which requires it. But the reverse is not the case; a capacity adequate for bodily response is not sufficient for all verbal responses, and so the former may be present when the latter is absent. Experiments of the type performed by Lazarus and McCleary are, however, sometimes cited in support of a more extensive theory. This is the view known as the doctrine of ' perceptual defence '. According to this view features of the world which are repugnant to a particular person may not be perceived. The personality may perhaps be regarded as preserving its unity by rejecting inharmonious facts: ultimately a man may fail to perceive his own desires and so develop neurotic symptoms through inability to control those desires. Experiments in support of this view may for example present words of embarrassing meaning in a threshold experiment and show that the threshold for these words is high (McGinnies 1949). There are various technical difficulties in that embarrassing words are possibly unfamiliar, which would raise the threshold, and also may be adequately perceived by subjects who are yet reluctant to say them aloud, especially to a professor. Perceptual defence is therefore a somewhat controversial topic (Howes and Solomon 1950; Singer 1956 reviews the literature). Yet clinical opinion is probably in favour of a mechanism of such a type, and certainly experiments in which a subject is presented with a large amount of complex stimulation provide evidence that perception is strongly selective along the lines of the perceiver's interests (Bartlett 1932).

A difficulty which may well be felt about perceptual defence is that it seems to suppose some kind of double mechanism: a word is perceived ' unconsciously ' so that it can be recognized as uncongenial and not perceived ' consciously '. The same difficulty arises in the less dramatic case of Bartlett's demonstrations of selective perception. If a civilian in war-time hears a story which contains an excuse for avoiding military service, and reports this excuse more lengthily than other parts of the story, must we suppose that the whole story has been perceived ' unconsciously ' in order that the point of acute personal interest should be picked out for conscious perception ? Both intuitively and from general arguments of biological economy, it seems unlikely. Yet at this point let us remember the filter theory developed at the beginning of this chapter. It is economical for a series of stimuli to be analysed first for simple physical properties conveying little information; so that a later mechanism need deal only with, say, sounds in a certain voice from a certain place rather than being swamped by all the incoming sounds. This means that the listener may know that a man's voice is striking his right ear and yet not know what that voice said. There need be no question of the man's voice being perceived in its entirety and then rejected as irrelevant. Similar arguments may apply to the case of perceptual defence, provided only that classes of words may behave in the same way as sensory channels do. Thus the filter might detect that a word belongs to the general class of sexual words without distinguishing which of those words it is: and pass the word to the later mechanism for more detailed analysis, if the filter is set to pass sexual words. The case would then be analogous to that of the word reaching the left ear, which is recognized as such by the filter and passed to a later mechanism because the filter is set to pass words from the left ear.

To say that this is possible does not mean that the writer necessarily supports the existence of perceptual defence on the present evidence. Yet certainly that theory does not require a completely duplicated perceptual mechanism, but merely a filter system of the kind we have found necessary for other reasons. The main factual point at which experimental evidence seems to be needed is the question whether a class of words can act in the same way as a sensory channel. It seems to be conceivable that they should do so: to take an everyday example, most people will notice that their own name has been mentioned in a conversation occurring at some distance and previously ignored. But the evidence is not compelling. This digression has served, however, to raise the possibility that the filter may have a permanent bias to pass or to reject certain classes of signals, independent of the temporary bias applied by instructions to the subject. The possibility of a permanent bias will be discussed again in later chapters. It will appear that there is much evidence for a bias in favour of certain kinds of stimulation; but the categories are less abstract than those of, say, sexual words as compared with others. They are more like those of, say, right ear signals as compared with left.

We may now turn to the last group of experiments showing disagreement between verbal and bodily response. These are those on ' automatization '. A practised action may be brought to the point at which the performer does not remember whether he has performed it or not: he is unable to give a verbal as well as a bodily response to the stimulus concerned. Such high degrees of practice are uncommon in the laboratory: from everyday life we may take the story of William James (1890) walking in a street in which he had once lived. He was preoccupied with other matters, and only became aware of his own automatic actions when climbing the stairs of the house he had formerly occupied. When earlier stages of learning are studied in the laboratory, it is usual to find that copious introspective reports are available in the initial period, but that after much practice less is reported (Solomons 1899). The bodily responses appear, but little is said about the task. This seems to be an effect on the same continuum as that reported by James, and it certainly seems that practice may reduce verbal response while leaving bodily response to the same situation intact.

As before, we may find it entirely reasonable that speech should disappear when other forms of response are still present. But it is interesting to consider why practice should have this particular effect. It will be remembered that in the last chapter an experiment by Poulton was cited to show that some tasks become with practice less dependent on the intake of information from the outside world. A task which cannot be done by an untrained man unless he can see the course of events continuously, may be possible to a trained man with only intermittent glimpses of the situation. This effect was described theoretically many years ago by Hull (1930). In his type of language, the response to each stimulus becomes conditioned to the proprioceptive stimuli from the previous response. Thus the appearance of the first stimulus may produce the whole series of responses even though later members of the stimulus sequence are not in fact presented. Our phrasing of the same statement would be that in a sequence which is often repeated in the same order, the first event conveys as much information as the entire sequence, and the other input events need not occur for the output to remain satisfactory. The other events become, in the language of information theory, ' redundant '. So if the stimulus side of a task contains redundancy, the worker will after practice still perform the task while taking in fewer events. Our formulation differs from that of Hull in the next step: because of this phenomenon, the capacity required for efficient performance will be reduced, and neural mechanism will be set free for the performance of other tasks. In fact William James did include among the characteristics of an automatized habit, that it interfered less with other activities. In the same way the present writer's experiments (Broadbent 1956a) show that practice on one task may reduce the amount of interference with another simultaneous task. The detailed findings were given in the last chapter: the practised task interferes with another task only at the instant when crucial information arrives and only to a degree dependent on the least amount of information needed to perform the task. The unpractised task interferes much more, as though the subject was not taking advantage of the redundancy in the stimulus side of the task. Perhaps a crucial feature of the results is the way in which some interference remains after practice. From the information theory point of view most tasks will produce some interference, as some minimal information from the environment will be needed. It is not clear that any alternative theory of automatization exists, but if it does it must account for the interference which remains after practice at the instant of arrival of crucial information. Other workers have reported similar results: thus Baker, Wylie and Gagné (1951) studied the interference on one task of another after varying degrees of practice on the first. They found that interference still existed up to the highest level of practice used. A particularly striking result is that of Bahrick, Noble and Fitts (1954), who showed that when a task with a repeating series of stimuli was practised there was less interference between it and another task. But the practised task contained stimuli in a random and unpredictable sequence, practice did not reduce the interference. This result strongly supports the present point of view: it is only by capitalizing on the predictable nature of the stream of stimuli that automatization can take place. (A closely similar account of effects of practice is given by Kay (1956).)

We have now considered the four groups of experiments on discrepancies between verbal and bodily response, and have found them consistent with cur general approach. One group, although superficially showing an inadequacy of verbal response, actually merely proves that verbal response often preserves no more information than bodily response; words do not give reliable information on the causes and processes producing the bodily response. A second group shows that verbal response is some-times still present when bodily response has ' fatigued ', but that this is rather rare. The last two groups show that verbal response may break down while bodily response is still dealing efficiently with the stream of stimulus events. Faint stimuli or prolonged practice may produce such a situation, and it seems to be fairly frequent. It is readily explained as due to the different stimulus-response coding present in verbal response, which demands a larger capacity of the organism and so makes verbal response more vulnerable. There is a clear advantage biologically in the effect of practice in reducing the capacity devoted to a particular task to the minimum, as this allows the simultaneous performance of other tasks.

Our distinction between verbal and bodily response seems reasonable, then. But it is not an absolute distinction. If a lengthy sequence of stimuli is dealt with by a bodily response or sequence of responses which does not start until after the stimulus sequence ends, or if in some similar way the capacity demanded by efficient bodily response is high, then the effects described for verbal response will also apply to bodily response. Conversely if a speaker practises a series of words repeatedly until he can reel it off on a given signal, it may be as automatic as any bodily response. A man who is engrossed in some skilled manual task may give only conventional and non-committal replies to questions. The distinctive quality of verbal response lies rather in the greater frequency with which sequences of stimuli appear in experiments on speech than in experiments on other topics: and in the fact that the ability to deal with sequences is a prerequisite for the development of sentence languages rather than isolated signs. This ability requires a large capacity and therefore a large brain. It is necessary not only for the use of language, but also for many other human peculiarities which involve long sequences of stimuli or responses.

### Relation to Earlier Approaches

Four earlier approaches are highly relevant to this attitude. The present section will consider the ways in which we can try to preserve the valuable contributions of each: for critical controversy is of only limited value, and in a science at an early stage like psychology, is likely to mean ignoring some of the facts.

In the first place, the traditional language of consciousness and attention deals largely with the problems we have mentioned. A work such as that of William James (1890) points out repeatedly the facts which are painfully restated in our different and unfamiliar terms. It is difficult to attend to two complicated tasks at once, though simple tasks may be made automatic. With practice they require little attention and fall almost out of consciousness. Most people recognize such statements as true and understand them without difficulty: and it is striking to compare James' statements about attention, made on the basis of everyday observation and introspection, with the theory of filtered information flow set out in this book, and based on artificial experiments. The great value of the traditional approach is that it points out a phenomenon of importance and does not allow it to be forgotten. Words, such as consciousness and attention, came originally from ordinary language because the facts of everyday intercourse emphasized these matters as important, and required verbal labels for them. Other sets of terms, not derived from everyday experience, have the disadvantage that they allow us to forget facts about behaviour which are obvious in everyday life.

Yet the traditional language has come off very badly in competition with other languages. The reason is undoubtedly that different people attach slightly different meanings to the words involved. Furthermore the words are often used with a frame of reference that causes great difficulties in practice. Consciousness is regarded as the experience of a subject who receives signals from the outer world but is himself a unity and the source of action. What then can we say of a man who turns out his electric fire while talking and cannot remember, on leaving the house, whether the fire is out or not? Was he conscious of turning out the fire? Did the action appear unconsciously? Or should we say it was conscious but at a low level of attention? Such alternatives seem to involve difficulties. Furthermore the terms cannot be applied to animals, whose nature is clearly close to our own, and an explanation of either man or animal would be easier if we could compare theories directly. It is equally difficult to relate a psychological theory in terms of subjective experience to physiological data, a fact which popular philosophers are constantly urging in support of the doctrine that no psychological theory can have a physiological basis. The approach set out in this book is an attempt to meet these difficulties while preserving the advantages of the traditional language.

Stimulus-response psychology has the great advantages of objectivity, of rejecting phenomenalism, and of emphasizing the selective and purposive aspects of behaviour. Theories in S–R terms have often been inadequate, and sometimes unclear—what approach in psychology has not? Yet on the whole it has been possible even for the opponents of Hull, Guthrie or Skinner to understand what their theories mean. This cannot be said for all other approaches. Furthermore the rejection of introspection has avoided the danger of trusting verbal accounts of bodily performance. We have seen good reasons for supporting this distrust, although not of course for neglecting verbal response altogether. One of the factors apt to be neglected by introspection is motive, and here also stimulus-response psychology has emphasized a desirable point. These advantages must be preserved in future approaches, and the present view attempts to do so. The main reasons for departing from stimulus-response language are the need for considering the coding of input into output, the need to consider the whole ensemble of possible stimuli rather than simply the presence or absence of each one, and the need to distinguish between the arrival of a stimulus at the sense-organ and use of the information it conveys. These points must be considered in view of recent experimental results, and it is difficult to do so in S–R terms.

5

The third view to be mentioned is also one which has protested against the consideration of isolated stimuli: Gestaltism. The supporters of that approach rightly urged that patterns and organizations of stimuli are highly important, and all modern views on perception are influenced by their criticisms. The informational approach differs in two main ways from the earlier one, though it may from some points of view be regarded as a new Gestaltism. First, it is not the pattern of present stimulation which is emphasized, but the ensemble of possible situations which might have been present yet are not. Secondly, it is not only the interrelation of present stimuli which is treated as important, but also the interrelation of stimuli in temporal sequences. The two kinds of combination have resemblances: just as the amount of information in a sentence increases very rapidly with the length of the sentence, so also does the information in a complex pattern increase very rapidly with the number of elements in the pattern. Just as a listener is likely to understand only one message in the complex jumble of sounds made up by mixing two messages, so also a complex visual display may be seen either as one pattern or as another. In the latter case different parts of the pattern will be 'figure' in the two alternative percepts, and the remainder of the pattern will be ' ground '. The relation of figure and ground in visual perception is clearly similar to that between selected and rejected speech messages: in both cases the former is reacted to in detail, while the latter receives only a general and undifferentiated response.

But we have considered sequences rather than simultaneous patterns in our analysis in this chapter, because the former must clearly involve mechanisms of greater capacity than do the latter. It is very unlikely that the nervous system should be capable of producing a different response for every different possible combination of simultaneous stimuli. That is, if the information in an extremely complex visual pattern is being preserved in response it is not likely that the information in an equally complex tactile pattern is also preserved in another simultaneous response. The number of sensory fibres is of the same order as the number of cells in the cortex, and therefore the number of combinations of sensory fibres is far greater. Yet it might conceivably be argued that by some curious coding the patterns of stimulation were preserved in patterns of activity in the cortex and so in patterns of response. When sequences of stimuli are considered this becomes impossible. There is no limit to the length of the sequence presented, short of the life of the organism, whereas simultaneous patterns have a limit set by the number of sensory fibres. The sequence must clearly convey far more information than each item within it; while each item itself may be a very complex pattern. As the sequence lengthens there must logically come a point at which the capacity required to respond to it adequately exceeds the capacity of the nervous system, no matter how large the latter may be.

To consider sequences was therefore logically desirable when arguing for a filter theory: if we had considered simultaneous patterns this theory would depend on the factual question of the actual capacity of the perceptual mechanism. By considering sequences we made it clear that the capacity must be too small whatever it is, since the sequence can be extended so indefinitely. The only factual question is whether human beings do respond at the end of sequences rather than with an individual response to every separate stimulus, and this fact the reader of this book illustrates. He will make a reaction to it after reading it: to do so he must have discarded a good deal of the information presented even if he used the capacity of his nervous system fully.

In addition to the lack of emphasis in Gestaltism on temporal sequences, their language did not always share the S–R virtue of wide intelligibility. It was not always possible for outsiders to divine the meaning of terms such as ' good figure '. These disadvantages the present approach seeks to avoid, while retaining the Gestaltist gains in the field of pattern perception.

The last view which we will consider is the closest to the present one, and has a clear historical connexion with it. This is the view set forth by Bartlett in *Remembering* (1932). That view is notable for many of the virtues attributed above to other approaches. It emphasizes facts of everyday importance, it gives a central role to the importance of motives and interests in selecting for perception part of the information striking the sense órgans. It considers patterns and situations rather than isolated stimuli, but it concerns itself with temporal sequences as much as or more than simultaneous patterns. Yet historically it seems to have been open to conflicting interpretations. Oldfield and Zangwill (1942) have discussed the history of Bartlett's approach, and have made it clear that the terms used have considerable ambiguity in their meaning. The word 'schema', which he uses, seems to have a different sense for him than for Head, from whom he borrowed it. It has been used in still other senses by more recent writers. Despite this difficulty, this approach takes into account features of behaviour ignored by all other views. The present attitude attempts to preserve some of these features.

The peculiar advantages of the Bartlettian approach can best be illustrated by considering Fig. 1 again. In Fig. 1A, a sequence of stimuli is dealt with by a series of responses, one following each stimulus. Such a mode of behaviour requires little capacity of the organism. In Fig. 1B there appears a mode which requires more capacity, and which we illustrated earlier by the reader's decision that this book was all nonsense. In this case the ensemble of responses is larger than that of the individual stimuli, but still smaller than that of sequences of stimuli. Each response can thus be partially determined by information from previous stimuli, though some of that information is discarded. As an example, suppose that we try to play blindfold chess: given that our memory mechanism for the movements of the king has an ensemble of 64 states. The king can at most choose each move from an ensemble of eight (forwards, backwards, to either side, and the two diagonals), so we can remember his first and second moves without difficulty. On his third move a crisis arises: our memory no longer has a capacity sufficient to store more moves, for there are more than 64 different possible sequences of three items each chosen from an ensemble of eight. It seems that we must forget earlier moves and so lose track of the game. Yet we can adopt a satisfactory compromise by remembering, not the king's last move, but the position he reached on completing it. There are only 64 such positions, so our memory mechanism is large enough for this purpose. When the king moves into one such position the event is determined not only by the immediately previous move but also in part by the whole sequence of past moves. To remember the present position of the king preserves a particular relevant part of the information in the sequence, while discarding the rest.

Such a mode of behaviour is closely paralleled by the handling of proprioceptive information in animals. The sequence of bodily movements is continually reported to the central nervous system, but no response appears to preserve all the information in that sequence of stimuli. Many responses, however, do preserve information on the present position of the body: in the simplest case, a normal man can say where his hand is with his eyes closed, although he cannot describe his movements for the last half-hour. More subtly, unless movements continually took into account the starting position of the limbs and the arrangement of the rest of the body, they would run into considerable difficulty. So our imaginary chess board case has a parallel in the perception of posture.

Henry Head (1920) noted many years ago that perception of posture might be disorganized by brain lesions even though proprioceptive sensitivity was normal. He therefore supposed that a ' schema ' existed in the brain, an organized residue of past sensations, and that each incoming sensation modified this schema but was not preserved individually. This point of view is clearly related to our chess board example, and so to the Fig. 1B mode of response to a sequence of stimuli. Bartlett (1932) extended this possible mechanism to broader fields, and regarded much of behaviour as schematically determined. It is clear that he included several rather different mechanisms under the one name of schema, and Oldfield and Zangwill distinguish some of them. It is equally true, however, that the general class of behaviour, in which the ensemble of responses is intermediate in size between the ensemble of individual stimuli and that of sequences of stimuli, also has a number of sub-categories. For example, in our chess board example each response (position of the king) is determined by the present stimulus (move of the king) and the last *response* (starting position of the king). In the example shown in Fig. 1B, however, each response is determined by the present stimulus and the last *stimulus*. Both examples are cases in which the individual response conveys only part of the information in the stimulus sequence, but in the chess board case this part is drawn equally from all portions of the sequence;

while in the Fig. 1B case the information comes predominantly from the portion of the sequence last before the response. Oldfield and Zangwill note that ' schema ' is sometimes used to refer to an organized product of past stimuli and sometimes of past reactions: it seems plausible to suggest that both modes of behaviour exist, the former being more determined by the immediate past and the latter less so. Yet neither is of the types illustrated in Fig. 1A or Fig. 1C, and so should be distinguished from them by some such label as ' schematic behaviour '.

Again, Bartlett refers in some places to the mechanical running off of a practised habit as an instance of schematic memory: though as Oldfield and Zangwill point out a mechanical running-off seems a very different process from the continually changing postural schema of Head. Yet habitual action and the postural schema are both instances of partial preservation of information from sequences. To illustrate this, let us consider the sequence

ABXTRABHQLABJCXSABFCULJABRDAB

At the close of such a sequence we may be unable to repeat it from memory, and yet may know that whenever A occurred it was followed by B. Such knowledge represents preservation of part of the information in the sequence, though not all of it. Similarly if we consider the sequence of stimuli which reaches any organism throughout its life, sub-sequences will repeat themselves. If the organism responds to the beginning of such a sub-sequence by a series of responses appropriate to the later stimuli of the sub-sequence, it is clearly preserving part of the information from the whole sequence of its life. It would only be preserving all the information if it could produce a response (such as a verbal one) indicating how many times the sub-sequence had occurred, what other stimuli had arrived before and after each presentation of the sub-sequence, and so on.

This type of partial preservation of information is clearly rather different from the other types we have considered, and in so far as the terminology used by Bartlett made the distinction obscure it was misleading. But the distinction between the forms of stimulus-response coding shown in Fig. 1 is obscured by most theories, and especially by S–R theories. Yet it is a highly important one, since the different modes require different capacities of the organism, and the use of the term ' schema ' has distinguished cases of the Fig. 1B type from cases of the Fig. 1A type. So far, however, we have not mentioned the Fig. 1C type, in which all the information in a sequence is preserved. Bartlett distinguishes a third type of behaviour besides the two already mentioned. This is exemplified in the recall of individual events, as when a man recalls going shopping yesterday and buying a large golliwog for his child. Such recall is distinct from that of familiar patterns, as when a man finds his way home or remembers how to ride a bicycle. Bartlett did not regard recall of individual events as schematic, but as requiring some higher order function with which he held consciousness to be associated. We too must draw a distinction between recall of individual events and of familiar patterns. The latter, as we have seen, is of the Fig. 1B type: the former is surely of the Fig. 1C type. When a man can make a different verbal response today dependent on the particular sequence of events which has occurred in his past life, he is preserving information from that sequence to a greater extent than when he performs habitual actions. It is one thing to respond appropriately to the words ' psycho-physical method of constant stimuli ', to be able to find one's way from Venice to Udine, and to recognize a woman as one's wife. But to recall that one married after taking one's degree but before going to Venice for the first time seems to be a quantitatively different type of function. In so far as the man remembering can recall the entire sequence of stimuli which has reached him, he must have a larger capacity than is needed for recognizing repeated subsequences.

In fact of course it would probably be impossible for the brain to produce a response preserving all the information from an entire life. But selected stimuli from points throughout that life do form a sequence capable of producing an appropriate response: we normally expect a man to be able to say whether his marriage was before or after his graduation, even though he may be doubtful of the names of the bridesmaids. Such recall requires a large capacity mechanism, just as understanding speech does, and we may agree with Bartlett that it forms a category of behaviour which is worth distinguishing.

The question arises whether it is legitimate or desirable to identify such a mode of response with ' consciousness '. Bartlett regarded the behaviourists of the time when he wrote as equating ' there is no problem of consciousness ' with ' there is no problem that cannot be stated without using that word'. The latter he felt was true, but the behaviourists passed illegitimately from it to the former proposition. Certainly no S–R theorist has ever emphasized the considerable difference between the three modes of response shown in Fig. 1, and this does seem to be connected with their lack of interest in human verbal behaviour. To the writer it seems that such words as ' consciousness ' are too broadly used for any exact definition, but from ordinary observation it may be thought that the adjective ' conscious ' is most properly applied to verbal rather than bodily acts. Introspection is almost always verbal, and when verbal and bodily response disagree as in the experiments mentioned earlier in the chapter, it is often said that the bodily actions are ' unconscious '. Yet many bodily actions are characterized as conscious or deliberate: in general these seem to be those which are determined by a whole sequence of past stimuli. For example, attending a graduation ceremony is likely to be regarded as a conscious act. It is a response which appears only once in each individual, and is determined by a long sequence of previous stimuli making up an under-graduate career. Switching off an electric fire on leaving a room, however, may be said to be done automatically or unconsciously: it is a response which often appears to a particular stimulus, and which is unaffected by the stimuli coming before or after the relevant one.

One might therefore make a plausible case for saying that the adjective ' conscious ' is applied to behaviour more often as the behaviour approximates to our type Fig. 1c. When a man can answer lengthy questions and especially when he can make verbal or bodily responses which take into account a whole sequence of events in his past history, we regard him as conscious. In such cases his capacity must be greater than when repeating a frequently performed sequence of actions, or when making a separate response to each incoming stimulus: and it is of course possible for men to perform such responses and yet to be regarded as unconscious. But we must not expect too close a correspondence between our present approach and the language of everyday life. For instance, as we have said earlier, type

Fig. 1c performance with its large demands, is unlikely to be possible for more than one sequence at the same time. This seems to correspond to the everyday notion of the indivisibility of consciousness. Yet the capacity of the nervous system could obviously be equally fully occupied by a large number of simultaneous type Fig. 1A or B tasks using large ensembles. The man would be performing a number of simultaneous tasks none of which would normally be regarded as fully conscious: yet he would be in a normal physiological state and might often be spoken of as conscious. Thus there seem to be certain dangers and ambiguities in the use of everyday language, despite the fact that it has preserved a fact about behaviour which is important and which is neglected by S–R language. The present approach tries to avoid these dangers, but to keep the great advantages of the Bartlettian view.

## CONCLUSION

The present chapter has gone far afield. In general it performs a purely logical function: it has demonstrated that the capacity of the brain will limit the number of tasks that can be performed simultaneously and so that part of the information presented must be discarded. This seems to the writer to be simply a ground-clearing process. The more interesting question to an experimentalist are the principles which govern the discarding of information, and with these we shall be concerned in later chapters. But the ground-clearing seems to be necessary at the present stage of psychology.

The later parts of the chapter try to show broader implications of this logical analysis, and to relate it to earlier views. In particular, three types of stimulus-response coding were distinguished, of which most verbal behaviour uses the one demanding the largest capacity. These distinctions are closely parallel to those made by Bartlett (1932). Such descriptive distinctions are not, of course, answers to problems. But it is better to state a problem clearly for further investigation than to ignore it, as theories other than Bartlett's have done. These general issues, however, may be left aside by readers who are unconvinced of their importance: and the argument of the first part of the chapter taken up with fresh illustrations in the next chapter.

# CHAPTER 4

# THE ASSESSMENT OF COMMUNICATIONS
# CHANNELS FOR EASE OF LISTENING

## The Multiplicity of Criteria

THE title of this chapter must not be taken in too broad a sense. We are not going to review all the known data on the intelligibility of speech through noise; such a purpose was disclaimed in the first chapter. We shall make, however, the point that no one experiment can fully assess a channel for all purposes: this point sometimes seems to have been neglected. In addition, we shall make some factual points of importance to the general argument of the book. Chief of these is the demonstration that listening to speech may be incompatible with perfect performance on a simultaneous non-verbal task, provided the latter represents the transmission of much information. This supports our abstract argument of the last chapter, and leads up to the application of our filter theory to non-verbal tasks in the next two chapters. A second point of importance is that the interference between two tasks may be increased, not only by increasing the amount of information presented in one task, but also by making that information more difficult to distinguish from the irrelevant background of stimulation. In ordinary language, one telephone may carry messages that are no more informative than those on a second, and yet the first telephone is so noisy that it requires more concentration to listen to it. One can doodle while conversing on the second telephone, but not on the first. These points are made by experiments which have not yet been formally published, and which will therefore be described in more detail than those mentioned previously.

To those unfamiliar with speech communication problems it may seem strange that no one experiment can assess a channel for all purposes. A simple example may make this more obvious. Let us suppose that we have to assess a radio system which will transmit only a narrow band of frequencies centred about 2000 c/s. There can be no one answer to the question:

how much has been lost by removing the low and high notes from speech? If the system is to be used under some circumstances, it may be that it will be heard extremely faintly. It might, for instance, be a portable radio for infantry to carry on patrols close to the enemy lines, where only the least possible sound can be made. Under such conditions the ear is in any case insensitive to frequencies much above or below 2000 c/s; and consequently the narrow band-width of the portable radio may be quite unimportant. On the other hand, the radio may be used in a place where the listener can turn it as loud as he likes, but unfortunately is a long way from the transmitting station, and so increases background noise as well as the speech he wishes to hear. At intensities well above threshold the ear becomes more equally sensitive to different parts of the spectrum, and so the loss of the information contained in the upper and lower frequencies may be a handicap in trying to understand speech at low signal-noise ratios. Finally, the radio may happen to be used in an aeroplane which makes considerable noise in the region around 2000 c/s, but rather little at any other frequency. (It would be an unusual aeroplane, but this is irrelevant.) In such a case our narrow band-width radio might be useless while one which passes an equally narrow band in another part of the spectrum is perfectly adequate.

These considerations are of course well known to telephone engineers, and in predicting the intelligibility of speech over a given system the spectrum of the noise and the levels of speech and noise must be considered. Much progress has been made towards the goal of calculating intelligibility from these data (Fletcher 1953), though perfection has not yet been reached. But in addition to assessment of a circuit by intelligibility testing there are other criteria which may be applied to it. An intelligibility test normally involves transmitting a standard list of words over the channel, and observing how many of them are correctly reported by a listener at the other end. High intelligibility may be scored by this method even though the listener complains that the speaker's voice is quite unrecognizable. He may also say on occasion that he is achieving high intelligibility scores only by considerable ' mental effort '. Richards and Swaffield (in Jackson 1953) give these three criteria, of intelligibility, absence of effort, and distinguishability from the original, as essential. They relate them to the capacity of the telephone circuit and point out that in general the last two criteria set higher standards than the first. This means that a telephone which has a satisfactory signal-noise ratio and gives high intelligibility scores may be unacceptable in practice, because it gives unrecognizable speech and requires ' effort '. To quantify these criteria, Richards and Swaffield use a standard sample of speech which is rapidly interrupted (on the average 500 times a second); they then vary the proportion of time for which the channel is interrupted until the speech is assessed by a listener as equal to the channel under consideration.

Periodic interruption of a channel in this way is a case of a distortion, other than the filtering out of certain frequencies or the introduction of noise. Another case is the transposition of all frequencies by a constant amount. Some experiments on this topic have been carried out to show that such distortion has an effect whose importance varies with the criteria applied, and these we will now consider. The shifting of all frequencies in a message by a constant amount is a distortion which may be produced in practice by a single side-band (SSB) modulation system, and thus is of some importance. One would expect from general Weber's Law principles that the distortion would have the most serious subjective effect at the lower frequencies, where it is relatively larger. For this reason its effect was compared with that of filtering out the lower frequencies.

A phonetically balanced word-list was recorded in two different random orders on tape. The list was List 3 of Test W–22 compiled by Hirsh et al. (1952): it contained fifty one-syllable words of familiar nature and giving a phonetic composition to the list as a whole which is similar to that of ordinary English. Although the balance is probably less perfect for the British listeners used in these experiments, than for the Americans used by Hirsh et al., the approximation was thought to be a reasonable one in the absence of adequate data on the British. The original tapes were then transmitted over an SSB radio system, and the output of the receiver recorded on other tapes. Five degrees of transposition of frequency were produced by suitable adjustment of the SSB system: 300 c/s and 200 c/s both upwards and downwards, and 0 c/s (absence of trans-position). With each degree of transposition, three levels of high-pass filtering were employed: removing the frequencies below 660, 440 and 0 c/s respectively. There were thus obtained fifteen different recordings, each of the same fifty words and each with a different combination of transposition and high-pass filtering.

The intelligibility of the various conditions was assessed in two ways: by mixing the speech with noise until the undistorted and unfiltered version gave a score of about 75 per cent correct, and by reducing the speech in intensity without adding noise, until intelligibility of the 'normal' version dropped to about the same point. Whichever course was adopted, all the recordings were played at the same intensity and signal-noise ratio to a number of subjects and the intelligibility scores of the various recordings compared. The two methods of assessment were used on different groups of subjects, and the order of presentation of conditions was of course suitably counterbalanced. When comparing the conditions under noisy circumstances, ten naval ratings were used as subjects, and their scores are shown in Table 1 (see p. 79).

It will be seen from Table 1 that both transposition and bass-cutting reduce intelligibility when noise is present. But the effect of transposition is much less when bass-cutting has been carried out. With 660 c/s bass cut, upward transposition has no effect at all; while with no bass cut upward transposition reduces the score of every subject ($p < 0.002$). Although down-ward transposition has a greater effect, which has long been known, this effect is greater when no bass cut is present. Once again, all subjects showed a larger difference in the one case than in the other ($p < 0.002$). In other words, once the speech had had the low frequencies removed transposition had little further effect on it: this is consistent with the view that transposition affects chiefly the low frequencies. One might expect that in that case transposition as well as bass-cutting would have little effect when the signal was made very faint, since that makes the low frequencies less important.

The second group of five subjects show that this is so, and the results appear in Table 2. (The 200 c/s transpositions have been omitted from the table, although they were presented to the subjects. Due to variation in tape quality the sound level was different in these recordings.) Both types of distortion are clearly less important in Table 2 than in Table 1. This not only confirms our suspicion that transposition has a greater effect on low frequencies, but also assures us that the very slight effects shown in the bottom line of Table 1 would not have been larger had the untransposed bass-cut speech been more intelligible in that table. In Table 2 the untransposed bass-cut speech gives as good a score as the completely normal speech in Table 1, yet transposition upward has no effect on it at all, and transposition downward has an effect significantly less ($p<0.01$) than in the top line of Table 1. Thus the absence of effect in the bottom line of Table 1 is not simply a statistical artifact due to ' the speech being so unintelligible it could get no worse '.

From a practical point of view, it should be noted that the filtered speech was in these experiments always kept at constant level per cycle within any one experiment. That is, when low frequencies were removed the upper parts of the spectrum were not raised in intensity to keep the total level of the speech constant. But in radio systems it will usually be possible to transmit a narrow band with more power than would be available for that band if other frequencies were also being transmitted. The lesson of these figures is that, when a satisfactory speech signal can be transmitted using high frequencies only, the effect of transposition will probably be unimportant. Further details of this work are given in an unpublished report (Broadbent 1955).

More generally, we have shown that other forms of distortion besides the filtering out of certain frequencies will have an effect which depends on the circumstances under which intelligibility is tested. Transposed speech will be little inferior to ordinary speech at low intensities, more so at higher intensities in noise, and very inferior in a noise whose energy is least at the low frequencies. But this is merely an illustration of the multiplicity of criteria to be applied to communication channels: and leads us to our main interest in this chapter, which is the assessment of channels by their effect on other simultaneous tasks.

*Transposed Speech and Simultaneous Tracking*

Both transposition of frequency and filtering out of the low frequencies have their effect by making unavailable the information carried by the lower end of the spectrum, as we have seen. But they do so in two different ways. Filtering removes the information altogether, leaving only the remainder of the spectrum. Transposition changes the familiar signal into an unfamiliar one at low frequencies, making it effectively into a noise, though not one which will produce any extra masking effect at higher frequencies. Thus the listener to transposed speech not only loses part of his information but also has to distinguish the remainder from other sounds. Correspondingly, transposed speech sounds peculiar and unnatural, requiring attention, while filtered speech is more straightforward to understand.

Two fresh experiments were performed to study the effect on a visual task of listening to distorted speech. It will be clear from the last chapter that the visual task should be one which requires the transmission of much information: that is, involving a rapid series of unpredictable stimuli. A high-speed tracking task was used to meet these conditions. A wavy line of brass contacts passed rapidly beneath a pointer whose position was controlled by the position of a hand-wheel. The line was screened from the subject's eyes until just before it reached the pointer, so that keeping the pointer on the line of contacts required continual attention. This tracking task is known as the triple tester, and since its war-time development it has been used a good deal as a standard task for experimental purposes: see, for example, Eysenck (1947). The score is the number of contacts touched in any run.

While performing this task, the subject was presented with the same recordings mentioned earlier in the chapter, but at a normal listening level and without noise. Only six conditions were used: the two downward transposed conditions and the untransposed one, each with 0 and with 660 c/s bass cut, and presented in a suitable random order. Table 3 shows the percentage of words which the six naval rating subjects were able to repeat correctly. In general the results are similar to those in Tables 1 and 2.

But our main interest in this experiment lies in Table 4: how was performance on the visual tracking task affected by listening? It is immediately obvious that bass-cutting and transposition have different effects. The latter, applied to unfiltered speech, causes a drop in performance on the visual task. All subjects showed the effect, so $p < 0.05$. But filtering has no such significant effect. This difference in the two kinds of distortion is suggestively parallel to the difference in the physical changes they produce in the signal: one simply removes information while the other converts it to meaningless sound. The latter therefore places a greater strain on the listener, since the same amount of remaining information must be distinguished from irrelevant sounds in that case but not in the other. This interpretation is supported by the effect of bass-cutting on transposed speech: it restores efficiency on the visual task to the original level, as would be expected if the cut was simply removing the meaningless irrelevant material. All subjects did better in the bass-cut condition than in the unfiltered one, with $-300$ c/s transposition, so $p < 0.05$.

In Tables 3 and 4 there are cases of equal intelligibility but unequal efficiency on the visual task, and also cases of unequal intelligibility but equal tracking performance. This is very strong evidence of the need for multiple criteria in assessing communications channels. It seems desirable to consider not only the intelligibility obtainable from a given speech system, but also the extent to which other tasks can be performed while using that system.

In addition, however, we have here evidence that the interference shown in the numerous experiments in Chapter 2 is not peculiar to speech tasks. A non-verbal task can also be affected. Admittedly it is not clear that the interference is of the same kind; it can hardly be due to the handling of too much information in the usual sense, since the differences in the listening task are only in the amount of irrelevant rather than relevant information. But we considered similar cases in Chapter 2, and argued in Chapter 3 that filtering would undoubtedly occupy part of the neural mechanism but that this was justified by the advantages it gained for the perceptual system proper. Making filtering more difficult might occupy more of the mechanism and so cause more interference with a simultaneous task. If so, the effect would be less likely to appear if the amount of information handled in the two simultaneous tasks was reduced. In support of this view, a fourth experiment was carried out in the same way as the last experiment but using only recordings of spoken digits instead of the list of fifty words. The ensemble of possibilities is here far smaller, and thus a smaller capacity is required. In keeping with this change in the situation, the various distortions produced no significant changes either in intelligibility or in the visual task. The detailed results are given by Broadbent (1955).

## Binaural Presentation and Simultaneous Tracking

Too general a conclusion could not be drawn from the results just given, since the case of transposed speech may be a special and peculiar one. Before we assert that non-verbal tasks can be impaired by bad speech communications, some other form of deterioration should be tested. In particular, the criticism should be noted that transposed speech is very rare in nature while filtered speech is ñot: a speaking tube or an echoing room is likely to produce filtering. It might be unfamiliarity which caused the visual task to deteriorate, rather than the presence of irrelevant sounds. The following experiment, however, shows a similar effect in a case in which the familiar situation is the more difficult to combine with a visual task.

The same tracking task was employed, and once again subjects were asked to listen while performing it. In this case, however, they did not have to repeat continually each word of a test list as it arrived. They were presented with a medley of irrelevant messages such as might pass between aircraft and the approach controllers of an airport. From time to time a particular call-sign was inserted unexpectedly amongst this babel, and the listener was asked to report that he had heard it. There were two conditions. In one case the irrelevant material and the call-sign were presented mixed through conventional head-phones. In the other case there was twice as much irrelevant material but half of it was presented to one ear alone and the other half to the other ear alone. The desired call-sign was unique in being presented to both ears simultaneously. From the results given in Chapter 2, this should favour correct hearing of the call-sign, particularly since binaural summation would increase the apparent loudness of the call-sign as opposed to the irrelevant background: as well as altering its apparent localization.

Twelve naval ratings performed this task, half receiving each condition first. The second of the two conditions described did, as expected, show more correct detections of the call-sign; though the difference was only significant at the end of the run. What was most striking, however, was a change in the efficiency of the tracking performance. The mean score was 982 with the binaurally separated presentation, and only 897 with the mixed presentation, $p < 0.05$. Once again the easier listening condition gives better simultaneous tracking. Further details are given by Broadbent (1953b).

The visual task, however, is still the same as in the previous experiment. A third investigation (Broadbent and Ford 1955) has compared the same two auditory conditions with a different visual task. To explain the choice of the latter it may be desirable to outline the practical purpose of these investigations. Pilots in radio contact with their home stations may hear other stations at the same time. The reason is simply that too many stations are using too few channels. If there are ten possible channels in a given frequency-band, and forty-five stations to use them, there is bound to be some overlap. However, if each station was assigned a pair of channels, every one of the forty-five could have a pair which was unique. Each station would share each of its channels with many other stations, but there would be no other station with the same pair of channels. If a pilot listened to two radios, one tuned to each of the channels of his own ground station, that would be the only station to be common to both radios. If one radio was heard on one ear and the other on the other, only the correct station would be heard on both ears. As a practical device the value of this technique may be limited, depending on the amount of overcrowding, on the availability of equipment, and so on. But it suggested the last experiment we considered, and led on to another similar experiment using pilots in the air as subjects. The visual task was in this case to perform a prescribed series of manoeuvres flying by instruments alone, while simultaneously listening to a radio transmission in order to pick out a particular call-sign. The same two varieties of listening were used. That is, the call was either mixed into ordinary head-phones with a number of irrelevant messages, or else split head-phones were used with a double number of irrelevant messages half coming to one ear and half to the other. In the latter case the call-sign was unique as being the only message heard on both ears at once.

The movements of the aircraft were recorded by photographing the instruments every 15 sec, the prescribed pattern of manoeuvres taking just over 15 min. The film records were afterwards analysed by examining each frame to see whether the height, speed and course were within certain set limits of the prescribed pattern: and the number of frames in which the limits were exceeded was totalled separately for each instrument.

Too much reliance must not be placed on the results, since the experiment was subject to the usual hazards of field studies in full measure: but they do confirm the laboratory findings. On six pilots studied, the altimeter was the instrument showing the most errors, followed by the direction indicator and the air-speed indicator in that order. The order probably reflects the severity of the limits chosen, and also the fact that the pattern required more changes of height than of the other variables, and more changes of direction than of speed. But the point of importance to us is that the most difficult part of the task, control of height, was performed significantly worse in the mixed listening condition ($p < 0.05$), which was as usual the more difficult way of listening. Control of speed, on the other hand, was unaffected: while direction showed a small and insignificant change in the direction of more errors in the more difficult listening condition.

This result again supports our view that complex non-verbal tasks may be impaired by a simultaneous listening task of some difficulty, though reduction in the difficulty of either may reduce the interference. Our three experiments have shown that tracking can be impaired either by transposed speech or by mixing relevant and irrelevant speech with no binaural cues to distinguish them: and that the latter condition will also impair the harder parts of the task of flying an aeroplane.

## GENERAL CONCLUSIONS

In this chapter we have seen difficulty of discrimination having to some extent the same effects as increase in the amount of information presented in a task. This is by no means unusual. One of the classic features of human behaviour which suggests the application of information theory is the fact that reaction time to a stimulus varies with the information conveyed by that stimulus (Hick 1952; Hyman 1953; Crossman 1953). The larger the ensemble from which the stimulus is drawn, the longer it takes to produce a reaction. But it has also been shown by Crossman (1955) that when the ensemble is kept at the same size the reaction time increases as the different possible stimuli are made more similar. It may be desirable to think of the stimuli used in any experiment as having positions in an ' information space ' made up of all the dimensions discriminable by the sense-organs. Discrimination takes a shorter time when the positions are farther apart as well as when they are few in number. Whatever the explanation for this correspondence between discrimination difficulty and amount of information, it seems well-established and it certainly seems reasonable that a larger mechanism should be required to recognize a small difference as real, against the background of unrelated nervous activity. As was said earlier in the chapter, this is connected with our statement in Chapter 3 that filtering would itself occupy some of the mechanism which would otherwise be available for information processing, so that a situation in which filtering is necessary may give a lower value for the capacity of the human being than a situation in which no filtering is necessary.

The argument of this book has been so far, first, that different speech tasks interfere with one another. This we ascribed to the limited capacity of the listener, which made necessary some selection among the information reaching the sense-organs. In the present short chapter we have shown that the addition of irrelevant sounds to a speech message made the latter interfere with a visual and non-verbal task. We have thus bridged the gap between verbal and non-verbal tasks, which our discussion in Chapter 3 encouraged us to think somewhat artificial: verbal tasks are very likely to be those with a high rate of information handling, but non-verbal tasks with such a high rate should show similar effects. In the next chapter we will abandon speech altogether, and enquire into the effects of meaningless sounds on visual, non-verbal, tasks.

Table 1. *The percentage of words correctly heard in noise under various kinds of distortion*

| Bass cut | Transposition of frequency | | | | |
|---|---|---|---|---|---|
| | −300 | −200 | 0 | 200 | 300 |
| 0 | 18 | 37 | 74 | 66 | 47 |
| 440 | 20 | 17 | 62 | 49 | 40 |
| 660 | 16 | 13 | 32 | 34 | 33 |

Table 2. *The percentage of words correctly heard at low intensity, under various kinds of distortion*

| Bass cut | Transposition of frequency | | |
|---|---|---|---|
| | −300 | 0 | 300 |
| 0 | 43 | 82 | 77 |
| 440 | 43 | 79 | 79 |
| 660 | 46 | 72 | 78 |

Table 3. *The percentage of words correctly heard with a simultaneous visual task*

| Bass cut | Transposition of frequency | | |
|---|---|---|---|
| | −300 | −200 | 0 |
| 0 | 63 | 86 | 97 |
| 660 | 67 | 58 | 81 |

*Table 4. The mean score on the visual task while listening to various distortions*

| Bass cut | Transposition of frequency | | |
|:---:|:---:|:---:|:---:|
| | −300 | −200 | 0 |
| 0 | 336 | 333 | 365 |
| 660 | 363 | 347 | 363 |

# CHAPTER 5

# THE EFFECTS OF NOISE ON BEHAVIOUR

A COMPREHENSIVE review of the effects of noise is fortunately not necessary, since Kryter (1950) and Berrien (1946) have reviewed the earlier work very thoroughly. Broadbent (1957a) has also given a more detailed account than is appropriate here. This is fortunate, because the practical importance of the problem has caused a fair number of papers to be written about it. In addition it is clear that some sounds are unpleasant, whether by learning or innately, and there is therefore a considerable literature of rather emotional type arguing that noise should be reduced. Examples of statements about noise ' driving us all mad ' and so on are given by Kryter. It need only be said that there is no evidence for such exaggerated claims: indeed, very little positive evidence of any effects on behaviour at all.

To summarize such evidence as is available, there are in the first place studies of industrial work before and after noise reduction. Some of these show improvements in efficiency: perhaps the best controlled are those of Weston and Adams (1932, 1935) who studied the output of weavers with and without ear-plugs. In one experiment they compared two groups over a period of time, while in another experiment ear-plugs were worn by the same workers on alternate weeks. Such precautions against practice or fatigue effects are not taken by some other industrial experimenters, whose results are therefore suspect. In both the Weston and Adams experiments the output with ear-plugs was greater than that without, though not dramatically so. Unfortunately the statistical methods of deciding significance which are now conventional were not then used, and the data for the individual workers in the two-group experiment are not given. In the alternate-week experiment all ten subjects are shown individually and every one shows the effect, so that it is certainly significant. The authors themselves preferred the two-group experiment because of changes in temperature and humidity from week to week in the other case. More serious than statistical points or minor variations in other variables, however, is the possibility that an experiment on the shop floor may be peculiarly open to ' suggestion ' effects, that the workers may approve of attempts to improve their lot and so try harder.   This point is made by Berrien and by Kryter, and it is a valid one: it does not disprove the results on weavers, but it makes laboratory confirmation with controls for suggestion desirable.   It is only fair to point out that half the subjects in the alternate week experiment gave the opinion that ear-plugs made no difference or were even positively undesirable: yet, as has been said, all subjects did better in the weeks when they wore plugs.   It seems a little difficult to ascribe this to suggestion.

Another minor point which bears on the role of suggestion and experimental novelty, is that the two groups in the second experiment were less far apart at the end of the experiment than they were at the beginning.   Weston and Adams point out that this may be a cyclic fluctuation and their graphs provide some evidence in support of this explanation; but equally the decrease in the effect might be due to the wearing off of the novelty, to the workers, of being used as subjects for an experiment.   A final point of interest is that the difference between the two groups is less at the beginning of the morning than it is later in the day, that is, the ' fatigue ' decline was greater in the unprotected workers.   This fact is of interest in view of laboratory findings to be mentioned later: but we should note that the alternate-week subjects did not give quite the same result.   The difference between plugs and unprotected ears was still least at a time during the morning, but this time was not at the beginning of the day but rather at mid-morning.   Possibly subjects who had worn ear-plugs one week might need to re-adapt themselves at the beginning of each day in the next week without plugs.   However, these last findings are worth rather little as evidence.

As has been said, other industrial studies are less well-controlled than those of Weston and Adams, and we may also criticize them on the same ground of liability to suggestion.   So laboratory studies must next be considered.   Many of these also are badly controlled, and have been adequately criticized by Kryter.   Of the remainder some show a slight but transient effect, and others no effect at all.   The former are of some interest to us, though perhaps of little practical importance, and should be mentioned in more detail.

### Transient Effects of Noise

A typical result is that of Ford (1929).   He asked his subjects to find a number of digits mixed in a jumble of letters, to add the digits together, and to write down the answer.   Eighteen such problems were given to each subject, and during the middle six, a klaxon horn was blown.   The first problem after the horn started to blow took longer than those done in the preliminary practice session in quiet: but this slowing-up effect rapidly disappeared.   Most interesting was the fact that another slowing occurred when the horn stopped after the twelfth problem.   In other words it seemed to be the change in the situation which interfered with the task, rather than the presence of a noise as such.

Rather similar results have been shown by Morgan (1916) for a coding task, and by Harmon (1933) for mental arithmetic, though Ford is rather unusual in the amount of emphasis he places on the effect of turning the noise off.   Pollock and Bartlett (1932) also found that a problem-solving task showed an initial effect of noise which wore off day by day, but in their case this may have been due to automatization of the task with practice. The repeated effect found by the other writers as the noise was turned on and off cannot be due to practice.   Some writers feel that the transience of the noise effect may be due to extra effort being brought in by the worker, and claim to support this by physiological measures of metabolism, etc.   But Harmon, for example, has found that metabolic effects return to normal as the noise continues, and so have more recent writers (Finkle and Poppen 1948).

In general it is agreed by most writers that the sudden onset of a noise may produce a very brief decline in efficiency, but that this will disappear as the noise continues.   For instance, Stevens et al. (1941), who were by no means believers in serious effects of noise, designed their noise experiments so that a steady sound of 90 db was present even in the ' quiet ' control conditions.   This was to prevent sudden sounds from outside the laboratory from reaching the subjects, since such sounds would have affected performance.   The precaution is a necessary one which the present writer has also adopted: there is no doubt that the transient effect from onset of a noise must be distinguished from the possible long-term effects, and therefore sudden noises should be excluded from experiments on the lasting effects. The latter are also of more practical interest than the former. But the interpretation of the transient effect raises points which will reappear in the more important case of prolonged noise. The onset of a sharp sound is known to be a stimulus for a ' startle response ' which involves general muscle contraction, blinking and so on: the sort of response which some people refer to as ' jumping out of my skin '. This response has been studied by Landis and Hunt (1939) and found to be still present in diminished form even in experienced pistol instructors when firing. This general undifferentiated response might be regarded as interfering with the response to the visual task: that is, the worker effectively stops responding for an instant and then begins again, because his task response could not occur at the same time as his startle response. Such a theory is plausible, but it would suggest that a man who had to make some response to the sound (other than the unlearned startle response) would also be hampered until the startle response had disappeared: any response to a novel sound should be less efficient than response to a more familiar one, just as visual tasks suffer more when a man has to ignore a novel sound, than when he has to ignore a familiar one. But responses to novel stimuli are in fact particularly efficient: it is worth digressing at this stage to consider the evidence on this topic.

A particularly good example was given in Chapter 2, when describing the experiments of Poulton (1956) on listening to messages from several loudspeakers. If the messages came more frequently from one loudspeaker, a message from the previously quiet speaker was more likely to be correctly heard than a message from the previously busy speaker. In terms of the filter theory we put forward earlier, the filter is biassed towards previously quiet channels, and information on busy channels has a lower chance of reaching the perceptual system. In ordinary speech, we attend to an unusual event rather than a simultaneous usual event. This fact is particularly curious because a rare event contributes more information than a common event, on the measure considered in Chapter 3: and a task requiring the analysis of more information might be expected to be more difficult. It seems well supported by experiments in other fields, however. For example, Hyman (1953), working with visual re-action times, found that as the ensemble of signals increased the reaction time went up, confirming the finding by Hick (1952) that reaction time was proportional to the information in the signal. When Hyman altered the frequency of the signals instead of having them equiprobable, he found once again that this decrease in the average information per signal did give a decrease in the average reaction time. But reactions to the least common signals were faster than they should have been on information calcula-tions. Once again there seemed to be an undue bias in favour of the unusual event.

Berlyne (1951a) also used visual reactions but required the subject to react only to one out of a group of simultaneous signals; and the most frequently chosen signal was recorded. After a sequence of similar groups, if a group was presented in which all members but one were familiar, the unusual signal was the most likely to be chosen. The same author, using rats (1950), has introduced the animals to particular objects, then removed them, and faced them later with some of the former objects and a new one. The animals spent more time investigating the new object than the previously experienced ones. As he points out, the time scale is in this case different, but once again the unusual stimulus is more likely to elicit a response.

If the response to a fresh stimulus is particularly efficient, it does not seem plausible that the inefficiency of work, done just after a noise has been turned on or off, should be due to a general decline in ability to respond, due to some competing startle response. Such a competing response should interfere with responses to the novel stimulus itself as well as with responses to other stimuli. It seems rather more likely that the man is unable to respond to visual stimuli from his task because he is taking in information from the ear; so he would actually be more efficient on responses to the auditory stimulation. Our view of the events within the man would be as follows.

His capacity is limited, and therefore a filter placed early in his nervous system selects only part of the information reaching his sense-organs. This will normally represent information necessary for his task.   The filter has a bias, however, towards channels on which any novel event occurs.   Thus the onset of a noise causes the filter to select auditory information, and so task information does not reach the perceptual system.   As the bias is only towards novel events, the *status quo* is rapidly reestablished and efficiency on the task returns to normal.   Stopping the noise will produce a similar temporary change.

As has been said, this view seems more plausible than that of a man thrown into a momentary inability to respond by any mode: but on either theory the fact that the onset of a noise causes a drop in the efficiency of a visual task is a limited capacity phenomenon.   We are passing now away from the verbal tasks we first considered, and have shown that under suitable conditions an irrelevant noise will interfere with a visual task.   But we must now emphasize the time for which the stimuli are applied: the interference appears only when the noise first begins.

The factual question which next requires an answer is: does any interference reappear after prolonged work ?   Is there any cumulative effect of noise ?   Or, in terms of our theory, when the filter has ceased to take in auditory information and returned to task information, does it ever return to the ear ?   If it does, this will mean that the bias of the filter towards novelty must not be taken to mean novelty at the senses; rather the bias is towards channels which have not recently passed information through the filter, and not necessarily towards channels on which no stimulation has recently occurred.   Both types of mechanism are logically possible; only experiment can decide which is in fact present, and such experiments are our next concern.

*Experiments Showing No Effects of Noise*

The various experiments we have already mentioned could be counted as showing no effect of noise other than a transient one. By the close of the work-period the subjects were usually performing as well in noise as in quiet.   But the period was extremely short, of the order of 10 min.   Most of the early experiments using longer work-periods are objectionable on statistical grounds. But the main evidence that performance can be maintained for long periods in noise comes from war-time researches, which are adequately based.   In one case, at Tufts College (1942), operators

were asked to follow a moving target for 4 hr.   A 2 min burst of
noise was presented at some time during this period, but did not
impair the work.   When it was presented towards the end of the
period, it actually improved efficiency; subjectively, the operators
reported that the novelty of the event relieved the monotony of
the long work-period.   Here again we seem to have a novelty
effect, though of a sort somewhat opposite to what might have
been expected: the operator does not attend to the novel sound
at the expense of his work.   There may, of course, have been a
highly transient drop in efficiency at the beginning of the noise,
comparable with that in the earlier experiments.   (Efficiency at
various points within the 2 min spell was not reported; Woodhead (1958) has recently reported that when a short burst of sound
is presented during a continuous rapid series of visual stimuli,
there is an interference on the few stimuli arriving just after the
bang but this disappears in a matter of seconds so that performance over a 4 min period is quite normal.)   But if so the re-
adjustment was no slower because of the prolonged time during
which task information had been arriving.   The filter may have
shifted channel, but if so the time of the shift was brief.   This
is a point which will be taken up again later: we shall see that the
presence of noise, according to one interpretation of the experiments, affects the probability of shifts of the filter, but not their
duration.

The second set of war-time experiments were done at Harvard
(Stevens et al. 1941).   In this case a large number of tasks were
used.   The subjects worked 7 hr days, and 115 db noise was presented on some days.   The noise used was predominantly low-
pitched, and was continuous.   Counter-balanced days were in
quiet, which was, as mentioned above, 90 db.   The noise ex-
posures were thus lengthy.   The tasks however were all restricted
to 15 min or less in length, in order to maintain motivation.   Each
subject was therefore changing from task to task at frequent
intervals, although the noise remained constant.   In addition there
were four 5 min breaks and one $\frac{1}{2}$ hr break during the day, all
spent in the noise.   The five subjects used were carefully selected:
they were all recommended by competent judges as generally
willing and able to work, and they were screened for auditory
and visual defects.   All of them had a high educational standard.

Certain tests used definitely showed an absence of any noise effect.   These included choice reaction time, card sorting, translating written codes, judging distance, and a task requiring the subject to keep a cathode-ray tube spot in a fixed position by the use of aircraft controls.   Another such task was the pursuit rotor, in which a small disc on a gramophone turn-table is followed with a stylus.

Some other tasks showed inconclusive results owing to high variability either between subjects or between performances of one subject.   These included speed of accommodation, dark adaptation, reversible perspective, hand steadiness and measures of muscle tension, metabolism, and breath rate.   There was also another task involving aircraft controls, this time used to direct a beam of light at a series of targets.   This task showed an apparent effect of noise both on speed and on accuracy, but it was later decided that the effect might have been due to auditory cues from the relays of the scoring mechanism: such cues would naturally be more helpful in the quieter condition.

What is to be concluded from these results ?   First, that the mere presence of considerable sound energy at the ear does not throw the entire nervous system into chaos.   Apart from the great practical importance of this result, it is quite consistent with our filter theory that only certain sensory stimuli are passed to the perceptual system.   At the same time, from our present point of view these experiments are precisely those which we would expect to minimize the effects of noise.

In most of the tasks used the rate of transmission of information through the man was low.   In, for instance, reversible perspective it is difficult to see whether any was transmitted at all: and in such tasks as hand steadiness or the pursuit rotor, there was no external independent source of information to which the man was responding.   Of course, when the man's action was not quite as intended—if his hand wandered—information on this fact would be fed back through the nervous system to produce a corrective action.   But this is true of any task, and when the hand is to be kept still or moved in a repeating pattern, the information transmitted must be less than when a series of different reactions is made to a series of different stimuli.

In the other tasks, although information might be transmitted through the man its rate of arrival is uneven and predictable. Thus in psychophysical experiments such as judging distance, or in tasks such as choice reaction, each signal occurs at a time which is roughly known to the subject and is preceded and followed by intervals in which little or no task information reaches the sense-organs. During these intervals the man could show good performance even though he closed his eyes. If something similar were to happen internally, if the filter were to cease to pass visual information, performance would not reveal the fact. The tasks of which this is probably least true are the two involving control of spots of light by aircraft controls: in these the information presented might be regarded as arriving more continuously. But one of them was regarded as fairly easy, and presumably therefore represented a low information rate, while the other did in fact show an effect although this was attributed to auditory cues.

In general, quite apart from the nature of the tasks, we would expect effects of noise to be slight in these experiments if we maintain the views put forward in the last section. We said there that apparently a novel stimulus, whether the beginning or ending of a noise, would tend to be passed by the filter. If noise continues steadily for some time (7 hr) while the task changes every 15 min, the task information is particularly likely to pass the filter and so no effect of noise would appear. Further, it should be noted that in this experiment all the tasks were practised by the subjects before the measurements were made: as we considered in Chapter 3, practice will alter task performance by reducing the amount of information needed for success. Practised tasks may well be more resistant to distracting stimulation, except when crucial information arrives.

The last experiment showing negative results which we shall consider is one by Viteles and Smith (1946). It is important because the conditions used were different from those of the Harvard experiments. The tasks were all longer: at least $\frac{1}{2}$ hr. They all involved quite high rates of transmission of information: for instance, they included coding using a typewriter, mental multiplication of three-place by two-place numbers, visual threading of mazes, the finding of particular locations in a grid of rows and columns, the inspection of two numerical series in search of cases in which both members of the pair were the same, and the tracing of a circular pattern by the use of two controls as in a lathe. The six subjects were not so rigidly selected: they had concluded their education after high school. Three noise levels were compared, 70, 80 and 90 db, the noise being that of an electric fan. This means, of course, that the highest noise level was the same as the ' quiet ' of the Harvard experiments. Four-hour work-periods were used, and three levels of temperature were also adopted.

Output of correct work certainly does not drop as the noise gets louder: on the multiplication and number checking tasks it was significantly greater at 90 than at 70 db. But output represents an average over the whole work-period of at least $\frac{1}{2}$ hr, so that brief failures to absorb visual information would not be reflected in it. Such brief failures might possibly be reflected in mistakes, which increase significantly in noise in the mental multiplication and lathe tasks. The locations task, on the other hand, shows significantly less errors at the highest noise level. It might possibly be said that the rate of handling information was least even in the locations task, and most continuous in the lathe, but such a statement requires fuller details of the actual situations than are available.

In general, then, this experiment shows no very clear and consistent effects of noise, despite the various differences between the conditions used, and those of the Harvard experiments. But in view of the results to be discussed later in this chapter this is not too surprising, since 90 db is the lowest level at which any positive effect has ever been demonstrated.

There are certain other experiments which have not been mentioned but which show negative results: they are cited in the various reviews of the topic mentioned at the beginning of the chapter, and are mostly on a smaller scale than those mentioned. They confirm, however, that many tasks can be performed quite as well in noise as in quiet after the very brief initial effect of turning on the noise. So far as the writer is aware, however, all of them possess at least one of the following characteristics: the noise is of less than 90 db, or the work-period or noise exposure are short, or the task is one in which there are numerous predictable instants in which no information will reach the worker. Many of the experiments possess more than one of these characteristics, as in the cases already discussed, and almost all use selected subjects. These are in no sense criticisms of the experiments, since it was essential to find out whether noise has any obvious cataclysmic effect before looking for more subtle changes. Nor does the fact that the negative experiments have these features in common necessarily mean that an experiment which did not have them would show any effect. Yet some experiments with positive results do exist, which will be discussed in the next section, and it is important to realize that this is not a direct factual conflict but merely a difference in experimental conditions.

## Experiments Showing Effects of Noise

The first experiment to be considered was deliberately designed to avoid the conditions which the negative experiments had in common. That is, the task and noise exposure were long, vital information might arrive at any time, the subjects were unselected except for normality of hearing, and the noise used was 100 db with roughly equal energy in each octave of the spectrum. The task was to observe continuously twenty steam-pressure gauges, and to turn a knob if any of the gauges showed more than a critical pressure. This task went on for $1\frac{1}{2}$ hr, during which fifteen signals were presented at various intervals and without warning. In other words the subject spent most of his time doing nothing but at any instant he might have to respond. The time taken to respond was recorded: as the display was deliberately a poor one, not based on the best human engineering principles, only about a third of the signals were seen in less than 10 sec.

A considerable amount of work had been done on this task with different subjects before the noise experiment began. The most relevant result at this point is that a practice effect appeared between the first two runs, but that if five runs were given on successive days the third and fourth runs were not inferior to the second and fifth. Accordingly in the noise experiment ten subjects were given 2 days work at 70 db, 2 days at 100 db, and a last one at 70 db. These subjects were naval ratings taken at random from a unit maintained in Cambridge. This source of supply had the advantage that the subjects were accustomed to working in very high noise levels, though not of course in the particular noise used in this case.

The effect was quite startling, the proportion of signals seen in less than 10 sec being 0·36 for quiet, and only 0·22 for noise, a drop of nearly 40 per cent. It must of course be remembered that this experiment had deliberately chosen conditions likely to produce an effect of noise: 40 per cent changes in efficiency will certainly not appear on all tasks. In addition to the original laboratory result on this twenty dials task (Broadbent 1954a), a closely similar task has been used by Loeb, Jeantheau and Weaver (1956) to compare efficiency in a stationary and moving tank, and showed lower performance in the latter condition. Naturally there was not only noise but also vibration involved in this case, so that its theoretical implications are less clear than those of the laboratory experiment, but it shows that similar effects appear under more realistic conditions.

To show that the amount of impairment depended on the task, another experiment was carried out (Broadbent 1954a) which was exactly the same as the original twenty dials one except that the signals were made easy to see. Instead of coming from badly designed dials, they were given by small flash-lamp bulbs. The proportion of signals seen within the critical time on the first run was over twice as many with this display as with the previous one. As was pointed out in the last chapter, distinguishing a signal from irrelevant background is a function requiring capacity, and a change in the display of this kind should therefore reduce the capacity needed and lessen effects of competing stimulation. (It must be added, lest the reader acquire a misleading impression of the way in which research is carried on, that this theoretical way of putting matters was not formulated before the experiment. An easier display was used because it had been found by other workers to minimize the effects of other stresses.) The effect of noise disappeared. As the altered task had not been previously used in quiet to confirm the absence of any difference between days, another ten subjects were tested in a counterbalanced order of noise and quiet: but there was still no difference on the average between the noisy days and the quiet days, when the whole group of twenty subjects was considered.

We next need to enquire whether this absence of effect on the twenty lights task means that the subjects are truly unaffected by the noise when doing this task: or whether it means that the subjects are affected but that the task is not one which reveals the fact in the score. Detailed analysis suggests the latter alternative, which is indeed the one supported by the point of view we are urging. Thus for example if the twenty lights are divided into those in the middle of the display and those at the edges, the former do show a significant deterioration in noise. This effect is diluted by the absence of effect on the other lights, and so does not appear in the overall results. Again, the length of the average sequence of signals unnoticed for more than 10 sec is longer in noise; that is, there is less tendency for periods of low efficiency to be evenly scattered throughout the work-period, they are rather concentrated at some time. In addition, the relative efficiency in noise goes down compared with that in quiet as the time since the beginning of the noise condition increases. Lastly, and most important of all, some subjects are far more affected than others. If we had considered only subjects who showed a practice effect between runs 1 and 2, similar to that shown by all subjects on the dials, we would have found an effect of noise similar to that on the dials. This individual difference is not of course a typological one: there are persons showing this pattern of behaviour in all degrees. But a correlation between the practice effect and the noise effect is significant. Furthermore, it will be shown in Chapter 7 that an independent test of susceptibility to noise is also related to educational achievement; which again bears on the interpretation of earlier experiments.

So far, then, we have shown that an effect of noise can appear when the particular conditions of earlier experiments are avoided. We have shown by changing the task and abolishing the effect, that it really is the particular nature of the work which is important, and not some peculiarity of the laboratory where the work was done. We also have some reason for thinking that the task which shows no effect, only does so because it fails to tell us everything about the man who is performing it. In various rather subtle ways performance is altered, although the average score remains the same. Both the tasks we have mentioned so far, however, are ' vigilance ' tasks, that is, they require the subject to watch for signals arriving at an uncertain time. The reality of the noise effect on such tasks seems fairly well-established: Jerison and Wing (1957) have shown that about 114 db noise produces a decrement in a task consisting of three clock tests performed simultaneously. (The clock test is discussed in the next chapter: in Jerison's case the rate of signalling was high, one signal every 20 sec on the average overall, but otherwise the task was similar.)* In addition Broussard, Walker and Roberts (1952), when investigating the effect of 90 db noise on the visual contrast threshold, found that reaction time to their near-threshold signals was longer in noise even though the threshold itself was normal. The extent to which their situation can be regarded as a vigilance task is discussed elsewhere (Broadbent 1957a); the conclusion was that it can.

It is desirable to consider also a task in which signals arrive at known times but frequently, so that the rate of arrival of information is even. This will act as a check on our original identification of the conditions necessary for a noise effect to appear; it might be that the length of the task and the lack of any opportunity for brief selection of a non-task source of information are not the important variables, and that there is some unsuspected feature of vigilance tasks which makes them vulnerable to noise. Furthermore, if we are to explain the numerous negative results from noise experiments, we cannot suppose that noise produces a lowering of efficiency which lasts throughout a long period. It must produce brief intervals of inefficiency, short enough to lie entirely in the gaps between the arrival of crucial information in, for instance, a psycho-physical experiment. Vigilance tasks can only detect this inefficiency because they sample the man's activity at unpredictable instants, and so do not allow him to arrange his brief periods of inefficiency so as to maintain task performance. An essential test of this view is to use a consecutive task in which the man's activity is continuously recorded; so that we can see whether he is affected by noise only for brief periods.

The task used (Broadbent 1953a) was one devised by Dr. J. A. Leonard. It consists of five separate lights, and five contacts each corresponding to a light. When a lamp goes on, the subject

---

* Jerison (1957) has found that noise does not affect a single clock-test performed by itself. This highly important result suggests that noise only affects tasks in which attention must be shifted regularly from one source to another; all the tasks showing effects are in fact of this type.

must touch the appropriate contact. As soon as he makes a reaction, another lamp lights. Consequently there is always something to do, and there are no rest intervals between the signals. If the man inserts such intervals by making a brief pause, possibly followed by faster work to make up, the fact is detected by a device which records the number of periods of 2 sec or more in which no response was made. In addition, any touches given to incorrect contacts are recorded. Practised subjects do tend to make such errors, surprising as it may seem at first sight, rather than to insert pauses in their performance. It will be noted that any error is a perfectly well-coordinated response, but does not correspond to the particular stimulus. That is, it seems to represent a failure in the intake of information rather than a breakdown on the response side. As noise experiments necessarily involve at least 2 days performance, in order to obtain quiet and noise scores from each subject, and so avoid the need for astronomical numbers of subjects to give an experiment sufficiently sensitive to overcome the large variability between individuals, errors rather than pauses are the main index of brief failures to take in task information.

This task was given to eighteen naval ratings for two $\frac{1}{2}$ hr periods on successive days. One day was in 100 db noise, half the subjects having this condition first and half second. As we might expect, the output of correct responses was not appreciably affected by noise: there was an insignificant drop of about 1 per cent. But the number of errors rose sharply: it averaged fifty-seven in noise and thirty-seven in quiet, a rise of over 50 per cent. A second group of fourteen subjects were used as a control for suggestion effects. They were seen individually and told that noise improves performance. But they still showed a rise in errors on noise of almost 50 per cent, so it does not seem likely that the original finding is due to suggestion. A very notable feature of these experiments was that the relative efficiency in noise again declined with time since the beginning of the test. If a 5 min work-period had been used noise would actually have been better than in quiet. As in other tests mentioned in this section, it seems that the length of the task is truly an important condition.

Another task in which the man is continually handling information and has no opportunity for a shift of attention to non-task stimuli, is one devised by Jerison (1954). Three lights face the subject, each flashing in a regular but slow rhythm and each with its own rate so that the sequence of lights does not repeat. The subject has to press a key when one of the three lights has flashed a prescribed number of times, say ten. So he has to keep continuous count of the three separate sequences of events, and even when he responds to one he cannot relax for an instant, as he must still remember the state of the other two channels. This task showed more errors in noise, the difference increasing as the length of time in the noise increased.*

By this stage we have reviewed a fair number of experiments, and the general conclusions are probably not clear to the reader. Let us state them in as simple a form as possible, before proceeding to a further test of the theory.

*The effect of noise thus far.*—Our survey thus far seems to require an effect of noise which is very comparable to blinking (Broadbent 1957a). Blinking is a function which has certain obvious characteristics. A blink usually lasts a definite brief period, though the frequency of blinks may be high or low. Each blink cuts off the incoming information to the nervous system instantaneously, but this does little harm for three reasons. First, if a man looks at some novel and important object he will temporarily suspend blinking. Secondly, although he cannot keep up this suspension of blinking indefinitely, he has some control over the time of occurrence of his blinks. As he goes on looking at an object he is more and more likely to blink, but if he knows that no crucial information will arrive at a certain time he can usually blink at that time, and so avoid interference with the task. Thirdly, he is able to continue acting even though he is not taking in information: he may follow a regularly wandering line with a pointer even while his eyes are shut, although he cannot of course do this with an irregularly wandering line. (These statements about blinking rest on experimental evidence by Drew (1950), and by Poulton and Gregory (1952).)

---

* A later analysis of the same task (Jerison 1956) showed that the effect appeared only between two independent groups of subjects, one working in noise and one in quiet. Once subjects had worked in noise they did not improve when given quiet conditions of work.

Now the effect of noise seems to imply an effect like blinking but within the nervous system. The man's eyes may be open, but he does not use the information from them. This failure must be brief, perhaps not as brief as a blink, but short enough that only errors on the five-choice task are affected. Output remains normal. The effect must also be brief enough to fit in between the crucial signals of the tasks used by the Harvard researches. The failures are also unimportant just after the beginning of a task, as blinks are: this appears from the change in relative efficiency in noise found in a number of experiments as time since the beginning of the task increased. It seems likely that when the task involves predictable safe periods in which nothing will happen, the failures can be made to occur at those times just as blinks can, and so leave the score unaffected. This helps to explain the difference between the earlier experiments and the later ones in which there are no safe periods free from the arrival of information. It is also necessary to suppose that the man can continue to act during these failures to assimilate information, just as he does when blinking; since workers in noise obviously do not stop dead for brief instants.

The resemblance between blinking and the inferred internal process is probably not coincidental, since the eyelids may well be used to assist the internal adjustments of the nervous system. But it seems necessary to suppose some such internal process to reconcile all the evidence we have reviewed: the only alternative is a failure of experimental technique on the part of some of those involved, and this does not seem plausible to the writer. The deduction of ' internal blinking ' from the experimental results proceeds as follows.

If the truth is that there is no effect of noise, the considerable changes found by some experiments become unintelligible. If the effect were a sustained lowering of efficiency, the negative results of the writer when measuring output on the five-choice task and of earlier workers using similar measures would be hard to explain. Thus the effect must be one of brief periods of inefficiency, increasing in frequency in noise. If these periods were due to a failure of response it would be hard to explain the observed possibility of continuous repetitive work in noise; and the fact that on the five-choice task, co-ordinated but incorrectly chosen responses, are the errors whose measured incidence increases. Only an increase in the frequency of brief periods of inefficiency on the perceptual side will fit all these experimental findings. That is, an effect like blinking but within the nervous system.

To say that noise produces brief failures of perception is thus entailed by the experimental results. But there remains the question of the nature of these failures. The experiments we have thus far considered are quite consistent with the view that all incoming information is temporarily blocked, as though the man was cut off from the outer world altogether for an instant. But the filter theory we have been putting forward in this book would suggest that the eyes are neglected only because information is being received from some other sense. In ordinary language, does the man attend to the noise and so neglect his work, or does his mind become a blank for an instant? These may be termed the distraction or paralysis theories.

This choice of possibilities is closely similar to that considered when the effects of turning on a noise were discussed. In that case too there was a possibility that the novel stimulus caused neglect of task information, and also a possibility that the novel stimulus caused a complete failure to deal with information of any kind. We decided tentatively, though not conclusively, in favour of the former, since novel stimuli themselves receive very adequate responses and so seem to be distracting rather than paralysing. The same argument can be applied in the present case, though more conclusively since the startle response can be left out of account. If different noises vary in their effect on a visual task, they may also vary when used as stimuli for an auditory task. On the distraction view, which our filter theory supports, the worst noise to ignore would be the easiest to notice, and so to use as a task stimulus. But on the paralysis view, the noise which causes the greatest disruption of a visual task should be the worst to use in an auditory task. It causes a general interference with response and must be supposed to do so whether it also provides task information or not.

*The effects of high and low pitched noise.*—The same five-choice task was used (Broadbent 1957b). Twenty-four subjects were used on this occasion, divided into three equal groups. Each group received its own intensity of noise: 80, 90 and 100 db. Each man worked for two ½ hr periods, on successive days, one day receiving a noise containing only frequencies above 2000 c/s, and the other day receiving a noise containing only frequencies below that point. The high-pitched noise produced more errors throughout, but the difference was insignificant at the two lower intensities. It was highly significant at 100 db: indeed, high-pitched 100 db noise produced twice as many errors as high or low pitched 80 or 90 db noise, which were all very similar to one another.

Two points immediately appear from this work as relevant to earlier experiments. First, the high frequencies seem to be disproportionately responsible for the effect. Use of predominantly low-pitched noise by some experimenters may have helped to obscure effects. Secondly, the effect appears sharply above 100 db, and experiments using lower levels would not therefore show it.

Our main interest, however, is in the fact that noise of different pitch varies in its effect on behaviour. Would it also vary in its effect on tasks in which it was itself a stimulus? To investigate this, reaction times to high and low pitched noises of various intensities were determined. An exact parallel to the effect of noise on a prolonged visual task would perhaps have been the use of noises as stimuli in a prolonged auditory task. But this was not done, as there are some reasons for doubting whether auditory vigilance is subject to quite the same rules as visual vigilance (see Chapter 9). Furthermore, the need to use intermittent noises when using them as signals automatically prevented an exact parallel with the experiments on visual vigilance in noise, since the noise was in that case continuous. Reaction times of the ordinary variety were therefore obtained. On a filter theory there might be no difference between different stimuli once the filter had selected them, the difference being rather between the probabilities of the correct class of sensory events being selected. The reaction times were therefore obtained in a way which gave a chance for failures of selection to show themselves. Each subject received five signals of one type followed by five signals of the other pitch, and so on until twenty-five signals of each type had been presented. No demonstration of the new signal was given before each group of five; the subjects were thus relatively unfamiliar with the signal at the start of each group of five reactions, but became less so as the series continued. Two separate groups of subjects were used, one having 100 db signals and one 75 db.

It has long been known that a more intense signal produces a faster reaction time, up to a certain level (Piéron 1952). Our experiments showing that a more intense sound interferes with work more than a fainter one, are themselves therefore in favour of a distraction rather than a paralysis theory of noise effects. If high pitched noise also produced faster reactions it would support this same view. Earlier experiments by Fessard and Kucharski (1935) and by Chocholle (1940) have disagreed on this point. Fessard and Kucharski found that high-pitched noise gave faster reactions, while Chocholle found all pitches gave equal times. The results of the experiment we are now considering resolve the conflict: it appeared that at the low intensity and with unfamiliar sounds the low-pitched stimulus gave a longer reaction time than the high-pitched one. At the higher intensity and with familiar sounds the two became equal. On examination of the procedure used by the two early researches, we find that Chocholle makes much of the need to familiarize the subjects with the particular stimulus being used: he therefore gave numerous trials with one kind of signal, and seems to have discarded early trials. Fessard and Kucharski, however, felt that fatigue should be avoided, and so gave very few trials. They were thus working with unfamiliar signals, and correspondingly showed shorter reaction times to high frequencies. Just as in the later experiment (Broadbent 1957b), the difference only appeared at low intensities.

It seems fair to interpret these results in favour of a distraction theory, then, as they exactly reverse the effects found when a visual task is done in noise. In the latter case low intensities and low frequencies produce the highest efficiency, in this case the lowest. In the visual case there is no difference between different pitches at low intensities, in this case there is none at high intensities. In the visual experiments the effect is greatest at the end of the run, and in this case at the beginning. It does not seem, therefore, that conditions which cause errors in the visual task also cause slow auditory reactions: on the contrary, they show fast ones and this suggests that the noise interferes with a visual task by itself controlling response rather than by disorganizing all response.    In terms of our filter theory, the filter selects the noise and so neglects the visual information.    In ordinary language, the effect of noise is to cause a wandering of attention rather than a complete mental blank.

Before leaving this experiment, there are two other points which should be made.    The first is the importance of interactions: high frequencies at low intensities have no effect, high frequencies at high intensities have a marked effect.    Equally, noise has no effect early in a task, but late in a task has a marked effect.    This seems to be a general rule of stress experiments, that variations from normal conditions have little effect in isolation, but that once the change has passed a certain point the effect is marked (Bartlett 1948).    There is another statistical interaction of interest in this experiment, however.    The subjects who received high-pitched noise at the highest intensity on the first day did worse throughout the experiment than subjects who received a more favourable condition on the first day.    This type of interaction has been neglected in the literature: almost the only example is a paper by Welford, Brown and Gabb (1950) on fatigue in air-crew.    They found that subjects who were faced with a particular task immediately after a long flight did badly, and also did badly when they returned to the task after a rest.    Other subjects who first came to the task fresh did well, and continued to do well even after a flight.    The explanation of this type of effect is not yet clear, and requires experiments of some complexity of design.    It may be that noise (or the after-effects of flying) affects the manner in which the task is learned and so all subsequent performance. Or it may be that the after-effects of the noise last over a long period which the intervening rest between sessions did not exhaust.    Other interpretations are possible.    Methodologically the possibility raises serious problems.    Most good noise experiments have used one group of subjects with counter-balanced presentation of conditions.    If noise has after-effects, this may not be adequate.    It is probably true to say that the results of all the work discussed in this chapter will remain valuable even if such after-effects are later established more reliably, but they may need some reinterpretation. Jerison (1956) has provided the first step towards putting the after-effects on a firm basis, by showing that a group, who first meet his task of keeping count of three sequences of events in noise, do worse on a later occasion in quiet than a group who first meet the task in quiet.

## Omissions in the Literature

The work we have surveyed is clearly not sufficient to allow satisfaction with our knowledge about noise. The major avenues which need future exploration should be briefly indicated.

In the first place, there is the absence of any data on very long-term habituation. The type of task which shows an effect of noise has not been given to people who have worked in noise for years, in the noise which they normally experience. This should be practical in the future, by taking tests which are known to show effects of noise to factories and similar places. There are some difficulties, however; ideally, the task should be continued in quiet for a very long period as well as given in a familiar noise. But for the moment we must be cautious about postulating effects on very highly experienced workers. A particular form of this warning applies to the difference between noises of high and low pitch. It must be admitted that, although the subjects used were familiar with noise, they were not familiar with the filtered noises used. Possibly after prolonged exposure the differences between the spectra would disappear. Kryter (1950) notes that this is true for subjective annoyance: the more high-pitched of two equally loud noises is initially reported as more annoying, but the difference becomes less with repeated exposure. Of course, with high-pitched noise of 100 db, some deafness would be produced by repeated exposure. It should also be noted that the experiments with positive results seem to show increasing noise effect if anything as the exposure goes on; this caution about very prolonged habituation is merely one which is logically necessary, and does not mean that there is any evidence for such habituation. The short-term habituation reported by some experiments is clearly not proof against long work-periods.

A second point is the need for more information on the more serious types of noise. Interrupted noise, both regular and irregular, needs to be tried. From our general view of the role of novel stimuli, it seems likely that interruption of a noise will increase the impairment produced by it.    Certainly intermittent noises are commonly reported as more annoying.    Again, in Chapter 2 a good deal of evidence was given about the importance of auditory localization in selective listening: it is chiefly important in allowing one channel to be ignored.    Vaguely localized sounds are reported as subjectively more annoying, and it may well be that a sound from a definite direction can more readily be ignored: the filter can reject more easily one particular auditory channel rather than all auditory channels.    Changes of localization in a noise of constant loudness may also affect its novelty and so degree of interference with a visual task.    Finally, it may be true not only that high-pitched sounds are worse than low but also that a narrow band-width sound is different from a broad band of frequencies.    A narrow band seems less loud for equal energy (Pollack 1952); it may also be easier to ignore one part of the spectrum than to ignore all parts.    Obviously there is much to be done on the question of the character of the noise.

A third point is the exploration of individual differences.    It is obvious to anyone that some people complain more about noise than others do; it was shown by Weston and Adams that those who complain more do in fact show greater benefit from ear-plugs (though the difference was not significant, and may of course have been a suggestion effect even if true).    Culpin and Smith (1930) showed that people rated as being of nervous temperament were more apt to complain of noise.    The individual differences on the twenty lights test seem, however, to be the first sign of marked differences in effect on performance.    This should certainly be pursued: more data on the role of individual differences will be considered in Chapter 7.

Fourthly, there is the possibility of effects on tasks other than vigilance tasks and those requiring continuous handling of information.    We shall see in Chapter 9 that there is some reason for regarding immediate memory and perception as involving the same mechanism.    If our filter is involved in immediate memory, and its operation is disturbed by noise, tasks using immediate memory may be disturbed even though the rate of arrival of information is not high and continuous.    Jerison's task already mentioned seems to be such a case, although the effects shown might in principle be accounted for purely by failure to take in information.* There may also be other effects of noise besides the effect on incoming information: it is interesting that noise shows no effect on gaps in performance in the five-choice task, since other stresses do (Wilkinson 1957). This may imply that noise produces a high level of outgoing activity, as well as periodic interruptions in the intake of information. But this is a matter for further research: it is relevant to the activation theory discussed in the next chapter.

Despite these gaping chasms in our knowledge, the writer feels that the position is a hopeful one. In his view of scientific method, a programme of research should start by asking very general questions and proceed to more detailed ones later. This is in fact what is happening with the problem of noise. First researches looked for a gross effect and showed that it did not exist. Then work was directed to possible less conspicuous effects by manipulating the experimental conditions, and an effect was found. The conditions of this effect were then made more precise and the avenues of future research which we have just mentioned should carry this process further. This, and not the misinterpreted form of hypothetico-deductive method which is broadly used today, is the true line of scientific advance. We shall return to this topic in the last chapter.

## PRACTICAL CONCLUSIONS ON NOISE

Although this is primarily a theoretical book, many of those who read it may be asked for opinions about effects of noise in industry. What answer should they make on the basis of existing evidence, bearing in mind that further research is needed? First, the work done in the particular practical case must be considered. Broadly speaking, if the task is one which might be disturbed by blinking (assuming that each blink was a second or so in length) it is one which may show effects of noise.

Many industrial tasks do not fall in this category and so would not be disturbed: they have frequent pauses in which no infor-

---

* Broadbent (1957e) has since found an effect of noise on a task involving a heavy immediate memory load. As with Jerison's task the effect carried over to subsequent work in quiet.

mation is reaching the worker, although he may be acting, and failures of attention will be concentrated at those times. But some tasks do need continuous reception of information, or at least rapid response to stimuli appearing at unpredictable times. These are the suspects. Even in such tasks, average output may be unaffected if any opportunity is allowed to the worker to speed up his work when he is attending to the task, and so to compensate for the momentary lapses in his attention. The most likely indices of effects of noise are accidents and scrappage rates, since these will presumably reflect failure to deal with unexpected situations. So far as the writer knows such indices have not been collected in any completely satisfactory industrial investigation, although in the related field of atmospheric conditions, industrial studies have long shown that accidents are a very sensitive index of poor conditions. There is here an opportunity for field research.

It may also be noted as of some interest that weavers, who were studied by Weston and Adams, do have to react to signals from their work at times they cannot always predict. Indeed, the effect found by those writers may be a genuine one despite its critics; it is certainly far smaller than the dramatic 40, 50 and 100 per cent changes which will appear in laboratory experiments when all factors are such as to maximize the effect.

Secondly, high-pitched noise seems to be worse than low. Admittedly there is no difference under some conditions, but when there was an effect it was always in that direction, and it therefore seems a good bet to reduce high frequencies first.

Thirdly, the main thing seems to be to bring the noise down to the 90 db level. This is still higher than many will regard as pleasant, but the most serious effects on efficiency appear to be above that level.

Fourthly, individual differences are important. If one person in a group complains of noise, it is dangerous to assume that he is unjustified. Scientific selection procedures would be nice, but do not yet exist.

Finally, any deliberate change in the noise level in an industrial situation should be accompanied by observation of its effects. This is because of our limited knowledge and especially because of possible differences in effects after very long-term habituation.

## GENERAL CONCLUSIONS

In Chapter 3 we said that the main interest for an experimentalist was in the principles which govern the selection of information to be passed to the perceptual system, and not in the fact that not all information was so passed. In this chapter we have found some such principles. They are that any novel stimulus is especially likely to be perceived, and so to prevent others from evoking reaction, that an intense stimulus is more likely to be perceived, and that a high-pitched noise is more likely to be perceived. All these three types of stimulation show greater efficiency on a task which requires reaction to them, and less efficiency on tasks which require them to be ignored. In the latter case, however, their effect on the main task is not to produce an even deterioration but to produce repeated brief failures. There is some evidence that these failures can be timed by the man himself so as to fall at periods when the task is delivering little information: but they can be detected by using suitable tasks.

These principles might in a sense have been otherwise. Our filter theory as first developed was almost purely a logical statement and not a factual one. The facts that the filter possesses enduring biasses in favour of certain classes of signals, and that it seems to stay only briefly on any channel which is designated as ' wrong ' by previous instructions, cannot be predicted simply by logical analysis of the problem. Have we nonetheless been biassed by our theory in interpreting the results ? It does not seem so. The fact that noise produces brief failures which are perceptual rather than motor in their nature seems inescapable except by casting doubts on the reliability of a rather large number of experimenters. The view that these failures reflect distraction rather than paralysis is less certain, but highly plausible in view of the opposite effects produced by requiring response to the previously ignored stimuli. We may perhaps note at this point that the contrast of distraction and paralysis is not ultimate: if the filter tends to swing towards a different channel it need not reach it, and may select neither type of information. Certainly the interpretation of effects of noise on visual tasks harmonizes well with the results of the multi-channel listening experiments. But the interpretation clearly has numerous consequences outside the field of noise experiments, and for this reason we shall now consider work done purely on prolonged tasks without noise at all, and see whether our interpretation fits the results. From our beginnings with the problem of listening to two voices at once, we have passed through the case of listening to a voice against noise while performing a visual task, and through the case of performing a visual task in noise. We turn now to cases in which no irrelevant stimuli, such as noise, are deliberately provided by the experimenter. Yet there are always such stimuli present, and we should therefore expect to find them operative. In everyday terms we expect to find that attention wanders even when an experimenter does not deliberately distract it.

# CHAPTER 6

# THE GENERAL NATURE OF VIGILANCE

## The Problem

THE experiments which we shall consider in this chapter mostly belong to a group known as ' vigilance ' tasks, whose chief feature is that a man responds only to very infrequent signals but may have to watch for them over long periods. The first such study was done by Mackworth during the war, in view of the problem of detecting submarines by radar from the air. Other experiments are now numerous, but many are equally directed at practical problems and therefore have not been published. The problem is indeed one which is not to be found in most contemporary text books and to a casual eye might well seem devoid of theoretical interest.

Our own concern with this problem is clear. We have come to the conclusion that after prolonged observation of one source of information, a man will show brief intervals in which he takes in information from other sources. His attention will wander. If this view is correct, it is in vigilance tasks that we may find evidence for it. But it would be unwise to consider the field only from our own theoretical point of view: the problem must be considered in its own right if due weight is to be given to alternative theories. To some readers, however, it may derive an additional interest from its bearing on the views we have already discussed.

It is also a problem of much intrinsic interest, even though it has little directly to do with auditory perception. Maintained observation of one source of stimuli is a task which is not only performed by radar operators but by all of us in many fields of life. It is especially present in learning, which is such a traditional field of psychology. Learning almost always requires sustained attention, and, as we said in the first chapter, it is useless to build theories about events in the deeper recesses of the organism until we understand how incoming information is handled. Similar considerations apply to problem-solving, and other traditional fields of psychology. But above all attention is a topic which has lately been neglected, but which was of great weight in text books of an earlier time. It is one of the most obvious features of human behaviour, and the principles which govern it should certainly form a part of our basic theoretical knowledge. It fell into bad odour because of the inability of introspective psychologists to agree with one another, or to provide objective evidence to back their assertions; but this is a condemnation of the technique used by introspectionists rather than of the problem. The technique originated by Mackworth is of great value in studying this basic problem of psychology, and the fact that it happens also to be of practical value should not offend the most squeamish. Indeed, it may even provoke them to reconsider their views on the relationship of pure and applied research. The great value of practical problems is that they force upon us difficulties which experiments done for theoretical reasons may ignore: it is in this way that the vigilance experiments have forced us to acknowledge again the importance of attention, which the theories of the past 30 years have not mentioned. Nobody would wish the wood of psychological learning to be invisible in the trees of *ad hoc* investigations made for particular practical reasons. Yet the most experimental of approaches to human beings can become as dogmatic as any armchair introspectionism, if the experiments are solely dictated by theory. The constant curb placed on speculation by the need to devise methods of educational selection, or to help those with brain injuries, or to design machinery for easy working, is a most valuable discipline.

If we adopt again our policy of looking first at the general facts and only coming later to theories, what must we say about vigilance? Mackworth's original experiment was a synthetic task embodying the most striking features of the work of a radar operator. The subject watched, not a radar screen, but a pointer moving round a clock-face in regular jumps, one every second. At rare intervals the pointer gave a jump of double length, which the subject had to report by pressing a key. In the first place, subjects were asked to work at this task for 2 hr. When $\frac{1}{2}$ hr periods within the session were compared, it was found that the first $\frac{1}{2}$ hr was considerably better than any other. This rather alarming finding was confirmed using a simulated radar screen, and also for an auditory task in which regular bursts of tone were heard. The subject had in this latter case to report rare bursts which were of extra length. When the results were communicated to the R.A.F., records of submarine detections at various times since the start of the operator's watch were examined and it appeared that a similar rapid drop in efficiency was occurring. The effect therefore seems to be something more than a peculiarity of the particular test first used, or even of the laboratory atmosphere.

On the other hand, Mackworth was able by manipulating the conditions to produce instances in which no decline in performance appeared after ½ hr. They are reported together with the original finding in his book (Mackworth 1950). And other experiments which had the same general characteristic of requiring watch for an infrequent signal proved to show no rapid decline; they will be considered later.

We are thus faced with the situation that some experiments show a very rapid deterioration in human performance, in a task in which the work output of the man is slight. This must have considerable bearing on our views of learning or of all tasks requiring continuous attention. Yet other experiments show no such decline and we must therefore search for the particular conditions which may produce the effect.

### Methods of Preventing Rapid Declines in Clock-Test Type Tasks

The first technique for keeping efficiency at a high level is to carry out the task with two men, each taking alternate ½ hr. This gave a roughly constant level of performance. That is, the ½ hr rests away from the task allowed the subject to return to it at full efficiency. Whatever the reason for the decline, it must therefore be one which rapidly disappears with rest.

A second technique is to keep the man at the task for the full 2 hr spell, but to call him up over a telephone system after 1 hr and ask him to do even better for the rest of the test. This produces a temporary return to full efficiency, which dies away after another ½ hr.

If a loudspeaker message is presented to the subject shortly after every signal, saying ' Yes, that's right ' if he had responded or ' You missed one there ' if he had not, efficiency was continuously maintained throughout the 2 hr period. This result was shown not only by the clock test, but also in the auditory test mentioned previously. In view of the ' motivational ' character of this knowledge of results and of the telephone message mentioned in the last paragraph, it is interesting and important to note that other methods of exhorting the subjects were ineffective. For example, if they were told that they must be especially vigilant when a pointer travelling over a map reached a certain region, there was no effect: the subjects showed a deterioration similar to those given no special instructions. It is also noticeable that giving the subjects dummy inert tablets did not affect their performance; while giving them benzedrine caused their performance to remain at the same level throughout the work period. All the above variations in conditions were first tried by Mackworth (1950).

Another somewhat ' motivational ' variable is the presence or absence of the experimenter. Fraser (1950) used the clock test to investigate another problem, the angle of the display relative to the horizontal. He found incidentally that he did not get the usual decline in efficiency after $\frac{1}{2}$ hr, and guessed that this might be due to his own presence in the room during the experiment. (In the original studies the subject was left alone as he would be in the practical situation.) Fraser (1953a) therefore made a direct comparison, and found that the presence of the experimenter did indeed improve performance sharply. In this case Fraser did not use the clock test, but a different task in which the subject had to watch a series of circles projected on a screen and report the occasional one which was of unusual size.

Characteristics of the task itself are also important. Thus Fraser (1957), using the same task, studied the effect of varying the difference between the signal circle and the ordinary ones: when the difference was small the decline was larger. Similarly if the display was unfocused so as to be difficult to see, a decline was more likely. These results resemble the differences mentioned in the last chapter between the twenty dials and the twenty lights tests, the poorer display showing greater effects of noise. The results also confirm findings given by Mackworth in his book for a synthetic radar task. When the echo to be detected was bright there was little decline in performance: when it was dim and difficult to see there was a sharp decline like that on the clock test. This result also seems to be comparable to differences found on the clock test between subjects: people who made few mistakes originally showed little decline in performance. People who made many mistakes initially did even worse after ½ hr. In general anything which reduces the visibility of the signal, including subject ability, seems to increase the chance of a rapid decline in performance.

One finding which is of very great theoretical interest was made by Fraser (1957). Using his same circle detection task, he varied the time for which each circle was visible before the next circle appeared. When it was visible for only 1 sec, the usual decline appeared with prolonged watch-keeping. When it was visible for more than 2 sec, no decline occurred. It will be remembered that in the original clock test situation, jumps of the pointer took place every second, so that the signal certainly took less than 1 sec.

Certain possible objections to this finding should be considered. First, in Mackworth's radar test the signal was visible for 4 sec, but a decline was observed. The radar test differed from the clock and from Fraser's task, in that signals might appear in a number of spatial positions; and unlike synthetic radar tasks used by Baker and Deese (to be described in the next section) the appearance of signals was unrelated to the position of the rotating sweep line. If therefore the watcher had to spread his observation over a large area he would only be able to look at any one point for a part of the time: the signal might therefore well have to be present for a longer time than it would in a situation not involving the search factor.

Secondly, Adams (1956) has performed an experiment similar to Fraser's but has found only a shift in overall performance, and not in decline during a run, when the brightness or duration of the signal were changed. To be exact, the effect of these signal variables on the decline was not statistically significant, although it did seem to be very slightly in the direction predicted by Fraser. It may be suggested that this was because Adams compared the various conditions on different groups of subjects, so that the very large individual differences in decline during a run (see Chapter 7) reduced the statistical sensitivity of the experiment.

Certainly the effect of signal brightness on decline has been found in other experiments, and is implied in results by Bakan which will be discussed later. However, the negative results of Adams should be borne in mind by the reader when assessing the validity of our argument later in the chapter, when the theoretical importance of the effect of signal duration will be discussed. With these exceptions experiments with long lasting signals have not usually found any decline in performance as the watch goes on.

We have now considered most of the experiments using the original clock test and highly similar variants, and it is clear that the rapid decline in performance which they sometimes show can be prevented by knowledge of results, by increasing the visibility of the signal, by outside stimuli such as a telephone message or the presence of the experimenter, by a brief rest, or by lengthening the time of appearance of the signal. There is one variant of the clock test which should be mentioned for the opposite reason, because it did not prevent the decline in efficiency. This is some work by Whittenburg, Ross and Andrews (1956), who gave an ordinary clock test, and compared it with a clock test in which the subject was equipped with two response keys. He had to press one of them when the long jump of the pointer was seen, just as in the orthodox clock test. But he also had to press the other key for each short jump of the pointer. This meant, of course, that he was continually active rather than sitting and simply watching as in previous clock tests. Yet Mackworth's original finding was confirmed under both conditions. The link which this result establishes between vigilance tasks and those which involve continuous work is highly important for theory, and this result will be mentioned repeatedly.

We may now turn to consider other vigilance tasks derived from the clock test. Some of these show striking declines in efficiency and others do not.

## Vigilance Tasks Differing from the Clock Test

Bakan (1955) has produced a variant on the vigilance technique which appears to be very sensitive. He delivered to the subject a regular series of light flashes. Occasionally one of these flashes would be slightly brighter than the others, and the subject had to report this. If he failed to do this, another flash with even more brightness was inserted and so on until the subject did report a flash. The intensity of the flash reported can then be used as a measure of the state of the subject. This type of measure gives more data from each experiment than do tasks in which a signal is simply reported present or absent. Bakan found a rise in threshold as the task proceeded in any one session.

Fraser (1953b) used a rather different method of achieving the same desirable end of a numerical measure from each signal rather than a detected-missed dichotomy. He presented a series of circles travelling across a screen, as described previously, and occasionally inserted a larger circle. The subject was required not merely to detect the circle, but also to judge the time at which it passed the centre of the screen. Such a judgement is naturally subject to constant errors, which are of no particular interest, so Fraser took as a measure the variance of each subject's judgements. The variance increased as time went on, and once again the test appeared highly sensitive.

Another task showing decrement is an auditory one, in which the subject had to listen to a stream of digits spoken at the rate of one a second. If required to detect, say, any occurrence of three successive identical digits, he showed little decrement, but if asked to respond to a more complex sequence such as ' any sequence in which an odd digit is followed by an even one and that by another odd one', decrement appeared. (Bakan 1952; Kappauf, Payne and Powe 1955.) This is comparable with the results of Fraser and Mackworth on signal difficulty mentioned earlier.

However, other vigilance tasks do not show any change in performance with prolonged work. Broadbent (1950) used the twenty dials test mentioned in the last chapter, in which twenty dials had to be watched and action taken if any of them showed a dangerous reading. In this case the signal remained visible until a response occurred: the time taken was measured and thus the dichotomy of detection or failure to report a signal was avoided. But the result was not the same as in Bakan's or Fraser's technique. The response time was no longer at the end of the work period than at the beginning. We shall consider reasons for this discrepancy in the next section: but it may be noted here that some connexion perhaps exists between this result and that of Fraser, mentioned in the last section, on the effect of extending the time for which a signal was present before being replaced by a non-signal stimulus.

Equally negative are the results of Elliott (1957), who used the same technique as Bakan but with auditory signals.    In his case the subject had to detect the presence or absence of a sound, rather than an increase in intensity in one member of a regular series of stimuli: this may conceivably be important.    On the other hand, in some of Elliott's experiments a regularly repeated sound of a different kind was present throughout the test, the signal being inserted immediately after this sound.    So from one point of view the task might be regarded as a discrimination.    The interval between the regular, no-response stimuli was different from that of Bakan, however, and so also was the interval between repetitions of the signal if the latter was not immediately detected. A last curious feature of Elliott's experiment was that his subjects were allowed to read or write as they chose during the course of the experiment; but that this had no effect on their performance. Such a course is only possible with an auditory task in which the stimulus is bound to reach the sense-organs whatever the subject's momentary activity.    A caution which should be given is that the absence of any decline during a run in Elliott's results does not mean that his subjects were achieving good performance throughout.    On the contrary, their thresholds were far above those obtained in a normal situation when the subject was expecting a signal: the fact that average performance can be moved up and down independently of the deterioration of performance from beginning to end of a session will concern us repeatedly.

A method resembling that of Bakan and Elliott was used by Bowen (1956) with visual signals.    In this case a spot of light was to be reported on a screen covered with twinkling ' noise ' spots. The signal was repeated again and again at the same intensity until the subject reported it.    The length of the series of repetitions necessary to secure response did not increase during the run, except with a very low signal rate of one signal per hour. Bowen found, however, that the rate at which the signal was repeated influenced performance.    This and another finding on the effect of the frequency with which signals were presented during the time of watch, will be considered after theories of vigilance have been examined.

Deese (1955) also reports having used a simulated radar task in which subjects had to watch a screen for targets. He failed to find a uniform decline in performance as time passed. In some of his experiments he used a technique very similar to Bakan's, increasing stimulus intensity until detection occurred: like Elliott, he was of course concerned with absolute detection rather than detection of an increase in intensity. In other experiments he inserted signals at a fixed intensity for one sweep of the scan on the radar screen, which meant that roughly 3 sec elapsed before that part of the screen was wiped clear.

Baker (1956) has carried out experiments with a simulated radar screen bearing a sweeping line of light comparable to that used on real radar screens. Signals might appear anywhere along the line of this sweep: records were made not only of the number detected but also of reaction time to each signal, and of the restlessness of the subject. The latter was recorded by contacts under his chair. The results from this test were a compromise; if signals came fairly evenly every 2 min (though not of course completely evenly) there was no increase in the number of missed signals but there was an increase in restlessness. If the timing of signals was changed to that of the clock test, in which some intervals were very much longer than others, the results were almost exactly like those of the clock test. This experiment also showed that the subjects could be biassed towards various parts of the display by altering the arrangement of the sweep; with a normal sweep they tend to see signals in the middle of the sweep line more than those at its ends.

The experiments we have cited show that some change takes place in men who do prolonged watch-keeping tasks, so that under certain conditions their performance deteriorates with time. Under other conditions either the change does not take place or else the measuring techniques cease to reveal it. It is now time to consider theories of this change.

*Theories of vigilance decrement.*—There seem to be at least four different ways of considering the experiments we have so far described: and it may well be that several of them are true. The first of them is to postulate an inhibitory state, similar to that supposed by behaviour theorists to explain the extinction of conditioned responses. It is indeed true that many of the phenomena of extinction resemble those of declining vigilance. The operations performed in observing extinction are to take a dog which has been conditioned, say, to salivate when a light flashes: to put the animal in a room by itself, and to make it watch the lamp for a prolonged period, receiving occasional flashes but not being given food when it salivates. The response then weakens. Equally the operations in observing decline of vigilance, are to take a human being, establish a particular response such as pressing the response-key when a flash appears on a radar screen: then to put the man in a room by himself and to make him watch the screen for a prolonged period, receiving occasional signals but not being given any reward for detecting them. The similarities are undoubted, and were pointed out by Mackworth (1950) in his description of the clock test results. There are certain qualifications and cautions which immediately spring to mind. Thus for example we cannot regard the decline of vigilance simply as an extinction of the conditioned response to a stimulus equated with the signal. If it were, the decline would be more rapid when signals are more frequent, whereas some results, to be mentioned later, show that the reverse is the case. One may quite legitimately say, however, that response to neutral features of the situation, such as the short non-signal pointer jumps in the clock test, is extinguished. This extinction may then generalize to the signal, which shares many characteristics with the non-signal stimuli. Subject to this kind of qualification, the parallel between the two situations seems fair: the telephone message experiment of Mackworth is a suggestive parallel to disinhibition, and the effect of knowledge of results resembles that of continued reinforcement in preventing extinction. There are other parallels, and we shall in a later chapter be asserting that extinction and decline in vigilance share the same explanation. But this is by no means to say that both are to be explained by an inhibitory construct; there are other ways of explaining extinction.

Deese (1955) gives some reasons for minimizing inhibition. (Incidentally he describes the writer as a supporter of the inhibitory theory, which is not and never has been the case. This is an easy confusion to make, since support for the parallel between vigilance and extinction is easily expressed in a way which can be misunderstood as an inhibitory theory of decline in vigilance.) It seems uneconomical to introduce two opposing states in the nervous system without first examining all ways to explain changes in vigilance as alterations in a single positive state of readiness to respond. Furthermore, performance in vigilance tasks does not merely decline: in Deese's experiments, in the writer's, and in others we have mentioned, it improves or oscillates. In the clock test there is evidence of a warm-up effect at the beginning of the task, and Deese finds signs of an end-spurt. Such effects require any inhibitory construct to take a rather complicated form.

A second way of considering vigilance results may be termed the 'expectancy' theory. This view receives rather stronger support from Deese, who has carried out some of the experiments relevant to it which we shall consider shortly. Briefly, the view is that response to a signal is a function of the probability of that signal, the probability being derived from the past incidence of signals. To some extent this is not a theory but a demonstrable fact. We have already considered many times the low information contributed by highly probable signals, and small quantities of information can be passed through a system of limited capacity faster than large quantities can. The empirical evidence that this does happen in man is provided by the experiments of Hick (1952), Hyman (1953) and Crossman (1953) which have already been cited. The question is, however, how far this factor comes into play in vigilance. Two illustrations of it were noted by Mackworth. In the clock test and the listening tests, where the spatial position of the signal was always known, it appeared that signals occurring very rapidly after other signals were badly seen. A plausible explanation of this effect was that such rapid sequences of signals were rare, signals being on the average infrequent, so that the second signal was not 'expected'. On the simulated radar test, however, this did not occur, and as in this test each signal appeared in a spatial position close to the previous one, spatial expectancy seemed a likely explanation.

One might possibly try to formulate an entire theory of vigilance in terms of expectancy; the decline in efficiency during a session in those tasks which show it could be ascribed to a gradual drop in expectancy from the normal fairly high level to a low level appropriate to a vigilance situation with few signals. But this needs some implausible assumptions. For example, both Bakan and Mackworth have found that a decrement appeared in a second test given a few days after the first. We would therefore have to suppose that expectancy at the beginning of the second test had reverted to a high level rather than remaining at the appropriate one. This seems curious, and abolishes one of the merits of the expectancy theory: the latter will explain a marked rise in efficiency produced in one run by a high signal density in another run, which has been demonstrated by Elliott (1957), but if expectancy does not carry over from run to run this explanation cannot hold. Nor does expectancy offer any explanation of the absence of decline in certain tasks. In particular there is the effect of signal duration shown by Fraser. One could possibly argue that any reduction in signal length when the probability of detection is not 100 per cent, will reduce the number of signals seen and so the estimated probability of seeing more. But this explanation ignores the fact that decrement fails to appear in long-signal tasks with very infrequent signals (the twenty dials test, and that of Bowen) and yet is present in short signal tasks with more frequent signals, such as the clock test and those of Bakan, Adams, Fraser and others.

The third approach to this problem may be called the activationist one. It is to consider a constant background of stimulation as a necessity for general efficiency. This approach also is mentioned by Deese: it harmonizes well with many modern approaches to the question of sleep and wakefulness. Kleitman (1939) held that wakefulness was maintained by a neural centre in the base of the brain, probably near the hypothalamus. This centre is kept active partly by sensory impulses: thus depriving a man of sensory stimulation causes him to go to sleep, and indeed most people do seek conditions of minimum stimulation for sleeping. Intense stimuli will wake somebody who is asleep, and in one who is awake they might be regarded as activating the wakefulness centre more and more. The latter keeps up the efficiency of the rest of the brain, perhaps by transmitting facilitating impulses up to the cortex. In monotonous surroundings, then, the whole level of nervous activity may be lower and so response to clock test signals less efficient. Once again, this type of theory seems to have some difficulty in handling the cases of

failure to decline in performance.   Why should the long signal of
the twenty dials test remain equally easy to see at the end of a
lengthy watch, when the short signal of the clock test does not ?

Finally, we may apply to vigilance tasks the view which we
suggested in the last chapter for noise experiments.   On this
view, it will be remembered, the information reaching the senses
is filtered and only part of it passes to the perceptual system.
This part will originally be determined by the instructions given
to the man: but the filter possesses a permanent bias in favour of
channels which have not recently been active.   This bias is
likely, after one source of information has been controlling
response for some time, to produce a change in the selected
channel: in ordinary terms, attention wanders.   Such a shift is,
however, temporary; the failure to take in information is intermittent, just as blinking is.

In explaining noise effects, we argued that the filter was more
likely to select auditory information briefly when an intense
noise was present.   If the theory is correct, however, shifts away
from the task should occur in any case, albeit less frequently.
Faint sounds, or proprioceptive stimuli, may provide the competing information; or stored material may even conceivably be
passed through the same filter.   In ordinary language, the man
notices odd features of his surroundings, or his own bodily sensations interpreted as discomfort, or day-dreams.   Such breaks in the
intake of task information will be brief, but will increase in
frequency as the task is continued.   One might therefore explain
vigilance decrement by supposing that the signals arriving later
in the task are more likely to fall in these brief instants and so be
missed.

As was said initially, these four points of view are not necessarily
incompatible.   One of them, the expectancy view, is almost
equivalent to the assertion that highly probable events place less
demand on the nervous system than improbable ones; that is,
that the concept of information derived from telephone systems
is applicable to human performance.   Two other views, the
inhibitory and the theory of the activation of the organism by
stimulation, might be described as holding that the capacity of
the nervous system declines under monotonous conditions.   The
last view holds that the capacity is employed in different directions

after prolonged work.    All these views may be true.    Let us now consider experiments relevant to them.

*Experiments on Inhibition and Expectancy*

The two first approaches may be considered together, because the experiments they suggest are similar.    One must add that there are in any case few researches relevant to the inhibitory approach.    Almost the only ones are some of Wilkinson (personal communication).    He observed performance when watching for a flash of light on a plain screen.    In one condition the subjects heard only an even noise background at a low intensity.    In another a regular buzz was inserted above this background every 4 sec.    The flash only occurred just after one of these buzzes, so that the subject could relax very briefly between buzzes.    In addition, this condition did of course provide more sensory stimulation, so that on an activation theory one might expect higher performance.    The average number of signals seen was in fact the same, but in the buzzer condition this average was achieved by higher efficiency at the beginning and lower efficiency at the end: the decrement was greater.    This fact argues against any activationist theory of decrement, though not necessarily of average performance.    Its relevance to an inhibitory theory is that one might describe the extra stimulus of the buzz as a source of extra responses to be extinguished, so that the total amount of inhibition present is increased.

This point is one which may help to explain the varying results of the vigilance tasks we have reviewed.    A repeated neutral stimulus was characteristic of the clock test, of Mackworth's listening test, of Fraser's variance test, and of Bakan's threshold test, all of which show a decline with prolonged performance.    There was no such repeated stimulus in the twenty dials test, or in the radar tasks of Bowen and of Deese; and these tasks showed no decline.    Unfortunately for this interpretation Mackworth's radar test and Baker's simulated radar task both show decrements but have no obvious repeated stimulus between the signals; admittedly both include the simulated sweep line of a radar set, rotating around the screen regularly.    But in one of Baker's conditions there was no sweep and if anything more decrement, and Deese's task included the sweep.    Another and more doubtful case is the work of Elliott; in his listening task there was sometimes a repeated neutral stimulus but no decrement. This might be explained by saying that the neutral stimulus was very different from the signal and so did not generalize; yet Wilkinson's was also very different.

Another similar exception is furnished by the effect of altering signal visibility in a number of experiments we have already considered. Here the monotonous stimuli were always present, but the decrement could be brought in or out by altering such parameters as the size or brightness or duration of the signal. These exceptions show that generalized inhibition from repeated negative stimuli similar to the desired signal is not a completely sufficient explanation of vigilance decrement. The presence of such stimuli may increase decrement compared with their absence, but it is not essential to have such stimuli to get decrement, nor does their presence ensure decrement.

The expectancy view lends itself to more experiments, such as those cited by Deese (1955). One can readily change the objective probability of a signal occurring, and observe the resulting changes in the performance of the man. If, for example, signals arrive every ½ min on the average the probability of a signal at any given time is higher than if the average interval between signals is 3 min. This type of experiment has been performed by several researchers, especially Deese (1955), Bowen (1956), and Jenkins (cited by Deese). There is no doubt that a higher average rate of signalling produces a higher average performance from the man, over the ranges studied. There may well be some upper limit where the absence of a signal becomes less usual than its presence: in such a case the man may be regarded as watching for non-signal, and one might expect that the lower the incidence of non-signals the lower his efficiency. But this is perhaps a point of little practical importance. Its theoretical interest is that an activation theory would also predict that a high rate of stimulation would produce greater efficiency but that this relation would hold, presumably, up to indefinitely high levels. An expectancy theory would predict optimum performance when signal and non-signal are equally probable, and a deterioration in the detection of either as it became less probable than the other.

A point which needs further investigation is the effect of varying the range of intervals between signals rather than the mean.    The object of studying this variable would be that the probability of a signal relevant to an expectancy theory is presumably probability at the time when it occurs.    If, for example, a signal occurred every minute exactly, the probability of a signal is highest 1 min after another signal.    Equally it seems likely from the arm-chair that a human observer would rapidly become very good at detecting such signals.    He might even do better than he would at detecting signals appearing at twice the frequency on the average, but with a range of intervals stretching from 5 to 55 sec. If this suggestion were supported by experiment, it would be another piece of evidence supporting the expectancy theory as against the activation one, since the latter might be expected to regard the mean interval between stimuli as more important than the range.    Some evidence of this kind comes from the work of Baker (1956) already cited, since his simulated radar task showed a decrement when the signals were given with the intervals used by Mackworth in the clock test; but not when the intervals varied over a smaller range.

This raises the question of the relation between decrement from the beginning of a run to the end, and poor performance throughout a run.    It will be remembered that Wilkinson's experiment showed no effect on the latter but a real effect on the former.    The expectancy results, on the other hand, show an effect on the latter with some doubt about the former.    Deese emphasizes that performance within a run may go up or down, while citing the effect of signal frequency upon the average performance for the whole run.    Bowen also showed his effect chiefly upon the average rather than the decline within a run, though his lowest rate of signalling did in fact produce a decline. Baker's experiment also shows increased decrement with a less probable signal.    But, as we said when first discussing the expectancy approach, it is clearly less well suited to explaining a decline than to explaining a steady low level of performance. Only if the subject has an expectancy at the beginning of the work-period which is higher than his expectancy at the end (i.e. if he expects initially that signals will be more frequent than they in fact are) will performance decline.    At first sight this makes the expectancy approach a good one for explaining the conflicting

9

results of different experiments: the subjects had different initial expectancies. But although this may well explain some of the differences, it cannot explain all of them. We have already noted that the various experiments on the effect of changing the visibility of a signal are not easily explained by expectancy; nor is the appearance of a decrement within the session on a familiar task, which Mackworth and Bakan both showed.

This possibility, that expectancy may explain average performance but not the trend within runs, should be compared with the point made in the last chapter about the effect of stimulus probability on reaction times. It will be remembered that, when the information presented to a man in a reaction time situation is decreased by making some signals more probable than others, his average speed of response increases correspondingly. But the infrequent kinds of signals, while giving slow reaction times, do not give times as slow as they should on a pure probability basis. That is, the speed of response averaged over the whole task does go up as the information is decreased and the mean probability increased. But the parts of the task do not follow a probability interpretation, any more than decline in performance during a vigilance task does. In both cases, it may be noted, it is the relatively novel and unusual stimulus which receives an unduly efficient response: but this is not a completely satisfactory formulation, since performance on certain vigilance tasks may sometimes improve during a run rather than deteriorate.

Before leaving expectancy, we may perhaps cite another approach which is closely related to it. Holland (1956, 1957) has suggested that the human watch-keeper may be regarded as making a series of observing responses, whose incidence will follow the rules found for rats making bar-pressing responses by Skinner (1938). The detection of a signal corresponds to a reinforcement, which in the case of the rat would be a presentation of food. In the animal situation, the food increases the rate of responding (subject to certain qualifications which we need not consider for the moment). Equally in the man, detecting a signal should increase the rate of making observing responses. Holland has set up a situation in which a man was given a brief glimpse of a signal-source whenever he pressed a key, and signals were inserted after varying time intervals or after varying numbers of key-pressings. Corresponding treatment of the rat causes the incidence of bar-pressing to follow the probability of reward, and closely similar results were obtained from Holland's human subjects.

This approach is closely connected with the attitude to animal conditioning which will be developed in later chapters; for the present, we may note simply that it has the advantages and also the disadvantages of the expectancy approach. It deals well with the average level of performance, but is on more doubtful ground when applied to the trend of performance during a run. Just as a decline in expectancy will only arise from a too-high initial level, so a drop in rate of bar-pressing by rats will only appear when the animals are shifted from a high incidence of reinforcement to a low one. Yet, as we remember, Coastal Command radar operators and industrial inspectors (Wyatt and Langdon 1932) continue to show decline in vigilance within their task-periods, even though the low incidence of signals must be perfectly familiar to them.

To summarize experiments on these two approaches, the inhibition view is better able to deal with declines within each run than with a low average for the whole run. The expectancy view is very satisfactory for explaining average performance, but less convincing to the writer when applied to trends within a run. Each approach has its advantages and disadvantages.

### Experiments on Activation and on Filter Theory

Some highly interesting experiments relevant to the activation theory have been performed in Montreal. The main feature was that all change in the stimulation delivered to the experimental subjects was reduced to a minimum for a prolonged period (Bexton, Heron and Scott 1954). This was done by keeping subjects in a small room on their own, providing them with blindfolding goggles, gloves, and similar means of reducing stimulation, and keeping them there for as long as they would stay. Despite good pay, the subjects were unwilling to endure these conditions for very long. Furthermore, their efficiency as measured by a number of tests declined considerably. When research workers, who were presumably more highly motivated, stayed in for longer periods, they became subject to gross distortions of the visual field. Shapes and sizes became unstable, so that it seemed that the normal mechanisms, which compensate for changes in the retinal image as objects change their position, had lost their efficiency.

As has been said, current physiological views on the role of stimulation in facilitating activity in the nervous system are in harmony with the results of these experiments. It has even been shown that reflexes become less efficient when they are not elicited for a long period (Eccles and McIntyre 1953). In some ways this trend is a reversal of an earlier fashion which emphasized the autonomy and spontaneity of the nervous system. Hebb (1955) has described how this change has caused him to alter his conceptual model of the nervous system. Formerly he held that spontaneous activity arose from the organism and was only controlled and guided by outside stimulation. Now he thinks rather that stimulation produces a level of activity in the organism, which may indeed be self-maintaining for a time, but derives ultimately from the outside stimulation. If this level is too low, efficiency will be low: and the same result may follow from too high a level of activation as in some emotional states.

Hebb's paper deserves to be read in the original; and it is certainly a very convincing formulation for understanding much human activity. The intensity with which stimulating problems are sought out, especially by the young, is difficult to fit in with many orthodox theories of motivation, and harmonizes much better with this one. At the same time, the search itself seems to be spontaneous. No stimulus arouses the demand for a stimulus, and to this extent the original emphasis on the initiating role of the nervous system preserved a real truth.

For our present purposes, the activation theory obviously has certain advantages. It can clearly cope with decline in performance during vigilance tasks, and also with low average performance. No matter how familiar the task, monotonous circumstances and deprivation of stimulation will still produce decreasing efficiency. Indeed, the difficulty becomes that of explaining why some vigilance tasks show so little decrement during a run. If the full decrement on the clock test is due to the absence of activating stimulation, why is there no decrement on the dials test, which seems to have no more? Furthermore, certain tasks which have been tried under various levels of stimulation have shown no change in the decline of performance with time, or even a worse decline. The noise experiments given in the last chapter are an example: why should performance in a high level of auditory stimulation be worse than in a low one?* Another example is provided by the experiment of Whittenburg, Ross and Andrews (1956), mentioned earlier, in which the clock test was performed with two keys, one to be pressed to each neutral stimulus and one for any signal stimulus. Wilkinson (1957), as part of an investigation of the effects of lack of sleep, used a vigilance task in which the subject pressed a key to neutral stimuli and refrained from action altogether when a signal occurred: the exact reverse of the normal situation. In both these experiments the constant action required of the subjects would produce considerable proprioceptive stimulation, as compared with the normal vigilance task in which they sit passively. Yet in neither experiment was there any difference in the amount of decrement shown.

This argument deserves closer attention, as the activation theory is otherwise so satisfactory. There seem to be two possible explanations which might be put forward. First, one might appeal to Hebb's statement that too high a level of activation is as bad for efficiency as too low a level. Consequently raising the stimulation level in these experiments was ineffective because the level was already too high. This explanation is inadequate. The decrement in the ordinary vigilance task is explained by the level being too low: if the level after raising the amount of stimulation is now too high, the rise in level must have covered the whole range from too low to too high. While this might conceivably be true of the noise experiments, it surely cannot be for the results of Wilkinson and of Whittenburg, Ross and Andrews. Furthermore, if this explanation is correct one would expect the effect of noise to get less as the period of work increases and the organism habituates to the stimulus; whereas the reverse is the case.

A second possible explanation is that from an activation point

* It should be noted that Helper (1957) has provided evidence that skin conductance is higher when working in noise, confirming that noise does in fact produce higher activation.

of view the important variable is the amount of information presented rather than the physical energy in the stimulation. This is not quite adequate as it stands, because some of the work supporting an activation theory has used irrelevant rather than relevant stimuli, so that in one sense the supporting stimuli contributed no information. For instance, inducing tension in the muscles by asking the man to hold a dynamometer increases his efficiency at certain tasks (Bourne 1955). We ought therefore to substitute ' change in stimulation ' for ' amount of information ' in the first sentence of this paragraph. In the case of relevant task stimuli this makes little difference, since information can only be conveyed by changes in stimulation. But the substituting of the alternative phrase allows us to include changes in irrelevant stimulation. An even better emendation might be to include both change and physical intensity of the stimuli by some weighted combination, since it seems likely that reducing the level of, say, the dynamometer tension, is not just as good as increasing it.

The remaining discrepancies are slight, but important. Why do some tasks, especially those with long signals, show no decrement as time goes on ? And why is it that noise increases errors although the speed of work is unaffected or even increased ?

We now turn to the filter theory which has been developed in preceding chapters. The most relevant experiments other than those already cited are ones which do not really count as vigilance tasks at all. The earliest of these is the work of Bills (1931) on prolonged performance of tasks such as colour-naming. If a man is presented with a series of colours, a fresh stimulus immediately following every response, it will be found that after some time he shows an occasional very slow response. Bills named these slow responses ' blocks '; and used as his criterion for detecting them twice the mean response latency. Blocks obeying this criterion increase in frequency after the man has been working for some time; but even so his mean response time need not increase. His activity becomes more variable without necessarily changing its average level in either direction. Mistakes may also appear in association with blocks; in general, the whole picture is one of intermittent failures in efficiency interspersed with normal performance.

In these experiments, whose results are supported by other

later workers such as Broadbent (1953a), the rate of presentation of stimuli depended on the subject himself. Bills and Shapin (1936) also examined the effect of presenting stimuli at a rate fixed mechanically at a value rather faster than people adopt under the voluntary ' unpaced ' condition. They found that this pacing delayed the onset of any decline in performance and was thus preferable to allowing the man to adopt his own rate of work. This fact agrees with the type of experiment which suggested the activation theory: the larger the number of stimuli presented in a given time the greater the efficiency of the man. It is also connected with the work of Conrad on the effect of speed of work, which will be discussed in Chapter 11.

But the situation is rather different when the rate of work is set by a machine sufficiently slowly for perfect performance. Broadbent (1953a) investigated this situation, using a task which is known to show Bill's blocks: the five-choice task of the last chapter. The rate of work was the same as the average which subjects could maintain under unpaced conditions. But they were unable to keep up a constant level of efficiency in the ' paced ' case, and their output of correct responses deteriorated after a time which had produced only blocks in the unpaced condition. The obvious interpretation of this result is that the man's behaviour, as distinct from the recorded performance, is changing in the same way whether performance is paced or unpaced. In the paced condition, each momentary block causes a loss of the opportunity to make a correct response, while he cannot improve his performance between blocks. In the unpaced case the increased variability of the man need not affect his average performance.

For ordinary repetitive tasks this argument may perhaps be acceptable; but it was used by Broadbent to explain differences between vigilance tasks which do and do not show decline in performance during a work-period. The suggestion was that the man's observation of a stream of signals was also subject to intermittent interruptions, with the result that tasks of a paced type, in which the signal was visible only for a brief period, would be affected by these interruptions. Tasks of an unpaced type, in which the signal was visible for an indefinite time, would be much less affected by them. In particular, the clock test would be expected to show an effect and the dials and lights tests would not. Fraser's experiment in which decrement would appear or disappear in the same task according to the length of time for which the signal was visible, is easily explained. It is also plausible that the tasks of Bowen, of Elliott, and of Deese, in which the signal was inserted again and again until seen, should show no decrement. On the other hand, it is a difficulty that Bakan's task, which also involved repeated insertion of signals, should show a decline. The explanation may lie in the interval between signal insertions, and in the other features of the task which affect activity between blocks.

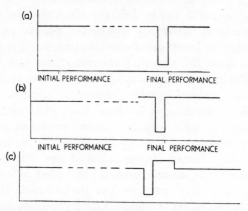

Fig. 2. Possible changes in the level of efficiency, following prolonged work.

This point should be examined further, with the aid of Fig. 2. In case *A* the effect of prolonged work is supposed to be simply an increase in the frequency of brief blocks in which signals are very unlikely to be detected. Between these blocks the probability of detection is unchanged. This type of model would obviously predict a deterioration in the detection of signals shorter than a block: they might appear in the middle of a block and disappear before the subject had recovered. But with signals lasting indefinitely, as in the dials, or repeated until seen, as in Bakan's method, the time before detection will still be longer on the average when blocks are occurring. It is only in Case *B* that the detection of long signals will be apparently unaffected. Here the probability of detection at times other than blocks has actually risen, so that the chance of a long signal lasting undetected for a certain length of time may be unchanged or actually changed in the direction of improved performance.

This shows that, while a blocking theory makes the prediction that tasks using short signals will give a decrement, the prediction for long signals is equivocal. It is even more so when we come to possibilities such as that in Case *C*. Here we might expect that continuous signals of indefinite length would be detected as quickly once blocking has set in as during normal performance, since each interval of low efficiency is followed by one of higher performance. But with a short signal repeated intermittently until seen, the outcome will depend on the interval between repetitions. If any signal striking the block was always followed by another striking the spurt, the score should be unaffected. If the interval between signal repetitions was bigger and a signal striking the block was not followed by another until after the spurt had finished, the effect on the score would be more serious. This kind of relationship may underlie the difference between Bakan's findings and those of other researchers; the data are insufficient to decide on the matter, but might perhaps be amplified by using Holland's technique mentioned earlier.

Another important point which should be mentioned here, although it depends somewhat on data to be given in Chapter 9, is that some kinds of stimuli may give rise to a delayed response even though they arrived during a block, provided they are not followed by another irrelevant stimulus. It will be remembered that in the description of Elliott's experiment it was noted that he (and also Bowen and Deese) required the subject to detect the presence or absence of a signal rather than the occurrence of a slightly higher intensity member of a series of stimuli. Bakan followed the latter course and this factor again may explain the difference between his results and those of others with a similar scoring system.

In general, then, the approach suggested by these experiments on blocking is not able to predict very specifically what will happen in experiments using long signals. It has the strong point that it will account for differences between short and long signals, which is a difficulty of most other approaches. But it obviously needs supplementing by some other principles which predict performance between blocks. In this context it is interesting to note a possible connexion between this approach and that of Holland mentioned earlier: provided that it is supposed that a series of instrumental responses shows blocking as the session proceeds, which is not a matter that has been given much emphasis by students of instrumental conditioning. However, Hurwitz (1957) has recently shown an effect in the bar-pressing behaviour of the rat which does seem analogous to blocking; we shall consider it in Chapter 8.

Even so, is it really fair to draw an analogy between tasks requiring continuous work and those of the vigilance type? At the time when this approach was first suggested, the analogy was indeed rather a long step and was justified only by the possible interpretation it gave of the differences between the clock test and the twenty dials. But since that time the gap between the two situations has been considerably narrowed by other experiments. The work of Whittenburg, Ross and Andrews, and of Wilkinson, has been cited several times. In their results it made no difference to vigilance performance whether the man was continually active or passive during the interval between signals. The step from the two-key clock test of Whittenburg Ross and Andrews to the five-choice serial reaction task, used by the writer for demonstrating 'blocks', is a very short one. In addition it has been shown by a number of recent experiments that the deterioration appearing in continuous work, which is usually loosely called 'fatigue', is due to a large extent to failures of perception and not to any breakdown of the mechanisms which organize response to clearly perceived events. These experiments will be described in a later section of the present chapter, as they are not really relevant to the question of the correct theory to apply to vigilance. But their existence is important when considering the justifiability of comparing continuous work with vigilance tasks. It is also noteworthy that Fraser's vigilance task (in which estimates of the time at which a moving signal crossed the middle of a screen became more variable with prolonged work) is closely compatible with the approach based on blocking.

A second question which should be discussed is the relation between blocking and filter theory, which has so far been left unstated and unjustified. As will be obvious from the chapter on effects of noise, the interpretation of blocking favoured by the writer is, that it represents an interruption in the intake of information from one source, owing to intake of information from another source. In other words, if we think of a filter selecting some of the information reaching the senses; then this filter ceases for a second or so to select task information, and rather selects some other kind of stimulation. As novel stimuli have a higher probability of passing the filter, these shifts in selection will not occur until after the task has been continued for some time. From the point of view of vigilance tasks alone, there is little to choose between this view and that of blocks as caused by an interruption in the intake of all information. The reasons for preferring the former view were discussed in the chapter on effects of noise: it makes intelligible the influence of noise in increasing the frequency of the momentary failures of efficiency. It harmonizes well with the fact that in the dials test the central dials are those best observed immediately after a signal but become less well monitored than the peripheral dials after an interval without signals (Broadbent 1950): this seems to indicate a tendency to shift the source of information used to control response. The ' shift of selection ' view is also supported by the fact that blocks in the five-choice task last about $1\frac{1}{2}$ sec, and this is in fact the time taken to shift selection twice, as will be seen in Chapter 9 (Broadbent 1954b). This view therefore seems probable, though the inference is bound to be less certain than that of an analogy between blocking experiments and vigilance.

To summarize the value of this approach, it covers some of the gaps in the other theories. It deals chiefly with changes in performance rather than with average performance over the whole run. And without help from other theories it cannot predict what will happen in tasks on which performance is determined by the average activity of the man over a period greater than a few seconds. However, at least this approach seems to indicate certain types of task on which decrement will definitely appear. The other approaches do not seem capable of giving unequivocal predictions, not because these approaches are completely untrue, but because so many variables are operative in tasks whose signals are visible for some time.　There is reasonable evidence for the effects of the variables emphasized by each theory, and it is likely that each of them requires further development rather than abandonment.

## A Synthesis of Views on Vigilance

Let us now give a brief consolidated account of the conclusions to which all these experiments seem to lead us, omitting the doubts and qualifications expressed above, for the sake of clarity. In the first place, the information striking the sense-organs is filtered, and only part of it is passed on to the centres in the brain which organize response.　Normally the filter passes that information which is relevant to the task set the man.　But occasionally the other irrelevant stimuli may be passed by the filter for a second or so, and during this time task information will not enter.　This event will appear as a pause or error in continuous work;　in a vigilance task it may mean failure to detect a brief signal, or a delay in detecting a long one.　In the latter case the delay may be countered under certain circumstances by a high level of activity between these ' blocks '.　That is, the level of activity when the filter is selecting task information is not fixed and may affect the time taken to detect signals. The frequency of shifts by the filter depends on the relative intensity and novelty of task and non-task stimuli, an increase in either of these qualities making a stimulus more likely to pass the filter.　For this reason a series of stimuli from the same source as the task stimulus, but requiring no reaction, may lower the efficiency of response to the task when at last it is required.

If the filter is passing task information, the speed with which any stimulus will be handled will naturally depend on the probability of that stimulus at that time.　A highly probable stimulus conveys little information and therefore response will occur rapidly:　remember the man in Chapter 3 with two keys and a variety of stimuli to report.　He could speed up his reporting by using a short response for the most common stimulus. In general, there will be an economical coding for any communication channel such that more probable messages are transmitted more rapidly, and the human nervous system is no exception.　Thus stimuli which occur at predictable times, and which are chosen from a small set of possible stimuli, will receive rapid response.

In addition to the effect of increasing probability of a stimulus in increasing the efficiency of reaction to that stimulus, a variety of events at the sense-organs is desirable if the efficiency of information handling is to be high. If the background of stimulation producing this effect is irrelevant to the prescribed task, it may cause an increase in the number of pauses or errors in the work, despite the increased efficiency in the intervals between pauses. But it should be noted that the pauses, or ' blocks ', will appear only after the work has been continued for a while: whereas the effects of stimulus probability and level of background stimulation may be present even at the beginning of a task, and remain unchanged throughout it.

Thus the average level of performance during a run is to be explained by activation and expectancy: whereas blocking explains the decline during the run.

This account includes all the approaches which we have outlined: and, although it requires considerable filling-in, it gives a reasonable account of performance on vigilance tasks. It also implies that performance on work requiring considerable overt muscular activity will also be impaired by the ' blocking ' mechanism, and that the decrement revealed in vigilance tasks is not peculiar to men watching for infrequent signals. There is some evidence that a perceptual element does enter into prolonged work of a more ordinary kind, and to this we must now turn.

### Perceptual ' Fatigue ' in Prolonged Work

Negative evidence is the first which should be mentioned. Prolonged work of a purely muscular nature does not show any downward trend very easily, unless the energy output of the muscles is exceedingly high. Naturally, if the muscles are required to perform at the limits of their strength for long periods, the work deteriorates. But when they are operating less intensively there are cases in which little decline can be found. Other cases do show a drop in efficiency, but as we shall see this may be due to differences in the stimulation reaching the man rather than to the repeated responses he is making. The fact that tasks of the five-choice type, discussed repeatedly in this chapter, show no decline in average output seems to indicate that repeated muscular activity is not in itself sufficient to produce a fall-off in response. Conrad and Hille (1955) found similar results when they measured the time taken in an actual industrial situation to pack jars into cartons; the mean time remained much the same throughout the day, although the variability increased just as that on the five-choice task did. (The classic 'fatigue' curves obtained from industry are somewhat suspect, because they take little account of the tendency of workers to spend time putting tools away at the end of the day: they may also be unwilling to start a fresh batch of work just before the official time to stop work. These factors will produce a spurious drop in output; it is essential to observe the actual time spent on working operations before drawing conclusions about the effect of prolonged work on performance. Although some tasks may deteriorate towards the end of the day, this jar-packing one did not.) The increasing variability of work is readily explained by the suggestion that the filter begins to select irrelevant information for occasional brief spells.

In the more complex task of flying aircraft, it has again been found that prolonged work does not affect ordinary measures of average performance. On the contrary (Bartlett 1943; Drew 1940) the deterioration is rather in the forgetting of peripheral tasks such as changing fuel-tanks; or in concentrating on one instrument in the cockpit to the exclusion of others. This result resembles those on industrial 'fatigue' and on the five-choice reaction task in that it makes it difficult to uphold the simple theory that repeated responses become less efficient. But these indications that the change occurring after prolonged work is rather increase in variability, do not by themselves show that the change is a perceptual rather than a motor one.

More positive in their implications are experiments using tasks on the border-line between vigilance and normal work. Once again, the experiments of Whittenburg, Ross and Andrews, and of Wilkinson are examples. The decline in efficiency when two keys are being pressed at a high rate seems likely to be perceptual in origin, since it is just as great when only one key is being pressed at rare and infrequent intervals. Another example of a border-line task is one used by Saldanha (1955), in which a vernier gauge had to be set to readings prescribed one after another by a mechanical device, each setting producing the next problem. Saldanha found that the rate of work did not decline with prolonged work, but that the size of errors increased. This can hardly be due solely to a decline in the efficiency of the motor system: if coordination was deteriorating, causing errors in adjustment, they would presumably be observed, and some attempt to correct them made. This would give slower performance and equal or increased errors depending on the extent to which the poor coordination could be offset by repeated attempts on each problem. The actual result, increased errors and unaffected speed, suggests that the errors were unnoticed, a failure of perception rather than response. It was also found that a rest away from the task restored efficiency, as would be expected, but that if a cancellation task using a quite different form of response was performed during the interval in the vernier task, recovery was not as final as with complete rest (Saldanha 1957).

Another border-line experiment is that of Siddall and Anderson (1955), on tracking. Prolonged tracking does not usually show any deterioration (Hoffman and Mead 1943). Siddall and Anderson felt that this might be the result of the varied stimulation which a constantly moving track provides. They therefore set up a compensatory tracking task, in which the subjects had to hold a pointer steady against a mark by cranking a hand-wheel at a constant rate. Errors in this task increased as time went on, which agrees well with the theory that the subjects did not notice their own errors in such a monotonous task.

Lastly, there are certain experiments in which the possibility of perceptual failure in prolonged work was deliberately set up in opposition to motor failure, for experimental testing. Some studies of lengthy tasks for the U.S. Air Force had made use of the Hullian concept of reactive inhibition. This concept will appear repeatedly in the next two chapters. In simplified form, it asserts that the occurrence of any response lowers the probability of that same response for a time. This postulate was found useful in explaining many of the phenomena of human prolonged work: for example, the fact that brief rests interspersed in the session often produce better performance.  But it was only on certain kinds of work that this was so.  For instance, the pursuit rotor, in which the subject has to follow with a stylus a small target dot on a gramophone turntable, shows a decline in performance when no rests are allowed.  The same is not true of a coordination test in which the subjects had to match the position of target lights by other lights operated by aircraft controls (Gagné 1953).  It was pointed out by Gagné that the tasks which seemed to show decline in efficiency with prolonged work (that is, to fit the reactive inhibition view) were those in which a repetitive series of stimuli were presented to the subject.  A less monotonous stimulus side to the task seemed to prevent decrement from appearing.  This suggested that decrement was a function of repeated stimulation rather than repeated response, if such a distinction could be made meaningful.

Two studies have now appeared in which the distinction is indeed made real.  One of them, by Adams (1955), required some subjects to spend the rest intervals watching somebody else perform the task.  This produced a decrement as compared with normal rests: and the response had clearly not been present although the stimulus pattern had been.  In the second study (Albright, Borreson and Marx 1956) performance with one hand was shown to impair temporarily performance with the other hand.  Again the overt response was different while the stimulus was the same.

All these facts strongly suggest that the deterioration found in human prolonged performance, is often a function of the number of times the stimulus situation has been presented, rather than a function of the number of previous responses.  In other words, they are quite consistent with our interpretation of vigilance.  The interruptions in the intake of information, ' internal blinks ' or ' blocks ', do seem to be a factor of importance in work of other sorts than watch-keeping.

## Conclusions on Vigilance and Filter Theory

Our survey of vigilance, and of prolonged work in general, shows that the filter theory developed in earlier chapters stands up reasonably well to this type of experimental test.  It requires supplementing with other principles, particularly those of expectancy and of activation theory. But the conception that the intake of information from the task is occasionally interrupted seems to be well-founded, and this may be interpreted plausibly as being due to passage of some irrelevant information through the filter.

In considering this aspect of human performance, the concept of reactive inhibition appeared. There is another way in which that concept has been used in this field: in relation to individual differences. As individual differences are in any case of interest and importance, we shall now turn to them as a preparation for a more detailed survey of reactive inhibition in general.

# CHAPTER 7

## SOME DATA ON INDIVIDUAL DIFFERENCES

IT has been noticed many times that some individuals show larger decrements from prolonged work than others do. Pavlov observed that certain dogs, when used for conditioning experiments, showed a greater liability to experimental extinction. That is, when a conditioned stimulus was given to them again and again they rapidly ceased to make any response. Other animals might continue to go on responding much longer without reward after the same amount of initial training. The former type he termed ' inhibitable ' and the latter ' excitable '. This is not to say that the latter type of dog had a more active type of behaviour throughout the experiment; the inhibitable type might well be more active initially, but showed a larger decrement with prolonged work. Pavlov himself regarded this individual difference as being parallel to differences in type of neurosis in human patients: the inhibitable extreme was analogous to hysterical disorders and the excitable to anxious ones. This appears to have been an analogy drawn on the basis of clinical observation, without any direct demonstration that patients of these types showed corresponding differences when used as subjects for conditioning experiments. The picture one can plausibly draw of the hysteric as a person who fails in persistence, whatever his initial level of performance, harmonizes suggestively with the types of animal described by Pavlov. But without support from experiment the analogy is a very tenuous one.

Recently, however, this view has reappeared in a more sophisticated form. Eysenck (1955a) has taken the Hullian postulate of reactive inhibition and suggested that hysterics show a greater rate of accumulation of this inhibition than do dysthymics (anxious and obsessional neurotics). The distinction between the two kinds of diagnosis is a fundamental one in Eysenck's earlier work. He has found that when a number of performance tests and questionnaire items are factor analysed, it is possible to describe the results by two factors. One of these can be made to correlate highly with a psychiatrist's opinion as to whether a given neurotic is dysthymic or hysteric; the other factor will correlate with the distinction between samples of neurotic persons and samples of unselected (presumably mostly normal) persons.

The rationale of such factor analysis has been a subject of controversy for many years. In its earlier forms it attempted to describe complex matrices of correlations by factors chosen for purely mathematical reasons: for example, if a group of tests $A$ correlated highly with one another, but not at all with another group of tests $B$, it could be argued that the inter-correlation was due to a single underlying factor which the tests of group $A$ assessed with more or less success but which was not involved in those of group $B$. This could be done purely from the set of correlations without any knowledge of the actual nature of the tests used. Unfortunately matrices of correlations do not always fit into such simple patterns, and it then becomes doubtful which of several possible descriptions in terms of factors is the best. Thus if the group $B$ tests correlate slightly with those of group $A$ but not as highly as the latter do with one another, should we describe the situation by one general factor measured to some degree by all the tests, with subsidiary factors accounting for the remaining inter-correlation? Or should we speak of several more equal factors? The decision as to which tests shall be regarded as the purest measures of a factor is also to some extent ambiguous. Decisions taken on purely mathematical grounds, as for example that as many tests as possible should be unrelated to as many factors as possible, although they may give an unequivocal set of factors, are somewhat questionable since the assumptions on which they are based may not be valid in any particular field of interest. For this reason many people have felt that the factors emerging were psychologically meaningless. The difficulty is a sophisticated form of the old problem of interpreting correlations. If there is a correlation between wearing spectacles and having bad eyesight, we do not decide on the underlying cause of the correlation mathematically: that might lead us to forbid the wearing of spectacles, as they obviously cause defective vision. Rather we interpret the mathematics by our knowledge of other facts. Similarly it was felt that the factors underlying matrices of correlations should be chosen for reasons outside those matrices.

Eysenck's work has attempted to meet this objection, since, having described the intercorrelations of numerous tests by two factors, he then fixes the final choice of these factors by psychological criteria. These criteria have been mentioned above: they are for the neuroticism factor the distinction between people under treatment for neurotic illness and those who are not, and for the second 'intraversion' factor the diagnosis of type of illness. In adopting this course he has considerably weakened the case of opponents of factor analysis, which is mostly based on the inadequacy of mathematical assumptions as a guide to disentangling empirical relationships. The mathematical aspect of factor analysis in Eysenck's work may be described as demonstrating that tests which discriminate between his criterion groups of people do inter-correlate when applied to only one group: the mathematics are used to extend the psychology and are not independent of it.

This remains true even though points of detail and of interpretation may well be questioned. For example, the different kinds of neurosis may need further dimensions to describe them than the two used by Eysenck; obsessionals may differ from anxiety states even though both have some features in common which are not shared by hysterics. Again, the independence of the two dimensions is a matter of some doubt, and might depend on the culture being investigated; a given degree of intraversion would be normal in some societies but might be neurotic in others. And even though tests which discriminate normals from neurotics do not distinguish one kind of neurotic from another, it is still possible that neurosis is caused by extremes or particular degrees either of extraversion or of intraversion. If there is a curvilinear relation between two quantities, it is possible for the product-moment correlation between them to be zero even though they are not independent: and factor analyses are normally carried out on product-moment correlations.

Such points of detail do not affect the value of the demonstration that dysthymics are more likely to work slowly rather than inaccurately, give high estimates of their own future performance, and answer questions about themselves in particular ways: and that normal people who do one of these things have a tendency to do the others.   However, a psychiatrist's opinion is itself a questionable criterion.   Even in physical complaints failures of diagnosis do occur (Irvine 1957) and opinions may differ even more in psychological disorders.   It is presumably for this reason that Eysenck has suggested the rate of accumulation of reactive inhibition as a mark of degree of extraversion.   There is some hope of tying degree of inhibition down to objective measures and so obtaining a criterion more satisfactory than psychiatrist's diagnosis.   The attempt is in fact to preserve the psychological basis for the dimension of personality, while at the same time avoiding the weaknesses of the original criterion.   It is perhaps unfortunate that the Hullian concept should have been chosen, since as we shall see in the next chapter reactive inhibition is open to a number of objections.   But if we translate the term as meaning simply ' decline in performance after repeated performance ', then the suggestion that this is a function appearing most markedly in persons showing the ' extravert ' pattern in other respects becomes an interesting possibility worth examination.

The preceding digression puts in some perspective the hypothesis that extraversion is characterized by a tendency to reactive inhibition.   Many, especially among experimental psychologists, will have doubts and reservations about both the crucial terms in this hypothesis.   But nobody can deny that certain features of the hysteric do to some extent appear together to the same degree in the same person.   Is one of these features a tendency to decline in efficiency after prolonged work ?

### Data from Vigilance Tasks

Almost everybody who has worked on vigilance has noticed the marked individual differences.   But it has not usually been possible to note any other features of the persons with the best or worst performances. Mackworth (1950) found that less deterioration appeared in more experienced watch-keepers, and in general in subjects who saw a high proportion of signals at the beginning of the run.   This seems likely to be connected with the effect of signal frequency which was discussed in the last chapter, and requires no assumption of differential rates of decrement peculiar to the individual. If he sees fewer, he deteriorates more, but it is his inability to see which is primary rather than his rate of deterioration. To eliminate this factor requires a vigilance task in which signals remain visible until detected, such as the twenty dials test. In the latter, individual differences in decrement within runs did not appear to be connected with initial level. On the contrary, they were correlated with the amount of improvement between runs. That is, people who got worse in one day's watch did relatively better on the second day than people who showed less deterioration within a watch (Broadbent 1950). This type of difference attracted attention because it resembled the differences described by Pavlov between his dogs; it was examined and proved significant at the $0.01$ level, tau $= 0.34$.

While this established individual differences in decrement and recovery from decrement, independent of the level of initial performance, it did not reveal any other features of the individuals showing the greatest decline. On some of the subjects in the initial group, however, there were also 'level of aspiration' data available. Levels of aspiration, so-called, are obtained by giving a subject repeated runs on a task, informing him of his performance after every run, and enquiring what he estimates he will score on the next run. It had been shown (Eysenck 1947) that dysthymics keep their estimates high relative to previous performance, the difference between the two being known as 'goal discrepancy'. A large goal discrepancy is thus associated with intraversion in Eysenck's sense. (At no point in this chapter do we use the word in its original clinical sense, which may be slightly different from that resulting from the use of hysterics and dysthymics as criterion groups.) For the present writer's purposes goal discrepancy was not used; the reasons will be discussed later. The score employed was highly correlated with goal discrepancy, however. It consisted of the sum of the goal discrepancies for each run, disregarding sign, so that a high score might be obtained by alternately high and negative goal discrepancies. To avoid confusing this score with the ordinary goal discrepancy, it will be called the 'triple tester index': the triple tester described in Chapter 4 was the task which the subject performed and on which he estimated his future performance.

A score representing decrement within runs was taken from the twenty dials test by subtracting the end of one run from the beginning of the next: this score correlated with the triple tester index, tau = − 0·46, which was significant at the 0·01 level on the twenty-one subjects used. (Product-moment correlations would have given higher numerical values than tau does, but it is doubtful whether the distributions involved are normal or the regressions linear, and tau was therefore employed.) The minus sign before the correlation indicates that the intraverts showed less deterioration during runs.

The twenty lights test is generally similar to the twenty dials: from the group of twenty subjects used in the noise experiment mentioned in Chapter 5, a score of temporary decrement was taken by adding up for each subject the amount of decrement on each 4 days. (Two of the days were of course in 100 db noise.) This score gave a tau with the triple tester index of − 0·42, which is significant at the 0·02 level. Slightly more data on the procedure used in obtaining these latter two correlations are to be found in the first cyclostyled report of the noise experiments (Broadbent 1951).

As has been argued in the last chapter, there may well be an analogy between vigilance tasks and continuous serial tasks such as the five-choice serial reaction task. On a third group of eighteen subjects, the decline in performance (as measured by number of correct responses on the latter task) from the first 10 min of a session to the second 10 min was determined for each of 2 days. One day was in 100 db noise. The decrement again correlated with the triple tester index, giving a tau of − 0·44, which is significant at the 0·02 level. It is extremely interesting to note that it is only the decrease in correct responses which gives this correlation. The increase in errors or of gaps without response does not correlate. In terms of the interpretation given in the last chapter, all subjects show a tendency for the filter to select information irrelevant to the task when they have been working for a time. These shifts of the filter appear as gaps or errors. But it is during the intervals between these gaps that the individual differences appear, some working harder when their performance is interspersed with gaps, while other individuals show impaired performance even during the time between gaps (Broadbent 1953a).

Thus far there seems to be some connexion between the triple tester index and resistance to the ill-effects of prolonged work. But it might well be argued, as all this research was carried out under research conditions and on naval ratings, that the correlation is due merely to the greater enthusiasm of some subjects for the research or some similar factor. It might be that persistence in real-life situations would not continue to correlate with the laboratory results. For this reason an attempt was made to confirm that high scorers on the triple tester index were resistant to the effects of prolonged work outside the laboratory. A sample of twenty-two naval ratings was divided into two groups according to whether or not they continued with some form of further training (usually evening classes or apprenticeships) after the age at which the law allowed them to leave school. The two groups differed significantly at the 0·05 level on the triple tester index, $t = 2·14$. (In this case the distributions appeared reasonably normal, so that $t$ rather than tau was employed.) The second real-life task examined was the Cambridge Tripos, and in particular in psychology. This examination is of course a lengthy one, and a number of undergraduates had given level of aspiration results as part of their practical work before taking the examination. Unfortunately there is no way of discovering the relative performance of each student at the beginning and end of the examination, so the assumption has to be made that those resistant to the effects of prolonged work would do well in the examination as a whole: not only because it is a long task itself but also because the preparatory work is lengthy. When the twenty-four male students on whom results were available were divided into those receiving first class or top second Honours on the one hand, and those receiving bottom second or third class Honours on the other, the former had the highest triple tester indices. For this difference tau was 0·33, which is only significant at the 0·05 level by a one-tail test. That is, we are only justified in accepting the finding if we would have regarded one in the opposite direction as due to chance. In view of the four previous results this is perhaps fair.

It should be said that in the latter two cases intelligence test scores were available for the subjects, and showed no relation with the triple tester index. (The test used was AH4.) There was also no correlation between the index and intelligence in other cases in which both scores were available for the same subjects. The results are therefore not due to a partial correlation with intelligence (Broadbent 1951).

Having thus made it unlikely that this individual difference is purely a laboratory affair, we must now turn to the validity of equating it with the dimension whose extremes are dysthymia and hysteria. As has been said, the triple tester index is not identical with the goal discrepancy score which is known to discriminate the two types of neurosis. There might therefore be some doubt about using it as a criterion. This is particularly true since in a very small-scale experiment the writer has been unable to find any correlation between it and a measure of extraversion taken from a questionnaire. The questionnaire score was therefore obtained from a number of subjects who were being used for certain other prolonged tasks. This questionnaire (Heron 1956) includes a number of questions which had been shown to give different answers from a hysteric group and a dysthymic group. There is of course no guarantee that the answers are truthful; this point should be emphasized, since there is sometimes misunderstanding about it. All that is known is that one type of answer comes from those diagnosed as hysteric and one from those diagnosed as more anxious types of neurotic. It may be that a particular type of person is more inclined to lie or attempt to play jokes on the experimenter; but the reasons for his answers do not concern us as long as we do not assume that they are truthful ones. It is quite sufficient for our purpose that a particular answer comes from hysterics, even though it may ' really ' mean that hysterics tell a particular lie.

The first task we may consider is one of performing mental subtractions. The subject observed a six-digit number through a slot until he felt sure that he knew it. Then he pressed a button which removed the six-digit number and presented a four-digit number. He subtracted the latter from the former, writing down the answer, and finally pressed the button for the next problem. Thirty such problems were performed at a sitting, and a measure of decrement after prolonged performance was obtained by taking the difference between the time for the first ten problems and that for the last ten. Fourteen subjects performed the task on two successive days; the decrement scores were summed for the two days. As eight of the subjects worked in 100 db noise on one of the days, four of them on the first and four on the second, it is desirable to consider the subjects as three separate samples for correlational purposes. Fortunately tau may be summed over three such groups, and the pooled value was in this case 0·50, which is just significant at the 0·05 level by a two-tailed test. The direction of the correlation was that expected; that is, the more extraverted the greater the deterioration with prolonged work. This result has not been published previously.

Another unpublished result is that of a similar correlation in the research of Baker (1956) mentioned in the previous chapter. In this case the task was, as will be remembered, to detect brief spots of light appearing on a simulated radar screen. The subject's chair was mounted on counters, so that his increasing restlessness as the task went on could be recorded. The amount of increase naturally depends on the initial level, some types of restlessness affecting the counters more than others. If the relative increase in restlessness is correlated with number of questions answered in extravert fashion, there is a tau of 0·50, which is significant at the 0·05 level on the fifteen subjects used. It is interesting and important, however, that there was no correlation between extraversion and decline in the number of signals detected on this task. We shall have cause later to emphasize that negative results mean little on groups of this size: but even so this fact is suggestively parallel to the failure to find a correlation between the triple tester index and increase in gaps or errors on the five-choice task. The individual difference is in the level of performance between gaps, and it was argued in the last chapter that tasks such as Baker's, using transient signals, are seriously affected by gaps.

A third unpublished correlation has been run between extraversion and the task used by Wilkinson (1957) in one of his experiments. He measured reaction times to unexpected signals occurring at rare intervals during a watch of 25 min. The trend of the results on mean reaction time was unrelated to the questionnaire replies, but it is argued by the present writer that this was because gaps would cause the most persistent of subjects to show some very slow reactions. On the other hand, such subjects would also show some very fast responses during the periods between gaps: so the increase in the range of the reaction times when the last five reactions were compared with the first five was calculated for each subject and correlated with intravert types of answer to the questionnaire. Tau was $0 \cdot 67$, which on twelve subjects is significant at the $0 \cdot 05$ level. Thus in this case the more extraverted subjects did not do relatively worse as time went on; they merely showed a smaller increase in the variability of their reaction times. The result is, however, quite in accordance with the views we have previously expressed; if the individual difference we are examining is largely one of performance between gaps, it will be variability rather than mean performance which will be affected in a task such as Wilkinson's.

So in summary there is some evidence that if people are ' extraverted ' in the sense that they perform some tasks more in the same way as hysterics do; then these people show a lower level of efficiency during the time between the gaps in performance which appear after prolonged work. There are a number of negative findings on other aspects of this individual difference which should now be mentioned. But it must first be pointed out that negative findings are worth far less than positive ones, on material of this type. A significant correlation reveals some real relationship, although our interpretation of it may be at fault. But a real relation may fail to be statistically significant simply because a small sample has happened to include one or two deviant subjects. Although the following data fit in with the writer's views, therefore, great caution must be used in accepting them until more copious results are available.

In the first place, in none of the questionnaire studies did the incidence of neurotic answers, as opposed to intravert-extravert ones, show any significant relation to prolonged work. Secondly, the leg persistence test (in which the subject sits with his unsupported leg outstretched for as long as he can) was obtained from eighteen subjects from whom scores on the five-choice task were also available. There was no significant correlation with decrement in performance. Although the number of subjects was small, particularly as once again they had not all been treated identically on the five-choice task and therefore a pooled tau had to be calculated, this result is to be expected from the previous one; although leg persistence does differentiate dysthymics from hysterics, it is very largely a measure of neuroticism (Eysenck 1947). If decrement on the five-choice task is not related to neuroticism, it should show little relation to leg persistence.

The importance of leg persistence from our point of view is that it obviously does not represent any transmission of information through the man whatsoever. If the peculiarities of extraverted people lie in the detection of events outside themselves, then such a task will hardly reveal them.

The results considered in this section are hardly perhaps more than suggestive. Nevertheless, they do give a reasonable probability to the view that extraverts deteriorate more with time in certain kinds of tasks. Let us now consider evidence for this conclusion from other sources.

*Extraversion and Decrement in Non-Vigilance Tasks*

In the first place, the work of Franks (1956) on classical conditioning should be mentioned. Franks conditioned the eyelid response in groups of dysthymics and of hysterics, and showed that the latter group reached the criterion level of response less rapidly. The same was true of conditioning of the PGR. A normal group lay in between the two neurotic groups. Rather similar findings were produced by Welch and Kubis (1947a, b) who found that cases showing clinical anxiety gave more rapid conditioning of the skin response than normal subjects did, and that hysterics were very difficult to condition.

In addition to these results, it has been found that the eyelid response conditions faster in people who score highly on a questionnaire scale of manifest anxiety: this is shown by Taylor (1951) and by Spence and Taylor (1951). At first sight it might therefore seem that there is an established relation between extraversion and reactive inhibition; but in fact there are considerable difficulties in the way of interpreting the results already given.

In the first place, the interpretation placed by Spence and his associates upon their results, does not mention reactive inhibition. They hold rather that anxiety is a general drive in the Hullian sense, a state whose reduction reinforces the occurrence of particular stimulus-response combinations. The more anxious individuals have a higher drive-state, and thus show more rapid learning. A similar though slightly different interpretation is that of Hilgard, Jones and Kaplan (1951), who regard the more rapid conditioning as due to a specific defensive drive which is stronger in the anxious subjects. This particular interpretation, as opposed to that of Spence's associates, is partially supported by the results of Bindra, Paterson and Strzelecki (1955), who failed to find any difference between two groups of high and low anxiety when using salivary, rather than eyelid or PGR conditioning. The same Taylor scale of ' manifest anxiety ' was used as in the work of Spence's associates. However, there may be other differences between the two procedures as well as the difference in the type of drive involved. For instance, if we prefer to emphasize reactive inhibition rather than drive strength, we may point to the interruption in the conditioning procedure, introduced by the need to insert a cotton wad into the subject's mouth every eight trials to test the strength of conditioning: such an interruption is unnecessary in the eyelid conditioning situation, and might have acted as a ' disinhibiting ' stimulus in the former case. Equally, if reactive inhibition with its rapid dissipation is the important variable, the interval between conditioning trials may be crucial. In the Spence and Taylor research it was only 20 sec, while in that of Bindra *et al.* it was about 1 min.

We may summarize these results as follows: if anxious individuals have a different level of drive to others, it is slightly more likely to be a different level of specific defensive drive rather than of general non-specific drive. But the results may equally well be due to differences in the rate of accumulation of reactive inhibition (bearing in mind the cautions about the use of Hullian terms which have already been mentioned and will be repeated later). The conditioning experiments so far employed do not distinguish between drive level, reactive inhibition, or for that matter any other of the variables which on a Hullian account of conditioning may raise and lower the level of performance. If it is asserted that the individual difference is in one of the concepts used by Hull rather than in any of the others it should be possible to make predictions which would differentiate between that possibility and the various others, and which would be testable experimentally; but this does not seem to have been done.

For example, the effect of varying the inter-trial interval could be determined. On a simple interpretation of the competing theories, differences in reactive inhibition should mean that the anxious individuals will be relatively much less impaired by shortening the interval between trials, so that the correlation of conditioning and anxiety would be less, and even possibly absent with long inter-trial intervals. On a drive-level theory, the inter-trial interval should affect all individuals in the same way, and the anxious individuals would be the best in all cases. No such result which would distinguish the various possible theories has as yet appeared from the conditioning situation, although it seems agreed that time taken to reach a given level of conditioning is an important individual difference and is somehow connected with anxiety.

Besides this difficulty of interpretation, there is a second difficulty of identifying what is meant by anxiety as a personality dimension. According to the work of Eysenck's associates on British subjects, hysterics score as highly on the Taylor scale of manifest anxiety as dysthymics do. In fact that scale might be regarded as a measure of neuroticism on Eysenck's two-factor system, rather than as a measure of intraversion. Franks (1956) found that on his subject sample the Taylor scale also failed to correlate with degree of conditioning.

There are at this point clearly difficulties of subject sampling. If one takes a group of neurotics who all happen to be anxiety states, one will obtain different results from them than from a sample of hysteric neurotics. If rate of conditioning were high in dysthymics and low in hysterics, one might falsely conclude from a sample of dysthymics that neurotics have a high conditioning rate. The possibility does exist on the existing data that this has happened in the results of Spence's associates : or some similar chance in those of Eysenck's school. The orientation of factors, for example, may be influenced by errors in the original psychiatric diagnosis. It is worth pointing out that, while the general distinction between anxious and hysterical types of neurosis is broadly agreed, there may be some difficulty in diagnosing individual cases. As the psychological process is often described, the hysteric's symptoms arise as an inadequate solution to a conflict which may well involve some anxiety in the usual sense of that word (Henderson and Gillespie 1947, p. 171). The contrast between the hysteric and the dysthymic is rather that the latter's anxiety is more persistent and 'long-range' in its scope: the hysteric may become quite calm and indifferent once he has established his symptom.

It is this kind of complex relation between anxiety as a general characteristic of neurotics on the one hand, and as a particular diagnostic feature of one kind of neurotic on the other, which makes it difficult to be sure of the reasons for the difference between the results of the followers of Spence and of Eysenck. Equally, it is not clear from existing data which, if either, of their theories is correct.

While on the subject of the ambiguity of ' anxiety ' as a characteristic of individuals, it is worth mentioning that a considerable literature now exists on the relationship between ' anxiety ' and educational attainment. For example, Lynn (1955) shows that children scoring highly on a questionnaire about worries and fears also have a higher reading attainment for their age. But it is not clear from these data alone whether these children are closer than the average to those features which all neurotics have in common: or whether on the other hand it is those features which distinguish the dysthymic from the hysteric which also appear in these highly attaining children. Both intraversion and neuroticism in various senses have been attributed to those who do well academically (Gough 1946, 1949 ; Vernon 1939 ; MacQuarry 1953); in some societies, of course, intraversion may well be more synonymous with social abnormality and so with neuroticism than it is in others. To sum up, there is little doubt that anxiety, in some sense of that word, contributes to rapid conditioning and to good academic achievement. But the exact sense in which this is true is somewhat uncertain. The individual differences may be due to drive or to reactive inhibition: to motivation or to fatigability, if one wishes to keep clear of Hullian terms. Or some other interpretation may be the correct one; the curve of number of CRs against successive trials in Franks' results is parallel in the dysthymic group to that for the hysteric group, though starting from a higher level. This suggests that the difference may be due to differences in the initial level of response—anxious people blink more often. The role of individual differences in conditioning has not been analysed sufficiently as yet to justify the equation of extraversion with one particular one of the many Hullian intervening variables.

Two other studies by Eysenck (1955b, 1956) attempt to break away from these difficulties by showing that individual differences are in the after-effects of exposure to a situation rather than in the initial response. In the first cited, Eysenck used the tactile figural after-effect on groups of hysteric and of dysthymic patients. This test is one in which subjects are first asked to determine the point on a wedge presented to the left hand, at which the apparent width is the same as that of a standard block presented to the right hand. Next the subject is asked to feel with his right hand another block of different width to the standard. Lastly, he makes another judgement of the standard. Many subjects under such conditions judge the standard differently on the second trial, the direction of the difference being away from the interpolated block. That is, if a very narrow block is presented during the interval, the standard afterwards feels wider. This change is known as a ' figural after-effect ' and ascribed by some theorists to satiation of the region of the cortex stimulated by the interpolated figure. The hypothesized satiation process is similar in some ways to reactive inhibition (Duncan 1956), provided one thinks of the inhibition as affecting a perceptual response rather than the overt one. At the same time some people may feel that the analogy is a tenuous one. Eysenck adopts it, at least provisionally, and then predicts from the theory that extraverts have a greater tendency to reactive inhibition that they should show larger figural after-effects. Although this may seem a large step, it should be noted that finding a correlation between the two situations is about the only way in which the analogy between figural after-effects and reactive inhibition can be verified. The use of individual differences in this way to verify general theories has been neglected.

Eysenck does in fact find larger effects in his hysterics, and a correlation between a questionnaire measure of extraversion and the size of the figural after-effect. Although the significance of some of the particular scores used in the experiment is rather doubtful, requiring one-tail tests to give results better than the 0·05 level, the overall effect reaches an acceptable level of significance. On the other hand, preliminary results by the writer on fifty normal subjects do not support Eysenck's findings, no doubt because of some difference in the figural after-effect technique employed. This discrepancy is still being explored.*

Eysenck (1956) used the pursuit rotor, described in the last chapter. A rest pause on this task produces an increment in performance which is often ascribed to recovery from reactive inhibition. When the amount of reactive inhibition is assessed in this way there are some signs of a correlation with extraversion. Two rest pauses were used, and the pooled measure of ' reminiscence ' (rise in performance after the pause) was not quite significantly related to extraversion. On the other hand, if the measure of reminiscence is taken from the first pause only, the correlation is significant. This is perhaps acceptable, as Hullian theory would expect reactive inhibition to play relatively less part in later runs owing to the development of conditioned inhibition. Most striking is a large and comfortably significant relation between reminiscence and neuroticism. This paper also includes interesting observations on the correlations between the various phenomena often observed on the pursuit rotor, such as warm-up, practice and decline from peak performance. These correlations may provide evidence on the extent to which the various phenomena are produced by common causes; we said earlier that correlational evidence is insufficiently used to test theories.

The general effect of these two papers, despite their weaknesses, is to make us more inclined to treat the individual difference which is characteristic of extraversion, as one which appears only after time spent in a situation. This does not necessarily rule out the possibility of differences in drive, since as Eysenck says a high drive state may produce greater resistance to reactive inhibition; but it does make it less likely that a simple difference in initial level of performance due to drive is operating.

---

* Since the above was written, data have been obtained from a modified psychophysical procedure which suggest that the intraverts are more influenced by their experience of the whole experiment. They are thus less susceptible to typical psychophysical errors in later determinations, and this characteristic would have simulated a smaller figural after-effect in the procedure used by Eysenck. This result supports the view advanced later in the chapter.

Before turning to experiments more distantly connected with this field, we shall consider one major study which is relevant to the distinction between drive and reactive inhibition. This is the work of Davis (1948) on individual differences in prolonged performance in a simulated aircraft cockpit. Davis found that control corrections tended to become rather more numerous than was best from the point of view of performance. The pilots used as subjects became, in fact, over-active. But in some this process became more and more developed, and was associated with subjective concern about the task and even with disturbance of sleep: in others there appeared a change to low frequency of corrections, so that errors persisted for a long time. The pilots were seen independently by psychiatrists, and each assessed as more liable to develop an anxious or a hysterical type of neurosis. If this classification was compared with one made from the experimental records, there was a significant relationship, the pilots more likely to give anxious neurotic symptoms being those who showed hyperactivity in the simulated cockpit.

Davis interpreted this result in terms of a drive theory, much as Spence and Taylor later interpreted the differences in rate of conditioning. But whereas the latter interpretation regarded the difference in drive level as present from the beginning, Davis treated it as developed by the situation itself. He regarded anticipatory tension as a reaction to a situation in which punishment may be delivered. Although a response, it has the effects of a primary drive such as hunger or thirst: that is, it increases the general level of activity and reduction in it will increase the probability of immediately previous responses recurring in future. These effects are normally adaptive and will result in the organism avoiding altogether situations which are damaging. But if for some reason the environmental situation is a peculiar one the mechanism may cease to be an adaptive one: thus in the simulated aircraft cockpit the hyperactivity actually decreases the chances of achieving success, and so produces more stimuli associated with punishment and so more tension. The process thus becomes out of control. In some individuals it may be stopped by the stimuli associated with punishment ceasing to arouse anxiety. This also is a maladaptive strategy, since it removes the hyper-activity at the cost of abolishing the mechanism which reinforces successful performance of the task.  In mentalistic terms, the man ceases to care.  The preference for one or the other of these maladaptive mechanisms will be individual and apply to other situations besides the performance of a skilled task: hence the correlation with psychiatrist's opinion.

Davis' views obviously owe a great deal to those of Mowrer (1950) and other exponents of ' acquired drives ' in learning theory; and it can be seen that they cut across the division of drive and reactive inhibition theories.  The difference is due to drive, but develops only as a result of exposure to the situation. Some of the results we shall next consider from experiments which do not involve prolonged work, can be readily interpreted in this way.

*Evidence other than Differences in Decrement*

In this section we shall examine some of the evidence that hysteria is associated with inadequate reaction to certain kinds of difficult situation, other than prolonged work.  For example, Foulds (1951, 1952) studied performance of a number of diagnostic groups on the Porteus maze test.  In this test the subject has a maze placed before him and is asked to trace a path through it with a pencil, without entering blind alleys or crossing the lines representing alley walls.  Groups of hysterics or psychopaths spend less time observing the maze before they start tracing it, than groups of dysthymics do.  They are also quicker in tracing the path once they begin.  These increases in speed are gained to some extent at the expense of an increase in errors.  Such a relation between speed and accuracy in the different types of neurotic has been mentioned previously as arising from Eysenck's work.  It is noteworthy, however, that anxiety states are not only slow starters but also make errors, being tremulous and wavy in their line drawing.  Reactive depressives and obsessionals are not only slow starters but also show the greater accuracy one would expect from their slowness.  The relation between speed, accuracy and diagnosis is not a simple one.

The chief interest in Foulds' work from the present point of view, however, is in the effect of distraction applied during the task.  The distraction used was for the experimenter to count aloud, one number every 2 sec, and for the patient to repeat each number after him. Under these conditions the dysthymics worked faster but the hysterics and psychopaths did not. There were some signs in both groups of a decline in accuracy. This result certainly suggests that the dysthymics were making some extra compensating reaction to the stress condition, such as the development of anticipatory tension postulated by Davis. At the same time it should be noted that this is not the interpretation favoured by Foulds himself, who says rather that the extra activity disrupts circular interfering activity (worry and rumination, for example) in the dysthymics. Certainly the improvement merely brings them up to the level of speed attained by normals, hysterics, and psychopaths. And there is no statistically significant evidence that the latter group deteriorate under the extra stress: merely that the dysthymics improve. Our earlier discussions of distraction will of course prevent us feeling any surprise at the absence of effect from a distraction of this sort; the counting conveys little information, and there is time between each count to deal with the maze-threading task.

Another experiment of this type, exposing the subjects to stressed and unstressed conditions, is that of Venables (1955). In this case the task was a choice reaction to one of two lights. A sequence of such signals was given to each subject, and then followed by another sequence in which the task was made more difficult. Sometimes the signal was a simple light, sometimes a light accompanied by ' green ' or ' yes ' from another stimulus source, in which case the response was the same as in the first simple sequence. But sometimes the signal was a light accompanied by ' red ' or ' no ' from the other source, in which case the response was the opposite to that in the simple case. After the mixed sequence which included these difficult signals, a final sequence was made up of simple lights and presented as the first sequence had been. Performance on these three sequences was compared for the unaccompanied light signals alone, so that in the middle sequence the more-or-less lasting effects of task difficulty were measured, as distinct from the momentary result of distraction. People clinically diagnosed as hysterics did worse in the middle sequence than in the other two; so also did those in a normal group (that is, composed of people not under treatment) who had high scores on the extraversion and neuroticism factors determined by a large test battery.  On the other hand people diagnosed as dysthymics, and normals with high neuroticism but low extraversion scores, did better in the middle sequence.  If an unselected normal group was considered, not excluding those with low neuroticism scores, significant correlations were found between extraversion and relatively low middle-sequence performance.  In this case the correlations were, however, fairly small.

While considering distraction, it should be noted that individual differences in the effect of noise on work are noted by many authors as being large.  It is pointed out by Eysenck (1950) that various German researches have shown that people of short, fat body build are slowed more in reaction time by distracting noises than people of tall, thin build are.  Such a difference in body-build has been associated by Eysenck (1947) with the extraversion-intraversion dimension.  It has also been shown by Sheldon and Stevens (1942) that this type of build is linked with extraversion as assessed by rating scales; although the latter are of course subject to the weakness that the rater's impression of any individual personality will doubtless be coloured by the beliefs current in our culture about a connexion between corpulence and sociability.  It should be noted that the German researchers were using body-build because of Kretschmer's association of body-build with the division of psychotics into schizophrenic and manic-depressive varieties.  Yet Eysenck (1952) showed that tests discriminating the latter were not those which discriminate the two types of neurotic.  And Venables and Tizard (1956a) showed that decrement in a five-choice serial reaction situation was characteristic of schizophrenics as opposed to depressives, a difference which would be in the wrong direction if we identify short, fat body-build with extraversion and work decrement.  There is here clearly an ambiguity of the same type as that discussed earlier, in the relation of anxiety as an indicator of neuroticism and anxiety as an index of intraversion.  The exact relation of the intraversion-extraversion distinction and that between the different types of psychotic deserves further work. It may be added at this point that the picture is further complicated by the variable of age.  Foulds noted that older subjects took longer before starting the Porteus maze, but were more accurate. Such a relation with age is not uncommon (Welford 1951). It is, of course, a shift in the intraverted direction: but body-build changes towards corpulence with increasing age. However, most of the studies in this chapter seem to have realized these complications, and held age constant. It still remains to be fully investigated in its effect on personality.

Other correlations with the effect of noise were reported by Broadbent (1954a). The twenty lights test showed a larger effect of noise on people who had a large practice effect between the two runs in quiet. As was mentioned previously, these are also the people who show large decrements during each run. And when the triple tester index was correlated with total score throughout the 4 days of the experiment, it was found that the relation was positive for that group of subjects who started with noise on their first day, and negative for those who started in quiet. (This fact was given only in the cyclostyled first report of the experiment, Broadbent 1951.) That is, if one accepts the index as a measure of extraversion, the extraverts do relatively worse throughout an experiment if they start in noise.*

To confirm and strengthen this finding, the data from the mental arithmetic task already mentioned in this chapter were examined. Eight of the subjects who had performed both under noise and under quiet conditions had also taken the Heron questionnaire. The product-moment correlation between extraversion and impairment by noise was just significant by a one-tail test. The result is strikingly similar to that of Foulds except that the distraction was in this case an intense stimulus rather than an additional task. It helps to confirm the previous finding on the twenty lights test, since the measure of extraversion is in this case more similar to that employed by other researches.

A last experiment bearing on the question of reaction to stress is that of Deese and his associates (Deese, Lazarus and Keenan 1953) who found that there was no relation between manifest anxiety and rate of learning until wrong responses were punished. When the latter step was taken, the anxious individuals learned

---

* It is not unusual for the conditions under which a task is first performed to determine efficiency on later trials under different conditions. We mentioned this point in Chapter 5, and cited the results of Welford, Brown and Gabb (1950) as supporting it.

faster. Here again therefore, it was reaction to stress which differentiated the two groups; and there seems a broad agreement throughout all the results we have considered that the extravert responds to stress less well. The caution must immediately be added that the stresses are all of the distraction type, or else punishment: it by no means follows that abnormal temperatures, lack of sleep, or other poor working conditions will affect the extraverts primarily. The point is theoretically important because Eysenck (1955b) has argued that all types of inhibition may be the same, and more prevalent in extraverts. This would mean that distraction could be classed as external inhibition, and the results we have considered would not then tell against the inhibition theory. Unless distraction is regarded as due to an inhibition like that responsible for extinction the fact that extraverts are differentiated by reaction to stress would be a point against the inhibition theory.

*Physiological affiliations.*—Before summing up, some rather different evidence should be stated. These are the possible connexions between extraversion and physiological events. First, brain injury has been supposed to produce inhibition over the surviving cortex (Eysenck 1955b). Petrie (1952) has indeed found that leucotomy increases the degree of extraversion as measured by Eysenck's methods. And Klein and Krech (1952) have also shown that the tactile figural after-effect was greater in the brain-injured, using exactly the same procedure as that afterwards employed by Eysenck to distinguish hysterics from dysthymics. This relation to brain injury undoubtedly needs further qualification, as its proponents are indeed aware; it can hardly apply to all brain injuries, but presumably only to those of certain types. Equally there is no evidence that it is due to inhibition in any physiological sense.

Chemical effects are also of some interest. For instance, Franks and Laverty (1955) showed that sodium amytal would accelerate the rate of extinction of an eyelid conditioned response, and there was also some evidence that it slowed original conditioning although this effect was less well established. Scores on a questionnaire measure of extraversion were increased by the drug. In terms of Eysenck's theory this means that sodium amytal produces cortical inhibition, and he cites evidence (Eysenck

1955a) that hysterics need less sodium amytal, when it is given for sedative purposes, than normals or dysthymics do. One may well, however, suspend judgement about cortical inhibition while accepting these results as a further demonstration of a connexion between questionnaire score and extinction. Changes of performance in the same individuals are a valuable supplement to correlations in different individuals.

A rather different line of evidence is provided by recent investigations of cholinesterase level in animals. It is known that the liberation of acetyl choline plays an important part in nervous function, and the concentration of cholinesterase (which catalyses conversion of this compound into others) in the brain is therefore likely to be connected with the degree to which nervous activity spreads or persists. The details of the connexion are, however, extremely unclear. Certain recent investigators have studied the effect of feeding animals on a substance which reduces cholinesterase level. Watson (1955) cites earlier unpublished work by R. W. Russell as showing that this kind of diet reduces the rate of extinction of conditioned responses: and he relates it to intraversion by noting that administration of cholinesterase does sometimes improve the state of schizophrenics. The latter group of psychotics is sometimes regarded as intraverted, though as we have seen they show marked work decrement in Venables' research, and do not score highly on Eysenck's intraversion scale (or, for that latter, lowly). Moreover, the therapeutic effects of choline treatment seem to be a little unreliable and are queried by some (Pare 1956).

Another study of cholinesterase level used the naturally appearing differences between animals rather than administration of some special treatment. This is the work of Krech, Rosenzweig, Bennett and Krueckel (1954). It deserves fairly close attention as the methods of research bear on our discussion of experimental extinction in the next chapter. Krech has long been noted for his interest in the systematic but incorrect choices made by rats in mazes. If alleys are made different from one another in several different ways, e.g. by being lighted as opposed to dark, having posts in them as opposed to being clear, and having circles over the entrance as opposed to squares, the rat will systematically react on the basis of one of these alternatives. It will go, say, into all the lighted alleys, even though this is not the correct choice and results in about 50 per cent of blind alleys. After a time this reaction to the light cue disappears and is replaced by reaction, say, to the right-hand alleys. Eventually the correct feature of the alleys is selected and the rat runs without errors. The preliminary systematic reactions are called by Krech ' hypotheses ' and their occurrence is generally agreed by investigators. There is a point of controversy in connexion with them, namely, whether any learning of the correct response occurs during response on the basis of the incorrect ' hypothesis '. Krechevsky (1938) has argued that it does not, that until the correct hypothesis is adopted the fact that only certain responses have been rewarded is irrelevant: this is supported by a demonstration that if the originally correct pair of stimuli are reversed in role, the original ' blind ' stimulus now becoming the ' correct ' stimulus and vice versa, there is no effect on learning provided that the reversal occurs during the period before the correct hypothesis is adopted. In ordinary terms, the suggestion is that the animal does not notice that only alleys with posts have been blinds, as long as it is reacting on the assumption that dark alleys are blinds. This view is strenuously denied by other theorists who hold that the correct response builds up in strength even while performance is on the basis of some other cue: and appears when response to this other cue has been extinguished to a weaker level.

This theoretical issue need not concern us for the moment, although we shall return to it. The present relevance is that Krech and his associates studied the preferred hypotheses of rats, and then killed them and examined the cholinesterase level in their brains. The maze used contrasted light/dark and right/left as features of alleys, and the first paper reported that animals reacting on the basis of position had relatively low cholinesterase levels in the sensory areas. From this one might think that these animals were oriented rather to the motor than the sensory side. But a later paper (Krech, Rosenzweig and Bennett 1956) shows rather that all animals initially react on the light cue, but that some abandon this hypothesis sooner in favour of the position one. These animals have high cholinesterase levels. This finding fits well with that already cited, that a high cholinesterase level increases the rate of extinction. Rosenzweig, Krech and

Bennett found that the high cholinesterase animals could be rapidly switched either to light or to position response by selective reinforcement of one cue or the other, while the low cholinesterase animals could not. The same authors showed that administering sodium pentobarbital gave the type of performance characteristic of low cholinesterase level (Rosenzweig, Krech and Bennett 1956). This forms a link with the sodium amytal experiments mentioned previously, the latter drug being a barbiturate as sodium pentobarbital is. The careful reader will note that the relationship is in the wrong direction; sodium amytal gave more extinction and sodium pentobarbital less. There are various conceivable excuses for this: the effect of drugs does reverse with changes in dose size, and the discrimination situation of Krech and his associates is possibly dependent on tendency to make positive responses as well as give up wrong ones. Animals which do well in it might not therefore be the ones which extinguish quickly in a simple situation. A rather similar relation between simple and discriminatory situations lies behind the finding that persons showing manifest anxiety do badly in complex tasks despite their more rapid acquisition of a simple conditioned response (Taylor and Spence 1952).

There is therefore only a tenuous connexion between this work and the intraversion-extraversion dimension. There is still a possibility that the individual differences discussed in this chapter are in some way connected with naturally occurring differences in the cholinesterase level in some part of the brain; but far more data will be needed before any very definite conclusion can be drawn.

One last point should be made. Rosenzweig, Krech and Bennett regard cholinesterase level as an index of cortical efficiency, and speak of the high level animals as being less ' stimulus-bound ' since they can shift from one dimension to another. Regardless of whether their differences are the same as those in extraversion, their phrasing may serve as a text in warning the reader against any impression from the earlier part of the chapter that extraverts are somehow inferior to intraverts. Poor performance in prolonged work or under distraction may well go with rapid adjustment to novel circumstances: the inferiority is specific to the particular task.

*A General View of the Problem*

It is difficult to consider the experiments we have been discussing without feeling that some important truth lies behind them. There are too many points of agreement between experimenters of quite different interests and assumptions for the whole body of data to be dismissed as trivial; caused perhaps by a concealed chance correlation in a particular sample of subjects. It seems certain that the individuals who do worse after prolonged work on some (not perhaps all) tasks have an undue chance of displaying features which are also characteristic of hysterics as opposed to dysthymics. But it cannot be said that any adequate account of this relationship exists. The main candidate is Eysenck's description of the hysteric as having a greater tendency to accumulate reactive inhibition. This formulation has some truth in it, but must be hedged around with a number of qualifications. It is also difficult to relate it to some of the hysteric's other characteristics such as his faster commencement of the Porteus maze in Foulds' experiments.

The difficulties of the reactive inhibition view may be divided into two classes. First, there are objections to regarding the hysteric as showing a decrease in the probability of any response which has occurred. It has already been noted that leg persistence does not seem to correlate with decrement in the five-choice task, and is admittedly a measure of neuroticism rather than extraversion. On the other hand, decrements in vigilance are not due to too much responding but, if anything, to too little: yet these decrements do correlate with measures of extraversion. Although in some cases, such as that of the pursuit rotor, decrements on work involving overt response have been shown to be greater in extraverts, we have considered evidence in the last chapter that decrement on the pursuit rotor is at least partially perceptual rather than motor. The figural after-effect is clearly a perceptual effect. We can hardly interpret ' reactive inhibition ' in a peripheralist sense if we are to uphold Eysenck's position; nor would he do so himself. To interpret freely the position he has taken up at one point (Eysenck 1955b) he seems to be thinking of the cortical events which follow on presentation of a stimulus, and regarding the depression of the probability of one such event as reactive inhibition of it. The position is in fact a centralist one.  The point is an important one, since as we shall see in the next chapter there is growing evidence that the extinction of conditioned responses is not to be explained by a simple peripheralist view of reactive inhibition.

To this caution there must be added another, that ' inhibition ' must not be thought of in any physiological sense.  While historically many have been tempted to suppose that a process of cortical inhibition underlies the extinction of conditioned responses, or figural after-effects, there is no particular reason for thinking that it does.  Physiologists do not usually look with favour upon spreading areas of excitation and inhibition conceived after the Pavlovian model;  and although they may yet change their views it is dangerous to take up a position which requires them to do so.  Inhibition must therefore be conceived operationally as ' the process whatever it may be which produces extinction '.

With these qualifications we have whittled down the inhibition view to a simple statement that hysterics show more rapid extinction.  But this raises the second type of difficulty for the theory.  If prolonged work produces more inhibition in intraverts, why are some scores affected differently from others ?  We have already mentioned that gaps and errors on the five-choice task have not been found to correlate with extraversion, that missed signals in Baker's task gave no correlation, and that on Wilkinson's task it was the range of reaction times rather than the mean which showed a greater change in some individuals, and those the intraverts.  We may add that preliminary trials by the writer at correlating extraversion with the effect of massing and spacing on rote learning, have been unsuccessful;  although in this case very few subjects were used.  (In Chapter 9 a view of rote learning will be indicated according to which, the effect of massing rote learning trials is related to ' blocks ' or ' gaps ' rather than to output on the five-choice task.)   It is not clear why the incidence of blocks should be unrelated to extraversion when decrements in output are;  there seems no reasonable ground for regarding one measure as a form of inhibition while the other is not.  Furthermore inhibition is itself a name covering a number of processes even if it is defined purely operationally.  Few theorists of extinction ascribe it to a single process;  most, like Hull, require two processes having different properties. Hinde (1954), in writing of response to repeated stimuli in innate behaviour, distinguishes four possibilities. With which of these should extraversion be paired ? And there is an additional step involved in deciding what other processes, such as figural after-effects, are to be taken as instances of inhibition. Finally, as has been said previously, there seems no connexion at all between inhibition and other characteristics of the extravert such as his preference for speed rather than accuracy and his different level of aspiration. In summary, Eysenck's theory of extraversion provides a working approach rather than an established theory, for it has not been related in sufficient detail to the various phenomena of behaviour to allow us to accept it on the same level as the various Hullian concepts.

Despite these difficulties, it may be argued that the inhibition view has been supported by positive results in the fields to which it has been applied, and made predictions. By the criterion of hypothetico-deductive method, therefore, it is to be supported. The writer does not uphold this interpretation of scientific method, as we shall see in Chapter 12. Briefly, the objection is that many other theories might make the same predictions, and that positive results therefore support them as well. To illustrate this point we may state another working approach on the nature of extraversion, this time from a rather different point of view. Although this approach is not definitely established, any more than Eysenck's is, there are two other advantages to doing so besides that of showing that inhibition is not the only principle capable of explaining these effects. First, we may encourage others to take an interest in this field even though they find the term ' inhibition ' uncongenial. Secondly, we may answer the point sometimes made against information theory models, that they cannot be applied to individual differences. This latter point is probably made because of a natural concern amongst psychologists that the more valuable and unique features of human beings should not be lost to view during the search for scientific understanding. To many who are acquainted chiefly with such machines as watches or steam-engines, the suggestion that analogies from machines should be applied to human beings carries the implication that personality is to be ignored. Yet the whole importance of the study of information flow in machines is that systems are now being produced which do possess individual features while obeying common laws. It would indeed be wrong if, as Hearnshaw (1956) supposes, the tradition of Galton was being ignored. But the analogy with machines is not intended to overthrow the study of individual differences: rather to extend it and place it on a more exact footing.

Let us consider a translating machine. In principle there are a number of ways of building such a machine, all based on the underlying conception of a machine which responds with words in one language when given words in another. At one extreme there is the type of machine which, when given one word, responds immediately with another word. At the other extreme there is the type which waits until a whole sentence has arrived and then responds with a whole sentence. To the latter one can say ' *Je viens de le voir* ' and obtain the answer ' I have just seen him '; whereas the former will probably say ' I come of the to see ' or something equally peculiar. At first sight, then, the latter machine has considerable advantages. Yet the former also has assets which are so great that most existing translating machines tend towards this extreme. First, the response is more rapid, although less accurate. This is of little importance in most translating machines, but it may be crucial in other types of system. Even in the case of translation, a machine in, say, an air-traffic control tower might find speed rather than accuracy desirable: provided the men who used it could interpret its peculiar syntax. Secondly, the vocabulary of words which can be handled by a machine of given size is far greater with the first type of machine than with the second. This can be seen from the principles discussed in Chapter 3. It is the advantage which weighs most with translating machine designers: a machine having an ensemble sufficient to cope with a reasonable vocabulary of words in all the possible sequences in which they might arrive would be unrealistically big.

In other fields the relative merits of speed and of accuracy may be more important; for the same antithesis will appear in, for example, systems for tracking moving objects. Some systems may move a gun to point to the detected position of a target, others may observe target position over a length of time and then move the gun to a position worked out from the whole of this sample of the target motion. One of these systems will be better with one kind of target, and the other with another. In general, the system which works on a short sample of information will be better with a target that changes its behaviour repeatedly; while that which works on a long sample of information will be better with a target moving in a smooth and predictable fashion.

The distinction between short and long sampling systems is common to a number of situations in which information is handled: each strategy has its own advantages. It would be surprising indeed if their relative value had not been considered in the design of nervous systems, and, since they are for many purposes closely balanced, one might expect some individuals to lean more towards one strategy and some rather towards the other. How would such individuals differ?

In the first place, as our original example showed, they would differ in speed and accuracy on certain tasks. Not on all: only on those to which our translating machine furnishes a fair analogy. Thus we would not expect any difference in time taken to run a mile, but we might well expect a difference in time spent observing a Porteus maze before commencing the run through it; this is taking in information, and the organism which takes a long sample will be longer in starting. This kind of difference in speed is, as we may recall, characteristic of the difference between intraverts and extraverts. Other differences which we have mentioned in this chapter can equally be described as features of short as opposed to long sampling systems.

Consider level of aspiration as an example. Each estimate of future performance given by the subject is based partly on immediately previous knowledge of his actual performance, and partly on the whole series of past performances. A long sampling system, one would suggest, would give a level of aspiration determined largely with reference to the mean of all past performances. A short sampling system would be guided by the last performance. In a task which does not vary much from one trial to another there may be little difference in these values: but in a task which is highly variable, the two kinds of strategy will give quite different values. If successive trials improve, for example, the long sampling system should extrapolate this tendency and so give consistently higher goal discrepancies than the short sampling system.   If on the other hand the trials vary randomly about a mean (which may or may not steadily increase) then the long sampling system will show alternate positive and negative goal discrepancies as real performance rises and falls above and below the mean (see Fig. 3).

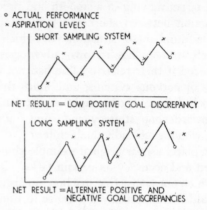

Fig. 3.   Levels of aspiration in a task with a fluctuating level of performance: as given by short and long sampling systems.

The finding that intraverts show higher goal discrepancies on the whole has already been mentioned.   What was left unclear in earlier pages was the reason for using the triple tester index, the arithmetical sum of all goal discrepancies for the particular subject *regardless of sign*.   A very high triple tester index may be achieved by alternate positive and negative discrepancies.   This type of score, rather than the orthodox goal discrepancy, was originally adopted for the theoretical reasons just given.   It is often equivalent to the more conventional score: but it should be mentioned that in none of the cases reported did the conventional score give a significant relationship, although it was in the same direction as that with the triple tester index.

The importance of this method of scoring will depend on the task: the triple tester is one which contains a large random element in each performance.   This may be responsible for the rather disappointingly low correlations between goal discrepancies on different tasks.   It has recently been claimed (Sutcliff 1955) that levels of aspiration are only consistent individual features when the task is one containing a large random element, which is quite reasonable on the present point of view. This interpretation also raises the point that differences between intraverts and extraverts may appear in more ordinary psycho-physical experiments, which should afford a better field for developing a sensitive test than does level of aspiration. On our interpretation the correlation of the latter with intraversion has nothing to do with subjective goals, but only with the difference between long and short sampling of the information on which the stated ' goal ' is based. Just as in the speed and accuracy case, the intravert corresponds to the long sampling system.

How would these contrasting systems react to stress? There are several reasons for arguing that the short sampling strategy makes any individual who adopts it more vulnerable to environmental factors which depress performance. On the one hand, any change in the mean performance over a past period would have less influence on present performance, just as the level of aspiration will be less influenced by the mean of past achievement. Again, the instructions given to the individual may be regarded as a remotely past stimulus which will count less in the present situation if the individual is short sampling. This would mean that the long sampling individuals would show evidence of compensating reactions to combat distraction or the effects of prolonged work (which previous chapters have regarded as closely similar). While both kinds of person would suffer deviations from the optimum performance, one kind would then react against this: and so we would have the individual differences in the trend of mean performance but not of gaps or errors which we mentioned earlier as a difficulty for the reactive inhibition view. We would have the agitated high frequency of corrections shown by Davis, in some individuals, and the high level of performance on reactions in a distraction stress situation shown by Venables. The differences would not, in general, be simply a matter of average performance but of the incidence of corrections and compensations.

In general, the difference between the extravert and the intravert is on this view that the former responds rapidly to changes in the conditions of his work; which may be disastrous if the changes are in the direction of making the work harder. But this is only provided that he already has an appropriate response to the new situation. It does not follow that he will learn a new response more rapidly than the intravert. The translating machine which we are using as an analogy does not learn new responses at all. The ' extraverted ' translating machine responds rapidly, and possibly inaccurately, to each word as it arrives: but the response word has been built in when the machine was manufactured. If we built a learning machine, provided with a feed-back on the effects of its past responses so that it will produce different ones in future if it has failed and keep to the same ones if it has succeeded it would have rather different characteristics to the simple machine. One might argue that the rate of learning would be faster if it gave a good deal of weight to knowledge of past results rather than to the present stimulus. If so, that part of the machine which received incoming information would resemble the long sampling type of simple translater rather than the short sampling type. The latter would not respond quickly to changes which demanded new responses. This analysis raises two important points. First, the traditional concept of perseveration is not equivalent to the view we have outlined. We would not necessarily expect individuals who change rapidly from one familiar type of response to another to be the same as those who can rapidly reverse a long-established response. Indeed, the lack of agreement between different tests of perseveration has in the past caused a number of investigators to abandon it, despite the suggestive results sometimes obtained from it.

The second important point is that predictions of rate of conditioning are rather unsatisfactory. We would expect extraverts to show rapid extinction, in massed trials with no disinhibiting stimuli; but rate of conditioning is a different matter. It may depend greatly on the spacing of trials, the initial level of response to the particular stimulus, and so on. This rather cautious attitude to conditionability seems justified by the nature of the evidence we considered earlier. We shall return in the next chapter to the relation between learning and the relative weighting of present and past stimuli; it is a highly complex topic.

Lastly, we should consider the question of figural after-effects and of the clinical symptoms of different types of neurosis. For the former, it could be argued that figural after-effect represents judgement of the present stimulus with reference only to the immediate past, and without considering the remotely past level of stimulation.   Thus one might conceivably find larger figural after-effects in the extraverted: but any modification in the procedure, such as altering the number and type of previous judgements, may remove or even reverse the effect.   It is for this reason that the writer's failure to duplicate Eysenck's results with a modified procedure was mentioned earlier.

On clinical symptoms, the less said the better, as almost any theory can be plausibly made to describe what facts we have on neurotic behaviour away from the laboratory.   However, the view that some neurotic personalities are inconsistent from day to day, persist without anxiety in maladaptive reactions, and are usually diagnosed hysteric or psychopathic, seems reasonably plausible. Dysthymics, on the other hand, show considerable compensatory behaviour and are acutely disturbed by the contrast between their present situation and behaviour, and their internal standards.

The foregoing views are not by any means to be regarded as more than tentative: but they show that other interpretations of these individual differences are possible without appealing to reactive inhibition, save perhaps in the completely operational sense of ' that which is responsible for extinction '.   Indeed it seems likely that many alternative explanations of the existing facts are possible, so that no one theory can claim a dominant position merely because it provides an account of existing data.

The results in this chapter are less adequate than any others in this book.   None the less, they suggest that individual differences in prolonged performance are highly important, and may be related to those differences which have appeared in the past in the clinical diagnosis of hysterics and dysthymics.   They have been included in the book primarily to attempt to stimulate interest in the problem; for clearly it is imperative that much attention should now be paid to individual differences in psycho-physics.   Whether one adheres to Eysenck's inhibitory interpretation, or whether one adopts the view just put forward which rather emphasizes the role of level of adaptation (Helson 1948), there seems to be some buried fact here awaiting the spades of future investigators.   For the moment we must leave it in this unsatisfactory state, and carry forward to the next chapter only a certain dissatisfaction with the phrase ' reactive inhibition '.

# CHAPTER 8

# THE NATURE OF EXTINCTION

AT this point we take a step whose value some may question. So far, our argument has passed from multiple channel listening, through the problem of listening while doing a visual task, to the problem of doing a visual task in meaningless noise. Then we considered visual tasks without any background of experimentally imposed noise, and lastly individual differences in these tasks. All these functions of human beings may well be related; but why should we now turn to animal behaviour? In the study of individual differences, we were hesitant in accepting a parallel between inhibition and extraversion. Should we not be equally cautious about any extrapolation from human behaviour to conditioning?

To some extent, this caution is highly justifiable. In Chapter 3 we considered behaviour from an informational point of view which made it quite clear that many functions possible to a large nervous system would be quite impossible to a smaller one. We cannot expect that every point we have made about human behaviour should be paralleled among animals. Yet the quantities of data we have surveyed have pressed us steadily towards certain general principles. Information entering the nervous system is filtered, and only part of it is passed on to emerge in response. The part which survives this process depends on various properties of the stimulus itself and also of the organism: intense stimuli are more likely to pass, so are novel ones, and those on particular channels such as high frequency sounds. Now the logical part of this argument applies as well to animals as to man. If our nervous systems are too small to handle simultaneously all the information which reaches us, so even more are theirs. A filtering process is even more necessary in such a case, and in fact we have already cited data from animals when trying to decide on the properties of stimuli which give them the priority in passing the filter: the results of Berlyne (1950) on novelty were from rats. We might equally well have cited those of Brown (1942) on intensity, rather than sticking to human data. We may therefore expect that the same general results which we have found in the human case should appear also in animals; though there may well be differences of detail, and no particular finding can therefore be applied directly to animals without confirmation by specific experiments. Confirmation from animal results is of general value for the interpretation we have put upon the human work: if there has been some error of reasoning in the account we have given, there may be no comparable results on animals. But if our interpretation has been correct, there should be at least some. As we said in an earlier chapter, the operations involved in extinguishing conditioned responses are very similar to those of measuring the efficiency of human watch-keeping. It is therefore in the extinction process that we may look for analogies. But first we should examine other existing explanations for extinction and see what kind of difficulties they meet.

## The Adequacy of Reactive Inhibition

Since the days of Pavlov, it has been usual to explain the disappearance of unreinforced conditioned responses after repeated elicitation as due to some inhibitory process. An extinguished response is not to be confused with a forgotten response, for two main reasons. First, the extinguished response may reappear if one gives the animal a rest free from presentations of the conditioned stimulus (' spontaneous recovery '). Secondly, the extinguished response may reappear if one gives a fresh stimulus together with that which has been conditioned and extinguished (' disinhibition '). Both these facts show that the tendency to produce the response is still present in the animal, but that some other factor is overlaying it. We therefore speak of ' inhibition ' of the response. The argument may actually be questioned, and we shall do so later, but it has been very widely accepted and may be left in the above form for the moment.

In Hull's formulation, as we indicated in the last chapter, this inhibitory potential is regarded as increasing every time a response occurs. When a stimulus-response combination is followed by food or some other ' reinforcement ', this produces an excitatory potential which balances out the inhibition. But once reinforcement stops, inhibition is unopposed, and the response gradually becomes less likely each time it occurs. The inhibitory potential is supposed to dissipate with time, while the excitatory potential does not (or at least dissipates more slowly) so that the response will recover after an interval. Disinhibition is explained by afferent stimulus interaction, whose unsatisfactory character was discussed in the first chapter.

How far is this explanation satisfactory? It has recently run into a number of difficulties, some of which have been considered elsewhere and will therefore be mentioned only briefly here (Broadbent 1959). They are of the same kind as the results which we mentioned in the chapter on vigilance as casting doubt on the motor origin of decrements in human work. Just as, in the human case, experiments have been done in which decrements are produced by purely perceptual work; so also in the animal case, extinction has been produced purely by stimulation without any response occurring. This may be done either by giving very faint stimuli which produce no response (Kimble and Kendall 1953), or else by removing part of the environment which is essential for response: for example, the lever in a Skinner box which the rat has been taught to press by following each response by food reinforcement (Hurwitz 1955). As in the human case this type of result implies that the process is more a central than a motor one. So does the finding that in maze-running, animals will go to different places on successive trials even though this means repeating the same motor response. Glanzer (1953) has suggested that this implies that repeated stimuli become satiated and so cease to produce an effect, and this certainly seems more plausible than the doctrine that repeated motor response is the source of inhibition. It is not altogether satisfactory, as Walker, Dember, Earle, Fliege and Karoly (1955) have shown that presentation of a goal-box stimulus away from its context in the maze does not produce the tendency to go to a different goal on the next trial. However, these authors agree that the motor response is unimportant: the animal responds alternately to different goals even when this means repeating the same response, as long as the goals are met in the maze. The experiments of Walker and his associates tell against reactive inhibition, even though they may necessitate some modification of Glanzer's formulation.

Other difficulties of the reactive inhibition view which have not been considered by Broadbent (1959) arise from a really detailed examination of the behaviour occurring in extinction. For instance, one of Hull's formulations suggested that the physical work done by the animal was positively related to inhibition, and it was indeed true that an animal which had to press a bar against a large resisting force in order to obtain food would make fewer pressings before extinguishing the response. But one ' bar-press ' is a very ambiguous unit. An animal may operate the bar by a large force for a short time, or by a weaker one for a longer time. It may linger on the bar or give it a quick sharp depression. The work of Hurwitz (1954) and of Trotter (1956) makes it clear that extinction is not necessarily quicker when the animal is doing more work. Nor does it do more work when freshly conditioned than when extinguished: on the contrary it may be inclined to hold the bar down more when not about to rush over to the food-trough for reinforcement, and this is the situation when extinction is well advanced.

Less crucial but still inconvenient for the inhibition view is the fact that spontaneously emitted responses, such as those in a Skinner box, do not die away evenly as extinction proceeds. The mean curve from a large number of animals may indeed be smooth, but the individual ones are very uneven. Hull postulates a random oscillatory process to account for such facts, but this is in any case an *ad hoc* postulate and seems unlikely when one examines the data in detail. For instance Hurwitz (1957) divides up the period of extinction into 2 min intervals, and considers separately the intervals in which the rat makes any responses and those in which he makes none. The latter become more frequent as extinction proceeds, but when the former are examined it is found that the mean number of responses in each remains the same throughout the extinction period. In fact, if the rat is responding it is doing so at roughly its initial rate. This activity merely becomes more interspersed with intervals of doing nothing at all as time goes on.

Such a finding is highly reminiscent of the results on con-tinuous human performance: blocks become more frequent, but the rate of work between them remains constant. In the human case the overall mean is unaffected, while in the animal it declines, and an inhibitory point of view may therefore seem more plausible in the case of the animal. But it requires a very specific type of postulated random oscillation, superimposed on increasing inhibitory potential, to produce Hurwitz's results. The variance of the oscillations must be increasing as mean performance decreases. It seems more plausible to say that the animal is alternating between two types of behaviour, responding and not responding. The probability of a shift from one state to the other changes during extinction, but the rate of responding in the appropriate state does not change.

These experimental results shed some doubt on the reactive inhibition postulate. Response does not seem to be necessary for extinction, and when response occurs it does not seem to decline smoothly during extinction as though it was being inhibited. Certain alternative views do exist, and to these we will now turn.

*Other views of extinction.*—Traditionally, the main alternative to a theory that the occurrence of each response builds up inhibition, is the hypothesis that other competing responses are established. These other responses are incompatible with the one being extinguished, just as lifting the leg is incompatible with putting it down. The original response therefore disappears. This theory has the advantage of simplicity. It holds out the hope that extinction can be accounted for without adding any fresh postulate to those required for explaining learning. Admittedly there will still be an inhibitory process superimposed on the original stimulus-response association, but the inhibition would itself be caused by another stimulus-response association and no new principles would be involved. In addition there is experimental evidence that other responses do appear in extinction. The animal does not simply lapse into immobility, but does something else. If it is given some reinforcement for a response incompatible with the original one, the extinction of the latter is accelerated. For instance, if the animal has been trained to raise its foot at a signal, shock being given for failure to respond, extinction can be got more quickly by giving food when the foot is pressed down.

Despite these points in its favour, the theory of interfering responses is not much favoured at the present day. It is vulnerable to certain logical objections: for instance, if stimulus $X$ produces response $A$, and this is supposed to be inhibited by the attachment of an incompatible response $B$ to $X$, how does $B$ appear in the first place? If $A$ has been firmly acquired before extinction begins, $X$ always produces $A$; and since $A$ is incompatible with $B$ this means that $B$ can never occur to be reinforced until $A$ has been prevented from occurring. This prevention must be due to some outside factor, itself requiring explanation.

In addition, the conditions which favour extinction are not those which favour the learning of new responses. That is, if we give a drug such as caffeine we get more rapid conditioning. But we get slower extinction, so that it is hard to explain extinction in this case as the conditioning of incompatible responses. A particularly important case is that of the time interval between trials: a rapid series of trials without intervening rests is bad for conditioning but favours extinction. This means, in essence, that the interfering response theory does not explain spontaneous recovery from extinction. For these reasons the general preference has been to reject the theory of extinction by competing response.

A rather different form of explanation in terms of relearning has recently been put forward by Uttley (1955). His contention is that each different possible sensory event produces a different event within the nervous system: thus far, this is similar to the informational approach we have been adopting throughout this book, though Uttley is concerned with rather different problems from those which have led us to concentrate on the filtering of incoming information. He then suggests that the brain stores the conditional probability of any event given any other, and if this probability exceeds some critical value, the occurrence of the conditional event will cause the other to be inferred. The output from the system after event $X$ will then be $A$ if $X$ has often been followed by $Y$, but $B$ if $X$ has not been followed by $Y$. Physically, this could be arranged by making some part of the brain take up a different state for each of the possible values of the conditional probability: the output is made to depend on the state actually reached. Uttley has in fact built various machines which illustrate the principle, and there is certainly nothing mystical or indefinite about it. This is important, because as we shall see at later stages, the consequences of the theory are somewhat similar to those of expectancy theories, which are repugnant to many psychologists on account of their mentalist overtones. If there is a vagueness in this type of theory, it is in the specification of the output, which cannot be assumed to be the same as the output to the inferred event. Ways of overcoming this vagueness, devised by Uttley and by Deutsch, will be discussed in Chapter 10: for the moment, it is worth noting that in fact a conditioned response is not identical with an unconditioned one. Rather it may be described anthropomorphically as the response which would be appropriate if the animal was expecting the unconditioned stimulus to follow the conditioned one. This anticipatory character of the response is an old story (Hilgard and Marquis 1940, p. 39), but it continues to be ignored by theories of the S–R type.

Uttley has pointed out that when stimuli are considered in triplets rather than pairs a number of surprising deductions can be made. Thus if $X$ has been regularly paired with $Y$, the system will infer $Y$ given $X$. If some third stimulus $Z$, which is less frequent than $X$, now occurs with $X$ for the first time since training on the combination of $X$ and $Y$ was begun, the system will not infer $Y$ from the $X + Z$ combination. This is comparable to the Pavlovian phenomenon of ' external inhibition '; given some unusual stimulus along with the conditioned stimulus, the animal does not produce the conditioned response. Repeated presentation of $X + Y + Z$ will, however, cause $Y$ to be inferred from $X + Z$ and the effect of external inhibition will therefore wear off after a number of repetitions. (There is a question of agreement with behavioural fact here, which we will return to later.)

If, after training, $X$ is repeatedly presented alone the probability of $Y$ following $X$ becomes low and therefore the output from the system will revert to being that originally given to $X$ alone. This is extinction. But the probability of $Y$ following $X + Z$ has naturally been unaffected by the presentation of $X$ alone: therefore the introduction of $Z$ with $X$ will cause an inference of $Y$. Equally an unusual stimulus will produce ' disinhibition ' of an extinguished response. Once again, repetition of $X + Z$ without

$Y$ will cause the two to have the same effect as $X$ by itself, and the disinhibitor will lose its properties with repeated presentation.

As so far expressed, this theory will not predict spontaneous recovery nor forgetting. The system assesses the conditional probability of $Y$ given $X$ by registering the total number of times $X$ has occurred without $Y$, and comparing it with the total number of times $X$ has been followed by $Y$. These total numbers remain the same if we do not present $X$ for 24 hr, and the response will therefore be just as extinguished at the end of that time as it was at the beginning. This does not, of course, correspond with the facts. In any case a system which gives equal weight to all past presentations is impractical, as it would become progressively harder to modify the inferences made by the system. Uttley therefore incorporates into his machines the principle that greater weight is given to events more recent in time. Thus if a system has been receiving $X$ and $Y$ independently for many years, it can acquire the inference that $Y$ will follow $X$ by a comparatively few paired presentations of the two events. These recent presentations outweigh the whole past history of the system. Twenty-four hours later, however, the paired presentations receive only the same weight as the numerous isolated presentations before them: and the system therefore reverts to its original output. For the best retention, therefore, training must be repeated over a considerable time: which corresponds with the observed facts. Furthermore exactly the same relation with time will apply to extinction. After 24 hr a rapidly developed extinction will have disappeared and will need to be renewed.

This device of inserting differential weighting into the storage of conditional probabilities has therefore allowed an explanation of spontaneous recovery. It will now be clear why, in the last chapter, we said that the length of time over which information was sampled was of importance to extinction. A system which uses primarily the present information and gives less weight to the past will extinguish and recover rapidly, and this must therefore be borne in mind when making predictions about the behaviour of extraverts from the views given in the last chapter. Unfortunately it seems clear that they will also learn and forget rapidly, and this is quite contrary to Eysenck's reactive inhibition view. There is not sufficient evidence to decide which view is correct; in any case the present view places great emphasis on the actual time intervals between successive trials. On a reactive inhibition view of extraversion, too long an interval between trials will merely minimize the individual differences due to that factor: on a view of extraversion as a short-sampling strategy in handling incoming information, long intervals may actually reverse the effect.

Let us now return to Uttley's explanation of extinction. As we have seen, it includes external inhibition, disinhibition, and spontaneous recovery. Furthermore it does so without postulating any inhibitory process, so that the argument for the necessity of such a process, based on disinhibition and spontaneous recovery, must be fallacious. But unfortunately certain details fit Uttley's explanation rather badly. For instance, if external inhibition by a stimulus $X$ is present on a conditioned stimulus $Y$, it can be eliminated by presenting $X$ and $Y$ together with reinforcement, as Uttley's theory would predict. But the theory would also predict that repeated presentation of $X$ alone without reinforcement would leave the external inhibition unaffected, or even possibly increase it. The conditional probability of food following $X + Y$ remains unaltered by such treatment. Yet Pavlov (1927, p. 46) clearly states that repeated application of many external inhibitors, without any other stimulus, causes them to lose their properties. In fact this agrees with the everyday experience that 'distracting' stimuli may interfere with efficiency, but lose their attention-getting quality when presented repeatedly alone. Some other factor, besides the storage of conditional probabilities, must be operative in external inhibition.

A similar factual discrepancy appears in the explanation of disinhibition. Uttley's explanation requires that the disinhibiting stimulus be one which has previously been present during conditioning, but which has not been present during the earlier extinction trials. If an unsophisticated view of the word 'stimulus' is taken, disinhibiting stimuli are known sometimes to be ones which have not been given during training. Examples are given by Pavlov (1927, pp. 63–6). One can perhaps answer this objection by saying that the disinhibitory stimuli, although not themselves previously present, possess some properties in common with stimuli which were presented earlier. If the physical stimulus is considered as a group of events, which is partially sampled on each successive presentation, any change in the situation during the process of extinction is likely to change the sample of events away from those which have been recently extinguished. This gives an increased probability that the next sample will include events which have not been extinguished; and so there will be a higher probability of response. This 'sampling' interpretation is in some ways similar to one of Estes (1950), and it makes disinhibition less of a difficulty to Uttley's theory than external inhibition was. A number of additional postulates are obviously needed, however, before the results of any particular treatment of the animal can be predicted. This is especially true since it is known (Pavlov 1927, p. 45; Konorski 1946, p. 21) that some stimuli are more likely to produce external inhibition than others are; that the same type of stimulus may be inhibitory when physically intense, and neutral or actually disinhibitory in its effects when physically weak: and that a stimulus may be inhibitory during its presentation and disinhibiting after it has ceased. These facts are not necessarily incompatible with Uttley's account, but they require very much more detailed explanation than a simple demonstration of the consequences of storing conditional probabilities.

The most serious discrepancy between theory and fact is over the effects of time intervals between trials. As has already been said, long rests between each presentation help conditioning but hinder extinction. The two processes should be affected in the same way according to Uttley's model. If extra weight is given to recent events (to explain spontaneous recovery) we would expect original conditioning to be more rapid with trials close together in time, which is not so. If on the other hand equal weight is given to recent and to more remote information, the explanation of spontaneous recovery has been lost.

The conclusion we may draw from this is that Uttley's account requires supplementing by other principles. This does not mean that it is false within the field it was originally intended to cover: indeed, to a very large extent it is a logical analysis and must be true. Some S–R theorists have remained unaware of the implications of their own principles for external inhibition, disinhibition, generalization, and so on. Yet it is quite clear from Uttley's analysis that some of these phenomena will follow simply from

S–R association without any further postulate. If one has an associationist postulate, one should choose other postulates only for facts which are not covered by simple association: Uttley demonstrates that some of the properties formerly given to ' inhibition ' are unnecessary. This in turn means that facts which have previously been neglected may be brought within the province of learning theory. For example, it is asserted (Konorski 1948, p. 146) that when a stimulus has been firmly established as an ' inhibitory ' one, a positive response may be rapidly established to this stimulus, but disappears the next day. That is, if stimulus $X$ has been repeatedly presented without being followed by food, extending the training over a very long period will bring the animal to a state in which presenting $X$ lowers the probability of any response appropriate to food. We then give food in conjunction with $X$ for a day, and develop a response of salivation to $X$. On the next day salivation does not appear to $X$, which we may describe as spontaneous recovery in reverse. This makes reactive inhibition look even less likely. But on Uttley's view it is very reasonable: more weight is given to recent information, and therefore the recently established conditioning fades with lapse of time just as extinction does. Marked fading would of course require a great deal of preliminary presentation of $X$ without food: the slight forgetting found in orthodox conditioning, when a day's rest is given, is presumably due to $X$ having been independent of food before the experiment began, rather than a definite sign of no-food.

Another neglected phenomenon to which Uttley has applied his system is that of ' induction '. This effect is usually described by theorists of classical conditioning in the following way. If an animal has been trained with several stimuli, so that some produce positive conditioned responses and others produce no response, presenting two stimuli in rapid succession will produce an interaction of their effects. An inhibitory stimulus preceded by a positive one is even less likely to give a response, and a positive stimulus preceded by a negative stimulus is even more likely to give a response. It is therefore argued, in terms of Pavlov's theory, that arousal of excitation at any point on the cortical analyser (or arousal of inhibition) will produce (induce) the opposite process at neighbouring points.

Uttley drew attention to the fact that, if stimuli $A$ and $B$ are applied alternately and food given only after $A$, the conditional probability of ' food following $A$ ' is not the only one to become high. ' Food following $A$ following $B$ ' is also high, and it might be fairly assumed that it may under certain circumstances be higher than the probability of food after the isolated event $A$. Equally, ' no-food following $B$ following $A$ ' has a high probability. With an animal trained by such a process of alternate presentation, we may well find that the positive stimulus gives an enhanced effect when preceded by a negative one and vice versa.

Is this explanation of ' induction ' a valid one ? It depends, of course, on the animals showing the effect having been trained in a particular way: just as the explanation of disinhibition does, and we expressed some doubts about the latter. But the reported demonstrations of induction do seem to involve training of the type which Uttley would suppose necessary. One of the clearest instances is given by Pavlov (1927, p. 197). It was found that a differentiation between two stimuli could not be broken down by continuing to apply them alternately and reinforcing both of them. It was necessary to cease the application of the previous positive stimulus, and to apply the other stimulus repeatedly with reinforcement, if both stimuli were to be changed into positive ones. This was interpreted as negative induction from the interpolated positive stimuli, but it fits Uttley's explanation perfectly.

It is likely that a good many of the reported instances of induction in the literature can be explained in the same way, and that the Pavlovian account of the phenomenon which leaves the method of training out of account is too simple. For instance, all the examples given by Pavlov (1927, pp. 188–201) seem to be reducible to Uttley's scheme. Konorski (1948, p. 17) admits that induction appears largely with differentiated stimuli, which means usually in the experiments conducted in the Pavlovian tradition that the positive and negative stimuli were presented alternately. As he says (p. 20) after a differentiation between two stimuli is established, they become a pair linked by inductive relations. The response to the positive stimulus, when the latter is presented between two trials of the negative one, is actually greater than it was before the negative stimulus was differentiated from it.

It is by no means certain that all instances of induction are of this type, and in particular some facts given by Konorski (1948, p. 18) are rather hard to fit into Uttley's scheme.  It appears that Podkopayev compared the effects of a positive conditioned stimulus applied during and after a training stimulus.  Differentiation in a classical or Pavlovian situation cannot be established with simultaneous presentation, so the animal cannot have been trained to discriminate the two stimuli when both were present. Yet the response to the positive stimulus was greater when the negative one was simultaneously present than when one followed the other.  Possibly this might be explained on the Uttley theory by supposing that extinction of the response to the negative stimulus had not proceeded far enough, but on the face of it the fact presents a difficulty.

One last instance of the explanation of classical conditioning phenomena by the registration of conditional probabilities in the nervous system should be mentioned.  Pavlov gives an account of an experiment using touch stimuli applied at various points on a dog's body and with various delays between stimulations (Pavlov 1927, p. 208).  The results are interpreted in terms of irradiation of inhibition followed by induced excitation.  This means that in the first stage of the experiment the application of one non-reinforced stimulus reduced the response at all the other points on the dog's body.  The animal was repeatedly experimented upon, and by the end of the process it was found that applying a non-reinforced stimulus actually increased the subsequent response to other places.  In terms of Uttley's theory, the animal had learned that the conditional probability of another stimulus was high following one non-reinforced stimulus.  No spatially spreading processes of inhibition and induced excitation are necessary.

Besides Uttley's theory, it is possible to produce other variations on the theme of counter-learning.  Hull himself included conditioned inhibition as well as reactive inhibition in his system, in order to explain the fact that repeated extinction abolishes spontaneous recovery and so causes permanent extinction: in fact, learning that the appropriate response to this stimulus is inaction.  This really means that Hull's system included both the possible interpretations of extinction.  Another variation is that of Razran (1956), who suggests that counter-conditioning forms a second stage in extinction; it follows a preliminary weakening of the response, due to absence of the proprioceptive stimuli present in the situation when reinforcement is given. This two-factor theory allows a counter-conditioning view to overcome the logical difficulty of the original arousal of the new incompatible response. It also allows some treatment of spontaneous recovery, which, if the writer has interpreted Razran correctly, is regarded in the same way as by Uttley. The effects of drugs are regarded as changing the proprioceptive input, so that they afford no difficulty. But it is not clear how this theory handles extinction-like phenomena which appear while reinforcement is still being given. One example of this is the depressing effect on conditioning of massing trials, which has been mentioned already. Another example is the so-called ' extinction with reinforcement ' (Pavlov 1927, Lecture XIV; Konorski 1948, p. 31). Repeated elicitation of a response by a conditioned stimulus tends to depress the response even though reinforcement is given, provided the process is carried on long enough.

Indeed, this is the typical difficulty of all alternatives to reactive inhibition. There are ' fatigue-like ' effects in conditioning even when reinforcement occurs: these assist extinction, so that the latter is not simply a process opposite to conditioning. Neither of the contending views seems therefore to be completely satisfactory, although both have their advantages.

## The Weakness of the Argument for Inhibition

In the last section, we showed that Uttley was able to give some account of spontaneous recovery and disinhibition without appealing to an inhibitory postulate. What, then, was the fallacy in the traditional argument that these two effects require inhibition to explain them ? Translating the problem into one of information-flow may help disclose the flaw.

When an unconditioned stimulus is delivered, the information about this event travels through the organism and eventually appears as an output, such as turning the head to examine the source of stimulation. After conditioning the first stages of this journey must be the same, but at some point the information takes a different course and emerges in a different output, such as salivating.   An analogy would be a railway system in which trains from London normally arrive at Chester, until the points are switched over at Crewe.   After that operation the trains from London arrive at Liverpool (see Fig. 4).   The application of the stimulus for an extinguished response corresponds to the departure of a train which would normally reach Liverpool, but which does not appear at that destination.   Spontaneous recovery would be the despatch of a pursuing train from London after a day's delay; the emergence of this train at Liverpool would reveal that the points were still in their post-conditioning position.   To preserve the flavour of the analogy, we might compare disinhibition to the despatch of a pursuing train immediately after the first one fails to appear, with an accompanying armed guard to foil any criminal attempts.

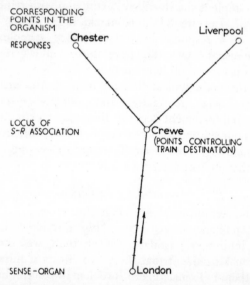

Fig. 4.   A railway system analogous to the flow of information through the nervous system in conditioning.   The locus of ' inhibition ' may be before that of S–R association: it is usually assumed that it is after it, for no good reason.

These pursuing trains prove only that the position of the points has not been completely reversed to the original state: they certainly do not prove, for instance, that the missing train

disappeared between Crewe and Liverpool.   The analogy therefore reveals that disinhibition and spontaneous recovery prove
at most that the change at the junction between the two lines of
information flow has not been completely reversed.   Uttley's
case is that even this is not completely proved: the change may
have been reversed for some trains and not for others.   As we
have seen, Uttley's criticism is not able to deal with all the
features of extinction, although it will handle many of them.
But there is another fallacy in the argument for inhibition: in
terms of the analogy, the train may disappear before reaching
Crewe rather than between Crewe and Liverpool.   The state of
affairs at Crewe is then quite irrelevant.   The normal account of
a response tending to occur but being inhibited gives the impression that the information travels from the senses through
the nervous system to a point beyond that at which its old path
diverges from its new one, and only then reaches a block or
interference which prevents the response from occurring.
Clearly there is nothing in disinhibition or spontaneous recovery
to warrant such an argument.   The information from an
extinguished conditioned stimulus may never travel far from the
sense-organ.

It is important here to distinguish linguistic and factual
arguments.   Some people speak of ' internal responses ' when
they wish to refer to events within the nervous system.   They
may wish to say that in extinction an internal response occurring
immediately after the sense-organs is inhibited, and so no further
responses are elicited by the internal ' stimuli ' arising from this
internal ' response '.   In fact, it is possible to speak of ' inhibition '
at an early stage in the nervous system, and to be clear in one's
own mind that there is no implication that any event whatever
has occurred at the place where S–R associations are modified.
This is true in much the same sense that it is true that mathematics
can be carried out with roman rather than with arabic numerals:
the inconvenience is considerable.   For example, we have already
cited in Chapter 6 the work of Adams showing that there is no
need for work to involve an overt response to produce a decrement
on the pursuit rotor.   People who merely watch the situation
show decrements.   Adams chooses to use Hullian terms to
describe his results;  one can speak of this experiment as showing

that reactive inhibition of the visual response is important, as well as that of the motor response. This is perfectly legitimate, but it is perhaps revealing that in a later paper Adams (1956) refers to a decline in the ability to detect signals as due to inhibition of the visual *effectors*: that is, to attribute the loss of information in transmission to a failure in the eye-muscles or some other part of the local loop controlling the adjustment of the senses. This may in fact be true, but it seems likely that Adams has been led into asserting it merely by the inconvenience of his language: there is no evidence for it. It seems desirable to avoid using language which carries such overtones.

However, too much weight should not be put on a minor phrase, and the choice of language is a matter of convenience, whereas the assertion of experimental results is not. In consequence, it should be made clear that the writer is not objecting to the word ' inhibition ' regardless of the way in which it is used, but only to the unwarranted implication that the process (whatever it is) occurs at a late stage in the nervous system. Many of those who use the word are no doubt aware of this danger. For the writer, it is too great a risk to be avoided while using the traditional word.

We may then agree that extinction may be associated with reception of the stimulus rather than with performance of the response: and this, it will be remembered, fits well into the framework of the experiments which shed doubt on reactive inhibition. Repeated presentation of faint stimuli causes extinction, even when no response has occurred: and an animal which has approached a black goal-box on one trial will approach a white box on the next even if this means turning the same way as before. It is now time to turn back to the concept of filtering sensory information which we have developed in previous chapters, and to see how well it will handle such results.

## Filter Theory in Extinction of Classical Conditioned Responses

In the following account we shall be too sweeping in certain respects and too cautious in others. That is, we shall apply filter theory in such a way as to account for as much as possible in extinction. This is far too sweeping, and later in a more cautious mood we shall have to admit that some features of extinction are better handled by other theories. On the other hand, we shall confine ourselves to phenomena which can be examined without raising the question of ' reinforcement theory ' of the Hullian type. That question will be raised in Chapter 10, but it should not be confused with the present one. What is said here about extinction may perhaps be acceptable to those who believe in reinforcement theory, whereas parts of Chapter 10 may not.

What would be the consequences, in a conditioning situation, of the filter operating on the principles we have developed in earlier chapters ? It would mean that all the stimuli falling on the animal's sense-organs could be regarded as competing to pass farther into the nervous system, and so eventually produce response. In this competition some stimuli would be more likely to succeed than others, depending on the class of stimuli to which they belong. For instance, more physically intense stimuli would be more likely to succeed, according to the results we mentioned in the chapter on noise; loud sounds interfered more with tasks to which they were irrelevant, and also produced greater efficiency in tasks to which they were relevant. Secondly, more novel stimuli would be more likely to succeed. Novelty, in this case, would mean that the stimuli came from a source which had not recently passed information through the filter: although it might well have presented information which had been rejected by the filter. The reason for describing novelty in this way is that in the noise experiments both task and noise were present throughout the work period, and the errors, which we interpret as shifts of the filter towards the noise, occurred only after some time. In an unchanging stimulus situation, the filter does not continue to select the same source of information indefinitely. Similar conclusions follow from the vigilance experiments mentioned in earlier chapters, though with less rigour, since in the competing stimuli there may be bodily sensations or other signals which were not present to the senses throughout the task. It may be added that an entirely fresh stimulus is more likely to be novel than one which has been present for some time even on this definition; but if two stimuli have both been present the one which has not passed the filter, and produced response, is the more novel.

Thirdly, the filter of any particular animal will be biassed in favour of certain sources of information, some biasses being fairly permanent and others shifting with the state of the animal. The differences between high and low pitched noise are an example of the former: we have not considered temporary shifts in the human case, except in the sense that instructions modify multiple channel listening. This category is intended to cover the fact that a man may notice food when he is hungry, but not when he has just eaten.

In view of this competition between various stimuli, it will obviously be highly difficult to produce any conditioned response unless all the other stimuli which might interfere with the conditioned one are reduced in priority. This will mean excluding all possible sources of changing stimulation such as the experimenter, or the sounds coming in from the street, and leaving the animal in the artificially static surroundings thus created until all their features have been passed through the filter. Once such a stage has been reached, a new stimulus will have a reasonably high priority for passing the filter and so may be used for conditioning. These precautions are well-known to exponents of classical conditioning: as Pavlov (1927, p. 29) put it ' the slightest alteration in the environment . . . immediately evokes the reflex which I referred to in the first lecture as the investigatory reflex. . . . However, if these neutral stimuli keep recurring, they spontaneously and rapidly weaken in their effect upon the hemispheres, thus bringing about bit by bit the removal of this obstacle to the establishment of a conditioned reflex '.

It may be noted that Pavlov reported difficulty in conditioning not only with conditioned stimuli which were very faint or accompanied by strange irrelevant stimuli; but also with extremely intense or completely strange conditioned stimuli. In the latter case, it appears that the animal did not make the unconditioned response: in our terms, the conditioned stimulus secured passage through the filter so effectively that the closely subsequent information about the appearance of food was rejected by the filter. For conditioning to occur both conditioned (CS) and unconditioned (US) stimuli must be admitted by the filter.

Given that CS and US are of priorities which are roughly equal and greater than those of any competing stimuli, conditioning may occur. But repeated presentation of CS, even when it is followed by US, will gradually reduce its priority and make it less likely to pass the filter. 'Extinction with reinforcement' will therefore occur. A rest away from the task will ensure that other types of information will pass through the filter and so restore the priority of the CS, thus producing 'spontaneous recovery'. A rather interesting point is that increasing the intensity of the CS may also help: and this is specifically mentioned by Pavlov (1927, p. 239) as being the case.

Although extinction will thus occur even when the US is presented after each CS, this latter arrangement naturally ensures that the filter passes information from a different source (that of food) after each CS presentation. The next CS therefore always follows selection of another channel by the filter, and this ensures some degree of novelty priority for it. When there is no reinforcement by a US, the filter may continue to select the source of CS information throughout an experiment. This will rapidly reduce the priority of that source of information, and thus cause even more rapid extinction.

After extinction and spontaneous recovery, the next phenomenon to be considered is disinhibition by some strange irrelevant stimulus. This may clearly be explained in the same way as the effect of reinforcement in opposing extinction. A high priority stimulus inserted between two presentations of an extinguished CS will ensure that the filter selects a different source of information and does not remain on the CS source during the interval between presentations. The effect will of course be only a temporary one, as indeed the effect of disinhibition actually is.

This use of the same explanation for disinhibition and for continued reinforcement is of course unusual in traditional theories, though Uttley links the two phenomena in a rather different way. It is worth noting that the effects of reinforcement are similar in certain ways to those of disinhibition. For example, it is noted by Pavlov (1927, p. 390) that the effect of a single US, during a series of CS presentations, is transient. An interval before the next CS reduces the effect of the reinforcement. This should be true if the US is a disinhibitor, but does not fit orthodox views of reinforcement of the Hullian type. It can be explained by Uttley, of course, by the reduced weighting of past events in assessing conditional probabilities.

Again, a disinhibitor loses its effect with repeated presentation. If reinforcement does likewise it might be better to give the CS presentation after every other or every third presentation rather than every time. This is quite contrary to simple (though not to present-day) reinforcement or contiguity theories. Yet it is true, and was noted by Pavlov (1927, p. 384). It has since become celebrated under the title of ' partial reinforcement '. The advantage of this type of treatment should be greater when trials are massed, and there is some evidence that this is so (Jenkins and Stanley (1950) have reviewed some of the data). But in general partial reinforcement has been mostly studied in instrumental rather than classical conditioning, and there is no doubt that rather different factors operate in the two situations. We shall consider instrumental conditioning later.

We thus have some sort of explanation of the principal facts of extinction: what of the more peripheral ones? External inhibition is an obvious candidate for explanation. Clearly any intense or novel stimulus will compete with the CS, not only before conditioning occurs, but also afterwards. When such a stimulus is applied, the CS will not pass through the filter and no conditioned response will occur. It need hardly be said that a sufficiently long time after the application of an external inhibitor the chance of the filter selecting the source of CS information will be actually increased, that is, there will be disinhibition. The length of time necessary for this will vary inversely with the intensity and novelty of the external inhibitor: it is not at all surprising to this view that the same kind of stimulus should be regarded as an external inhibitor during its action and a disinhibitor afterwards, or an external inhibitor when very intense and a disinhibitor when weaker. These points were mentioned earlier, it will be recalled, as difficulties of the Uttley interpretation. Another such point is the loss of effectiveness of external inhibitors when they are presented repeatedly, even without CS or US.

Induction cannot be completely explained by the filter mechanism, but positive induction can sometimes be handled by treating it like disinhibition. That is, presenting a negative stimulus will actually increase response to a subsequent positive stimulus, because the filter has had to shift from one source of information to another. Pavlov could not assimilate negative induction to disinhibition because the negative stimulus had no observable response attached to it: disinhibition was supposed to be due to the investigatory reaction, and, as this did not appear in the cases described as positive induction, the latter could not be due to the same mechanism as disinhibition (Pavlov 1927, p. 191).

If this is the case, one would expect that the more different the event which represents the negative stimulus from that which represents the positive stimulus, the greater the ' inductive' effect on the latter. This is because the filter selects a source of information rather than a single signal: that is, it passes a class of stimuli having certain features in common. In the multi-channel listening experiments, it will be remembered, a series of different words spoken by the same person were all passed by the filter. Thus if positive and negative signals are very similar, they may both represent signals of the same class: in such a case passing the negative stimulus through the filter adds no novelty priority to the positive stimulus. So we might expect the enhancement of response to a positive stimulus by a preceding negative one to be greater when the two stimuli are very different. There is some evidence in Pavlov (1927, pp. 215–18) that this is the case. The negative stimuli in all the cases mentioned on those pages seem to be ones which have been established by direct extinction of the stimulus concerned, or by differentiation in which there is some reason to believe that the positive stimuli from which differentiation was made were not those used as positive stimuli in the induction experiment. That is, the training was not of the sort which Uttley supposes necessary for the production of induction effects. In the more usual case when the positive and negative stimuli are a pair differentiated from one another (presumably by alternate presentation) the positive and negative induction effects are greater the more similar the two stimuli (Konorski 1948, p. 17; Pavlov 1927, p. 193). This sounds an ominous note for the filter theory explanation of positive induction.

Two last points to which filter theory is relevant are so-called ' paradoxical phase ', and the difficulty of backward conditioning.

The first of these is a name for the fact that animals do sometimes behave abnormally in their responsiveness to stimuli of different intensities. The usual behaviour is to respond more efficiently to more intense stimuli, as filter theory would predict. But some kinds of treatment of the animal will disturb this order of priority, so that faint stimuli actually become as likely as, or more likely than, intense stimuli to elicit response. As our explanation regards intensity as important not in itself, but in the priority it confers on a stimulus in competing with other stimuli, this is not surprising. We would expect, for instance, that prolonged presentation of stimuli would reverse their initial order of priority, since those which had passed the filter least often would have the highest ' novelty ' priority. This is indeed one of the techniques for developing paradoxical phase (Pavlov 1927, p. 273). In human beings, it is interesting to note that schizophrenics show an abnormal relation between stimulus intensity and reaction time (Venables and Tizard 1956b). The reversal of rank order of stimuli after prolonged presentation has been noted already as appearing in watch-keeping over a number of dials. Those which are the best observed initially are the worst after a prolonged interval without any signals being delivered (Broadbent 1950).

Backward conditioning is the name given to the technique of presenting the CS after the US. It is very difficult to establish a response to the CS alone by this technique. Fairly clearly, this is a form of external inhibition: the food interferes with learning of the CS. To filter theory, the food is a high priority stimulus and its presentation therefore prevents the (probably lower priority) CS from passing the filter. It may be noted however than an Uttley-type explanation could also be applied: with the orthodox order of presentation, the probability is high of US occurring with CS following nothing, since CS followed nothing during training. But with the backward order CS followed US, so the probability of US occurring with CS following nothing is low.

## Limits and Merits of the Various Theories

The foregoing account of filter theory as applied to extinction largely follows an earlier statement by the present writer (Broadbent 1953c). Even at that time, however, weaknesses were apparent.  While positive induction was explained in terms of a parallel with disinhibition, negative induction presented a difficulty.  There was no obvious reason why the presentation of a positive stimulus should actually decrease the chance of a succeeding negative stimulus producing a response.  The caution was therefore given that the explanation of such phenomena was only tentative, and a particular case of negative induction was explained as due to 'expectancy' (Broadbent 1953c, p. 337).  Following a series of stimuli of one kind, it was argued, the probability of a stimulus of another kind was low.  One of Pavlov's examples of negative induction was in fact that a CS for salivation was less likely to receive response following a series of CSs for defensive responses against shock.  This could be fitted to some extent by an expectancy theory, though without any great confidence; and no explanation at all was advanced for more typical cases of negative induction.  Since that time Uttley's explanation in terms of the conditional probabilities established by the Pavlovian method of differential training seems to provide an account of the majority of cases, both of positive and of negative induction.  Furthermore, filter theory accounts only for temporary extinction.  Permanent extinction, from which spontaneous recovery is not apparent, must be explained by some theory of the Uttley type; after repeated pairing of the CS with no-food, the animal develops a response of no-salivation to that CS.  Is there any advantage in retaining filter theory, then?  Might it not be more parsimonious to use one theory alone?

In the first place, let us summarize the pros and cons of the traditional views, namely counter-conditioning and reactive inhibition.  The former has difficulty in accounting for the effects of massing and spacing trials, and for spontaneous recovery.  Its explanation of disinhibition is unclear, and it offers no obvious answer to the problem of extinction with continued reinforcement.  And if the new response to the CS is incompatible with the old one, some additional postulate such as that of Razran is necessary to explain how the new response appears for the first time.

The reactive inhibition view cannot handle permanent extinction without supplementation by counter-conditioning.  It can deal with massing and spacing, with spontaneous recovery, and with extinction with continued reinforcement by suitable choice of values for the various factors in the equations. It does not explain disinhibition clearly, nor external inhibition, and it does not explain how extinction can take place without occurrence of the response, nor how responses can be repeated provided the stimuli eliciting them are changed.

Uttley's conditional probability theory, and the filter theory, are modifications of these traditional views in the direction of centralism. The occurrence of response is unimportant to either of them: the important processes take place at an earlier stage in the nervous system. This gives them the following advantages.

Uttley's system does not need a postulate resembling Razran's, to explain how the new response appears for the first time. As soon as the probabilities of events at the sense-organs change, the stored representations of those probabilities within the organism change: the disappearance of response to the CS is because the inference CS-food is no longer valid, and not because of some overt incompatible response. Furthermore, by giving heavy weighting to recent events, the system will explain spontaneous recovery: but not massing and spacing. On the contrary, if recent events are heavily weighted learning should be fastest with massed trials. The explanation of disinhibition is clearer than in older brands of counter-conditioning theory, but assumes a particular kind of past experience on the part of the animal. That is, it applies only if an event which has occurred infrequently during training occurs also in extinction when the disinhibiting stimulus is applied. The fact that the same kind of stimulus may be inhibitory when intense and disinhibitory when weak is not considered. The explanation given for external inhibition is fairly definitely inadequate; and there is still no explanation for extinction with continued reinforcement.

As Uttley's view is a modified form of counter-conditioning, so filter theory is a modified form of reactive inhibition. It has the advantage over its predecessor that it will explain such facts as the alternation by rats of the stimulus which they approach in a two-choice situation, even though this means repeating the same response. It can also make some sort of explanation for the experiments which show extinction without performance of the response; but it should be noted that Uttley's theory will handle these as well as filter theory does. For example, in Hurwitz (1955) experiment a rat is placed in a Skinner box with no lever present, and this lowers the number of bar-pressings in a subsequent trial period. This might be because the filter has passed information about the box recently and so rejects it now, with the result that few responses to it appear. But it might also be that the probability ' food in this box ' has become low: which might explain why, for example, Deese (1951) claims that spontaneous recovery from this form of extinction is less than that from the normal form. Again, a CS to a leg-flexion response was presented by Kimble and Kendall (1953) at low intensity so that no response occurred. This produced more extinction than an equal number of presentations of a normally intense CS. But the US was shock, given only if the CR did not occur. Consequently the weak stimulus gave more opportunity for the probability of ' shock following extended leg following CS ' to become low, whereas the intense CS did not give such opportunities—the leg was always flexed. Thus it is only spontaneous alternation, which cannot be interpreted in terms of conditional probabilities, which unequivocally supports filter theory as against Uttley's system. (It should be noted that Glanzer's suggestion that stimuli become satiated after repeated exposure is similar in many ways to filter theory and possesses the same advantages of explaining spontaneous alternation of place. It must be modified, however, to take into account the work of Walker, Dember, Earl, Fliege and Karoly (1955) showing that presenting a stimulus outside the maze does not produce more choices of the opposite stimulus inside the maze. In terms of filter theory, it is not whether a stimulus has reached the sense-organ that matters: but whether it has recently passed the filter. Our only objective information about this latter condition is that a response to the particular stimulus has occurred. So presenting a stimulus outside the choice situation may well leave behaviour in the maze itself unaffected.)

Filter theory also provides an explanation for disinhibition which readily accounts for the importance of stimulus intensity, and does not assume any particular past experience for the occurrence of disinhibition and of external inhibition. It will explain the disappearance of the latter as the inhibitor is presented repeatedly alone. In addition it possesses all the advantages of reactive inhibition: but, like the latter concept, it cannot explain permanent extinction, nor spontaneous recovery 'in reverse'. The latter phenomenon we mentioned earlier; it is the finding that when a chronically extinguished response is reinforced, it may be restored but will be found to have disappeared again next day.

It seems clear that reactive inhibition and counter-conditioning are open to fatal objections. They cannot even be combined, as Hull attempted to do, since the combination of $I_r$ and $_sI_r$ does not predict the results of spontaneous alternation experiments, nor those of extinction without response: nor provide any explanation for disinhibition. The choice lies between the two more recent theories, or, to be exact, between a theory based on conditional probabilities alone and one which also includes aspects of filter theory. Some parts of Uttley's approach must be included to account for permanent extinction.

A glance back at the objections to Uttley's theory will show that it cannot be accepted by itself. We are left with the combination of the two approaches; the nervous system stores conditional probabilities of events provided that information on the occurrence of those events passes through a filter at the input end of the system. Since the filter rejects information arriving on channels which have recently been passing information through the filter, repeated presentation of the same stimulus will produce failure to respond. A rest away from the situation will restore the *status quo*; but if a CS is presented without food on many occasions the stored conditional probability will be changed, and the response to that CS will become inaction.

This gives an outline of the way to combine the two theories; what of the details? In some cases both theories explain the same facts, with varying degrees of efficiency. First, let us consider spontaneous recovery. The explanation by filter theory cannot be sufficient because of ' spontaneous recovery in reverse '. So we must include the extra weighting of recent events from Uttley's approach. Yet the latter would not explain massing and spacing, so that filter theory must be kept in and both factors will therefore be operative in spontaneous recovery.

Secondly, external inhibition is dealt with in very unsatisfactory fashion by Uttley's account. Filter theory is required to explain the waning of the effectiveness of an external inhibitor when presented repeatedly. While it is no doubt true that the probability of ' food following CS plus unusual S ' will be lower than that of ' food following CS alone ', the filter will reject a good deal of the information accompanying the CS and it may therefore be doubted whether this particular form of external inhibition is of great practical importance compared with that explained by filter theory.

Thirdly, in the case of induction, the merits of the theories are exactly reversed. Filter theory is very much strained in explaining induction, whereas conditional probabilities do so easily. There may be a few cases in which the original explanation advanced by filter theory is correct, but most of those reported are based on the type of training supposed by Uttley to be necessary.

Fourth and last, we come to the difficult question of disinhibition. It is difficult because each theory has its own merits. An explanation in terms of conditional probabilities requires a particular training for the animal. Furthermore, it does not explain the differences between different stimuli in their effects. Filter theory does not have these weaknesses, but it seems to explain only the disinhibition which follows a stimulus and not that which occurs when CS and disinhibiting stimulus arrive simultaneously. We shall shortly return to the precise rôle of each theory in explaining disinhibition, but as this question leads on to those discussed in the next chapter we will first consider the rather different question of the relation of extinction in classical conditioning to that in instrumental conditioning. The matter is important, because disinhibition is more difficult to show in the instrumental situation and has in the past been denied by those working with that type of experiment (Skinner 1938).

## On the Relation of Classical to Instrumental Conditioning

It cannot have escaped the careful reader that most of the ' facts ' cited in the present chapter come from Pavlov, with some expansion by Konorski. As this work was done many years ago, and is technically faulty in many respects by modern standards, why is such reliance placed upon it rather than upon the copious modern animal studies ? The reason is a very simple one. Any glance through a journal will show that the majority of studies of animal behaviour employ instrumental rather than classical conditioning. The distinction is that, in the classical case, a CS is repeatedly presented with a US. The response to the latter is used as the dependent variable: when it occurs to the CS alone, conditioning has taken place. In instrumental conditioning there is normally no CS other than the continuously present stimuli arising from the apparatus. The response is one which appears spontaneously in the situation, and reinforcement is given by presenting some stimulus such as food which does not normally produce the response which is to be conditioned. The spontaneously occurring response increases in frequency after being reinforced, and extinguishes if reinforcement is abandoned.

Our concern throughout this book has been with the filtering of incoming information. We laid it down that the filter tends to select continually fresh sources of information. Consequently if the animal is placed in an unchanging situation, the various features of it will be passed through the filter each in turn (in order of priority) until all the information about the situation has entered the nervous system. This means that in unchanging surroundings response to some one feature of the situation will sooner or later occur, regardless of the priority of that feature for passing the filter. The occurrence of such responses will depend, on the average, on other factors such as the stored conditional probabilities of various events within the organism. Thus if pressing a bar is followed by food on one occasion in every four, bar-pressing will be more frequent than if food follows only once in every ten presses. Furthermore the rate of pressing will be low immediately after a reinforcement (when the probability of another is low) and rise immediately before the next. If food is no longer given, the rate of response will die away until it reaches the pre-conditioning level at the time when the probability of food following bar-pressing is equal to that of food following no-bar-pressing. In general this means that equally conditioned animals will tend to make the same number of responses in all in extinction, even if some other factor alters the rate at which responses are made. For instance, if some extraneous factor such as electric shock is applied on one day, this may cause fewer responses to be made on that day because of other interfering activities. But correspondingly more responses will be made on later days to keep the total number of responses in extinction the same: since otherwise the number of instances in which food had followed bar-pressing would be in excess of that holding in the original state of the animal.

All these are in fact characteristics of instrumental conditioning, of which the best general account remains Skinner's (1938) classic text.* This strongly supports the interpretation that mean rate of response depends on the conditional probability of reinforcement following that response. But there are other and more negative aspects of instrumental conditioning: for on our interpretation the operation of the filter should appear in the detailed structure of the sequence of response but not in its mean rate. Thus if a trained animal is placed in a Skinner box for a series of extinction trials, we would expect long inter-response intervals when the filter selected irrelevant information and short ones when it did not. The latter would be the case more rarely as time went on, so that the mean rate of responding would die away to zero: but it would be made up of bursts of activity interspersed with periods of little response when the animal is otherwise engaged. This type of detail has not greatly interested those who work with Skinner boxes; although Anger (1956) has shown that reinforcement of particular inter-response intervals makes those intervals more probable, he does not report the changes in the distribution of intervals as each session proceeds. Hurwitz (1957) has however reported such an analysis (as we said above), and his results confirm our suggestion that detailed study of the records will show an increase in the number of long inter-response intervals without a corresponding decrease in the number of short ones: that is a widening of the distribution rather than a shift of the mean time.

Disinhibition forms a negative instance of importance. Skinner (1938, p. 97) tried to disinhibit a bar-pressing response while it

---

* Ferster and Skinner's (1957) monumental work is not yet sufficiently familiar to the writer to be considered here: it contains a large number of results of importance from the present point of view, and the reader should consult it.

was being extinguished, but failed.  As we would put it, he would merely alter the priorities of various features of the environment by his presentation of a fresh stimulus: this might cause delay in responding, or the appearance of a response earlier than would otherwise be the case, depending on the intensity of the extra stimulus.  Indeed Skinner reported that this was the case, but that there was no change in the mean rate of responding: and this we would expect.  His failure to obtain disinhibition was due to the fact that the instrumental situation is not sensitive to brief ' blocks ' in the responsiveness of the animal.  Classical conditioning on the other hand is very sensitive.  If a CS arrives and disappears while the filter is passing some other kind of information, no response will occur.  A preliminary stimulus which heightens the priority of the CS just at the instant when it occurs will greatly improve the chances of response.  In the instrumental case the most that can be expected is a brief intermittency in the rate of response.

It may be added that disinhibition has since been shown in an instrumental response, by Gagné (1941).  Instead of measuring rate of bar-pressing, he used running to food in a runway, and stimulated with click sounds.  As he was measuring over a short time-scale, he did find enhancement of response in extinction by the disinhibitor.  Skinner himself (1938, p. 101) noted that extra stimuli would facilitate response temporarily.  He was merely concerned to argue that they did not alter the depression of response rate on the average which appears in experimental extinction, and that this depression is not inhibitory in nature.  The argument is perfectly sound and the writer is in full agreement with it: none the less Skinner's results do not ' cast grave doubts on the reality of the phenomenon reported by Pavlov '.  They merely show that instrumental conditioning is different from the classical variety.  If one is interested primarily in the establishment of stored conditional probabilities instrumental conditioning is the technique to use.  If one is interested in the filtering of incoming information, classical conditioning is preferable and has in consequence been cited in this chapter.

While on this subject, we may hark back to our discussion of human vigilance.  We argued in the human case that the mean efficiency of observation depended on the probability of a signal, while the operation of the filter superimposed moment-to-moment variations on this mean efficiency. As the latter increased with time spent in a situation, short signals would show a rapid decrement as the work period continued. The efficiency of detecting long signals would show no such decrement, but merely reflect the probability of signal occurrence. The distinction is the same which we have now drawn between classical and instrumental conditioning. Holland's analogy, mentioned in Chapter 6, between instrumental conditioning and detection of a signal of indefinite length, is valid and important. The proper analogy to detecting short signals, however, is the classical conditioning situation or the discriminated operant using short stimuli. In neither case can conditioning be taken as an ultimate principle: the situation requires the kind of analysis which we have tried to give it. The behaviour of the animal is the same in both classical and instrumental conditioning, but when we alter the operations performed in observing it we alter the results of our observations.

*Disinhibition*

We turn now lastly to the question of disinhibition. As we noted earlier, filter theory has the disadvantage of predicting disinhibition only in cases in which the CS follows the disinhibitor. A similar difficulty occurs in the conditional probability explanation of induction: we mentioned earlier that in some experiments of Podkopayev (Konorski 1948, p. 18) a positive stimulus had more effect when delivered at the same time as a negative stimulus than when delivered afterwards. This is difficult to explain if positive induction is the result of training the animal by using alternate positive and negative stimuli.

Both these difficulties might be overcome by suggesting that information from two simultaneous stimuli may pass through the filter successively. Thus when Podkopayev's two stimuli were applied, the filter selected first the source of the negative stimulus and then shifted to the source of the positive stimulus. The latter information, having been temporarily stored, was then passed through the filter and produced its enhanced response. A delay in applying the positive stimulus until after the end of the negative one would allow the filter to shift away to some third channel. However plausible the translation of events from simultaneous to successive may seem, there is as yet no direct evidence for or against it in animals; we shall consider some similar cases in man in the next chapter.

There are two other difficulties in the theory of disinhibition. First there is disinhibition of delay. If a CS is followed by a US only after a delay of, say, 3 min, a conditioned response may be established in which the CS is followed after 3 min by response even though no US has occurred. An extra stimulus applied during the delay will disrupt it by producing the response immediately (Pavlov 1927, p. 93). This does not fit the filter theory of disinhibition, although the phenomenon seems closely similar to the effect of an extra stimulus applied with the stimulus for an extinguished response.

The second difficulty is that of disinhibition when a response is being overlaid by a new incompatible response. In such a case (Hamilton and Krechevsky 1933) applying a shock may cause the old response to reappear. This is suspiciously like ' spontaneous recovery in reverse ' and raises the same kind of difficulty for filter theory. If we regard the stimulus as the same for both old and new responses, the operation of the filter should have no effect on their relative probabilities. If on the other hand the stimulus is regarded as slightly different for the two responses, no extra stimulus should cause the filter to do other than prefer the more novel of the two conditioned stimuli.

A possible way out of these difficulties is as follows. To explain ' spontaneous recovery in reverse ', we have to say that events carry more weight in the assessment of conditional probabilities when they are recent than when some time has passed since their arrival. We have pointed out repeatedly, starting in Chapter 3, that information can be stored in different ways with different degrees of efficiency, and that in determining output at any instant the input must be sampled for a length of time which may extend some little way into the past.

Let us combine these points, which are respectively established by experiment and by logic, into a further speculative suggestion. If a system has two storage devices, it may give more weight to recent events by storing much of the information from them in one store but only passing selected items of information to the other store. In terms of Fig. 1 in Chapter 3, one store would operate on a Type C basis and the other on Type B. As was explained in Chapter 3, the latter requires a smaller capacity than the former and so should be able to deal with information from a considerable portion of the organism's past history. The former, however, needs a large capacity and so will hold the information from only a few recent events.

Such short and long term storage systems are common in modern machines. For example, a translating machine which is to type out English might contain the stored rule ' *i* before *e* except after *c* '. This rule would probably be built in by the designer, though in theory a machine could be designed to learn it for itself. The storage is in any case relatively permanent. A short term store would also be needed to store the information ' *c* has just occurred '. This storage is extremely temporary, since the arrival of the next letter will displace the item in store. Typically, long term stores in machines are based on structural change in the machine, such as the plugging of leads into certain sockets. Short term storage is more usually by functional methods such as the transmission of a certain sequence of pulses around a closed circuit again and again until the information is required.

The likelihood of such a dual storage system in animals is increased by the recent work of Andjus, Knopfelmacher, Russell, and Smith (1956). They froze rats some time after the animals had learned a maze. This treatment prevented any electrical activity from continuing in the animal's brain, though of course structure was unaffected. Retention of the maze was scarcely affected. On the other hand, they quote an earlier unpublished research by Ransmeier, which showed impairment of retention by freezing (or any other drastic treatment) given less than 1 min after learning the maze. It thus appears that storage of recent events is mediated by a different and less structural type of store than storage of more remote events.

How does this possibility help to explain disinhibition? The short term store, because of the strain on its capacity, may be regarded as the system which is guarded by the filter we have so often mentioned. If we consider delayed conditioning, the occurrence of a CS passes the filter and enters the short term store. After the appropriate interval the correct output is produced. But during the interval other stimuli will strike the sense-organs.

Either the filter will exclude them, or they will enter the temporary store and displace the information on the recent occurrence of the CS.   In the latter case the output occurs too soon and the phenomenon is regarded as disinhibition; in the former case the other stimulus is ignored and might be regarded as inhibited by the ' inhibition of delay '.

This account is slightly too simple.   Complete displacement of the information concerning the CS would prevent response altogether.   Although this is reported for very intense stimuli (Pavlov 1927, p. 95), it is not the disinhibition effect.   What is needed for the latter is that part of the available capacity should be taken up by the extra stimuli, so that only the general fact that a CS has occurred remains in store, without detailed information on time intervals: disinhibition of delay will appear only with stimuli that are not too intense or otherwise of very high priority.

We may now turn to orthodox disinhibition.   If a previously established CS has begun to receive no reinforcement, this information is in the temporary store and so causes a temporary adjustment of response.   On the next day the temporary store has been cleared, and the non-reinforced trials have scarcely influenced the permanent store, so that response returns to its original pre-extinction state.   A similar result may be achieved without a delay of a day by presenting an extra stimulus even during the session on which extinction is begun.   The extra information occupies the temporary store, leaving capacity available only for the registration of the occurrence of the CS and not for the recent alteration in the reinforcement schedule. The output is therefore determined by the permanent store: disinhibition.   If the extra information places too much of a demand on the capacity of the short term store, even the occurrence of the CS will not be registered.   This is the external inhibition which too intense a stimulus may produce.

The foregoing argument may be easier to understand if we consider again the machine which types English.   Normally $i$ is followed by $e$.   When $c$ occurs this ceases to be true, but after an interval in which other letters arrive it becomes true again. Interpolating an extra letter after the $c$ will restore the normal relationship unless the interpolation prevents the occurrence of $i$ from being detected by the machine.

This more complex and speculative theory has no difficulty with disinhibition either of delay or of a response which is being overlaid on another incompatible response. It represents an extension of Uttley's postulate that recent events carry more weight than more remote ones: the recent events are in the temporary store and the past ones in the permanent store, and the two stores have roughly equal weight in determining response, so that one recent event carries more weight among the few in its store than one long past event does among the many in the other store. But there are other ways in which differential weighting could be achieved, and it may be that one of them would give a better explanation of the remaining puzzles in disinhibition than would the one we have just described. Although the dual natures of storage in machines have often been pointed out as possibly of biological importance, there has been no direct evidence of a dual system in animals other than the experiments on freezing mentioned earlier. We have here at least pointed out that a dual system would harmonize with some of the peculiarities of behaviour; in the next chapter we shall be considering direct experiments on a short term system in man.

### GENERAL CONCLUSIONS

We have seen that the older theories of extinction meet certain crucial difficulties. The phenomena of extinction can be explained, however, by a combination of our filter theory with Uttley's postulated mechanism for assessing conditional probabilities of events. The two theories provide, in some cases, competing interpretations of the same events, and these are the points at which further advance is necessary. But it is clear that no inhibitory theory is needed.

The problems which remain suggest, first, that simultaneous stimuli might receive successive passage through the filter; and secondly, that there might be a temporary storage system of limited capacity distinct from the long term storage responsible for the retention of the bulk of experience. Both these possibilities are illuminated by experiments on human beings which we shall now examine.

# CHAPTER 9

# IMMEDIATE MEMORY AND THE SHIFTING OF ATTENTION

IN this chapter we come full circle, back to the problems of multi-channel listening. The data to be considered are those on short-term memory for information coming from various sources: although we are now back in the field of human performance, the reader will remember that our ignorance of the nature and limits of short-term memory was a considerable handicap in coming to any final conclusion about extinction in the last chapter. In Chapter 2 we considered multi-channel listening as though filtering was complete in its action at any one time; that is, as though a message which was rejected at the time of its arrival could never pass through the filter later and produce a response. This over-simplification was for expository purposes only, to set out the conception of filtering without adding the necessary qualifying statements which are undoubtedly needed. By now the reader has probably grasped the basic idea of filtering incoming information, and although he may disagree on a good many points with the views put forward in earlier chapters, he has probably conceded that something of the sort does take place in some of the situations we have considered. The time is now ripe to return to multi-channel communication.

The difficulty of immediate memory first presented itself in the field when the advantages of spatial separation of loud-speakers were being measured (Broadbent 1954b). As we said in Chapter 2, the merit of this type of auditory display is in providing information for the filter to use. That is, spatial separation was useful when some of the messages were to be ignored, but less useful as more of the information did in fact require response and could not be filtered out. But it was noticed that the improvement in performance with spatially separated loudspeakers was not only in the understanding of the messages once detected; in addition, more attempts were made to answer relevant messages.

This had the following implications. Pairs of messages were arriving at the listener's ears, each message starting with a call-sign. In each pair one of the call-signs was that of the listener and marked out that message as relevant. Yet if more attempts were made to answer relevant messages, it must mean that the listener had heard both call-signs and that spatial separation of the loudspeakers had helped him to do this. What became of filter theory if the listener could hear two channels on which call-sign information arrived simultaneously?

Introspectively, the answer was simple. One does indeed listen to only one channel at a time, and so to only one call-sign: but if that call-sign appears irrelevant one can change channels and still hear the relevant call-sign and message on the other channel. There seemed to be a kind of ' double-take '; the sounds one had previously ignored now struck home to consciousness. The experience is a familiar one, and has been described by Hebb (1949). But it is one which different people describe in different words, and we have already said that it is unwise to rely on verbal accounts of the way in which responses are organized. An attempt was therefore made to establish various objective measures of this type of performance.

A first indication that the interpretation was correct was obtained by presenting series of call-signs without any subsequent messages and at various speeds. At slow speeds spatial separation was still helpful, but at fast speeds it ceased to be so. This was to be expected if the information on the two channels was handled by the perceptual mechanism successively and so took longer in the separated case. In introspective terms, at higher speeds one could not listen first to one channel and then to the other; another pair of call-signs would arrive before the process was finished. It is important to note that by ' slow speed ' here we mean that a pair of call-signs arrived only every 2 sec. ' Fast speed ' means faster than one pair every second. So the process of listening to a call-sign, shifting to another channel, listening to another call-sign, and shifting back again, was taking more than 1 sec and less than 2 sec (on these subjects).

This then suggested the following modification of the familiar memory-span experiment used so commonly in intelligence testing. Normally one presents a series of six or eight digits, rather like a telephone number, and asks the subject to repeat them back immediately. In the experiment we are now considering the listener was given a pair of head-phones in which each ear was connected to a separate channel, and two lists of digits were presented simultaneously. Thus one ear might receive 723 while the other ear simultaneously received 945. The listener was asked to reproduce all six digits in any order he chose: and surprisingly enough was often able to do so. When he could, the order of reproduction was in the vast majority of cases either, 723945, or else 945723. That is, all the information from one channel appeared in response before any of the information from the other channel. A response of the type 792435, alternating channels, was never obtained.

The experiment was also performed with deliberate instructions to the subjects to alternate channels and so give the digits in the order in which they actually reached the ears. This was virtually impossible: although some subjects did achieve it to a limited extent, it seems likely that it was done by a preliminary response to the information in some other order followed by a transposition of this order into the required one before the digits were reproduced publicly. Such a transposition is known from intelligence testing to be possible though more difficult than normal memory span: one can repeat a telephone number backwards, but not so long a number as one can forwards.

All the above results apply only at a speech rate of two digits/sec on each channel, a fairly normal speed. When slower rates were used it appeared that alternation of channels was still very difficult at one digit/sec, but quite possible at one digit every 2 sec. This fits in with the earlier deduction that a complete cycle of two perceptions and two shifts of the filter occupies a time between 1–2 sec. Naturally this applies only to individuals of the type studied, namely British naval ratings.

Before drawing any far-reaching conclusions from these results (which were all given by Broadbent 1954b) it is necessary to be sure that they are not due to some peculiarity of the relation between the two ears. One ear produces more activity on the opposite side of the cortex than the other ear does, and vice versa, and this peculiar form of immediate memory might therefore be due to the division of the cortex into two hemispheres, and fail to apply when other senses are used for delivering the information. Another set of experiments (Broadbent 1956c) made sure that this was not the case. They were similar to the split memory-span experiment already mentioned, but instead of using the two ears they used the eye and ear simultaneously. In another variation different frequency regions were stimulated, by mixing two tape recordings each containing three digits, but passing one of the recordings (before mixing) through a filter rejecting low frequencies. In both these cases results generally similar to the binaural case were found, being most clear-cut with the eye and ear, and less frequent when two voices of different spectra were employed. In the eye and ear case it was especially striking that half the individuals studied reproduced the auditory information first and then the visual second, so that the effect cannot be due to some persistent auditory after-effect absent from other senses.

Two other differences between the various sensory channels should be noticed. First, an experiment with voices differing in their frequency characteristics showed that instructions to alternate channels could be obeyed at a rate of speaking of one digit every $1\frac{1}{2}$ sec on each channel, as opposed to the 2 sec found with the two ears. As the time for each perception is presumably the same, this implies that the time for shifting from one channel to another is shorter when the channels are different sound frequencies than when they are different ears. This is perhaps an appropriate point at which to mention the experiments of Cherry and Taylor (1954), which are also related to the time taken to shift channels. They presented speech to one ear at a time; at intervals the speech was turned off and delivered to the other ear instead, then returned to the original ear, and so on. At slow switching rates this produced no difficulty, nor at fast switching rates where no attempt was made by the listener to follow the shifts from ear to ear. By measuring the intelligibility of the speech a point of maximum difficulty was found, when the mean switching rate was rather greater than a complete 3 c/s. That is, the speech was on in one ear for just less than $\frac{1}{6}$ sec.

They suggest that the listener shifts attention from one ear to the other, but that this shift takes $\frac{1}{6}$ sec and so attention does not arrive at the other ear in time to hear anything. This is not an unduly different estimate from the one given earlier: two shifts would then take $\frac{1}{3}$ sec, and if perception of a digit takes $\frac{1}{2}$ sec this would give $1\frac{1}{3}$ sec for the whole cycle of shifting between ears. Remembering that naval ratings are probably slower than most laboratory subjects, this is not too different from the time of $1\frac{1}{2}$–2 sec found in the memory span experiments.

But there are other reasons for doubting whether Cherry and Taylor have hit on the only possible interpretation of their results. They report a control experiment in which the speech was switched on and off in one ear only, the other being left unstimulated. As they note, intelligibility at slow switching rates remains only 50 per cent instead of rising to the 100 per cent level found with switching between the two ears. But the minimum intelligibility is still at the 3 c/s point. This cannot be due to any shifting of attention, and it is not altogether clear what does explain it. (The finding of the control experiment agrees with results of Miller and Licklider 1950.)

Schubert and Parker (1955) have since confirmed Cherry and Taylor's results, but with the very interesting addition that inserting noise into the ear which is temporarily not receiving speech, reduces the size of the dip in intelligibility in the region of 3 c/s switching rate. (It also seems to shift it upwards to nearer the region of 6 c/s.) They therefore ascribe the result to a short-lasting contralateral inhibitory off-effect. Like Cherry and Taylor's explanation, this ignores the fact that the same switching frequency in one ear alone produces more difficulty than other frequencies; unless one supposes that the inhibitory off-effect is ipsilateral as well as contralateral. In any case, the dip is still present with noise insertion, even though it is reduced.

The present writer is thus doubtful whether this finding can be taken as evidence for the time taken to shift attention. An alternative explanation which might be offered is that the ear, like any other information handling system, samples the input over a certain length of time before taking a decision on the nature of the input during that time. If the time is by preference about $\frac{1}{3}$ sec, a switching rate which allows the speech to be present for only the first half of each sample impairs the chance of a correct decision as to the nature of the sound delivered to the ear. A frequency much lower than 3 c/s would allow 50 per cent of samples to acquire adequate information, and so give 50 per cent intelligibility. A higher frequency will allow each sample to contain more than one burst of speech and so restore its adequacy. Inserting noise between each burst of speech might blur the dip if we assume that sampling time normally starts from the onset of a sound in the ear. Desynchronizing the ear's sampling and the switching of the speech would upset the relation we have been considering. This suggestion is a digression from the main theme of this chapter, but will become important again in Chapter 11 when we consider the psychological refractory period. It is mentioned here because Cherry and Taylor's work raises it.

Whatever we conclude about the time for an individual shift of attention (or, as we would put it, of the filter) it is important to note that the 2 sec cycle found in the memory span experiments agrees with the length of the ' blocks ' found in continuous work after it has been continued for some time. In Chapter 6 we interpreted such blocks as due to a shift away from the task and back again.

To revert to the immediate memory experiments, the second important difference between different sensory channels is that presenting information to the eye and ear simultaneously gives at least as good retention as presenting all the information to one sense only and successively. This is important because it suggests that whatever the processes through which information passes in this type of memory span, they are at least as efficient as those of ordinary memory span. The experiments using two ears or two frequency bands are not sufficient to prove this, because in those situations performance is inferior to ordinary memory span. This was thought from the first to be due to a perceptual rather than a memory difficulty: the filter has more difficulty in passing information from one ear and rejecting that from the other than it does in passing the eye and rejecting the ear. A control experiment had shown that even irrelevant digits on the other ear produce a comparable deterioration. But the eye and ear experiments make this tentative conclusion firmer: no abnormally inefficient storage system is involved in these cases of successive response to simultaneous stimuli.

*The Problem of Short-term Storage*

Given all the results mentioned so far in this chapter, it is clear that we can take it as a quite common occurrence for information reaching the senses at the same time to emerge from the effectors successively: to change, metaphorically speaking, from line abreast to line astern. It is not a peculiar function of some one combination of sense-organs.

Fig. 5 illustrates the problem which immediately arises. There must be an earlier stage in the nervous system at which the information can pass simultaneously, which is labelled *S* in the figure. There is a later stage which can only pass the information successively, which we have labelled *P*. The question of acute interest is the point of transition from *S* to *P*. The

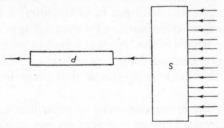

Fig. 5.    The type of flow diagram implied by the experiments considered in Chapter 9.

immediate memory experiments have shown that this is not at a point close to the muscles: undoubtedly it is true that the mouth cannot take up a shape suitable for saying two digits simultaneously, but if this were the only reason for the successive emergence of the information the problem would be trivial. However, the fact that the digits cannot emerge in the actual order of their arrival but only grouped by sensory channels shows that the transition from *S* to *P* must take place farther back in the nervous system.

Equally, the experiments with different sensory channels show that the junction of *S* and *P* does not lie in some specific sense-organ; the next problem is to locate it more precisely within the nervous system. The alternatives seem to be twofold. Either the *S* system is a normal stage in the processing of information, entitled to the full box it is given in Fig. 5; or else it is an extra introduced only for momentary overloads of information, and perhaps more fairly represented as in Fig. 6. This diagram emphasizes the fact that at the time of changeover there must come a point at which part of the information has already entered the $P$ system, but the rest is still in the $S$ system. It may be that the $S$ system exists only for this period of changeover, that it is essentially a storage mechanism for excess information while the $P$ system is already handling as much as its capacity will warrant. Thus in our modified memory span experiments, it may be that some of the information passes straight into the $P$ system and only the extra is delayed in the $S$ system.

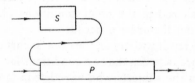

Fig. 6. A variant on Fig. 5, to emphasize the possibility that the $S$ system may only be used in the simultaneous stimulation case.

The next step, then, is to distinguish between the possible flow diagrams shown in Figs. 5 and 6. The technique used to do this will need some previous explanation of other experiments on immediate memory.

*Order Effects in Immediate Memory*

Anyone who is familiar with modern learning theory is aware that a list of items learnt by heart are not equally difficult throughout. The beginning and end of the list present less difficulty than the middle, and the point of greatest difficulty lies between the middle and the end. Experiments on immediate memory, using only one presentation, are less frequent than those in which a list is presented repeatedly until learnt: but there are some such experiments, and they show that this serial order of difficulty is roughly the same even in immediate memory. In the latter case, however, the difference between the two halves of the list seems rather greater than the difference between the last items and the middle ones: the most noticeable feature of errors in immediate memory is that they tend to be in the second half of the list of items, though possibly the last item of all is slightly better recalled than those before it. A typical experiment is that of Robinson and Brown (1926). The same finding has appeared in the work of Kay and Poulton (1951), which includes some other facts which should be considered.

They compared two conditions: one in which the subject knew in advance that he would have to recall the items in their order of arrival, and one in which he did not know whether he would have to recall the items in the same order or with the second half of the list first. In the latter condition the order of recall was prescribed by the experimenter after the items had been presented. As has been said in the last paragraph, in the orthodox condition orthodox serial order effects were found; but they were altered in the other condition, when the subject was in doubt about the order of recall.

If the order of recall was in fact the same as that of presentation, the only difference between the two conditions lay in the subject's knowledge. Yet the subjects who were left in ignorance did not do better on the last item than on those preceding: and they did do better on the first item of the second half than on the items before and after it. In other words the usual bow-shaped curve of difficulty is influenced by the memorizer's state at the time when the information arrives. Most important from our point of view, however, is the fact that the first half of the list was still recalled better than the second half. This difference depends on the order of presentation and recall and not, in this experiment, on previous knowledge. When the order of recall was in fact reversed, the two halves of the list showed equal numbers of errors: thus the order of recall as well as that of presentation influences the results, and their effects may be regarded as cancelling out when they are in opposite directions.

Brown (1954) performed some similar experiments with important differences. Instead of presenting all the information in one stream, he delivered two different lists simultaneously. Each list had its own kind of item: thus one might consist of numbers and the other of arrows pointing in different directions. They were seen by the subject on a moving paper belt, and he had to respond to them while they arrived as well as attempting to recall them afterwards. The various possible conditions were that the subject might have to give one list alone, or the other list alone, or one list and then the other. In some cases the recall conditions were known before presentation, and in others they were left ambiguous until after presentation.

As far as serial order is concerned, Brown's results show that the efficiency of recall of a list is lower when the other list has previously been recalled than when recall of one list only is required. This result comes from comparisons made with the same amount of knowledge during presentation, that is, no knowledge. These findings confirm those of Kay and Poulton on the effect of recall order on reproduction: the difference from Kay and Poulton, in that the items were presented simultaneously and not in the opposite order to that of recall, is a valuable control. The earlier result might have been due to differences in the time elapsing since presentation of the items.

Other findings of Brown's which may be mentioned while the reader still has the experimental conditions in mind, are that the conditions with prior knowledge of recall order are better than those without, except for the case when the other list has to be recalled first. That is, memorizing more material than is needed for recall is a handicap: and ignorance of the order of recall depresses the first items to be recalled. It does not significantly depress the last items.

Another experiment on recall order is that of Lawrence and Laberge (1956). They used visual material, tachistoscopically displayed for $\frac{1}{10}$ sec. Two cards at a time were shown, and each card contained several objects of the same shape and colour. There were thus six facts to be reported: two numbers, two shapes, and two colours. If the subjects were given prior instructions to concentrate on one of these dimensions, errors tended to be made on the others. But if the order of recall was laid down by the experimenter (without orders to concentrate on one dimension) exactly similar results are obtained: the errors are made on the last dimensions reported. The authors concluded that the traditional ' selective perception ' account of the effects of instructions to concentrate was unnecessary. The results could be explained in terms of recall order. This interpretation will have to be considered later: for the moment the important point is that the first items recalled were the most efficiently reproduced.

Lastly, in all the experiments by the present writer on memory span using two channels of presentation, the first items to be recorded were also the most likely to be correct. This was true even if the subjects were told in advance which of the channels to record first: that is, the results were not recalled first because they were right. They were right because they were recalled first.

To summarize all these results: if information enters a man successively and leaves him in the same order, the first items are the best recalled. This does not depend on his knowledge that recall will be required in that order. Nor does it depend on the items entering in a serial order; as long as they leave in an order the effect will appear. If the order of leaving is opposite to the order of entry, the effects may cancel out.

In terms of the analysis made in the last section of this chapter, this seems to mean that the first information to pass through the $P$ system is the most likely to emerge successfully. It is a fair assumption that the $P$ system is involved in ordinary memory span, even though the $S$ system may not be. In any case, the serial order effects apply even in the simultaneous stimulation case from which our $P$ system was defined.

This means that by varying the time at which instructions are given for a particular order of recall, we should be able to detect the time at which the $P$ system operates. If we present two simultaneous sets of digits, and only say after the presentation that we require a particular order of recall, the system shown in Fig. 5 might still be able to feed the information to the $P$ system in the right order. Thus the information required to be recalled first would in fact be the best recalled.

The system shown in Fig. 6, on the other hand, would pass information straight into the $P$ system as it arrived. As the recall instructions had not then been given, the order of passage into the $P$ system could not be determined by the instructions and may or may not correspond with them. If it does not, the order will require to be transposed—with the results shown by Kay and Poulton. We would thus expect the serial order effect to be greatly reduced or even abolished by giving instructions for recall only after the information had been delivered, if the system is of the Fig. 6 type. If it is of the Fig. 5 type, serial order effect will be normal, as we said in the last paragraph.

### The Effect of Instructions Before and After Stimulation

An experiment was therefore designed in which three digits were presented to one ear, and three to the other simultaneously: the order of recall was prescribed by the experimenter either before or after stimulation (Broadbent 1957c). Efficiency on the ear indicated for prior recall was compared with that on the other ear. When the recall order was prescribed before stimulation, the first channel always received a much more efficient response than the second. In the other condition an unexpected result appeared. In early stages of practice the normal serial order effect was shown: in later stages it almost disappeared, and the two channels were handled with approximately equal efficiency.

So we must conclude that our original antithesis was a false one. The listener can function either in the fashion of Fig. 5 or in that of Fig. 6. Further, he changes towards the latter as he becomes more familiar with the situation. The reason for his doing so is evident when one examines the overall level of efficiency shown by the subjects as opposed to the relative level on the two ears. When they show the usual serial order effect they perform much worse than at later stages of practice, when they have lost the usual order effect. Subjects who are informed of the order of recall before the stimuli arrive do much better at early stages of practice than do their colleagues left in ignorance. At the later stage of practice there is no significant difference between prescribing recall order before or after stimulation, so far as overall efficiency is concerned. It looks therefore as though the system shown in Fig. 5 was an inefficient one, and it is preferable to operate as in Fig. 6.

Before considering this conclusion further we ought perhaps to compare these results with those of the other workers who have prescribed recall order after stimulation: namely, Brown, and Lawrence and Laberge. Brown's results are in general in agreement with the present ones. He does not find, in his experiment using simultaneous presentation, the sort of serial order effect reported by the present writer for low levels of practice. That is, his subjects always did equally well on both halves of the list if they were uninformed of recall order at the time of presentation. This may be for one of two reasons: his subjects were all given a day's practice before results were taken, so that they may have been aware of the greater efficiency of the Fig. 6 type of performance. Secondly, he required response during presentation, and this may encourage the use of the $P$ system at that time. He did obtain a serial order effect when successive presentation of the two halves of the list was used, just as Kay and Poulton did: but this is of course not comparable to simultaneous presentation.

Thus far the agreement is fairly good. But Lawrence and Laberge's results are a different matter. They found, it will be remembered, that they obtained a normal serial order effect even when the order of recall was prescribed after presentation: and in conjunction with a normal overall level of efficiency. They very properly therefore decided that no selective factor need be supposed to operate at the time of stimulation, and that the selectivity which appears in response is due purely to memory and response factors. How can we reconcile, first, their results with those of Brown and of the writer: secondly, their interpretation with filter theory?

Two obvious differences exist between their conditions and those of the other experiments. First, the actual time taken by stimulation was only $\frac{1}{10}$ sec, as opposed to a time of the order of seconds in the other experiments. This means that a Fig. 6 type system would not have much time to pass any information through the $P$ system while stimulation was actually in progress. The difference from a type of system resembling that in Fig. 5 would therefore be less than in the other experiments. It also means that any detrimental memory factors would have longer to operate in the other experiments and so to produce greater inefficiency.

The second difference in Lawrence and Laberge's experiment is that they do not report the spontaneous order of recall in their type of task. They are, of course, considering stimulus dimensions rather than channels of incoming information, as was necessary if their results were to be comparable with those of classic experiments on selective perception. It may be advisable to enlarge at this point on the differences between the concepts of dimension and channel. Any stimulus event, as we have said before, has a number of characteristics by virtue of which it conveys information. Different events may be the same in some characteristics but different in others: thus they may be the same colour but different in shape. The filter which we have been supposing, passes the information from events which have some characteristics in common. Thus it may pass right-hand side sounds and reject those coming from the left-hand side of the head. Now admittedly the colours of several objects have in common the characteristic of affecting colour receptors rather than, say, touch ones. But it seems plausible that the filter would operate more readily on some characteristic in which not only the dimension but the point on that dimension is common to several events. Such a characteristic does exist in Lawrence and Laberge's experiments: it is spatial position. One colour, shape, and number were observed in one place and one in the other. If the filter operated on the basis of place, the natural response of the subjects would have been ' 2 red squares, 4 blue circles ' rather than ' 2, 4, red, blue, squares, circles '. But this was a recall order which they were never instructed to employ. The importance of this is that, if the subjects were to operate as Fig. 6 systems, the first information through the $P$ system would be the shape, colour, and number of the objects on one card, and this information would therefore be better retained than that from the other card. When recall was required beginning, say, with both colours, recall order would undoubtedly exercise its normal effect and would not be cancelled out by instances in which the subject had happened to pick exactly the opposite order for the first passage of information through the $P$ system. Thus they could operate as Fig. 6 systems, attain the correspondingly high level of efficiency, and yet show the serial order effect due to the order of recall.

Both these possible reasons for the disagreement with Lawrence and Laberge's results could be tested experimentally. Thus if the latter one is true, a repetition of the experiment with ' left first ' and ' right first ' as the instructions for recall would make the results approximate to those found in the writer's experiment. If the former explanation were true, the same change in results could be achieved simply by delaying the provision of recall order instructions for some time after stimulation.

But it is not in fact very important what explanation is given for the divergence of results in the two types of situation. The writer's results certainly do not require that any selection exists among the various stimuli reaching the senses, at the time of their arrival: only that part of the information is selected for passing on to a later mechanism. This latter system, as we saw in Chapter 3, is limited chiefly by the extent to which it holds information from earlier instants in the history of the organism. As we said in that chapter, two single isolated stimuli are less likely to interfere with one another than two streams of speech, and from one point of view one might say that this is because of limitations of memory rather than perception. However, to the writer it seems artificial to distinguish between ' perception ' and ' memory for stimuli arriving a second or so previously ', and he would therefore have preferred to describe Lawrence and Laberge's results as showing that the selective nature of perception appears only as the percept develops and not at the moment of stimulation. The point shows clearly the difficulties which words such as ' perception ' and ' memory ' produce when they are used in anything more than a very rough general sense, to indicate a field of interest. In the flow diagrams of Figs. 5 and 6, the box $P$ might be called ' memory ' in view of Lawrence and Laberge's results; to the writer the word ' perception ' includes immediate memory, so that he labelled the box $P$ for perception, $S$ standing for storage. But as to some people perception excludes all memory it is better to keep to letters. If there is any real question of fact involved here it is over the doubt whether Fig. 5 or Fig. 6 most nearly represents events within the organism in these simultaneous stimulation situations.

We may now return to a puzzling feature of the results of the writer's experiments: Fig. 5 performance is rather inefficient, and this looks as though the $S$ system is an imperfect one. Avoiding passage through the $S$ system, as some information is able to do in the Fig. 6 type of performance, produces better results. But it has been pointed out earlier that when the eye and ear are the two sensory channels for delivering the information, performance is at least as good with simultaneous presentation as in the successive presentation of ordinary memory span. The former must involve the $S$ system for some of the information, the latter apparently need not.   So one would have thought, if the $S$ system was simply a poor one, that simultaneous presentation would be worse than successive.

The best way of reconciling these results seems to be that one should adopt the possibility that the $S$ system is only an inefficient one when information stays in it for some time.   Thus if the process of delivering the stimuli takes a considerable time, Fig. 5 performance is liable to be poor.   Fig. 6 performance allows all the information to leave the $S$ system rather more quickly, and so is more efficient.   This is, of course, the first of the explanations advanced earlier for Lawrence and Laberge's results.   In their situation the process of stimulation was rapidly over, and the withdrawal of it from the $S$ system could begin sooner.   Thus efficiency with Fig. 5 performance would be nearly the same as with Fig. 6 performance.

This means that the information in the $S$ system is being lost in a matter of seconds:  a very rapid decay indeed.   It is possible to examine this suggestion directly:  in addition it is closely linked to a theory of immediate memory which we may now consider.

### The ' Rehearsal and Fading Trace ' Theory of Immediate Memory

Brown (1955) performed a number of other experiments on immediate memory, besides those on serial order effect which we have already mentioned.   Many of them were of the type usually described as ' retroactive inhibition ' experiments.   That is, the recall was separated from the presentation by some other activity. In most retroactive inhibition experiments, the original learning is carried on over many repeated presentations of the information, and the interpolated activity is also a learning task.   Some interference is usually found.   Brown's situation was thus unusual in employing only one presentation of the original material, and in using for interpolated activity a series of stimuli which required response but which were not to be memorized.   He was able to show fairly severe interference in this way.   In control experiments he showed that the amount recalled was not particularly affected by varying the time interval between presentation and recall.   He also showed that the amount of interference depended upon the amount of original material and on the number of interpolated stimuli. If there were few items to be recalled, many interpolated stimuli were needed to produce interference.

All this agrees well with everyday experience. If we are told a telephone number, the time taken to walk across the room and dial the number makes little difference to our efficiency, so long as no other action is required of us. To be asked a question between hearing the number and dialling it will, if we have to answer the question, interfere severely. And of course a long modern number shows the effects of interference more than the short numbers of country exchanges in the past. Introspectively, most people would say that this was because they rehearsed the number internally between hearing it and dialling it. If anything interfered with the process of saying the number over and over subvocally, it would be forgotten.

Brown therefore suggested a theory based on this introspective account: the presented material forms a trace which decays rapidly, but can be restored by rehearsal. Since all the items cannot be rehearsed simultaneously, there is a limit to the number of items which can be kept in existence as traces by rehearsing each in turn and returning to the first when the last has been rehearsed. Beyond a number fixed by the rate of decay, and the rate of rehearsal, the first trace will have disappeared completely before the last has been rehearsed. If this number of items has been reached, any other activity which interferes with rehearsal will cause a failure of recall. If the number of traces is small, the extra activity may be carried out during the interval between successive rehearsals: the traces may safely be allowed to decay a little before the next rehearsal. Brown found, as would be expected, that the precise time at which the interpolated activity was introduced between presentation and recall was not important. There were other features of his results which supported this theory: for instance (Brown 1954) the effect of extra activity seemed to be less where the material recalled took the form of spatially oriented arrows rather than numbers, and it seems likely that rehearsal is less important with such material.

In terms of our analysis, this theory amounts to the suggestion that information can stay in the $S$ system only for a limited time: but after passing through the $P$ system it can be returned to the $S$ system. The identity of the $S$ system in the two cases, before and after passage through the $P$ system, is perhaps open to doubt: it may be that the store which lies before the $P$ system is not the same as that which lies after it. But for parsimony we may perhaps assume that they are identical for the moment. The theory thus becomes one of recurrent circuit type, in which information is passed continuously around a loop until required. As has been said, this is in fact a common device for short term storage in machines; although in the latter application each part of the equipment is usually only able to pass one item at a time, whereas in the present case the $S$ system can hold them all simultaneously. However, this is merely a matter of definitions: if we considered a loop in a machine in two sections, one much smaller than the remainder, it would be true that all the information could be in the large part simultaneously but the small part only successively. The analogy may be sufficiently close, therefore: but our more general formulation includes the possibility that the underlying mechanism of the system may be, say, successive excitation of a series of synapses which gradually change threshold between excitations. Any speculative physiologist could produce a number of possible mechanisms, and it would be a pity to commit oneself to any one of them.

The possibility that the $S$ system can hold information only for a limited time is therefore of some general interest, as well as providing an explanation for the discrepancy mentioned in the last section. An experiment was therefore set up (Broadbent 1957c) in which the $P$ system was kept occupied for various lengths of time after the arrival of information by another channel. Thus there would be increasing opportunity for the $S$ system to show a decline in efficiency with time. The arrangement was to deliver six digits to one ear, and to present two other digits to the other ear at some time during the arrival of the six. The listener was instructed to report first the six and then the two. This he was able to do quite well when the two digits arrived just before the end of the six: but much less well if they arrived earlier. In other words if the two digits were in the $S$ system for more than a second or so before their admission to the $P$ system, they were less efficiently recalled. It is also of interest that the second of the two digits was more efficiently recalled than the first: it had, of course, been in store for shorter time.

These results seem to confirm Brown's suggestion, though there are perhaps other theories with which they might also be consistent. However, the view of immediate memory as a circulation of information from a temporary store through a limited capacity system and back again, repeated until response is required, seems to harmonize a number of results and at the moment is the most probable suggestion.

Another result bears no direct relation to Brown's theory but is of some interest for other reasons. This is the effect of inserting irrelevant items before or after the relevant ones in the $S$ system. For instance, suppose six digits are presented to each ear, and the listener is asked to give first all six from the right ear and then, say, the first two from the left ear. This task is almost impossible: apparently irrelevant items place some extra load on the system. Their effect is practically as great whether they come before or after the relevant ones. This result may be contrasted with the negligible effect of irrelevant items on one ear when all the relevant items are on the other ear (Cherry 1953). As we have said previously, the filter which selects information for the $P$ system chooses all events having some characteristic in common. If relevant and irrelevant items are on the same channel, the effect of the latter is considerable.

Another group of results should also be considered, because of their relevance to the theory of immediate memory, although they do not concern simultaneous stimulation. These are results on the effect of varying the amount of information per item in an orthodox memory span situation. It has been found by Pollack (1953) that the percentage of information lost in such a situation depends on the number of items presented and not on the information per item. This means that the amount of information in a span is not constant: it is greater, for instance, in remembering a series of letters than a series of digits. In the former case, each item is drawn from a larger ensemble of items, and as the number of items recalled is much the same the amount of information is greater. Miller (1956) has reported an intriguing result based on the same fact: the span for items having a low information content can be improved by training subjects the conversion between such items and items having a high information content. For instance, binary numbers in which each digit is either 1 or 0 can be translated into the familiar decimal numbers in which each digit can take any value from 0 to 9. If the subject is trained in such translation he can translate a series of ones and zeros into ordinary numbers as they are presented. He can then handle a normal memory span of about seven or eight digits, and retranslate into binary numbers when asked for recall. His apparent span for binary digits is then much greater, as each decimal digit is the equivalent of several binary ones. But this increase in span depends on training in recoding one set of items into another: without such training the span is determined by number of items and not by information per item. A rather similar effect is found by Aborn and Rubenstein (1952) who varied the amount of information in a span by restricting transition probabilities between items rather than the size of the vocabulary of items. They reported results favourable to a view of immediate memory as a store of constant capacity in informational terms, rather than of a constant number of items. Learning of transition probabilities is rather more similar to Miller's recoding technique than learning of vocabulary size is. Even in this case, however, the constant capacity relation broke down when large numbers of items were being used.

At first sight, this general finding that immediate memory does not have a constant capacity fits readily into the ' recurrent circuit ' theory of immediate memory. If we were dealing simply with a passive store it would be reasonable to expect it to hold a constant amount of information. If the limit to the span is set by the number of items which can be passed through the $P$ system before the $S$ system loses the first of them, it is more plausible that a constant number of items should be the limit.

But the matter is not completely simple. The limit on the $P$ system is presumably one of rate of handling information: indeed, this must be so if we are to suppose that the filter we have postulated in earlier chapters lies between the $S$ and $P$ systems and serves the purpose of securing the most economical use of the latter. Remember the experiments showing that stimuli of low information content interfere less with one another than do those of high information content. If then, items of low information content can pass through the $P$ system more rapidly, why cannot more of them be circulated before the expiry of the time limit for information in the $S$ system ?

Various answers to this difficulty are possible. First, one might suggest that to some extent the filter needs to change channel for every fresh item: the time taken for rehearsal is then largely a question of the product of the number of items and the time taken for a shift of the filter. As the latter is unrelated to the information in the item, the total time for rehearsal will be much the same even though each item takes only a short time to pass into the $P$ system. It is indeed true that the span is slightly longer for low information items, as might be expected from the slight reduction in rehearsal time per item which would occur on this theory. But although this suggestion was put forward by the writer (Broadbent 1957d) he feels somewhat dissatisfied with it. It is very implausible to suppose shifts of the filter between each item when the whole purpose of the latter is to pass items with a common characteristic. Furthermore, the number of successive items which are completely identical is of course greater in binary numbers than in decimal ones, so that fewer shifts would be required in the former case. It might be interesting to know whether longer spans are possible when there are more runs of similar items and therefore, on this view, fewer filter shifts. But for these reasons the explanation seems rather unlikely.

A second possibility is that the time limit for items remaining in the $S$ system is shorter when the items are of low information content. The number of items rehearsed before the time limit is reached will then be the same even though rehearsal is faster. The objection to this view is that it is an *ad hoc* postulate: any difficulty can always be met if we suppose some extra feature of the theory to do so. In itself the postulate is not too unlikely: low information items tend, to use an unsatisfactory word, to be more similar to one another than do high information items. Yet if there are a certain number of dimensions on which items can differ, low information items can of course differ on more of them, thus providing a redundancy which should be valuable in resisting the effects of time on the storage system.

Perhaps the most hopeful suggestion is one by Brown himself (personal communication). He points out that the order of items contains part of the information in the span, and progressively more as the information per item decreases. If information on the order of items is lost more easily than information on the nature of items, there would tend to be a limit to the number independent of the information per item.  A possible criticism which occurs to the writer is that this mechanism would set a limit to the span without any need for the postulate that the *S* system possesses a time limit, so that the facts are being over-explained and we ought to discard one or other postulate.

All these explanations should be testable by experiment, and future work may therefore decide which of them is the correct one.  However, the fact that span is limited by number of items rather than by information is obviously not a crucial difficulty for the ' recurrent circuit ' theory of memory.

*Implications of these results for earlier problems.*—The facts about immediate memory which we have been considering have a bearing on each of the topics we have considered in earlier chapters.  In the first place, we can see that multi-channel listening is likely to be eased by the fact that momentary peaks in the rate of arrival of information can be handled.  The peaks must be only momentary, but as long as the man is not asked to store items on one channel for too long while dealing with another channel, he will be able to cope with both.  We can see, too, that Mowbray's experiments described in Chapter 2 were under conditions which would minimize this possibility: as he used continuous streams of information there would be no opportunity for a shift from one channel to another and analysis of stored information.  In his experiment using items of information (rather than continuous streams) the items were embedded in irrelevant material; the latter would lower the chance of the relevant information being withdrawn from the *S* system if the *P* system was handling another channel when it arrived.

But this does not invalidate the general conclusion that there is a limit to the capacity of the perceptual system, nor the conception of a filter which selects part of the presented information for feeding to that perceptual system.  The experiments considered in Chapter 2 are of value as establishing these points, but the conclusions are equally implicit in the experiments on split memory span.  The qualification simply needs to be added that the filter does not operate at the sense-organs, but only at a stage after a storage system of a very temporary kind.  This emphasizes the central rather than peripheral nature of the filter.

When we come to the effects of noise and of prolonged work, there are several points to be considered. We interpreted the ' blocks ' and errors in continuous work, and the failures to detect infrequent signals, as due to a shift of the filter to a non-task source of information. The fact that the time taken for a double shift seems to be of the same order as a block confirms this interpretation; both are roughly between 1–2 sec.

In addition, however, the fact that a signal can produce response after a delay, even though some other information is being handled at the time of its arrival, means that we must modify our conclusions about the effect of length of signal on decrement in vigilance tasks. We said that a signal lasting only 1 sec or less might occur during a block, and so produce no response. There was a fair amount of evidence to support this conclusion. But from our present point of view it should be possible for the signal to produce a delayed response without being missed altogether.

Reaction times do indeed increase in vigilance tasks under stress conditions. Mackworth (1950) gives such times for the clock test both for simple prolonged work and for work in heat and high humidity. It is interesting to see that the distributions of reaction times cross over at rather over 1 sec: under stress conditions responses slower than this become more frequent than they are normally, and faster responses are less frequent (Mackworth 1950, p. 42). The mode of the distribution does not shift very far: that is, if a response appears in less than a second it takes much the usual time. All these features would be expected if the delayed responses were due to signals arriving during blocks producing a response after the conclusion of the block.

Why, however, do any misses at all occur ? The answer may lie in the other neutral stimuli which precede and follow the signal. In the clock test each double jump of the pointer is interpolated amongst repeated single jumps. As we have seen in this chapter, if the $P$ system is occupied on one channel and a relevant stimulus occurs on another channel, the chance of recovering information about the latter stimulus from store decreases sharply with the presence of other irrelevant stimuli before and after it on the same channel. Thus the details of the clock test situation minimize the role of delayed responses and emphasise complete failures of response. The same is true of other tasks which show marked decrements in many individuals: for instance Bakan's or Fraser's. The importance of repeated irrelevant stimuli was noted in Chapter 6; the reason for it is now rather more clear.

Some missed signals do of course occur even in tasks such as Mackworth's radar test in which there do not appear to be other neutral or irrelevant stimuli to prevent delayed reaction. One reason for this may be that the filter is selecting non-task information for longer than the minimum period of a second: in which case the rapid decline in efficiency of the $S$ system becomes important. A second explanation may be that the peripheral filtering systems come into play: the eyes may actually be pointing in the wrong direction for detecting the stimulus. In such a case, as the information never enters the nervous system it cannot produce a response even after a delay. It is interesting that this possibility may not apply to auditory signals: as peripheral processes of adjustment are of less importance in the ear, the information usually enters the nervous system, and so may produce delayed responses in vigilance situations rather than complete failures of response. This is a possible explanation of the deviant results of Elliott in the vigilance situation, since he used auditory signals. The other cases of auditory vigilance, Mackworth's and that of Bakan (1952) employed interpolated neutral signals so that delayed responses were unlikely. However, as we noted in Chapter 6, there may be other reasons for the difference between Elliott's results and those of other vigilance tasks.

When we turn to individual differences, the chief point to note is that the suggested distinction between extremes of extraversion and of intraversion (short as opposed to long sampling of information before action) does not imply that the temporary store is more important than the long term store in extraverts. On the contrary, the establishment of habitual actions is the process closest to the insertion of information into long term store, and this is a question of input-output relations, which we distinguished previously from sampling time. The differences between individuals considered in Chapter 8 may rather be explained by a difference in the length of time which corresponds to an item in the short term store.

Lastly, when we come to Chapter 8, we can see that we now have reasonable evidence for the existence of a short term store like that postulated at the end of that chapter to account for various puzzling features of disinhibition. It may now be opportune to consider the effect of our general findings on theories of learning: in the first place, as applied to human rote learning.

*Implications of these results for rote learning.*—It has probably not escaped the reader that by supposing the $S$ system to store items only for a limited time we have given some explanation of the fact that the first items through the $P$ system are the most efficiently recalled. This can be seen most clearly when the person memorizing is acting in the way shown in Fig. 5. As both channels feed information into the $S$ system simultaneously, the first channel to discharge into the $P$ system is that which runs least risk of exceeding the time limit in the $S$ system, and so failing to be recalled.

The same explanation can be applied to each of the cases of simultaneous stimulation, cited earlier when we wished to establish that the first items through the $P$ system were the best recalled. What, however, of the cases of successive stimulation, in which the first items through the $P$ system were also the first to be presented and so do not gain any advantage over the later ones? The serial order effect here will depend on relative rates of presentation and of passage through the $P$ system. It may further be noted that passage through the $P$ system may be at different speeds depending on whether or not response is required: if items are merely returning to the $S$ system they may go through faster than if they are issuing in response. This possibility is reinforced by such facts as that silent reading is faster than overt reading: Brown (1955) reports an experiment to show this, although it depends to some extent on the honesty of the subject's introspection that all the items have been silently read.

To avoid confusion we will give different names to the two possible rates of passage through the $P$ system; the rate when the information is not appearing in response will be called 'rehearsal' rate, and the rate when response is occurring will be called 'recall' rate. Those who dislike identifying our $P$ system with that responsible for consciously reported subvocal rehearsal will perhaps excuse us on this occasion.

We thus have three rates: presentation, rehearsal, and recall. Of these the middle one is probably the fastest; and if it is faster than recall, the earlier items in the sequence will, on their final circulation, spend less time in the $S$ system than the final items do. To see this, consider that the last rehearsal starts at time 0 and lasts for, say, 2 sec. If the process of overt recall starts at this time, 0 plus 2, and lasts for 4 sec, the interval between rehearsal and recall of the first item is 2 sec. But the interval between rehearsal and recall of the last item is 4 sec, and the last item therefore runs more risk of failure of recall.

If on the other hand presentation rate is slower than rehearsal, the first items will go into the $S$ system through the $P$ system, and will be delayed there until the later ones have passed through the $P$ system: this will cause the final items to be better recalled than those before them. We thus have two opposing tendencies which will counter-balance in varying degrees to produce a curve of difficulty in which the hardest part of the sequence is somewhere between the two ends.

The two counter-balancing effects have been shown by Poulton (1953b) for the different but analogous case of presenting two series of items one after the other. If recall of the first series is complete before presentation of the second, the two naturally each show normal difficulty. When presentation of the second overlaps recall of the first, there is a deleterious effect on the end of the first list and the beginning of the second, causing the two together to give a bow-shaped curve of difficulty. In mentalistic terms, recall of List 1 and perception of List 2 cannot be performed simultaneously: this means that if List 1 is recalled completely before any attention is given to List 2, the first items of the latter will have faded beyond recall. Any attempt to observe List 2 before List 1 has been recalled will delay the reproduction of the last items of List 1, and so cause failures. In our terms, List 1 arrives and passes through the $P$ system to the $S$ one. When List 2 is arriving, the filter may either select List 1 and pass the information from that list to the output, or select List 2 and pass that information to $S$. The former strategy will mean that List 2 stays in $S$ for a long time, the earlier items being the most affected. The latter strategy will mean that List 1 stays in $S$ for too long: the best compromise is to start passing List 1 to the output but to select List 2 for recirculation before List 1 has all emerged. Thus the beginning of List 2 and the end of List 1 suffer most.

Another consequence of this point of view will be that slow presentation and fast recall will enhance the advantage of the beginning of the list, while the reverse conditions will give the advantage to the end of the list. The combination of slow presentation and slow recall will be worse all through than the combination of fast presentation and recall. All these predictions have been confirmed by Conrad (personal communication and 1957). They apply, of course, only to speeds too fast to allow rehearsal during presentation or recall.

One fact about serial order may appear to have been forgotten, namely, the change in the effect when a list presented in one order is recalled in the reverse order. This is readily handled: change in order can only be produced by the information entering the $S$ system in one order (either from the sense-organs or from the $P$ system) and being removed to the $P$ system in a different order. A reversal in order will mean that the first items to enter the $S$ system will stay there longer than the others, and longer than the mean if there had been no reversal. A change in order will therefore mean a drop in the efficiency of the first items as compared with the later ones, and a net decrease in span. As we have seen, these effects do occur.

Serial order has been the subject of a number of previous theories, though it has usually been considered in more long-term rather than immediate memory. At the same time our views may be expected to apply to long-term learning, since we cannot expect information to enter the long-term store without passing through the $P$ system. The factors we have indicated above should therefore appear in, say, rote learning experiments. The best theory of such experiments is that of Hull *et al.* (1940): they draw the analogy between trace conditioning and the attachment of each item in a list to the other items. The last item is not only an immediate response to the stimulus of the previous item, but also a trace response to the first item and to each of the others. With each such trace there is associated an inhibition: and there are more traces in action when the list is halfway through than at any other point, as may be seen by connecting up each item to all the others graphically. Thus the greatest difficulty will be in the middle of the list. As inhibition dissipates with time, massed learning trials will show the effect more clearly than will trials separated by intervals. For the same reason, performance may actually improve for a few minutes before the normal 'forgetting' decline sets in, after partial learning by massed trials. This improvement is known as 'reminiscence'; it should be greatest in the middle of the list as the inhibition is greatest there. As we shall see, the effect does occur but is rather dependent on the conditions of the experiment.

The advantages of this theory are several. In the first place, its manner of presentation is usually acclaimed. In the later form (Hull *et al.* 1940) it is highly quantitative and may therefore be regarded as automatically superior to our own view, which is restricted to predictions of the type '*X* will do better than *Y* '. But the quantitative character is largely spurious: it depends on the appropriate choice of constants in the equations, and constants determined for the learning of lists of one length do not hold for the learning of lists of another length. The true merit of the theory appears rather in its early non-quantitative form (Hull 1935). It there makes precise non-quantitative predictions for a number of different situations which have been indicated in the last paragraph. These predictions were experimentally testable, and the paper exercised a very valuable influence. We shall see in Chapter 12 why the qualitative rather than the quantitative form is to be regarded as the superior from the point of view of scientific method.

There are certain difficulties in the Hullian view, despite its harmonization of much data. It allows insufficient play for the role of previous instructions, which as we saw in the experiment of Kay and Poulton (1951), may greatly alter serial order effects. In that experiment the possibility that recall might have to be in a different order changed the relative difficulty of the last items. Other workers (e.g. Krueger 1932) have shown that instructions to the learner to concentrate on particular parts of the list produce corresponding changes in the errors in different parts. A number of the other facts cited in this chapter on the effect of reversing order in recall, of varying presentation and recall rates, and of presenting stimuli simultaneously, are similarly outside the scope of Hullian theory.

The question of presentation rate is a particularly intriguing one. All the effects of massing and spacing, reminiscence, and serial order, apply chiefly to nonsense syllables learned at a rate of one syllable every 2 sec. If the rate is slowed to one syllable every 4 sec, the effects largely disappear. It may be added that reminiscence is somewhat elusive even at the 2 sec rate; it seems to be more likely if the subject is required to correct errors he may have made in anticipating the next syllable to appear, by reading out the syllable which actually occurred. The opposite instructions may produce difficulty in showing reminiscence (Buxton and Bakan 1949).

Finally, the effect of massing as opposed to spacing trials is attributed by the Hullian theory to inhibition, which dissipates with time to produce reminiscence. But if this were so the effect of massing should disappear as longer and longer intervals are allowed before recall. In general this is not true: spacing trials produces benefits on retention as well as on rate of learning. Underwood (1952, 1953) has admittedly produced evidence more in conformity with Hullian theory, but his results are exceptional. As he has indicated (Underwood and Richardson 1955) the effect of massing which persists into retention seems to be due to generalization from other lists. That is, if subjects have learned many other lists, they tend after massed practice on a fresh list to make mistakes in retention tests. If they have learned few other lists, spacing does not show an advantage in retention although it does do so in rate of original learning. Most experiments have been done with subjects who had learned a number of lists, and so the conclusion that spacing favours retention was widely accepted. Hullian theory, however, provided no prior explanation of the necessity for a particular kind of experience in the demonstration of effects of spacing. It can perhaps provide a *post hoc* explanation by arguing that a massed list learning situation is very similar to other massed learning situations and therefore responses appropriate to those other situations appear and interfere with the correct ones.

There thus seem to be certain difficulties in the Hullian account, despite its merits. Our own views naturally deal with the facts cited in this chapter, since they were designed to do so. We must now see if they will suggest any explanation for the other difficulties of the trace conditioning theory.

Anybody who has acted as a subject for a rote-learning experiment will agree that it is a highly monotonous situation requiring continuous reception of information from one source, the window of the memory drum. This is a description which would also apply to vigilance tasks, and indeed there seems no reason why the results of experiments on prolonged perception should not apply to rote learning. No doubt other factors will be acting in addition, but the information must pass the $P$ system if it is to enter the permanent store. Now we said in the case of vigilance tasks that the decrement with time took the form of interruptions in the intake of information. They become increasingly frequent, although performance in between them may be unaffected. The interval between successive responses when such a ' block ' occurs in continuous work is between 1–2 sec, so that the interruption in the intake of information is presumably of the order of 1 sec. In the rote-learning situation each item appears for a limited time, during which the subject has to observe and say it and then to attempt to say the next item before the latter appears. A block of 1 sec will leave little time for these two operations and is likely to cause one or both of them to remain undone. The time available will be even less if incorrect anticipations have to be put right. It will be noted that a decrement of this sort applies both to learning and to performance: if the syllables have never passed the filter they will not be learned and retention will be inferior. This situation is more likely to occur in massed learning than in spaced learning. So also, after partial learning, some of the syllables, whose connexion with their adjacent syllables has been learned, will not pass the filter and there will be a reduction in the number of correct anticipations. This will only be true after a long series of runs through the list on the memory drum without a pause to allow the filter to select other information; a brief rest will eliminate ' blocks ' and so allow better performance —the reminiscence effect.

As the decrement is one produced by short blocks rather than an even decline in performance, a 4 sec presentation rate will allow ample time even when a block occurs and so will not show these various effects. It is interesting to notice that, from our previous argument in Chapter 6, unpaced learning should produce the same result as the 4 sec rate, even if the average rate of work is faster than one item every 4 sec. Husband (1929) does report absence of massing and spacing effects in unpaced learning of a finger maze.

An advantage of this type of interpretation is that it explains the sensitivity of the various phenomena, such as reminiscence, to changes in conditions. A 2 sec presentation rate should, in view of the 1 sec length of interruptions in information intake, be only just fast enough to show the effects. A faster rate, or increasing the time demanded by the task by such instructions as ' spell out the syllables ' will make the effects more likely to appear.

We thus have some success in applying our views to the facts traditionally explained by the Hullian trace-conditioning hypothesis. Two cautions should be given. First, our postulated recurrent circuit system seems to be necessary to explain immediate memory. But experiments are rare in which any account is taken of the possibility of a short-term and a separate long-term store operating on different principles. As a result we cannot say whether the long-term store has any properties of its own contributing to the results explained by traditional rcte learning theory. Properties of the immediate memory system need to be excluded before we can say what the long-term system is like, and they have not been. So we must not assume too confidently that the properties of the short-term system will account for all the phenomena of massing and spacing, serial order, reminiscence and so on. More experiments are needed. But there are already a number of minor findings in the literature which are of great significance once we recognize the distinction between two varieties of storage. For example, on our view material rote learned to a criterion of a few correct repetitions is partly in the long-term and partly in the short-term store. The latter is sensitive to ill treatment: it will be lost rapidly with interpolated activity and therefore with time, but it can be restored by a few fresh presentations of the material. In fact it is often noted in retroactive inhibition experiments that the effect of an interpolated activity is not to return the originally learned material to an earlier stage of learning; retroactive inhibition is greater when

measured on the first few trials after the interpolated activity than
when there has been an opportunity to bring back some items into
short-term storage (Melton and Irwin 1940; Melton and von
Lackum 1941).

So-called ' overlearning ', in which the material is presented
again and again after apparent mastery has been achieved, will
transfer more and more information into the permanent store.
Overlearning does in fact change the forgetting curve, the effects
of retroactive inhibition, and it decreases the signs of ' remote
associations '. This last finding means that if a list is learned to
criterion, the learner will show an advantage on a new list made
up of the same items in a different order. If the old list is overlearned, there is little saving on a list in derived order (see Woodworth 1938, p. 30).

Another difference which needs examination is that between
sensory material and sequences of movements. The latter are
possibly less appropriate to a recurrent circuit mechanism: at
least there are less conscious reports of rehearsal in bodily skills,
than in learning involving sequences of stimuli. Phenomena
which depend on the storing of part of the information in the short-
term store should therefore be less marked in bodily skills: that
is, forgetting should be slower, and retroactive inhibition less.
In general, such skills should behave like overlearned material.
They should, however, show some effects of massing and spacing,
and reminiscence, because those effects are due to failure of the
filter to select information for action and so will appear even if
recirculation is not used with the particular material. And of
course there is probably no skill so completely motor that no
sensory learning is involved in it; the differences will only be of
degree. The differences and resemblances between bodily skills
and verbal material do seem to support this interpretation
(Woodworth 1938, p. 152). All these points need to be
examined with the possibility of two different mechanisms in
mind.

The second caution is that this interpretation is not so much in
opposition to the Hullian view as a development of the latter. In
Hull's early non-quantitative papers he did point out genuine and
surprising similarities between conditioning and rote learning,
and the writer supports these similarities. He would hold that

the phenomena of trace conditioning are due to the same mechanism as those of immediate memory: the behaviour of a dog given a stimulus for a trace response is very similar to that of a man given a telephone number for immediate reproduction. Dog or man must ignore any other stimuli which arrive before response occurs, or else they will fail to make the response. As a compromise the man may make a note of the number if he is interrupted before he can dial it; the dog may salivate when given a stimulus which is disinhibiting but not intense enough to be externally inhibiting. Thus there is a continuity between the present view and the Hullian one: the writer would regard the development as the necessary step from observing similarities in behaviour to considering the psychological mechanisms responsible for the similarities. The quantitative development of behavioural measures before the mechanism is understood is a false step: it tends to be autistic, much of the quantification in Hullian views being quite unrelated to any experiment, and it has therefore been rejected by the present writer: but the behavioural facts classed together are very similar in the Hullian view and in this one. We are trying to develop rather than refute.

## CONCLUSIONS

In summary then, we have considered a good deal of evidence which supports a view of an immediate memory mechanism distinct from that used for long-term memory. The conception is that information is held in a short-term store with a very limited time span. From this store it may be passed selectively by a filter through some mechanism of limited capacity from which it is returned to store; this furnishes a method of indefinitely long storage as long as no response to other stimuli is required. The various findings cited show that this mechanism clears up certain details of the results mentioned in previous chapters: the filter is still a necessary postulate, but its operation is not quite as simple as it was earlier assumed to be. And the implications of the principle that ' only information which passes the filter can be stored for long periods ' seem capable of explaining a surprising number of findings usually dealt with by learning theory, and some which are an embarrassment to traditional theories. The time has now come to return to the animal case for the last time, and to consider how far our filter system can clear up difficulties in that field.

# CHAPTER 10

# THE SELECTIVE NATURE OF LEARNING

As was said in Chapter 1, the problem of learning is to a great extent that of explaining why only some things are learned. Early simple views of conditioning held that repeated association of any two stimuli one after the other would cause the response to the second to become attached to the first. This was, of course, taking conditioning as a self-sufficient principle rather than a useful situation in which to study more analytic postulates about behaviour. But it is related to more sophisticated approaches, such as Uttley's postulation of storage of conditional probabilities of any event given any other. The early views became unsatisfactory when detailed study of behaviour showed that the response finally appearing in any situation was not necessarily the most frequently or the most recently associated with the stimulus: rather it was a biologically useful one, the response which secured some end useful to the animal. Such a conception is vague and never obtained currency in that form: but a more satisfactory version of it appeared in the reinforcement postulate, that there were certain kinds of treatment (for an animal in a given bodily state) which when given immediately after a stimulus-response combination would make that combination more probable in the future. Here was a reason why responses of turning into blind-alleys in mazes were eliminated and responses of turning towards food-boxes were established. A reasonable amount of selection by the learning process was thus explained.

Although broadly successful the reinforcement postulate fits a little uneasily at the edges. There are certain instances in which some degree of learning seems to take place without reinforcement. For example, there is sensory pre-conditioning, in which two stimuli are repeatedly presented in association, and one of them afterwards made a stimulus for a conditioned response. The other stimulus is then unduly likely to produce the same response (Brogden 1939). Another instance is latent learning, in which an animal is allowed to run a maze without reward: after a reward is introduced the performance at maze running improves extremely rapidly, showing that some learning has taken place during the unrewarded training.   A third difficulty is partial reinforcement: if in an instrumental conditioning situation the reinforcement is given only after every tenth response rather than every time, the response may be harder to establish but is also harder to extinguish.   Yet, as the response has been followed by reinforcement less often, it should on a simple interpretation of the reinforcement postulate be less well established. These are classic objections to the reinforcement postulate: more recently there have been experiments on the exploration of their surroundings by rats, some of which have been mentioned previously (Berlyne 1950; Montgomery 1952), and which suggest that much activity takes place without the reinforcement normally considered necessary.

These objections can be answered by complicating simple reinforcement theory: there is a possible appeal to secondary reinforcement, a principle according to which a stimulus previously associated with a reinforcement is itself reinforcing.   This would explain sensory preconditioning, provided that we suppose some general secondary reinforcing power for the second stimulus. Some explanation can be given for latent learning: provided that a distinction is introduced between the building up of habit strength and the performance of response.   It might, for instance, be argued that the former is a linear function of drive and the latter a multiplicative function, so that introduction of reward improves performance relative to habit strength (Hull 1952). Partial reinforcement again can be explained by linkage of the responses into sequences, each sequence receiving a primary reinforcement.   Such explanations have the disadvantage of blurring the value of the reinforcement principle.   When secondary reinforcement is of such importance, why is not everything learned ?   Why does not the rat in a maze learn to enter blind alleys, since he only meets them during trials that end in reward and so should have been secondarily reinforced ?   Why are not a host of minor responses built up in strength because they happen to occur before stimuli that have acquired secondary reward characteristics ?   The explanation must lie in the differential strength of primary and secondary reinforcement, the latter becoming weaker as it becomes more indirect. Possibly a quantitative theory capable of accounting both for partial reinforcement at very low ratios and also for the elimination of blind alleys in mazes could be constructed. But the writer is sceptical of its chances: partial reinforcement needs a very slight attenuation of reinforcement as it becomes more secondary, while eliminating blinds needs a sharp attenuation.

The suggestion that novel stimuli are themselves reinforcers (Berlyne 1950) is another possibility accounting for some of these results, but it meets the same difficulties as secondary reinforcement. For example, the sharp improvement in latent learning performance when reward is introduced needs rather specific assumptions about the relation between learning and performance and such assumptions could only be validated by very detailed experimental evidence from other situations than the latent learning one. In default of such evidence, explaining the latent learning results in that way becomes *ad hoc* postulation.

Criticism of this type cannot be pushed too far. In the present book we have repeatedly argued from experiments to theoretical generalizations, and in each field studied we have met difficulties which do not fit the generalization. For the most part these difficulties have been met only by showing that they are not crucial, and that there are various possible explanations for them. Further information would allow us to decide which explanation was true; but if any theory is to be stated in an advancing science it must contain frontiers at which detailed advance is still to be made. The answers of reinforcement theorists to their critics are of this same kind: they show that the objections are not crucial and that various extra postulates might account for the facts. So long as reinforcement theory remains a sound organizing framework which gives meaning to the field as a whole, they do not feel justified in dropping it without alternative.

The selective nature of learning could also be explained by postulating a selective operation on the information entering the nervous system; in fact, by supposing a filter like the one we have been considering. Let us first consider evidence from classical conditioning experiments to show that such a filter does appear in learning.

*Stimulus Dynamisms*

To avoid needless disagreement, it should be said at once that the next section will be perfectly innocuous to many reinforcement theorists. The Hullian system allows, for example, that intense stimuli are more likely to produce response. This property is known as stimulus intensity dynamism. By saying that intensity confers priority in a competition to pass through a filter at the entrance to the nervous system, we are merely adding to the Hullian statement about behaviour, a statement about the mechanism responsible for behaviour. Reinforcement theorists may regard this addition as speculative, since they sometimes accept uncritically the view that statements about internal processes are operationally untestable. But at least the addition is not in conflict with reinforcement. Nor is there any reason why other stimulus properties should not be scaled in a fashion similar to intensity; in fact as soon as stimuli affecting different sense-organs are involved, one must apply some weighting factor in computing the intensity dynamism to be assigned to each. One might argue, for instance, that pain stimuli possess a high degree of such dynamism; it is often reported with some surprise (e.g. Pavlov 1927, p. 30) that such stimuli make very effective conditioned stimuli despite the interfering reactions which they originally arouse.

The postulate of afferent stimulus interaction, which we also discussed in Chapter 1, provides a niche in the Hullian system for the effects of presenting two stimuli at once; the latter situation is of course one which filter theory would regard as important, because the filter might discard the information conveyed by one stimulus although it would not have done so had the stimulus been unaccompanied by another. One example of this was given in Chapter 1. To take another (Pavlov 1927, p. 142), if we present a tone plus a light stimulus to a dog and follow the combination by food, we soon establish salivation as a conditioned response to the pair of stimuli. The light stimulus alone, however, is completely ineffective in eliciting the response. As we would now put it, the tone has higher priority and so in simultaneous presentation the light information never passes the filter. Consequently it never becomes a conditioned stimulus, in this type of experiment. Pavlov relates this fact to the effect of stimulus intensity and, on the previously cited page, remarks that presenting two equally intense sounds establishes responses to both sounds when presented singly.  If one sound is presented at a much lower intensity than the other, however, it is over-shadowed by the other just as the light is overshadowed by the sound.  It is unfortunate that sounds were used, as one would mask the other under some circumstances and Pavlov's account is not sufficiently detailed to exclude this possibility.  But another experiment (Pavlov 1927, p. 270) showed that over-shadowing of a light by a sound did not apply when the sound was faint.  Nor was a touch overshadowed by a weak sound, although with stronger sounds this was normally the case.

Overshadowing shows certain features which act as a control against it being a purely sensory phenomenon.  For instance, a response can be attached to either stimulus if they are presented singly rather than simultaneously.  Even the overshadowed one must therefore be capable of affecting the sense-organs.  Further-more, when the combination of stimuli was reinforced repeatedly after the establishment of responses to each component separately, the ' weaker stimulus ' (to use Pavlov's phrase) did not become overshadowed.  As we would put it, once the filter has selected information of a certain type and the high probability of reward following events of that type has been established, that type of information keeps a high priority.   It is also possible to extinguish response to the stronger stimulus while leaving the combination unaffected, by differential reinforcement.  Pavlov does not seem to report the effect of this treatment on the weaker stimulus: it might possibly cease to be overshadowed on the present view, though the point is not crucial.

These results do seem to require slight modifications to the orthodox stimulus interaction and dynamism postulates: the two should be inter-related, dynamism affecting the outcome of inter-action.  Interaction should also be regarded as affected by the establishment of a response to one of the two stimuli, but this probably needs no fresh postulate.  The response can be regarded as giving rise to a third stimulus which changes the interaction.  With these slight modifications there is no difficulty in accommo-dating the results given so far within the framework of Hullian theory.

Another finding of interest to us is a repeated finding by Lashley (e.g. 1938) in his experiments on generalization. The latter is the tendency, after a stimulus has been attached to a response, for other stimuli differing in certain respects to produce the same response. Lashley found that if a stimulus possessed various features, generalization was much greater when some of them were changed, than when others were. As we would put it, some of the information conveyed by an event passes the filter but some of it does not. Only that which does do so becomes essential to the conditioned stimulus, and so events can differ from the original in respects which were rejected by the filter during conditioning, and still elicit response. It appears that an interpretation of this finding as due to ' afferent stimulus inter-action ' is acceptable to Hullians (e.g. Blum and Blum 1949, p. 48).

The most dubious, for a reinforcement theorist, of the facts to be mentioned here are those concerning the continuity of learning. This is a topic which has been dealt with elsewhere (Broadbent 1959) and will be handled in less detail here. It is, as we said in Chapter 7, an agreed fact that rats in mazes will react systematically to some incorrect stimulus for a series of trials before reaching correct performance. During such systematic responses the correct stimulus-response combination occurs and is followed by reinforcement on a proportion of the trials, half if a two-choice maze is used. Does this reinforcement affect the probability of future correct response, or is it irrelevant as long as the animal is reacting on the ' hypothesis ' that some other stimulus is correct ? We might expect the latter, if we think of the filter as discarding information other than that which is controlling response. As a matter of parsimony, however, most Hullians and to some extent S–R theorists of other persuasions have contended that the probability of the correct response is unaffected by the systematic responses to some other stimulus: in predicting response at any stage of learning we should take account of the number of reinforcements given to the particular response throughout the experiment and not only those since the correct hypothesis was adopted.

The issue is tested by, for example, experiments in which the positive and negative stimuli are interchanged before the animal reaches correct performance. If it is responding, say, to light rather than dark alleys, the first few reinforcements may be given whenever the animal happens to turn left rather than right in its response to light alleys. Then in later trials, still before the correct solution has been found, the reinforcement is given for right turns rather than left ones. If the animal is ignoring the distinction between right and left as long as it is responding to light as opposed to dark, then this reversed pre-training technique should show no slower learning than a more usual procedure in which right turns are reinforced throughout. Some workers say that this is so, but others deny it.

From our point of view we would say that the need for filtering only exists in so far as a large amount of information is presented to the organism: if there is only a little reaching the senses it may all pass the filter even though not all of it is being used to control response. Consequently reversed pre-training might well slow learning when an animal faces a choice between two alleys distinguished in very few ways. If there are a large number of alternative ' hypotheses ', it is impossible for the information about all of them to enter the animal and so filtering will occur: reversed pre-training will then show less effect than in a simpler situation, possibly none at all. An experiment which suits this interpretation is that of Lawrence and Mason (1955). They trained rats to make a choice, then reversed the positive and negative stimuli and trained again, then reversed again and so on. The rate of reversal was faster when the alleys of the maze were distinguished in only two ways, than when a third dimension was added and varied independently of the correct stimulus. That is, if the animal was learning to distinguish black from white alleys, the addition of high hurdles in the entrance to some alleys and low hurdles in the entrance to others slowed the learning. (The hurdles were of course irrelevant to the correctness of the alley.) Furthermore, systematic runs of responses to one stimulus dimension (' hypothesis behaviour ') were less common when there were fewer differences between alleys. This is just what we would expect if filtering only becomes important as the amount of presented information increases.

Experiments showing no effect from reversed pre-training do normally employ alleys differing in several ways, and also use rather difficult discriminations (Blum and Blum 1949). The latter is to some extent equivalent to presenting much information, as we noted in Chapter 4: closely similar stimuli take longer to produce reactions, and interfere more with other tasks, just as stimuli of high information content do. Moreover, decreasing the magnitude of differences in one dimension may well lower the priority of that dimension for passing the filter, just as decreasing the magnitude of an isolated stimulus does. It is thus very plausible on a filter theory that reversed pre-training should sometimes show an effect but on other occasions cease to do so. No other view seems to give an adequate account of the different results of different experiments: Blum and Blum (1949) make an attempt to do so, but it does not seem altogether satisfactory (Broadbent 1959). Ehrenfreund (1948) showed that placement of the correct stimuli relative to the animal's senses may affect the appearance of continuity learning, reversed pre-training only having an effect if the stimuli were in a prominent position. This is sometimes referred to as supporting continuity theory, but it merely illustrates that some stimuli are more likely to pass the filter than others.

Thus there is a fair amount of evidence for the operation of a filter in animal learning; the phenomena which it produces are recognized in the Hullian system by the postulates of stimulus dynamism and interaction, and an account of them merely expands that system without contradicting it. One may regret that animal psychologists have been so little interested in amplifying these postulates and have largely confined themselves to instrumental rather than classical conditioning. Pavlov's data are not by modern standards adequate, and it should be possible to shed much light on perception by studying the stimuli which are most likely to overshadow others, the effect of small time intervals between stimuli, and so on. All this may well be admitted by reinforcement theorists without compromising their own position.

## Filter Theory as a Substitute for Reinforcement

Since there is likely to be a filter selecting the stimuli which are and are not used for learning, can the reinforcement postulate be dropped for the sake of parsimony? We said that intense or novel stimuli are likely to pass the filter and that some kinds of stimuli (such as high frequency sounds in man) also possess a high priority. It is difficult to avoid supposing that an animal in a ' drive ' state, e.g. one of food deprivation, has a temporary modification of the filter, such that reinforcing stimuli (food, in the example) are particularly likely to pass the filter. If now we suppose that some mechanism within the organism stores the conditional probabilities of all events about which information passes the filter, it is clear that the repeated association of two intense stimuli is likely to be stored. So also it is likely that all conditional probabilities involving ' reinforcing ' stimuli will stand a good chance of being stored. If $X$ is always followed by $Z$ in the outside world, the stored conditional probability of $Z$ when $X$ has occurred will depend on the number of occasions on which $Z$ has passed the filter when $X$ has done so. A high priority for $Z$ will mean that whenever $X$ passes the filter $Z$ will also be likely to do so if it occurs, and therefore the stored probability of $Z$ given $X$ will be high. This is true even if $X$ has rather a low probability, since when $X$ is rejected by the filter on one of its occurrences that does not affect the stored probabilities of all other events given $X$. But if the priority of $Z$ is low, the frequent occurrence of $X$ and $Z$ in close proximity in the outside world will not necessarily result in a high stored probability of $Z$ given $X$; for if $X$ passes the filter on one of its occurrences $Z$ may well fail to do so, and the relationship will therefore not be stored.

Thus it follows that the events associated with reinforcers will be learned, and those which are followed by events of lower priority will not be learned. In the main, this will give behaviour similar to that to be expected on reinforcement theory; presenting reinforcement will greatly facilitate learning. But there will be exceptions, since events which succeed in passing the filter will be stored even though they are not reinforcers. Thus the probability of an end-box stimulus following a right turn in a maze and an alley-wall stimulus following a left turn will be stored after exploration of the maze; introduction of reward will then improve performance considerably. Presenting two stimuli in sequence may give the second a high probability following the first, so that attachment of the second to a conditioned response will cause that response to appear to the first stimulus. In this case, however, care must be taken to avoid rejection of either stimulus by the filter. They must be reasonably intense and novel events: the repeated presentation alone may be sufficient to cause rejection of the events by the filter. Sensory pre-conditioning will therefore be rather difficult to establish, as indeed it is (Reid 1952).

Partial reinforcement affords no difficulty: response may be supposed simply to keep step with the instantaneous probability of reinforcement following response. As some responses are closely followed by reinforcement, information on them and on the reinforcement will pass the filter and the corresponding conditional probability be stored. A low ratio of reinforcement will naturally raise the conditional probability slowly, and so cause slow conditioning: if reinforcement is given at set infrequent time intervals the response rate will be slow. If on the other hand the reinforcement is given after a certain number of responses the rate will be high in order to achieve the situation in which reinforcement is highly probable. (A more careful account of the relation between probability of reinforcement and response rate will be given later.) Corresponding to the slow acquisition of response the rate of extinction will be low, since omissions of reinforcement will have little effect on conditional probability in a case where the numbers of responses concerned are much greater than they are in high ratios of reinforcement. To take a hypothetical example, after ten reinforced responses the probability of reinforcement following response is unity. After ten responses followed by reinforcement interspersed among ninety unreinforced responses, the probability of reinforcement following response is one-tenth. In the first case two unreinforced responses lower the probability to five-sixths, a fall of a sixth. In the second case, twenty unreinforced responses lower the probability from one-tenth to one-twelfth, a fall of a sixtieth. As changes in the conditional probability are slower, then, following partial rein-forcement, extinction is naturally more difficult. The low rate of responding immediately following each reinforcement also fits this interpretation well, while being contrary to a simple view of reinforcement theory: essentially however the statement that the rate of responding drops at that time because the probability of reinforcement is then low, is the same as the statement that response is attached to the stimuli produced by many unreinforced responses, such stimuli having always been present when reinforcement was given.   Orthodox S–R theory can thus explain partial reinforcement; but the advantage of filter theory is that it can explain partial reinforcement without losing sight of the fact that in most everyday cases response strength does vary with the amount of reinforcement.   Reinforcement theory requires the persistence of stimuli due to past responses in this case; yet if such persistence were to occur in situations other than the partial reinforcement one, all responses would be established primarily to the traces of previous unreinforced ones and so would occur most readily following a sequence of ' useless ' actions.   This does not seem to happen.   Filter theory provides an explanation of the difference between the partial reinforcement situation and others;   by emphasizing the similarity of the response which is ultimately reinforced and those which must be counted to assess the probability of reinforcement.   As bar-pressing is the response which is reinforced, the filter passes information about the occurrence of bar-presses even when they are not reinforced;   the performance of a long sequence of different responses followed by one reinforcement at the end of the sequence would be more difficult to establish than the sequence of similar responses used in the Skinner box.   However, some similar explanation can probably be translated into the language of reinforcement theory.

Various features of latent learning are explicable on the view we have been putting forward.   For instance, if the drive state of an animal is increased, the filter will presumably reject stimuli irrelevant to that drive even more firmly.   Information about water may have a reasonable priority for a rat satiated for all drives, and so pass the filter if the animal is given enough explora-tion time.   But a hungry rat will have a higher priority for food information, and therefore a lower priority for water information: the filter will be more likely to pass the former and therefore to reject the latter.   If therefore a latent learning experiment is done in which the animal runs a maze for food reward while water is in the maze, and if the next day the animal is made thirsty, the probability of correct response will be lower if the hunger on the first day is greater.   This does seem to be the case: at one time there was even a belief that latent learning could not be shown at all by animals under strong drives; even though this has had to be modified, it still seems to be easier to show the effect with weak drives. (Much of the literature, at least up to the date of the review, is given by Thistlethwaite 1951; Kendler 1952, and Thistlethwaite 1952 should also be read with this reference.)

Other factors which hinder the appearance of latent learning in T-mazes are those of asymmetry. If the animals have strong position habits, regularly turning right or left, it is difficult to make them show latent learning. So also is it difficult when the reward used in the preliminary training is placed on one side only of the T-maze, rather than both. And some experiments using black and white alleys have failed to show latent learning: which may have been owing to the marked preference of rats for black alleys. All these relationships harmonize with filter theory: if other information has a high priority for passing the filter, the information about the reinforcer which will be required in the crucial runs has a lower probability of entering the store. Systematic responses thus suggest that latent learning will be slight. Equally it is important not only that the animal should enter a particular alley but that the corresponding information should pass the filter: thus, forcing the rat into particular alleys by mechanical means seems to produce less learning than allowing the animal to make its own choices, which ensures that information is passing the filter.

The various conditions given by Thistlethwaite (1951) as favouring latent learning all therefore seem to be readily explicable from the point of view of filter theory. So may they be to reinforcement theory, given sufficient extra postulates. The main reason for preferring the former view is simply one of parsimony: we must have a filter to account for the phenomena admitted by reinforcement theorists under the headings of stimulus dynamism and interaction. Why therefore must we also have a reinforcement postulate if the filter alone will do the work?

To this advocates of reinforcement theory may well counter that our formulation is inferior on other grounds of scientific style. The fact that it is non-quantitative, and inductive rather than hypothetico-deductive will be considered in Chapter 12. We must deal now with the more serious criticism that it explains only part of the facts: it speaks of selecting part of the incoming information, but it offers no scheme to explain what happens to that information once selected. It may be an acceptable view scientifically that some part of the brain has a number of possible states, that each of these states corresponds to a particular conditional probability of one event when another has occurred, and that in consequence the actual conditional probability is reflected in the state of the brain. But, the reinforcement theorist may argue, unless some way is specified for this probability to issue in response, the whole approach depends on anthropomorphism. It will be forced to postulate some unexplained process which decides on the response having been provided with the conditional probabilities: in short, a ' little man '. If this criticism were true it would be a serious one, since it would mean that the problem had simply been pushed farther back into the nervous system. It is the hint of such a defeatist approach which seems to upset S–R theorists when faced with the use of terms such as 'expectancy' or 'consciousness'. (Consider, for instance, the views of Jenkins and Stanley (1950) on an expectancy interpretation of partial reinforcement.) The writer would agree that our problems are not to be solved by giving them anthropomorphic names; but this does not mean that a theory based on conditional probabilities need fall under such a criticism. Let us now turn to recent attempts to describe the process of selecting response when conditional probabilities are stored within the nervous system.

*Theories of Response*

Uttley (1955) puts forward a simple account of the manner in which a response may occur when it and no other is followed by reward. If, say, a bell rings and the animal is given food provided it raises its paw, the simple theories we have considered so far will not explain the paw-raising. Uttley says that the combined probability of bell, food, and paw-raising becomes high. If then the bell is objectively present and the sensory mechanisms corresponding to food are activated from within the animal (' drive '), the occurrence of paw-lifting will have a high probability and this may be assumed linked to effector systems which will ensure that it does occur.

This theory is highly simplified, and ignores order effects:

in training the food may follow the response, while in the appearance of the learned response arousal of the drive precedes response.  The nervous system must also be able to distinguish between actual occurrence of a response and inferred occurrence; if these two are different it is not clear how the animal takes the step from one to another.  To make this point clearer, it is as though the animal had observed frequently in the past that bell, food, and response occurred together and so when food and response appear it infers that the bell is going to ring.  Yet it takes no action to produce the ringing.  If bell and food occur together it may predict its own response, but why should it take action to produce that response ?  These are really detail points, which do not seem to have been expanded by Uttley himself, who is more concerned with the assessment of probabilities involved.

Deutsch (1953, 1956) has gone further into the production of sequences of behaviour.  His system is still developing, and may have changed further before this book appears, but the early presentations provide sufficient for our purpose.  The first gives an account of simple behaviour sequences and the second a modified account of complex sequences such as those in insightful learning.  For simplicity it is easiest to consider the earlier system first: consider, say, the sequence of behaviour involved in some instinctive activity such as the courtship of lower animals.

Deutsch postulates a row of ' links ' in the nervous system to explain each such behaviour sequence.  A link is a functional unit, that is, its physiological structure is unspecified and it is defined merely by its functions.  The link at one end of the row is activated by, say, changes in the chemical constituency of the blood, and the activation spreads along the row.  If a link is activated and there is no further link in the row to which it can transmit this activity, the motor output of the organism is varied.  To each link there is attached an ' analyser ', which is a complete neural system for recognizing some environmental situation.  When that situation occurs the analyser fires, and this switches off the attached link.

A moment's thought will show that the effect of this is as follows: if an animal is in the physiological state appropriate for mating, a row of links will be active.  The link at the end of this row farthest from that aroused physiologically will be, say, the link corresponding to an analyser set for the sight of a female.  Various kinds of behaviour will appear, not necessarily random muscle contractions but fairly complex organized activities such as locomotion, calling, and so on.  As these activities vary the environment, it will sooner or later happen that a female appears and the last link in the row will be switched off.  This leaves the next link in the row active: its analyser may correspond to the sensory pattern produced by a display posture on the part of the male.  He therefore behaves in a variety of ways until he takes up this display posture, which switches off that link. The next may be attached to an analyser for some particular posture on the part of the female, and the male will not proceed further with mating until she provides this stimulus.  When she does, the next link to be active may be that attached to an analyser for another posture on the part of the male, and activity will proceed until this posture is taken up.  In this way the animal will proceed through a series of situations, continually ' seeking ' the next step in the chain.  By ' seeking ' one means merely that varied activity will persist until that step is reached. As it is supposed that the motor output present when an analyser fires off will be the first to occur when the corresponding link next controls output, an animal which has proceeded through the sequence once will do so smoothly and rapidly in the future.

The system can be applied to learned sequences, by supposing that rows of links are formed by the ordered stimulation of corresponding analysers, the final stimulation of an analyser already attached to a row joining the new portion on to that already existing.  Thus if, say, the sequence of events corresponding to the path through a maze terminates in the sight of food, activation of the hunger drive will cause seeking of the entrance to the maze and, if given opportunity, running of the maze.  (It will of course be noticed that if an analyser halfway along the row fires this means that the sequence will proceed from that point, as the switching off of the link cuts off the more remote parts of the row; a trained animal shown a female does not ignore her and seek the beginning of the maze.  There may however be some preference for a previously traversed sequence rather than some fresh way of reaching the consummatory situation, subject to the results of spontaneous alternation experiments.)

The postulates already mentioned have certain disadvantages. Thus if an animal runs a maze in one direction its output will be in exactly the wrong sense for rapid running in the reverse direction: although the maze will ultimately be traversed in reverse if there is some motive for doing so, progress should be extraordinarily slow. This does not agree with experience. Furthermore, learning a maze under one incentive should not assist performance with a fresh incentive, which is of course not the case. A rat taught to run to food when hungry will also run to water when thirsty. The second version of the theory avoids these difficulties, and also accounts for insight, latent learning, and similar phenomena.

There are two types of alteration in the postulates. First, analysers are now supposed to fire in varying degrees according to the strength of the corresponding stimulation. Motor output controlled by the end link remains the same as long as the corresponding analyser is firing to an increasing extent: it varies only when the firing is decreasing. The animal is thus ' sucked in ' towards the stimulus corresponding to the analyser of the end link. If during this process the analyser of a link closer to the other end of the row is stimulated, that link decreases the amount of activity it transmits and increases its control of the motor output. To go back to our original example, the animal might when first aroused indulge in random activity until he caught the scent of a female, and then proceed in such a way that the scent became stronger. But he does not go on blindly until the scent reaches maximum intensity, because as soon as he sees the female this reduces the importance of scent and increases that of sight. Furthermore, stimulation of an analyser $A$ without stimulation of the next one $B$ shortly afterwards decreases the sensitivity of the link $A$ to activation by $B$: so that the animal will not go on for ever trying to proceed by a blocked path if there is some other open to it.

The second group of alterations concern the possibility of spread of activity from row to row. It is supposed that when an analyser is common to two links on different rows any activation of one link spreads through to the other. This takes care of one of the difficulties mentioned earlier: if, for example, an animal has learned a maze for food reward, it is only necessary to attach the end-box analyser to the water analyser for the benefits of previous training to be used in running to water: the end-box analyser being in common to the row based on hunger and the new row based on thirst. The difficulty of, for instance, retracing is met by the first set of alterations to the postulates; if an output which causes decrease in the next stimulus is immediately suspended progress along a row in either direction should be fast. To use engineering terms, the feedback loop is much tighter in the later set of postulates.

The great advantage of this system over S–R ones is that it accounts for the appetitive character of behaviour, the tendency to produce smooth and immediate shifts in motor output to preserve a constant sequence of stimulation even though the environment is abnormal. It has long been known, for instance, that an animal taught a maze by one form of response will perform it by some other form: that is, if it ran through the maze during training it will swim through it if the maze is filled with water. It has even been reported recently by Gleitman (1955) and confirmed by McNamara, Long and Wike (1956) that animals pulled through a maze as passengers will run through it correctly on subsequent trials. Such learning may well be inferior, however, to a training technique which ensured that information did enter the nervous system: in our terms, that the filter selected the relevant information, or in Deutsch's that the links were in fact switched off in the right sequence. These cases of ' response equivalence ' are easily and neatly handled by Deutsch's theory. Of course with a sufficient degree of complication the same explanation may be framed in S–R terms. One might suggest that each stimulus produces random responses of which the ones leading to the secondary reinforcement of the next stimulus are made more probable: the final responses to the last stimuli in the series are given the primary reinforcement of, say, food. The phrasing does not matter, save that Deutsch's is far more convenient and concentrates attention on the essential aspects of the process. S–R language implies largely an open-chain type of system (in engineering terms) while systems of the closed-loop type seem more likely biologically. The closed-loop type of system is used in engineering practice to provide response equivalence: we prefer not to insert a simple heating system in a building, since on a warm or cold day that would give an undesired result. Instead we may insert a thermostat-controlled heating system which will adjust the level to a desirable temperature no matter what the abnormalities of the environment. (For cheapness we may use ourselves as the sensitive element in the thermostat, poking the fire if we feel cold and letting it go low if we are warm, but the principle is the same.) Similarly it seems likely that biological systems are of the closed-loop type, producing behaviour appropriate to securing particular stimulation. Deutsch's terminology is also useful in considering the effect of, say, stimulating taste-receptors while not allowing food to enter the stomach. This type of experiment has been performed a good deal lately, and readily fits into the scheme proposed (Deutsch 1953).

Some thought will show the reader that a system of this type would develop in a trained animal into a mesh of analysers ordered in a manner corresponding to the ordering in space and time of the environment. Rows of links would run in all directions across this mesh, with the result that introducing a reward at any point would immediately activate links corresponding to distant analysers. If the animal was then placed near the stimuli corresponding to such analysers it would find its way to the reward: latent learning. Under some circumstances it may fail to do this. For instance, if there is a two-choice maze in which the animal has been run when hungry and if there are similar stimuli in both alleys but water in only one alley, making the animal thirsty will produce activation of the various links starting from that corresponding to water. Because some analysers are in common to both alleys, there will be transfer of activation to the other alley and so along the row corresponding to it. At the choice-point there may be little difference between the activation of the end-links corresponding to the two paths, and the animal may therefore take the wrong turning. This type of failure will be less likely if the water is very near the choice-point and the stimuli common to the two alleys are in the end-boxes; and Deutsch (1956) cites experiments which show that this is so.

The bad effects of asymmetric reward on latent learning are also intelligible on this system. If food is placed in one alley only, a hungry animal will firmly attach the links corresponding to that alley into a row, while the links for the other alley will have higher thresholds for activation passing from one to another. If there is water in the other alley, making the animal thirsty will produce activation not only of the row for that alley, but also of the food alley through common analysers. As the thresholds between links in the food alley are low, the activation will spread along that row more completely and at the choice-point the food alley may actually be the one to secure response. Deutsch points out that this damaging effect from strong irrelevant motivation on latent learning should only apply if the irrelevant drive is in fact rewarded: Strange (1950) found latent learning of the position of food after exposure of the maze given to thirsty rats without any water reward. Gleitman (1950) did not do so, however, and the discrepancy is not explained.

## On the Relation Between Various Theories

Deutsch's views are of importance as providing the link between stored representations of the order of events in the environment on the one hand, and response on the other. He is concerned largely with behaviour sequences such as maze running, and less with the effects of temporal sequences of stimuli such as those in classical conditioning, or with levels of reinforcement less than 100 per cent. His interests therefore are different to those of Uttley, but the two views are complementary. We may introduce Uttley's contribution into Deutsch's system by supposing that the thresholds between two links are an inverse measure of the probability of one analyser firing after the other in the past history of the animal. Thus in, say, the partial reinforcement situation the activity of the link whose analyser corresponds to ' stimuli resulting from bar-pressing ' will be greater when food is more probable and less when it is less probable. As we saw earlier, this will give behaviour the characteristics which it does have in the partial reinforcement situation. The assessment of probabilities will carry with it the other consequences mentioned in Uttley's views: in particular, the relative roles of recent and remotely past stimuli will be different.   Deutsch notes (1956, p. 124) that there are certain phenomena such as those of delayed reaction which he does not cover.

This combined Uttley-Deutsch approach has some limitations, even so.   Both theories require an enormous capacity for the nervous system if all the information reaching the sense-organs is to be stored.   And neither claims to cover the various experiments on filtering of incoming information, which we have discussed previously.   There is no reason, however, why the storage of conditional probabilities and the production of responses in such a way as to produce a sequence of stimuli terminating in reinforcement, should not be supplemented by a selective operation on the incoming information.   There remains the question of the role of such a filter in the explanation of particular experiments: as we have seen, Uttley's view explains some facts which filter theory also explained.   In some cases, such as induction, the view that the reported behaviour was the result of the conditional probability of the various stimuli seemed probable.   In other cases filter theory was the more satisfactory: for instance, disinhibition seemed likely to be due to dominance over the short-term storage system by some irrelevant stimulus, so that the long-term storage system became the prime factor in determining response.   There are some similar cases of overlap between Deutsch's views and those of filter theory, and these must now be considered.

In the first place, some of the facts about latent learning which Deutsch explains were also accounted for by filter theory: notably the effect of asymmetrical reward.   It certainly seems fair to explain the failure of latent learning, when alleys have many stimuli in common, by a spread of excitation from one alley to another: but it seems a little unsatisfactory also to postulate spread of excitation when the alleys do not have food stimuli in common.   Furthermore the case of asymmetry of reward seems highly similar to those of asymmetry of position habits and of asymmetry of colour of alleys.   Deutsch might perhaps explain these effects also by the lowering of thresholds between links in the favoured alley, since the fact that it was favoured showed that it led to some kind of reinforcement: but asymmetry of these other kinds differs from asymmetry of reward in one respect. Asymmetric reward is of course always given in the alley opposite to that which contains the incentive which will become relevant in the trials to test for latent learning. But position and colour are independent of the other factors and therefore may sometimes favour the alley which an animal should choose if it is to show latent learning. So Deutsch's interpretation does not seem so applicable to colour and position asymmetry. Rather one might describe the facts as showing that the animals are under the control of a row of links, which does not include analysers for the information which interests the experimenter: and therefore that this information is not stored.

This brings us to a more analytic examination of the points of contact of this theory and of filter theory. If the two are to be combined, it will mean that the firing of some analysers in Deutsch's scheme is incompatible with that of others. Or at least that the effect of that firing on the inter-connection of links is non-existent: the information strikes the sensory system but is not stored. This does appear to be provided for in Deutsch's postulates (1956, p. 118). The threshold of excitation of a link is a function, not of successive firings of the analyser on that link and that on the next link, but of the number of times the link has been switched off. This presupposes not only a sequence of stimuli but also the activation of the row of links. Unless the row is activated, unless information of that type is being selected, it will not be stored.

As the postulates are stated at the time of writing (it must be remembered that they may have changed by the time this is read) they might be mistaken for a reinforcement theory. The attachment of ordered analysers to links is said only to take place when an analyser already attached to a row is fired. But it is not essential to the system that no ordering of analysers should take place unless primary or secondary reinforcement follows it. One might rather deduce from the postulates that ordering of analysers would occur in any case but that the importance of reinforcement was in the attachment of the freshly ordered analysers to rows which were liable to activation. Unless a row is attached to such an active row, the probability of sequential stimulation of the analysers while the corresponding links are active is low; and therefore the threshold for excitation passing from one link to the next will remain high. If this deduction were made the theory would become, like filter theory, one in which reward adds to the probability of learning but is not essential to it.

We might, then, escape the difficulty of interpreting failure of latent learning with asymmetric cues. Our final argument would be in this form: incoming information is selected on the basis of its own qualities (intensity, novelty, and the hierarchy of different senses) and of the motivational state of the system. That is, information of the type appropriate to any analyser attached to a link on an active row has a high priority. In the latent learning case, a tendency of the animal to respond to colour or position of the alleys during preliminary training implies that a row of links attached to analysers for these characteristics is active. Therefore information of other kinds is less likely to pass the filter and establish a representation in which its relation to the choice-point is correctly preserved. Unless such an interpretation of Deutsch's theory is adopted it is quite difficult to decide precisely how the asymmetric cases of latent learning (and the ill effects of forced choice) should be explained. But in general the arguments for filtering of information are not from the same field as those for Deutsch's system: the two approaches are almost completely complementary rather than competitive.

We have thus reached a satisfactory combination of three views: filter theory stating the information which enters the store, Uttley's theory dealing with the relative strengths of the attachments between different events on which information has passed the filter, and Deutsch's dealing with the production of a response by this storage system when a drive is applied to the animal. A word should also be said here about the relation of this combined approach to earlier theories, which have been somewhat neglected in our own presentation. We have considered the general merits of a cybernetic approach to some extent in Chapter 3, and will return to its advantages in Chapter 12. Here, however, it is desirable to pay due respect to other approaches.

To a great extent the S–R approach is a language in which factually different theories may be expressed. Thus although the view given in this chapter is different from that given in Hull's *Principles of Behavior* it does not follow that a view like the present one could not be expressed in S–R terms. Some aspects of Berlyne's approach (1951) do indeed seem to provide such an expression: the views of Spence, quoted by Hilgard (1956, pp. 414–19) from personal communication, are also related to this approach. The objection to using S–R terms is one of convenience and not one of essence. For instance, if one supposes that the selective nature of perception is due to the establishment of an internal response incompatible with certain other internal responses, one may be led into supposing that the principles governing the habit strengths of such internal responses are the same as those governing external responses. With careful formulation this danger may be avoided, but it seems a useful device to keep the words ' stimulus ' and ' response ' for observables, and to speak of ' information ' when drawing legitimate inferences about unobservables. The choice of a different language does not imply contempt for the past achievements of S–R theorists: on the contrary their emphasis on the selective nature of learning and on the necessity for objective phraseology has been of great value. Furthermore there is much in behaviour which falls outside the scope of the topics we have discussed, but on which our knowledge is purely due to S–R theorists.

Perhaps the closest historical connexion with the present view of animal behaviour is that of the Tolmanist approach. Many of the arguments we have used are familiar to those who have read the writings of cognitive theorists: if we have omitted to cite these writings, it is deliberate rather than an oversight. The reason is simply one of presentation. The use of words derived from human experience (such as ' cognition ') has, in the writer's belief, emphasized genuine weaknesses in behaviour theory. But the vagueness and anthropomorphic associations of these words have offended some people to such an extent that they have neglected the validity of Tolmanist criticism. Furthermore the difficulty of demonstrating learning without reinforcement is itself a sign that Tolmanism has underemphasized the importance of that factor in learning as well as in performance. Neither learning nor performance depend completely upon reinforcement, but both are facilitated by it.

By adopting different terms, it may be hoped that we have avoided the emotional reactions which are sometimes aroused by the phrases of cognitive theorists: each of the three sections of the present view has in fact been embodied in a mechanical model (Broadbent 1957d; Uttley 1955; Deutsch 1954). It can hardly be urged that such views are mystical or incapable of physical realization. What merits they have are undoubtedly based, however, on previous work both of cognitive and of S–R theorists. This is as it should be in science.

# CHAPTER 11

# RECENT VIEWS ON SKILL

IN the last chapter we tried to fit our views into a general approach to animal behaviour; in the present one we will do the same for human skilled behaviour. Both cases are not described in as much detail as they would merit if we were not principally concerned with the theory of attention. There are a good many fields of research on skill which do come into contact with the topics we have discussed: but there are of course other aspects which we shall leave unmentioned.

*Refractoriness*

The first topic which deserves mention is that of ' the psychological refractory period '. The basic observation which has produced interest in this subject is that when two stimuli are presented for reaction the time taken to respond to the second stimulus is sometimes unduly long when the stimuli occur close together in time. The earlier experiments on the subject have been reviewed by Welford (1952): following the distinction made by Davis (1956a) we may say that the evidence falls into three categories. There are experiments on continuous tracking of a moving target, in which corrections are made by the operator at his own discretion. These corrections are usually made at intervals no closer together than $\frac{1}{2}$ sec (Craik 1948). There are also experiments on step-tracking: that is, distinct movements of definite length. Here the operator may be following a straight line with a pencil, and be faced with a sudden jump in the line to a new position parallel to the first. He has to move the pencil over to the new position: it is found that if another step back to the original position is required less than roughly $\frac{1}{2}$ sec after the first, the second response is delayed (Vince 1948). Thirdly there are experiments on ungraded responses (such as key-pressing in which movement need not be exactly controlled), or on the stopping of movements. For instance, simple key-pressing reactions to sounds, with varying intervals between the stimuli, have been reported as showing slow response when the stimuli are only $\frac{1}{2}$ sec apart (Telford 1931). The stopping of a movement which is carried out in zig-zag fashion along a double row of contacts may be difficult if only $\frac{1}{3}$ sec is allowed between the signal and the time at which the contact is reached where movement is to be stopped (Poulton 1950). It is possible, however, if twice that interval is allowed.

There is further and later evidence which casts doubt on the generality of each of these conclusions. It will be easiest to consider it while examining the various theories advanced to explain the results.

The theory which deserves first consideration is that formulated by Welford (1952). He contended that the results were due to ' the central processes concerned with two separate stimuli not being able to co-exist '. As they would take a definite time for each stimulus, the process concerned with the second stimulus could not begin until after that for the first stimulus had ended. The time between the arrival of the second stimulus and the end of the central processes for the first stimulus would then be added on to the reaction time for the second stimulus. This would only account, however, for delays when the two stimuli were separated by less than one reaction time. Delays were reported, as mentioned earlier, with intervals as long as $\frac{1}{2}$ sec, and these could not be due to any ' organizing time ' for the first reaction. A suggestion of Hick was therefore adopted by Welford; he argued that with many responses feed-back information on the performance of the response was necessary, and would occupy the same nervous mechanism as that concerned with stimuli from the outer world. Thus for short periods after key-points in the response (such as the beginning and end of the step-movements of the pencil in the experiments mentioned earlier) the second incoming stimulus would not be handled.

This means that if a man is following a line with a pencil, and a step to a new position appears, there will be a short delay before the pencil begins to move up. If a second step reversing the first appears during the delay, the pencil will begin to move up, but will then reverse the movement after an interval of one reaction time from the start of the movement. This is the normal refractoriness appearing with inter-signal intervals of less than one reaction time.   But if the inter-signal interval is slightly longer, if the second step occurs just after the beginning of the movement, the ' central processes ' will be occupied with feed-back information and the reversal of the movement will not occur until one reaction-time from the end of the time spent on feed-back information.   A similar situation will apply just after the end of the movement.   Thus there will be three values of the inter-signal interval at which the second stimulus will give long reaction times.   One will be at very small values, one at values just longer than one reaction time, and the third at values just longer than one reaction-time plus the time taken to reach the end of the movement.   In between these points there will be two values of the inter-signal interval at which the second signal will have a nearly normal reaction-time: when it occurs just before the start of the movement, and when it occurs just before the end.   Welford (1952, p. 6) shows that this is in fact the case. He noted that practised subjects may dispense with the feed-back information, especially in ungraded responses (1952, p. 16). This must indeed be true in such experiments as those of Quastler (1956) on the maximum rate of transmission of information through the man: in those results signals are being dealt with much faster than two a second.   Davis (1956a) has confirmed that two stimuli separated by more than one reaction-time may each show normal reaction-times on highly practised subjects, using key-pressing responses.   He did find the delay, with a second stimulus occurring during the first reaction-time, which Welford would predict.

Another point which Welford considers (1952, p. 8) and which we shall see to be important in connexion with the next theory, is the effect of extremely small intervals between two stimuli. When such intervals are present, the second reaction-time may be normal: the first reaction-time under such circumstances is likely to be longer than usual.   Welford suggests that this may occur either because response is deliberately withheld for a short time to ensure that no second stimulus is about to arrive; or because some irrelevant central activity occupies the analysing mechanism until a short period after the first stimulus has arrived. If the second stimulus occurs during this time reactions to both stimuli may be initiated together.   Davis (1956a) did not find any such ' grouping ' of stimuli, the delay in the second response being longest when the two stimuli were simultaneous. He also found no negative correlation between reaction times to the two stimuli. However, the phenomenon is well-established by other results: its absence in this case is perhaps due to the fact that Davis's two practised subjects were always required to respond first with one key and then with the other, so that the order of response was well established. They were also instructed to respond rapidly to the first stimulus without voluntary delays, and their results showed that they obeyed this instruction. This might well exclude both the mechanisms suggested by Welford as producing ' grouping '. The absence of negative correlations, incidentally, is not crucial since very long pauses before the two responses were initiated would cause both to give long reaction times.

This theory is clearly of great interest to us. It supposes what is essentially a perceptual system of limited capacity. Although the original formulation was in terms of stimuli, their probability was intended also to be relevant (Hick and Welford 1956). The central organizing time for highly probable stimuli is supposed shorter than that for improbable ones, and thus the limitation is essentially one of rate of handling information. The theory also requires a short-term store for information arriving while the perceptual system is fully occupied. Both these requirements we have supposed in our own approach for other reasons, and this helps to strengthen our confidence in Welford's theory. There are, however, two slight difficulties which suggest that modifications to the theory may be necessary. One is the question of grouping already mentioned. Welford's plausible interpretations of the phenomenon were put forward in the older framework of stimulus and response, and not in informational terms. The two stimuli contribute no less information even if the perceptual system delayed handling the first of them until after the second had arrived. How, then, can the second be undelayed ? This objection cannot be met by suggesting that the information from the first stimulus is delayed sufficiently to allow that from the second to be undelayed: with a limited capacity channel and a normal second reaction time this should mean that the response to the first stimulus will be the second to occur, which has not been reported. It might be the case, however, in the step-tracking experiments in which the second response is the opposite to the first. Much of the evidence for grouping comes from such experiments, since sometimes in such a situation there may be no response if the two stimuli are separated by only a very small time interval. This might be regarded as the second response appearing first. We will consider another interpretation later.

The second difficulty comes from the fact that much of the time elapsing between stimulus and response is due to peripheral processes. The information must travel from the senses to the brain, and from the brain to the muscles. There seems no reason why the latter time for the first response should not overlap the former time for the second response. It is only the central processes which can be supposed incapable of dealing with both items of information simultaneously, as Welford himself says (1952, p. 3). Yet the amount of delay for the second stimulus can be calculated by supposing that it cannot occur before two full reaction times after the first stimulus. That is

$$RT_2 = 2RT_1 - I$$

where  $RT_1$ = reaction time to first stimulus
$RT_2$ = reaction time to second stimulus
$I$ = interval between stimuli

$$I < RT_1 \text{ (When } I > RT_1, RT_2 = RT_1).$$

This is confirmed by Davis (1956a). In other words the amount of delay of the second reaction is larger than can be accounted for by the time taken by the central processes alone in dealing with the first stimulus.

Leaving this difficulty in the air, we will now proceed to the second theory. This is the parsimonious view that all the results can be accounted for by the instantaneous probability of the stimuli: the second stimulus does not usually arrive immediately after the first, so when that event does occur the response time is long. The possibility seems to have been first put forward by Poulton (1950) and was also adopted by Elithorn and Lawrence (1956). Neither of these papers provide experimental evidence which is completely crucial. Poulton showed, as mentioned earlier, that an unexpected signal to stop a movement took longer to have its effect than the signal to start the movement. The latter was preceded by a warning signal and so was expected. As Welford (1952, p. 10) points out, the possibility is not excluded that the central mechanisms are occupied by feed-back information when a movement is in progress. But in any event, all theories stated in informational terms take the probability of the stimulus into account, so that demonstrating its importance is no blow to such theories. The question at issue is whether an additional delay occurs with small inter-signal intervals.

Elithorn and Lawrence used two light signals, one on each side of a fixation point, and the right and left hands for the corresponding responses. After a warning signal either the right or left stimulus arrived ½ sec later. The other stimulus occurred after a further interval varying from 0 to 0·95 sec. Response times to the first stimulus were not reported: those to the second were fast at extremely short intervals, slow at about 0·1 sec, and then increasingly faster. There was some sign of further slowing at the very longest intervals.

Their discussion of these results was unhappily worded. In the first place they contrasted expectancy theory with Welford's approach, although as Hick and Welford (1956) point out Welford's theory was itself an expectancy one so that this was a false antithesis. Secondly they referred to the occurrence of the first stimulus as lowering the probability of the one on the other side. Both Hick and Welford, and also Davis (1956b), seized on this point, for it is undoubtedly fallacious. The temporal uncertainty of the stimulus on the other side remains unchanged: and the probability that the next event will be on the other side is actually raised. Despite the validity of this criticism, Elithorn and Lawrence appear to have in mind a theory to which the criticism does not apply. They have merely used an unfortunate phrase to express it.

The essence of their position is that different stimulus-response processes can co-exist: in information theory terms, this may be translated as the contention that human beings can operate as several parallel and independent channels rather than as only one. When operating as two independent channels, reaction time to a stimulus is determined solely by the probability of that stimulus, and unaffected by the processes in the other channel. If we now consider the distribution of time intervals between the warning signal and the occurrence of, say, the right-hand light, we find that on 55 per cent of trials, that light went on $\frac{1}{2}$ sec after the warning signal. The remaining 45 per cent of trials were evenly divided between nine longer time intervals. This means that if we determine the probability of a stimulus occurring at a given time interval provided that it has not occurred at any shorter interval, the resulting cumulative probability is high for the shortest interval, then low, and then increasingly high. This variation of temporal uncertainty is entirely independent of events in the other channel. As reaction time does follow this probability, Elithorn and Lawrence's results are perfectly in accordance with the hypothesis that the man is operating as two independent channels (though also as we shall see consistent with the single channel view). Our belief that this is the core of their argument is strengthened by the fact that they do plot the distribution of stimuli at different intervals after the warning signal on one side alone (p. 126).

How far can this interpretation be applied to the earlier experiments? In general stimuli have come from the same source rather than from different sources and very short inter-signal intervals have been no more frequent than those of any other length. Thus the cumulative probability of a signal given that one has not already occurred will increase with time since the first signal, and the shortest interval should give the longest reaction time and so apparently provide evidence for refractoriness. On the other hand, Davis (1956a) pointed out that the longest intervals did not give the shortest reaction times either in his results or in those of Elithorn and Lawrence: and that there was no independent evidence that reaction time would follow the cumulative probability of a signal over a range of fore-periods in the way postulated. Mowrer (1940) had indeed shown that, when one length of fore-period was more common than any other, reaction time was shorter than at any other value of fore-period; but this affords no evidence for the case when all fore-periods are equally frequent.

We might expect, however, an analogy with other psycho-physical judgements. In these, judgements are often biassed towards a 'level of adaptation' which is the middle of the presented range when all values in the range are given equally frequently. When one value is given more frequently, the level of adaptation shifts towards it (Helson 1948). Thus we might expect the subjective estimate of the distribution of a range of time intervals (occurring objectively with equal frequency) to be peaked in the middle of the range. If one interval is given more often than the others, the peak of the subjective distribution would lie between the mid-point of the range and the most common interval.

We might expect then that if a signal is given after a warning signal, and if several different time intervals are used equally frequently, reaction time will follow a compromise course between two extremes. On the one hand, there will be a tendency for the reaction to become faster as the interval becomes longer, since on any one trial the probability of a signal given no previous one is higher as the interval is longer. On the other hand, there will be a tendency for reactions at the mean interval to be faster than those at shorter or longer intervals, since the mean appears subjectively more probable. The compromise between these two extremes would give a U-shaped curve in which short intervals would give very long reaction times, long intervals medium reaction times, and medium intervals the shortest times. Davis (1956a) discusses these various possibilities, and notes that his own results do show reactions at medium intervals which are faster than reaction times to the first of the two closely paired signals. Welford (1952, p. 8) has noted that long intervals seem to give long reaction times in the earlier experiments. Davis therefore accepts the role of range of inter-signal intervals in making the reactions at medium intervals faster, but he is sceptical of the value of the cumulative probability, interpretation with its prediction that the optimum inter-signal interval will be above the mean of the range. Klemmer (1956) has since shown in a task without the complication of double stimuli that reaction to a stimulus preceded by a warning signal at one of a range of intervals is fastest at an interval between the mean and the upper end of the range. Davis's scepticism may thus be unduly cautious: the suggestion that refractoriness is a range effect similar to those found in other psychophysical situations is fairly plausible, if one only considers the data already mentioned from ungraded response situations. A true test of its adequacy would require the use of a set of inter-signal intervals in which the shortest were the most frequent and the longest the least frequent. If cumulative probability was constant for all intervals and the short intervals still gave longer reaction times than the long intervals, this would demonstrate the inadequacy of the independent channel theory.

Pending such an experiment, there are two facts which seem to the writer conclusive evidence against independent channels. The first comes from the step-tracking experiments mentioned earlier. The varying probability of signals at different inter-signal intervals can provide no explanation of the optima at 0·2, 0·4 and 0·7 sec, separated by long reaction times at 0·3 and 0·5 sec. The explanation given by Welford, it will be remembered, is that feed-back information from the response interferes at the two intermediate intervals: this explanation seems adequate. The second fact is the result of control experiments by Elithorn and Lawrence in which only the second stimulus was presented. Reaction time was faster than in the two-stimulus case when the time since the warning signal was less than about 0·75 sec: in other words, the slow reaction times in the two-stimulus case at about 0·1 sec inter-signal interval were due to interaction between the two stimuli. This argument is not quite watertight, since the subjects knew that only one stimulus was to be delivered in these control trials; they might therefore have combined the two independent channels, which they used in the main experiment, into a single one of higher capacity. Yet this in itself would mean that the supposed two channels are not perfectly separate.

These two points seem therefore to require some addition to a purely probabilistic point of view, an addition of Welford's type being adequate. Furthermore, the results of Elithorn and Lawrence are perfectly consistent with Welford's views: he had allowed for rapid reaction time to a second stimulus ' grouped ' with the first, and he had said that refractoriness might in trained subjects apply only at inter-stimulus intervals much shorter than ½ sec, because of the neglect of feed-back. Our conclusion about the theory of refractoriness as an artifact of stimulus probability must therefore be negative: the organism cannot be perfectly represented by two independent channels. It may well be, however, that with sufficient training men may be able to bring themselves effectively to that state, even though it has not yet been shown unequivocally. We would expect that if this were done, the capacity of each of the channels would be rather less than that for a man trained to act as a single channel. Thus if the man had been trained to react to any of six possible signals to the point where the occurrence of one did not interfere with responses to others, he would not be able to respond faster if given a short session of simple reaction times to one of the signals. However, it remains speculative whether such training is possible.

Three further theories of refractoriness should now be mentioned. One is the simple view that output from the nervous system is withheld while feed-back information is being handled, not because of the limited capacity of the perceptual system, but because a new output may blur environmental changes. This is most clearly seen in compensatory tracking, where a target has to be held in the centre of a sight or on the middle of a cathode-ray tube. Here any movement of the operator's controls may produce a movement of the spot which will mask movements produced by objective target motion. Thus it may be useful to suspend response while target motion is being observed, and vice versa. This theory is clearly not applicable to the case of ungraded responses and therefore cannot be satisfactory by itself. It raises some interesting points: for example, it suggests that the intermittency of tracking corrections noted by Craik (1948) would be more noticeable in compensatory than in pursuit tracking. In the latter case target motion is separated from the movement produced by the operator's controls: for instance, one spot on a cathode-ray tube may move about and the operator be asked to follow it with another spot. Pursuit tracking is under certain circumstances superior to compensatory (Poulton 1952a) and we might expect if refractoriness is eliminated or reduced in pursuit tracking that the advantage would be greater with high frequency target motion. The operator could follow such high frequencies more rapidly. This does seem to be the case (Chernikoff, Birmingham and Taylor 1956). With pursuit tracking it does not seem that there is any sharp upper limit to the frequency which can be followed by a human being (Noble,

Fitts and Warren 1955).    But error does increase with frequency, largely because the output from the man ceases to be synchronized with the target motion even though it is oscillating at the same frequency.   This lack of synchronization appears in a frequency range varying with the individual: just below this frequency range, phase errors appear which last for a constant time rather than a constant number of cycles of target motion.   Noble, Fitts and Warren interpreted these results as showing that the movement of the target is intermittently sampled and an output of the same frequency generated.   The increase of error with frequency is due to the constancy of the time interval between samples. Thus something corresponding to refractoriness does seem to appear even in pursuit tracking, and the theory advanced in this paragraph cannot be fully adequate.   But it does show that extra refractoriness due to feed-back on the Welford principle may affect tracking situations of different kinds to different degrees.

A fourth theory is that the central processes require a brief rest after handling the information from each stimulus.   The trouble with this view, as Welford has pointed out (1952, p. 2) is that it is an *ad hoc* postulate with no apparent reason for it.   The writer does not therefore favour it, but it may yet be needed to explain the odd fact, mentioned earlier, that refractoriness appears to last a full reaction time despite the peripheral processes which account for part of that time.   Davis (1957) has indeed suggested it as an explanation for the fact that refractoriness of normal length appears between a visual and an auditory signal, despite the fact that reaction time to auditory signals is shorter than that to the visual signals normally employed.   Thus in this case refractoriness is of more than one reaction time; it could be explained, as Davis suggests, by supposing that the central mechanisms become refractory after each item of information passes through them.   Another possibility mentioned by Davis is that the extra time is occupied in shifting from one channel to the other.

A fifth theory may now be mentioned, which appears in a paper by North (1954).   This is the view that no stimulus can act instantaneously, but rather that there is a continuous sequence of changes at the sense-organs and each decision to respond is taken on the basis of a sample of these changes over a finite period of time.   At a simple level this seems to be entailed by the fact that activity will be proceeding in other sensory nerve fibres, and that the occurrence of an environmental event can therefore be confidently detected only by comparing the activity in a group of fibres with that in other fibres over some small period of time. Once the activity has remained different for such a period of time, it may be attributed to the environment rather than to chance. Some success has been achieved in deducing various psycho-physical relationships from such a view (Gregory 1956).

On a more complex level, the waveform of speech arriving at the ear forms a sequence of events to which discrete responses are made. There is some evidence that several successive changes take place before a decision is reached: for example, if an artificially generated burst of noise is followed by a vowel-like group of harmonics, the sequence of sounds is heard as a plosive consonant and vowel. The particular consonant heard depends on the central frequency of the burst of noise: but it also depends on the vowel which follows (Liberman, Delattre and Cooper 1952). The reason is, briefly, that in making a plosive consonant the mouth takes up a position which varies with the consonant. On the succeeding vowel being articulated, the mouth must move to a new position and the harmonics sounded in the vowel will show this ' transition ' as it is called, at their beginning (Cooper, Delattre, Liberman, Borst and Gerstman 1952). From the listener's point of view, this means that a sequence of sounds represents the ' stimulus ' for the consonant and vowel, but that one cannot separate out the ' stimulus for the consonant '.

Again, it will be remembered that Cherry and Taylor drew attention to the impairment of the understanding of speech caused by switching the speech on and off at a rate of about a complete 3 c/s. We interpreted this also as an interference with sampling the incoming sensory information over a finite time. If the listener makes three decisions per second as to the nature of the sounds he is hearing, basing each decision on a sample $\frac{1}{3}$ sec long prior to making the decision, he will make about 50 per cent correct decisions when the speech is on or off for periods of more than $\frac{1}{3}$ sec. That is, half his samples will be empty and half full. At the other extreme, very short and frequent interruptions will leave each sample with an adequate amount of information, as the speech sounds do not change very rapidly and so closely spaced interruptions will not cause any particular sounds to be missed altogether. The number of correct decisions will be minimal when each sample contains all its information concentrated in one half of the sampled time: and this, as we have said, is when the speech arrives in samples of about $\frac{1}{6}$ sec in length.

In the reaction time situation, we might suggest that the incoming information can only enter the perceptual system in segments of a given length—say $\frac{1}{3}$ sec to agree with the results of Cherry and Taylor. The minimum reaction time will then occur only when the stimulus arrives towards the end of a segment. In such a case the reaction time will equal merely the sensory and motor conduction times plus the central decision time, the latter depending on the probability of the signal.

If the stimulus occurs earlier in a sample there will be an extra time added to the reaction time, owing to the delay before the sample enters the perceptual system. This will affect the variance of normal reaction times, which does not in fact behave as one would have expected on the simplest informational model (Hick 1952). In reaction time situations, however, it may be possible for a prepared individual to close his sample just after the end of the fore-period: that is, just after the stimulus. Any succeeding stimulus will necessarily fall in the next sample, and therefore receive an extra delay equal to the length of the sample minus the interval between the two stimuli. With the suggested sample length of $\frac{1}{3}$ sec, this will account for the various data we have mentioned on refractoriness in ungraded responses. It need hardly be said that if the two stimuli fall in the same sample the second can receive a normally rapid response, but that this will involve a slow reaction to the first stimulus.

Bearing in mind our discussion of individual differences in Chapter 7 it will be realized that the length of sample is likely to be different in different people. Welford indeed suggests (1952, p. 15) that refractoriness is longer in older people. If the random activity of the nervous system is greater in older people, they might indeed find it desirable to adopt a longer sampling time for incoming information; this is according to the view that this time allows the signal to be distinguished from its random background (Gregory 1956). Older persons were also noted in

Chapter 7 as behaving like intraverts in certain ways. Little can be said about possible individual differences in refractoriness beyond remarking that most of the experiments seem to have been done on very small numbers of subjects, and any individual differences would be very disturbing to the generality of the results.

This view is essentially a modification of Welford's. It has two advantages: first, it allows grouping of stimuli without reversal of the order of response, since the capacity of the decision process is not the only factor limiting the speed of information handling. Secondly, it explains why refractoriness lasts a full reaction time and not merely the central organizing time: it does so by regarding the equivalence of sampling time and visual reaction time as a coincidence. Other reactions with different sensory and motor conduction times may well show the same period of refractoriness. All in all, this is the view which the writer thinks most probable.

But there are weaknesses in this view as compared with the original one of Welford. First, no clear explanation is given of the man's ability to close his sample after the first signal. Secondly, the triple refractoriness found in step-tracking is not easily handled: Welford allows feed-back information to occupy the central processes for a mere 0·15 sec, which is much shorter than our supposed sampling time. One might possibly assume a different sampling time for proprioceptive information; or more probably suggest that the refractoriness is in this case not due to feedback, but to a decreasing periodicity of the sampling from the time of the first signal. A signal near the end of the first sample, after the first signal will show no refractoriness; but a signal at the beginning of the second sample will, and so on. If this were so, it should occur also in experiments with ungraded responses, and there is little sign of that. Davis (1956a) does find longer reaction times with inter-signal intervals of 0·50 sec than with 0·60 or 0·40. But the finding is hardly a large or reliable one.

In summary, refractoriness is clearly a phenomenon of limited capacity on all the theories advanced. Certainly in some cases the human being acts as a single communication channel and therefore cannot deal with two signals in rapid succession. It may be that he can train himself to act as several lower capacity channels in independence; but this has not been proved. Thus in skilled performance the same questions of selecting information for action and discarding irrelevant data, which we have considered throughout this book, will be important.

## Anticipation

Because of delays due to sensory and motor conduction times, to the limited capacity of the system which connects them, and possibly to the segmentation of incoming information, response is bound to lag somewhat behind events at the sense-organs. Any means of cutting down this lag is highly advantageous biologically, and various means are in fact adopted in human skilled performance to do so. These means are usually grouped under the name ' anticipation ', though that name may carry some overtones which are unintended. Some of the aspects of anticipation have been mentioned earlier, since they were relevant to results discussed in previous chapters.

In the first place, it is possible for information necessary for subsequent actions to arrive while other actions are being carried out. That is, sensory and motor conduction times can overlap as we suggested in the last section. In a rough sense this has been known since the early studies of Bryan and Harter (1899) on the performance of telegraphists, and the analysis of processes such as reading aloud (Vernon 1931). It is notable that telegraphists are not writing the words corresponding to the sounds reaching their ears, but rather previous words. So also the reader is not fixating the words he is saying, but later words. However, there are pauses in writing and speaking, and possibly the analysis of incoming information might take place during those pauses. Detailed examination of skilled performance shows that this is not so. Thus Leonard (1953) required subjects to make a series of hand movements from a central point to outer points and back again. In one condition the outer point to be touched next was signalled at the time when the central point was touched: in another condition the next outer point was signalled as the last one was touched. Thus in the second condition the information was available at a time when a movement to a known point (the centre) was still to be made before the information was used, whereas in the first condition the information was to be used as soon as possible after its arrival. Measurement of the time spent at the centre showed that the second condition reduced this time sharply: thus the information was certainly being taken in and processed sooner when it was presented sooner. But the other times spent at the outer points, or in transit between the points did not increase correspondingly: thus the processing of the incoming information was overlapping with movement of the hand back to the central point.

There are limits to the extent to which this overlapping is useful. Poulton (1954) showed that when a series of signals is arriving for a series of responses, it is rather harmful to provide the signals more than one item before the responses to which they are appropriate. It will be remembered from Chapter 9 that, in another of Poulton's experiments (1953b), when a series of items was presented and response did not begin until halfway through the series, there was considerable loss of information. On the other hand, it was quite possible to receive half the series, respond to it, receive the other half, and respond to that. In other words the number of items which can be held in store somewhere within the organism is much less if a continuous series of stimuli and responses is in progress than if the input and output of information can proceed alternately, the store being cleared by each output. As we put it in Chapter 9, this means that the information passes through the $P$ system as it leaves the organism as well as when it arrives or is recirculated: therefore input and output cannot be completely overlapped.

The difficulty is of course connected with the rapid loss of information which is left in the $S$ system without opportunity to enter the $P$ system: input and output often take place at too high a rate to allow recirculation of stored information during the intervals between the passage of incoming and outgoing items through the $P$ system. But at low rates of input and output there is much less difficulty in storing several items. This can be conveniently demonstrated by laying out a number of playing cards face up, and finding the fastest rate at which a victim can name these cards when pointed out in a random order by the experimenter. If he is now asked to name the cards one or two steps behind the experimenter's pointing, he cannot do so at the same rate. If the rate of choosing cards is slowed down, however, he can manage to keep several cards behind.    This has been shown more formally by Poulton (1954).    It means that the rate of transmission of information through the man decreases when naming behind the experimenter's pointing, as compared with the case of naming while he points.

The fact that the limited capacity $P$ system is used for output as well as for input thus limits the value of this first kind of anticipation.    It is sometimes called ' receptor-effector anticipation ' or more briefly ' the eye-hand span '.    But the reason why items must pass through the $P$ system again when leaving the organism, having already passed through it when entering, is by no means clear: this point was passed over hastily in Chapter 9 although the observant reader may have noticed it.    It was reasonable that continual recirculation through the $P$ system should be necessary when holding items in immediate memory for a time longer than that possible for the $S$ system.    But there is no apparent advantage in passing outgoing items through the $P$ system: on the contrary, there are the disadvantages of interfering with recirculation of other items and with the reception of fresh information.    The fact remains, that although a man can easily remember a six-digit number, he will find it very difficult to repeat back random numbers six digits behind a speaker who reads them at a rate of two per sec.    Thus output must interfere with input; the difficulty is why?    One might, as in the case of refractoriness, appeal to the importance of feed-back information about the progress of response.    Possibly the $P$ system is occupied not by the outgoing information but by the monitoring of response to ensure that it is in accordance with intention.    But this is made rather unlikely by the next broad category of anticipation to be discussed, and we will therefore return to the problem of overlapping input and output after we have examined this second category of anticipation.

This is the phenomenon known as ' perceptual anticipation '. When a tennis player strikes a ball, the stroke is not controlled by information coming from the ball at the instant when the racket reaches it.    Nor is receptor-effector anticipation sufficient to bring about success: the eye indeed records the position of the ball well in advance of the movement, but the position is not that at which the blow is struck, because the ball moves during the reaction time.    The movement, however, obeys rules which the player has frequently observed to be followed previously: the stimulus ' ball leaving the opponent's racket along a certain type of path ' is followed by a sequence of stimuli which has occurred previously. Response to the last member of this sequence is initiated before the whole series has occurred objectively: so that response and event occur simultaneously and the racket strikes the ball.

This is the form of anticipation which has been mentioned previously. Its importance is shown by the fact that tracking performance on a target moving with simple harmonic motion, and no opportunity for receptor-effector anticipation, will show a lag between input and output. Repeated experience of the target-motion, however, will abolish this lag (Poulton 1952a). Furthermore once this stage has been reached tracking performance is not seriously affected by blinking the eyes or by objective momentary interference with vision (Poulton 1952b). The objective occurrence of the sequence of stimuli is not now necessary: it can be filled in subjectively provided some of its members are observed.

The possibility of thus attaching events into sequences which have previously occurred is doubtless the basis for the very long eye-hand spans which occur in practised tasks when the transition probabilities of events are not equal. For instance, a telegraphist taking down plain language may be very many words behind in his writing, despite the fact already noted that with random sequences of stimuli at high rates the eye-hand span is only a few items. A long sequence of words, however, is an item in this sense, and thus in such a task the eye-hand span can extend over considerable periods of time.

This immediately raises the question of the role of the $P$ system during this time. From what we have said it might be that in dealing with a sequence of events the information from the first is passed through the $P$ system, that this is sufficient to initiate a series of responses; and that the $P$ system is occupied with these responses until such time as another event must be detected to produce another series of responses. In ordinary language, we might guess that the telegraphist hears a few words, predicts the remainder of the sentence from his knowledge of English and the topics usually discussed on his line, and so can write the whole sentence. Most of the time his attention is occupied, we might say, with his writing: he interrupts it from time to time to listen to a few more words and so keep his transcription in correspondence with the real message. On such a view the skilled man with a long eye-hand span is performing rather like the man who repeats digits several places behind the person speaking them, if they are said very slowly. Perceptual anticipation would thus allow the elimination of lags in response, and make the task independent of the objective occurrence of external events. It would also make it more possible to combine the task with other tasks, since reduction of the total demand on the $P$ system would allow other items of incoming information to pass through it. It will be remembered that it was found by Broadbent (1956a) for the multi-channel listening case, that practice on one channel reduced interference with another channel except at the actual instant when items of information arrived simultaneously on both channels. So also Bahrick, Noble and Fitts (1954) found that practice in responding to a regular series of stimuli allowed that task to be combined more effectively with another; whereas practice had no such effect when the series had no regularly repeating character.

It may be questioned, however, whether this is all the benefit to be drawn from perceptual anticipation. It may be that feedback on the progress of response need not be continuous: that in perceptual anticipation the demand on the $P$ system is reduced not only because fewer items of incoming information need be handled but also because fewer items of outgoing information need be the concern of the $P$ system. If this were so the interference of a practised task with another task would depend chiefly, not on the complexity and time-consuming character of the movements demanded by the practised task, but rather on the signals from the environment which originate those movements. Thus if two men were trained to respond to light signals, one by pressing a key and the other by typing out a nursery rhyme, sufficient training might nearly equate the amount of interference showed on some simultaneous task. This point requires further and rather more laborious investigation.

Why, on such a view, should the $P$ system be used in response at all, since it is not necessary to handle feed-back information?

(This of course does not necessarily imply that there is no control of response by sensory feed-back, but only that that information does not pass through the $P$ system: rather as the control of room temperature by a thermostat does not require the occupant to take any action after the first setting of the thermostat.) One might suggest that when the sequence of responses is not a frequent one the $P$ system is used to ensure that the order within the sequence is correct. On such a view the passage of information through the system during response (the evidence for which was mentioned earlier) has nothing to do with feedback but only with the initiation of response: just as in a computing machine, there may be sub-routines for common mathematical processes which will run themselves off once initiated. Such sub-routines will still need to be started off in the proper sequence. However, this is a topic which deserves further experiment.

In summary, anticipation falls into two varieties. One of these, receptor-effector anticipation, is limited by the fact that input to and output from the organism are to some extent incompatible. Thus at high rates of transmission of information through the man, there cannot be too large an amount within the nervous system at one time: the eye-hand span must be short. At lower rates the span can be increased by using the short-term storage method of recirculating through the $P$ system during intervals in the arrival and departure of information. Perceptual anticipation, on the other hand, depends on long-term storage and greatly lessens the demand on the $P$ system. It is the basis of the fact that human beings can be treated as mathematically equivalent to communication channels, since they adjust themselves to an optimal coding, and thus improbable signals take longer to elicit response than probable signals do.*

### Speed and Load

So far we have been considering skills in which there is only one source of signals. But there are very many practical cases in which this is not so: in flying an aircraft, attending several cotton looms, driving through traffic or attempting to score in a football game there are many sources of information each transmitting at its own rate. (The concept of ' source ' will require further elaboration later.)

* A more detailed review of anticipation is given by Poulton (1957).

Experimentally, this situation can be examined by setting up a display consisting of a number of dials, each bearing a pointer and one or more fixed marks. When the pointer on a dial is touching a mark, a simple response is required. The speed of rotation of the pointers on the various dials must be different, as otherwise the sequence of signals would repeat itself: and the effects on response of varying the number of dials and the average number of signals per minute can both be studied.

In such a task there are effects from altering the number of dials even with the same number of signals per minute: and from altering the signals per minute even with the same number of dials (Conrad 1951). To consider the latter effect first: as the demanded rate of response increases, it is not surprising to find that more signals occur without receiving a response. It is more unexpected that the rate of response does none the less increase: in fact it is not impossible for a man faced with a very rapid series of signals to respond at a rate which is faster than the rate of signalling used in a previous or subsequent experiment on the effects of lower rates. Yet in the other experiment he still did not produce a perfect performance, since his responses were then at a rate even slower than the signals.

This ' energizing ' effect of a high rate of stimulation is probably responsible for the good effects sometimes reported from pacing a worker mechanically (e.g. Bills and Shapin 1936). If a high rate of signalling is presented, the number of responses will be greater than with a low rate; or, probably, than with signals produced by the man's own responses so that he works at his own speed. This is not contradictory to the statements about pacing in Chapters 5 and 6: there we were concerned with the fact that a man may, as a period of unpaced work increases, keep up the same average by a few much slower and many slightly faster responses. This he cannot do when paced mechanically at a constant rate equal to the mean. But it is still true that if paced above his natural mean he will increase his mean. One would expect that such a benefit can only be attained at the expense of a proportion of missed signals even if the worker is fresh. These would be an embarrassment in, for instance, conveyor belt assembly work; they would represent unfinished jobs to be taken off the line at a later point and returned to the beginning.   In general, mechanical pacing is undesirable if its rate is the same as that produced by the worker when left to his own devices, as he will miss items after prolonged work due to his increased variability.   This effect may be removed, as Conrad and Hille (1955) have shown, by such devices as pacing two workers by one machine; when one girl missed an item due to a moment of inefficiency, the other was able to retrieve it.   Another practical answer to the assembly problem (though of little theoretical interest) is to put barriers across a conveyor opposite each worker so that items accumulate in a pool, giving a task which is unpaced but with the considerable advantages of the conveyor from the point of view of the production engineer. There may be some advantage in mechanical pacing at a rate faster than the man would naturally work, provided the job is one in which missed signals do not matter.

The reasons for this effect of speed are not clear.   It might be an activating effect of high levels of stimulation, or it might be that as signals become more probable so response becomes more rapid.   Both these views are of course similar to those put forward in Chapter 6 when discussing the effect of rate of signalling on vigilance; whatever the explanation these results at high rates of signalling are clearly similar to those at low rates.

High rates of signalling produce omissions but have relatively little effect on the number of errors of timing.   If we examine the number of responses made early or late to their corresponding signals, we find an effect of ' load ', that is, of altering the number of dials while keeping the total number of signals per minute from the whole display constant (Conrad 1955b).   Close scrutiny of the results shows that the mechanism of these timing errors is one which depends on the occurrence of other responses.   A late response is more likely to occur when other responses have occurred shortly before the signal in question: and an early response is more likely when other responses occur immediately after the signal.   The effect of this is to produce a rate of responding which is more constant than the rate at which signals arrive; clumps of nearly simultaneous stimuli are converted into evenly spaced responses.   (The responses, it should be noted, had to be performed by one hand and only one at a time.)

Now when a number of sources are independently generating

signals the number of short intervals between signals goes up
with the number of sources (Conrad 1955a; Cox and Smith 1953).
With a large number of dials one is more likely to have two signals
at once than with a small number, even if the rate of signalling
from each dial is reduced by the same factor as the number of
dials is increased. Thus the number of timing errors, and also
of missed signals, increases when the number of sources of
information increases. A rather curious point is that when the
worker is provided with some control of the average rate of
signalling, he picks the same rate regardless of the number of
dials (Conrad and Hille 1957). This naturally means that he
makes more mistakes at the high loads.

A different approach giving similar results is that of Mackworth
and Mackworth (1956). Instead of using dials they used a row
of windows, each carrying a fixed card bearing six symbols. In
the windows there appeared from time to time other moving
cards each also bearing six symbols. The subject had to report
the number of similarities between each fixed card and each of
the moving cards appearing in its window. Errors were again a
function both of number of cards per minute and of number of
windows. In this case there was no opportunity to observe the
imminent appearance of a card in a window, as there was the
imminent arrival of a pointer at a mark in the dial experiments.
Thus errors of timing were not relevant. The total number of
correct responses was approximately (though not exactly) proportional to the product of cards per minute and number of
windows. This useful approximation may be a source of some
confusion if thought of simply as Errors $= K \times$ Speed $\times$ Load:
it does not mean that a worker can watch twice as many machines
if each machine requires attention only half as often. The
' Speed ' term is total speed and not speed per source: so doubling
the number of machines watched should multiply errors by two
even if the rate of signalling from each machine is halved.

Mackworth and Mackworth found that a convenient index for
the difficulty of each card in their task was provided by the degree
of overlap with other cards. For each card one may take the
number of seconds for which it is visible while Card $A$ is also
visible, the number for which it is visible while Card $B$ is also
visible, and so on. The total of these numbers forms an overlap

index for the card: and as the number of windows goes up this index shows more numerous sharp peaks. As we said earlier, with several independent sources there is a higher probability of overlap than with few. The overlap index for any card is also highly correlated with the number of omissions on that card. The breakdown of a task in which there are a number of sources of information is thus largely a question of the number of times at which information arrives from two sources simultaneously. However, this factor alone is not quite sufficient to explain the increase in errors as load increases. There is a residual element which may be due to some such factor as the need to search a larger area before detecting the presence of a card. Speculatively, one may connect this residual factor with the failure of Conrad's subjects to slow down the display sufficiently to compensate for their own inefficiency as the load increased.

In general, all these results fit closely into our conception of an organism with a limited capacity adapting itself to make the best use of that capacity. As we would put it, the filter selects one channel of information at a time, and any need to handle more causes failure to transmit the information. One 'channel', however, is not quite equivalent to o1e ' source ', as that word has been used in discussions of speed and load. A channel presents a number of events possessing some characteristic in common, such as stimulating the same sense organ. A source in the load experiments presents signals which not only come from the same spatial position but are incompatible with one another. A pointer cannot be at two positions simultaneously, nor can a window be occupied by two cards. If there were two concentric pointers revolving on the same dial, they might be separate sources but the same channel, as those words have been used. Thus the relation between speed and load experiments and the filtering of incoming information is not completely worked out: but they have much in common.

## Preferred Control-Display Relationships

It is undoubtedly true that one cannot always transmit the same amount of information through a man when one presents it in two different ways. For example, if the effects of his control movements appear on his display only after several integrations have been performed upon them—that is, after a time lag—he is less able to keep stable control of the situation than he can with a more immediate display-control relationship (Birmingham and Taylor 1954). Providing him with a differentiated version of the display, which responds at once to control movements, may allow perfect control even though this display does not correspond to any event in the real world. A familar example of the merits of a differentiated display is the artificial horizon, which responds to control movements more rapidly than the airspeed indicator and altimeter do: a more sophisticated example is the optimum display for helicopters (Taylor and Birmingham 1956). The point of theoretical interest is that the movements required of a man in response to, say, a disturbance of an aircraft by turbulent air, are exactly the same whatever the display provided for him. Thus the information transmitted through him must be the same if performance is successful. Nevertheless the task is easy with one display and difficult with another.

This fact, which may be called the problem of coding, is one of great concern to information theorists since it means that one cannot simply apply the theorems of information theory to human performance without considering the particular coding employed in the case in question. We shall not go into the problem very deeply here; indeed there is probably no satisfactory way of dealing with it at the moment and certainly no agreed way. We may note, however, that it is a problem to which information theory has called attention rather than a weakness raised by some other approach. In fact it is difficult to formulate the problem in any other language, such as that of S–R theory.

Two points about preferred control-display relations do concern us, however. One is that some of the difficulties are due to the operation of the filter and of the other mechanisms we have discussed in this book. To take the example of the effect of lag between control and display, the difficulty here may be that of short-term storage when continuous input and output have to be kept flowing. The problem has already been discussed in this chapter: one might suggest that the effect of lags in a discontinuous task (such as aiming darts at a target) is less disastrous than it is in a continuous task such as flying an aircraft on airspeed indicator and altimeter alone. In the first case the output can be stored until its effect is known, while in the second it cannot. But, so far as the writer is aware, no experiment has been performed to compare the effect of lags on continuous and discontinuous tasks of equal difficulty.

Another and perhaps more obvious example is the case of reaction times to a situation well-known in the classical literature. These are reactions in which the various signals are independent and not alternate. Thus one might have two lights and three keys: one response for one light, one for the other, and the third response for both lights simultaneously. The amount of information transmitted through the man is the same as in an orthodox three-choice situation with three lights and three keys. Yet the reaction time is considerably longer in the unorthodox situation. The fact has recently come into prominence because the combining of direction indicators on cars with the brake lights transforms an orthodox into a complication situation, and so sharply increases the reaction time (Gibbs 1952; Dunlap and Wells 1910). One may suggest that this is because the information has to arrive by two channels on all occasions, whereas in the orthodox situation it need only be assimilated from one channel: the others are not independent and their state can be inferred. An alternative possibility which has much merit is that this is a change in the dimensions of the input signals. A given amount of information can be conveyed by $x$ signals each having $y$ possible values, or by $p$ signals each having $q$ possible values, so long as $x \log y = p \log q$. But the change from one type of code to the other normally requires a delay line in physical systems (Fano 1949), and it is reasonable that it should do so in biological ones.

Whatever the true explanation of these cases, it is clear that the kind of system we have been postulating will handle information presented in some ways better than it will that arriving in others. Filtering and storage of information normally lead to efficient use of a limited neural mechanism, but they will place restrictions on the speed with which items of information can arrive (no matter how small the ensemble from which the items are drawn), and on the number of sensory channels by which they arrive (particularly when they arrive quickly). It is interesting to note that Quastler (1956) puts similar limits on information handling as the result of attempts to determine maximum rates of transmission through human beings. The rate, say in typewriting, is sub-optimal either with very small numbers of keys, to be hit exceedingly rapidly, or with very large numbers, which cause confusion.

Perhaps more important is the question of abolishing coding difficulties by training. Many of the instances in which tasks take unduly long to learn can be explained as the result of long attachment of some different response to the stimuli presented. For instance, if we see a dial giving too low a reading and are asked to correct this with a knob, we normally turn the knob clockwise. If we are driving a strange car, and wish to turn to the right we normally turn the top of the steering-wheel to the right. (For a number of experiments on this subject, see Chapanis, Garner and Morgan 1949.) A particularly good example is that if we compare several spatial arrangements of display and control we find that some patterns are better than others; but that each pattern of display is better with the same pattern of control (Fitts and Seeger 1953). Indeed it may be possible to improve efficiency on a task by replacing a normally good display by a bad one, as long as the control is also the particular bad one which suits that display. This effect is known as ' stimulus-response compatibility '. A clue to the learned nature of many preferred control-display relationships is found in the fact that Americans normally assume a toggle-switch, such as a wall-switch for an electric light, to point downwards when it is off. Englishmen assume the opposite, most switches in England operating in the opposite sense to those in America. In this case the preferred direction is built up on a conventional basis, but in many cases it is inherent in the physical nature of everyday experience (Gibbs 1951). Every time we pick something up or point at it, we strengthen the tendency to make a movement to the right to reach something seen at the right.

Such relationships can be reversed by training. Many cars have door-handles which work in the opposite direction to those in houses, but the owner of the car does not lock himself in when he tries to get out. His passengers may, but he has had sufficient training to reverse the normal response. How far does this possible reversal with retraining make it unnecessary to change display-control relations in industrial practice ?

There are two dangers in relying on training to reverse an established habit. In the first place, we have seen previously that a given level of performance may be due partly to long-term and partly to short-term storage of information. When an old habit is replaced by a new one, it is the latter which most benefits from the short-term storage. But short-term storage is of limited capacity: any irrelevant incoming information which succeeds in passing the filter will interfere with storage of the new habit. Thus under distraction or similar stresses there may be reversion to the old way of performing the task, even though stress-free performance is satisfactory.

This danger could be overcome simply by giving far more practice, until the new relationship is also stored in the long-term store—overlearned in the traditional phrase. It is doubtful whether Englishmen living in America are unduly troubled by light-switches after a learning period in which any distraction causes reversion to the old pattern. But when the new relation to be learned is one which contradicts everyday experience it cannot be established unconditionally in the long-term store. Even after much training as a pilot one cannot base one's life on the ground on the assumption that every action will be followed by a lag before its effects appear. Thus the correct type of performance in the air must be kept in operation by a short-term storage of the fact that ' this is not the usual situation '. Once again, interference with short-term storage may cause disruption of the established performance.

The relative importance of these two possibilities has not been assessed: but certainly it has been shown that after training on an abnormal control-display relation performance may be worse than normal under stress even though satisfactory under normal conditions (Vince 1950; Garvey 1957).

## CONCLUSIONS

The picture of skilled performance built up by modern researches is one of a complex interaction between man and environment. Continuously the skilled man must select the correct cues from the environment, take decisions upon them which may possibly involve prediction of the future, and initiate sequences of responses whose progress is controlled by feed-back, either through the original decision-making mechanism, or through lower-order loops. The processes of filtering the information from the senses, of passing it through a limited capacity channel, and of storing it temporarily are only part of the total skilled performance. But they are of the same general nature as the other processes involved, and harmonize with the broad view of skill which is now developing.

# CHAPTER 12

# RETROSPECT AND PROSPECT

WE are now nearing the end of our journey, and have finished discussing experimental results. In each field examined we have tried to follow the plan of first stating the factual results and the broad generalizations resulting from them: then going on to the various theories met with in that field, and the experiments supporting or disproving those theories. More tentatively we have tried to choose the most probable theory or combination of theories, and finally to advance rather speculative explanations for the remaining inadequacies of the theory. This means of progress has various disadvantages. For example, it is difficult for the reader to plough through masses of data before he is clear about the generalizations which those results illustrate. It may also be unclear how the conclusions in different chapters are related. More serious, by this stage in the argument it may be a little unclear what conclusions are to be regarded as well-founded and what is merely a tentative conclusion for further experiment. For this reason the first step to be taken in this last chapter is to put together formally our main conclusions.

## SUMMARY OF PRINCIPLES

(A) A nervous system acts to some extent as a single communication channel, so that it is meaningful to regard it as having a limited capacity.

(B) A selective operation is performed upon the input to this channel, the operation taking the form of selecting information from all sensory events having some feature in common. Physical features identified as able to act as a basis for this selection include the intensity, pitch, and spatial localization of sounds.

(C) The selection is not completely random, and the probability of a particular class of events being selected is increased by certain properties of the events and by certain states of the organism.

(D) Properties of the events which increase the probability of the information, conveyed by them, passing the limited capacity channel include the following: physical intensity, time since the last information from that class of events entered the limited capacity channel, high frequency of sounds as opposed to low (in man), sounds as opposed to visual stimuli or touch as opposed to heat (in dogs).

(E) States of the organism which increase the probability of selection of classes of events are those normally described by animal psychologists as ' drives '. When an organism is in a drive state it is more likely to select those events which are usually described as primary reinforcements for that drive. Thus food has a high probability of being selected if the animal has been deprived of food for 24 hr. In addition all classes of events which have previously been selected closely before such reinforcers or before events leading to such reinforcers (see Principles (F) and (G) ) are more likely to be selected in future.

(F) Given that two signals have been selected one after another, the conditional probability of the second given the detected occurrence of the first is stored within the nervous system in a long-term (relatively slowly decaying) store.

(G) In accordance with Deutsch's postulates, when an animal is in a drive state it will indulge in appetitive behaviour until one of the temporarily high priority events occurs at its sense-organs. Its behaviour will then vary in such a way that it receives that ordered series of stimuli which, from a count of past conditional probabilities, has the highest probability of terminating in the primary reinforcement for that drive.

(H) Incoming information may be held in a temporary store at a stage previous to the limited capacity channel: it will then pass through the channel when the class of events to which it belongs is next selected. The maximum time of storage possible in this way is of the order of seconds.

(I) To evade the limitations of (H) it is possible for information to return to temporary store after passage through the limited capacity channel: this provides storage of unlimited time at the cost of reducing the capacity of the channel still further and possibly to zero. (Long-term storage does not affect the capacity of the channel, but rather is the means for adjusting the internal coding to the probabilities of external events; so that the limit on the channel is an informational one and not simply one of a number of simultaneous stimuli.)

(J) A shift of the selective process from one class of events to another takes a time which is not negligible compared with the minimum time spent on any one class.

Of the above principles, (E) and (G) are the most tentative. The remainder seem to the writer to be reasonably well founded: the doubtful ones were included in their logical order for the sake of completeness. Certain other possibilities are worth further investigation, but cannot be regarded as even tentatively established. These include:

(K) There is a minimum time during which information from one class of event is sampled before any action is taken about it.

(L) This minimum time is shorter in persons who are extraverted, by Eysenck's operational definition of that word.

An information-flow diagram incorporating the more probable principles is shown in Fig. 7.

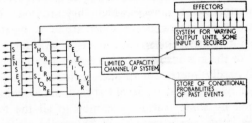

Fig. 7. A tentative information-flow diagram for the organism, as conceived at the present time. This diagram includes many of the views put forward by various workers in recent years: it covers Brown's research on immediate memory, Deutsch's and Uttley's on learning and the work on anticipation and refractoriness as well as that on noise, multi-channel listening and prolonged performance.

## Major Implications of These Principles

Now that these principles are stated thus baldly, it may be urged that they are not particularly surprising. Do we not know that attention is limited, that noises distract us, that we consciously rehearse any matter which must be remembered for a short period, and so on? What gain is there from putting these everyday experiences into this stilted language? They have already been formulated by the classical introspective psychologists: why is time and effort wasted on rephrasing them?

There are two answers to this objection. First, it is indeed true that the principles lead to no prediction which is contrary to every-day observation. It would be a poor set of scientific principles which did do so: though it is not uncommon for psychologists to feel that they ought to contradict common beliefs about behaviour.

But secondly, as a matter of history it is not true that these principles are obvious nor that they were adequately formulated by classical psychologists. It is quite possible to say that mentalistic statements are consistent with them: to say that our limited capacity single channel is to be equated with the unitary attention of the introspectionists. Indeed, the writer believes that the one is simply a more exact version of the other. But a view of attention as unitary might also be taken to mean that a man cannot perform two tasks at once: which experimental evidence shows to be untrue. A view of noise as distracting might be taken to mean that card-sorting or mental arithmetic will be worse performed in noise; which they are not. It is worth listing a few of these conclusions which are by no means obvious.

(1) The interference between two tasks will increase as the probability of the stimuli in each decreases: two highly probable stimuli will hardly interfere with one another.

(2) When relevant and irrelevant stimuli are arriving together, distinguished by some features common to all the former and none of the latter, performance will be greatly assisted if these features are of certain kinds. (That is, if they are amongst those on which the filter can operate.)

(3) The effect of prolonged work and also of continuous distracting stimuli will be greatest at the end of the work-period, and will consist of intermittent failures in the intake of information. Tasks in which a great deal of perceptual anticipation is possible will therefore not show such effects.

(4) When two groups of stimuli arrive simultaneously at the sense-organs, the probability of efficient reaction to one of them will fall off very rapidly with the interval between its arrival and the end of the other group, provided the other group has to receive a prior reaction. But immediate memory is not normally very sensitive to time.

(5) The most difficult of a series of items held in immediate memory will be nearer the beginning of the list if the presentation rate is fast and the recall rate slow, and nearer the end if the reverse is true.

These conclusions are not exhaustive, but they illustrate points which have certainly not been proved in previous accounts of attention. Admittedly some of them may have been stated: for example, William James (1890, Chapter XI) states the third of the above conclusions, in the form that voluntary as opposed to involuntary attention cannot be continuous. Voluntary attention rather is a continual returning of attention to its object when it wanders away. This the present writer believes to be a remark of great insight, as is the whole of James's chapter; but without objective experimentation we have no way of deciding between James and the misguided enthusiasts who hold that noise makes it impossible for any task to be performed, no matter what the nature of the work.

Other conclusions from these principles are by no means certain, but are conceivably possible, and ought to be considered by theorists in the appropriate fields. For instance:

(6) Some of the phenomena of temporary extinction may be due to failure of the conditioned stimulus to be selected.

(7) The great value of reinforcement in facilitating learning (as opposed to performance) may lie in the high priority which re-inforcers have for passage through the limited capacity channel, and therefore the greater effect they have on the stored proba-bilities. Other high priority stimuli would do the same if per-formance were secured.

(8) The phenomena of rote learning usually considered by theorists may be very largely due to properties of the short-term storage system, and not to those of the long-term system. In many laboratory experiments performance is carried only just above a criterion of mastery, when part of the information is still only in the short-term store. The phenomena thus change with overlearning.

## Characteristics of the Present Approach

There are various features of our line of argument which may have concerned some readers: in particular the fact that this is a non-positivistic approach, and attempts to find out what happens inside the organism. It may also be doubted whether the use of terms from communication theory has been of value; and whether the inductive approach ending in qualitative principles is perhaps inferior to a hypothetico-deductive approach starting from quantitative postulates and proceeding to numerical predictions which can then be tested. Of these three objections the first two are specific to this field, while the last raises general questions of scientific method, and will be left till later.

Psychologists are nowadays chary of postulating events within the organism. In this attitude they can look for support to modern physics, which also has had to take into account the relation between the process of making observations and the concepts used in theorizing. In addition it may be thought proper to strike out a separate field for psychology, peculiar to itself. The nervous system is the province of physiology; psychologists should study behaviour and are entitled to seek out regularities in that field just as, say, biochemists do within their own field of observation.

But there are certain differences between the cases of physics and psychology. In the former science certain concepts may be inherently unobservable. It seems likely that no conceivable observation can overcome the uncertainty about the position and velocity of an electron, since determining one disturbs the other. Events within the skull are not inherently unobservable: they are merely inaccessible to our present techniques. The proper analogy for the most speculative statements in psychology is not with, say, a proposition about velocity through the ether, where there is some doubt whether the proposition is meaningful. It is rather with propositions about mountains on the other side of the moon, which are perfectly meaningful but rather difficult to test. The mountains are as difficult to observe as the velocity, but the reasons for the difficulty are purely technological.

Another example closer to our own field might be the statement: ' The nervous message consists of a series of discrete pulses detectable by their electrical characteristics '. At first sight this a perfectly straightforward statement about observables. But suppose it had been made before the development of modern amplifiers: it would not be meaningless although it could not at that time be directly tested. Some such theories incapable (at the time) of direct testing have nevertheless proved of great scientific value: for example, Helmholtz's resonance theory of hearing or for that matter Rutherford's telephone theory. Additional point is given to this example by the fact that these theories are now known to be only partly true: yet nobody could deny their contribution, which has largely resulted in our knowing the facts which prove them insufficient.

When dealing with macroscopic events statements about unobservables are not necessarily mystical or scientifically useless. The clues to the value of such a statement are, first, the degree of exactness in the statement, and secondly the plausibility of an assumption of causality between the unobservables and observables. It is necessary that we should know what kind of observation would test the statement even if we cannot at the moment make it. It is also necessary, if the statement is to be worth making even though meaningful, that we should be able to make inferences about the unobservable from observation. For instance, if we were the first people to investigate dew formation, we might put forward the hypothesis that the unobservable process was an electrical one because most conducting materials show different rates of dew formation from non-conducting materials. This might then be tested by examining electrically non-conducting materials which differed in other ways (Burniston Brown 1950).

In our own approach we have tried to make our hypothetical constructs of such a kind that they could be recognized if it were possible to observe them directly: a filter or a short-term store might take different physiological forms, but it could be decided with reasonable ease whether any particular physiological structure was or was not describable by these terms. In addition the language of information flow depends on causal relationships; to hark back to Chapter 3, we can only be sure that there are two states of the brain intervening between two different responses because we assume causality to operate. If this assumption is invalid, if appropriate responses ' just happen ', then our argument is fallacious. But it is doubtful whether any scientific psychology can be based on a denial of causality.

The fact that the one assumption of causality allows one to draw valid inferences about events, within the brain is now recognized by the ' operationists ', who are sometimes regarded as the standard-bearers of a positivist psychology (Garner, Hake and Eriksen 1956). Broadly speaking, if two different stimuli produce the same response one is justified in assuming some common event within the nervous system: if some kind of treatment abolishes the effect of one stimulus but not that of the other, that treatment must act before the point at which the two causal lines become one. By this type of argument we can draw valid inferences about events which are not directly observable.

The need to issue in experiments which do involve observables is truly essential. Statements about mountains on the other side of the moon are meaningful, they may be either true or false, but they are at the moment of little use to science unless they could be shown to affect, say, the tides on earth. Much of the discussion of cybernetic principles which has taken place in recent years is of the same order as discussion of moon mountains. Computing machines operate on a binary basis; they have long-term and short-term stores; servo systems seek goals by negative feed-back. But it is often urged that these analogies are of no worth unless there is evidence that organisms operate in the same way: and it is sometimes assumed as a further step that no such evidence exists. This book has been intended to show that nervous systems are networks of the type shown in Fig. 7, and of no other type. As has been admitted, the evidence for parts of the system is weaker than that for others: but a general layout of this type is entailed by the detailed evidence about behaviour which we have surveyed.

The same hypothesis might have been described in other terms, for example in those of stimulus and response. In brief the use of cybernetic language has had four main advantages. First, it has allowed us to keep the words stimulus and response for observables. If we were to describe the system of Fig. 7 in S–R terms, we would need to speak of internal responses: this carries with it a danger common also to speculative physiology, that if we use words normally given an objective meaning we will think our theory objective even though it be wildly specu-lative. Unobservable responses figure frequently in modern S–R theories; the writer dislikes them.

A second and related point is that we rid ourselves of undesired overtones. S–R terms press us constantly towards open-chain models of the nervous system, towards a peripheralism which is by no means always justified. Some events must take place within the nervous system; by speaking of ' responses ' we beg the question whether a given event is central or peripheral.

Thirdly, a description of the integrative action of the nervous system in terms of information flow will be readily attached to physiological knowledge when the latter becomes available. For example, recent studies of the electrical activity in the cochlear nucleus following a click sound, have shown that it can be modified by centrifugal messages. If a cat is shown a mouse just before the click is sounded, there is no electrical activity of the type which normally follows a click (Hernandez-Peon, Scherrer and Jouvet 1956). If the click is repeated without any other stimulus, the cochlear nucleus potentials habituate, that is they do not appear when the click is given. Converting the click into a conditioned stimulus for a response to shock (Galambos, Sheatz and Vernier 1956) keeps the cochlear nucleus potentials at their normal level; extinction of the response makes them disappear. All this is obviously a physiological mechanism which could form the basis of the box marked ' selective filter ' in Fig. 7. (But not a completely satisfactory basis, since it is doubtful if there is room for the ' short-term store ' before the cochlear nucleus.)

This readiness to connect with the neighbouring sciences is highly desirable. Chemistry could hardly have reached its present state if its theoretical concepts had not been formulated in terms which would allow a bridge to be built to physics. This is not necessarily to say that psychology alone is incapable of providing ultimately satisfying explanations, and must always appeal for them to physiology (Farrell 1955). On the contrary, it may often be preferable to explain a physiological fact by reference to its role in a well-understood psychological function: to say, for instance, that the effects shown by the cochlear nucleus potential are explicable as the operation of the filter with which we are familiar from behavioural data. But whichever way the explanations are operated it is desirable to leave room for contact with physiology. Originally S–R theory may have been intended to do so, but it has become increasingly detached as time went on. The physiological basis of an excitatory potential, a reflex reserve, or a cognitive map might be hard to recognize.

On the other hand, psychology is undoubtedly a field large enough to form an autonomous science. To use hypothetical constructs made up from physiological terms is to lay oneself open to the danger of having one's psychological theory disproved by some irrelevant physiological research. The most eminent and convincing of contemporary speculative physiologists is Hebb (1949): the psychological essence of his theory is that the perception of patterns can be accounted for by the linking of unit elements in the nervous system into sequences. This theory is worded physiologically so that the elements of the theory are identified as cell assemblies and phase sequences. Should a physiological experiment cast doubt on the latter, the psychological side of the theory will be in danger of being neglected: although it may well be true even though the elements are not physically what Hebb supposed them to be. Such a fate has already overtaken the Gestaltists: their unlikely physiology has produced neglect of their genuine psychological achievements. Thus information theory is desirable as allowing future contact with physiology but never assuming physiological detail.

The proper relation between the physiologist and the psychologist may be regarded as analogous to that between the automobile mechanic and the test driver. Each of these men has his own domain of knowledge: no wise man will believe anything but the simplest assertion about a car engine before it has been proved on the road, any more than a wise man believes speculative physiology before it has been tested in psychological experiments. And for many purposes a knowledge of the mechanism is not essential to the driver; no more so than a knowledge of the problems of driving is essential to the mechanic. (In the scientific field, one may note, the psychologist usually knows much more of physiology than the physiologist does about behaviour.) Nevertheless, the driver and the mechanic are handling the same car and ought to speak a language which can be applied to the problems of either.

The last advantage of information theory terms is, as we have said, that they emphasize the relationship between the stimulus

now present and the others which might have been present but
are not.  This relation is, as the last sentence shows, cumbrous
to express in any other language.  But it appears repeatedly in
the study of skill, of attention, and of perception generally as a
matter of the first importance.  If the use of information theory
concepts had no other advantage but this, they would still be
justified.

## On the Limits of Hypothetico-deductive Method

We are reversing, in the course of this book, the plan of many
books on psychology.  They often start with a general discussion
of scientific method, then set up postulates, and then discuss
predictions from those postulates.  The type of such books is
that of Hull (1943).  We, on the other hand, have discussed
results first, then theories, and finally broad principles.  Now
we are coming to the discussion of scientific method.  This
inversion is deliberate, as we said in the first chapter.  So also
is the omission of highly specific quantitative elements in the
principles finally drawn up.  We may seem therefore to be
running contrary to the whole trend of scientific psychology.
Hull's methodology has been highly praised by such authorities
as Hilgard (1948), and has been given as a reason for preferring
his system by some, such as Berlyne (1951a).  The writer has
elsewhere considered formally the merits and demerits of a
highly quantitative hypothetico-deductive method (Broadbent
1956b); we shall now indicate only the main conclusions.

In the first place, Hull deserves the highest credit for insisting
that all postulates should be tested by making deductions from
them which are experimentally testable.  The early papers in
which this case is put (Hull 1930, 1935, 1937) are of truly great
quality: and the recognition that such concepts as ' purpose '
do not imply a reversal of the normal order of causality, an action
on the present by the future, had a valuable influence.  In our
own language, 'purpose' implies a representation within the organism of some situation, and a feed-back system which modifies the
output so that the situation is attained.  All this Hull recognized.

Yet just as in psychology S–R theory is inadequate because it
does not consider the other stimuli which might have been present
but are not, so also in scientific method the hypothetico-deductive

approach is inadequate unless it is recognized that there are other possible hypotheses which might have been tested. When we set up a set of postulates for experimental testing, the appearance of a favourable result supports our postulates only in so far as it disproves contradictory and incompatible postulates. Naturally it does not support our postulates against others which predict the same outcome. We may wish, very naturally, to reduce these other hypotheses to the smallest number we can. To do this means that our own hypothesis must be worded not only exactly (so that we can tell which experimental results would disprove it) but also very quantitatively (so that there are more experimental results which would be incompatible with it). For example, the hypothesis put forward in Chapter 9 predicts that normally speaking the point of greatest difficulty in a memorized list of items will be between the middle and the end of the list. The hypothesis put forward by Hull *et al.* (1940) gives a prediction of the exact item which will be the most difficult (which will in fact be one of those between the middle and the end of the list). Obviously if an experiment is done, some of the possible results would disprove both theories, some would be consistent with both; and the remainder would disprove Hull's theory but be consistent with that in Chapter 9. For this reason a result favouring Hull's theory would be far more convincing than one which merely supports the theory of Chapter 9. The former result excludes more of the competing theories; and this is the unrecognized reason why many people admire Hull's quantitative methodology, and have probably felt dissatisfied with the less quantitative predictions made in this book. A verification of a quantitative theory excludes more possibilities than a verification of a qualitative theory.

The point is similar to the well-known principle that predicting an unlikely event (such as the appearance of an unknown planet) is more convincing evidence in support of a theory than is predicting a very likely one: this principle has given philosophers and theorists of scientific method a good deal of trouble. In the form of Bayes' Theorem it is undoubtedly sound; the probability of a theory after an experiment has been performed is related directly to the probability of the theory before the experiment and inversely to the prior probability of the particular experimental result. But in practice these two prior probabilities are unknown, and Bayes' Theorem is therefore somewhat unrealistic. To apply it, it is possible to use the more doubtful Bayes' Axiom, that when the outcome of an event is unknown each of the possible results is equally probable. This certainly is untrue in any ordinary sense of probability: but the approach we are advocating here might be described as a justification of acting on Bayes' Axiom because it is the best possible strategy.

To revert to our discussion of quantitative and qualitative theories, it might seem that we have cut the ground away from under our own feet: we have argued that quantitative theories are preferable because verification of their predictions is more convincing. This is true provided the predictions are in fact verified; but they will not always be. Unless we have some extra-sensory perception which allows us to set up correct hypotheses with a greater than chance frequency, in advance of experimentation, we will have a correct hypothesis in only a proportion of our investigations. If there are $n$ hypotheses and we choose one for test, we will pick the correct one on only $1/n$ occasions (assuming the impossibility of guessing correctly without evidence). What will we learn from disproving our pet hypothesis? That depends on the alternatives we have set up. If we have formulated all the $n$ hypotheses which logically might explain the problem that concerns us, and if we have performed an experiment with $n$ possible results, one for each hypothesis, it will not matter much whether our favourite is verified or not. One of the others is sure to be. But usually exponents of hypothetico-deductive method formulate only one major hypothesis: and failure to verify it means only that one of the other $n-1$ hypotheses is true, without giving any indication of which one. In such a case it can be proved (Broadbent 1956b) that the optimal scientific strategy, on the average, is to formulate our major hypothesis only as the general class of hypotheses consistent with $n/2$ of the possible experimental results. The more alternative theories are formulated prior to the experiment, the more restricted it is possible to make each of them: if there are $p$ theories, each should be consistent with $n/(p + 1)$ of the experimental results.

To put this argument in a more familiar form, consider the

game 'Twenty Questions'. If we know that an object is mineral, and can only ask questions to be answered 'Yes' or 'No', it is not a good strategy to ask if the object is the third diamond from the left in the crown of the Queen of England. Admittedly a 'Yes' answer to such a question will be highly satisfactory: but a 'No' answer will provide almost no suggestion for further advance. The best questions are very general ones such as 'Is it metal or not?' In a succession of games, the best questions will be answered 'Yes' on fifty per cent of the occasions when they are asked: this is certainly not true of the question about the crown diamond. In the same way it is more useful at early stages of a science to formulate theories in such a way as to predict only general results, and to have few (if possible, no) other theories consistent with those results. The ideal at early stages is to perform experiments with only two possible results, and to say 'If A occurs, a theory of this general type must be true; if B occurs, it cannot be'. At later stages, when many classes of theory have been eliminated, this will lead one to ask quantitative questions just as at late stages of 'Twenty Questions' it may be appropriate to ask the question about the crown diamond.

The formulation of highly quantitative theories must depart from the ideal in one of two ways. If the theory is tested by experiments having only two possible results, other theories besides the one formulated will be consistent with the result actually obtained. If on the other hand the experiment has a large number of possible results, then on the average quantitative theories will be rapidly disproved without any compensating advantage: little is learned by disproving a quantitative theory. Hull's theorizing in its later form shows both these weaknesses. Cotton (1955) has pointed out that the theory gives a highly complex expression for particular observed relations: the experiment used to test the truth of the theory shows only that the observed relation belongs to a very large class of expressions amongst which that predicted from Hull's theory is one. On the other hand, when this way of escape was not taken, as in the mathematico-deductive theory of rote learning (Hull *et al.* 1940), then the theory was rapidly disproved. As is said by Hilgard (1948, p. 328) ' his efforts to predict the form of the serial position curve seemed rather promising when a crude approximation was accepted, but when the details were taken seriously an enormously complicated *ad hoc* system was needed. This did not meet the test of interchangeable constants, and the whole enterprise has ended in a stalemate.' So will the majority of honest attempts to test highly quantitative theories, because of their own logical nature.

If we take into account, as information theory has taught us, the whole ensemble of possible explanations for any scientific problem: then the most rapid advance will be made by dividing this ensemble into classes of equal size and performing experiments each of which picks out one of these classes and rejects all the others. In practical cases it may not be possible to reach this ideal, but we can at least approach it. To do so will mean starting by the examination of broad fields of experimental results, rather in the positivist tradition whose chief advocate is now Skinner. The setting-up of generalizations from these results is in fact the rejection of all theories inconsistent with the generalizations, and the acceptance of the remaining class as containing the adequate explanation. The next step takes us beyond the pure positivist, however, since it consists in dividing the possible explanations into two or more classes and attempting to decide between these new classes; and the explanations to be tested at this stage go beyond the original observations. For instance, when Andjus, Knopfelmacher, Russell and Smith (1956) subject animals to freezing after they have learned a maze, they are dividing explanations of behaviour into those which depend on storing experience solely by some continued process in the nervous system, and those which regard at least part of the storage as due to changes in structure: their findings show that the latter class of theories contains the correct explanation. The positivist would disapprove of such an enquiry, but as we have seen earlier his objections are not valid. These objections give the impression of being to some extent a reaction against the tendency of psychologists to 'test' theories by verifying a prediction made also by many other theories: in so far as the Skinner approach is such a reaction against this tendency we can heartily sympathize with it. There can be no legitimate objection, however, to theories which include hypothetical constructs provided that those theories are tested by predictions which few (if possible, no) other theories would make.

The proper road for progress then is to set up theories which are not at first detailed, although they must be capable of disproof. As research advances the theory will become continually more detailed, until one reaches the stage at which further advance is made by giving exact values to constants previously left unspecified in equations whose general form was known. At this later stage it may be convenient for teaching or expository purposes to reverse the logical process by which knowledge has been gained: to state a set of postulates and deduce from them the facts known to be true from experiment. But this is merely an expository device. It is a highly inefficient strategy to state postulates and deduce predictions unless the postulates have been reached by the gradual narrowing down of possibilities.

The history of science bears out this argument. It is very surprising that Hull (1943, p. 7) should set up Euclidean geometry as a model for the scientific endeavour: geometry is of course a logical exercise without any necessary correspondence with reality. It may be useful practice in rigorous thinking to deduce the exact consequences of a set of arbitrary postulates, but it is not science. Where adequate explanations of objective events have been reached, it is rather by a process of narrowing down the possibilities like that we have described. The example of Newton's *Principia*, given by Hull, is misleading; while it is indeed true that that great work was written in geometrical form, it was based on centuries of previous advance in which competing theories had been eliminated. The history of astronomy is older than our records, and had issued by Newton's time in well-established lower-order theories such as Kepler's formulation of the elliptical motion of planets. Furthermore, the expository technique of the *Principia* is not that of Newton's own earlier work, such as that on optics. It seems likely that he was forced away from his own conception of scientific method by the pressure of rather backward-looking criticism from those who surrounded him (Burniston Brown 1950). Rather than regard the geometric form of the *Principia* as the ideal, it might be plausible to call it a relic of the scholastic age surviving into that of modern science.

Newton's *New Theory of Light and Colours* followed the plan we have set before ourselves: it started with observations, considered possible explanations, and after checking the suggested explanations and eliminating some, concluded with a statement of principles which were entailed by the whole series of results. In other fields of science the same process can be seen: in chemistry elements were classified, generalizations established about the relative weights of each involved in any reaction, and the atomic theory devised to explain these generalizations. The next step was the periodic table of the elements in order of atomic weights and so to contemporary theories of atomic structure and valency. In biology the gradual establishment of truths concerning geographical distribution and homology of structure was essential to the great theoretical principles of the *Origin of Species*. From the philosopher's arm-chair it might be said that logically some genius might have enunciated 300 years ago the principles of modern atomic or evolutionary theory, deduced their consequences, and had them verified over the intervening centuries as technology advanced. The fact remains that this did not happen, for the very good reason that 300 years ago any other set of equally detailed principles seemed as likely: and therefore less ambitious theories were first established.

The proper road for psychology is therefore by way of more modest theorizing. The introductory chapters of Hull (1943) on the value of hypotheses are sound, but need supplementing. Either we must confine our attention to miniature systems for a restricted field of behaviour, as Hilgard (1948) argues; or we must have more general, less detailed theories for the broad field. In the writer's view both are necessary, since the miniature system can never be tested on an intact organism without some assumptions about matters outside the scope of that system.

## On the Status of Scientific Methodology

Hull (1937) compared scientific method with philosophical speculation, to the disadvantage of the latter. He took as an example of the latter the statement ' besides God no substance can be, nor can be conceived '. Such a statement is not observationally testable and thus can only be urged by argument and persuasion. The problem of human nature, Hull argued, should be attacked by the scientific rather than the philosophic approach. With this conclusion the writer is strongly in agreement; but unfortunately there is a difficulty which can best be expressed by describing theories of scientific method as themselves philosophical. If we say that we believe in effects of noise on behaviour, and are challenged, we can cite experimental evidence in our aid. But if we say that we believe in evidence, and are challenged, we can cite no experiments to prove our point. All we can do is to argue and persuade, as Hull did. The logical status of the two beliefs, in noise and in evidence, is different: one is a statement within a language and the other a statement about the rules of that language. Once we decide to play Canasta, the rules prescribe our behaviour; but there is nothing in the rules to stop the man who wants to play Bridge instead. Unless one distinguishes between statements about and within languages, one finds oneself in the sort of logical tangle illustrated by the paradoxical statement ' everything I say is false '. And when the distinction is made, one finds that Hull's statement ' a satisfactory scientific theory should begin with a set of explicitly stated postulates ' is of the same class as ' besides God no substance can be, nor can be conceived '.

It is important to realize this, for two main reasons. The first of these concerns disagreements between those who accept Hull's fundamental belief in the value of experimental testing; such disagreement may arise about the particular statement quoted in the last paragraph, or about the use of S–R terminology, or about similar procedural beliefs. It is essential that no reader of this book should be led, by the criticisms we have sometimes made of S–R theory, into thinking that any cybernetic theory is necessarily better than any S–R theory. On the contrary, many enthusiasts for the language of communication engineers have fallen into the pitfalls of premature quantification and of ' verifying ' complex theories by a few simple experiments, which we have discussed in connexion with S–R theories. Conversely, many S–R theorists have stated in their own language, relationships which cyberneticists have afterwards ' discovered ': Hull (1937) gives an outline account of behaviour in terms of negative feed-back and of a stored representation of external events. As has been said in Chapter 10, the latest views of

Spence seem suggestively similar to those we have advanced, when allowance is made for a due process of translation. It would be unwise to magnify the differences, which are to a great extent of the same kind as those between arabic and roman numerals, or the various early notations for writing calculus. As these analogies show, this is not to say that one language is as good as another; the writer believes that cybernetic language is as great an advance over S–R terminology as arabic over roman numerals. But the important thing in arithmetic is the correctness of the calculation, and the important thing in psychology is the structure of the relationships between the various theoretical concepts, rather than the words used as labels for them or the mode of presentation employed.

Appreciation of this unimportance of language as opposed to meaning should be reciprocal: when S–R theorists adopt an explanation of reasoning in terms of sequences of internal responses, it is not a victory for that theory but merely a translation of the position of cognitive theorists into a different language. Both Hull and Spence seem to have had such an appreciation of the distinction between words and their referents; but it is to be suspected that some of their supporters have not.

There is a second reason for emphasizing the extent to which adopting, say, the hypothetico-deductive method, is an arbitrary choice rather than something which can be proved correct. This is that it gives us more understanding of the real issues at stake between those who believe in the scientific approach and those who do not. Hull challenged those who do not wish to explain human behaviour in the same terms as other natural phenomena to produce a testable system based on non-physical postulates. But this was a misunderstanding; such people reject the whole conception of testable systems in this field. This position cannot be proved incorrect, but only opposed by persuasion, argument, and the testimony of the fruits of scientific method in the lives of those brought up in it, and in its practical results in fields of application. The persuasion will be futile unless it is based on an understanding of the opponent's point of view.

Behind the rejection of attempts to predict and understand behaviour in terms of non-mental concepts, there often lies an unwillingness to deny the values of everyday experience. The shape of a snow-flake, or of a mountain may be impressive; but most of us yield more respect and affection to the wisdom, fortitude, and compassion of certain human beings. To reduce these qualities to the operation of the same laws which produce even beautiful natural objects seems almost to be a closing of the eyes to them. Any of us, who believe in the scientific approach, who is wanting in this respect and affection reinforces this interpretation. Yet, as Spence (1940) has said in other words, our concepts should be judged not by the discrepancy between their own nature and everyday experience, but by the agreement between experience and the effects which the interplay of our constructs would produce. The actions of great men will not be changed when we know more of the underlying structure behind them: the phenomena remain the same whatever formulae we find for their description. In the same way to understand the anatomy of a man is not to abolish or deny the beauty of his intact body: without such knowledge that beauty can neither be repaired when it is damaged nor represented artistically to heighten its value. Compassion also will be more effective when it is based on fuller knowledge of human behaviour.

For these reasons a book such as this cannot come to a rounded conclusion and say, there is no more advance possible to this method. The scientific quest must be renewed: not to denigrate man, but to raise him up. And to the writer the belief in experimental method seems merely a translation into the idiom of our time of the injunction to be, not only as innocent as doves, but also as wise as serpents. It would be well to combine it with other precepts from the same source.

# REFERENCES

ABORN, M. and RUBENSTEIN, H. (1952). Information theory and immediate recall. *J. exp. Psychol.* **44**, 260–6.

ADAMS, J. A. (1955). A source of decrement in psychomotor skills. *J. exp. Psychol.* **49**, 390–4.

ADAMS, J. A. (1956). Vigilance in the detection of low intensity visual stimuli. *J. exp. Psychol.* **52**, 204–8.

ADRIAN, E. D. (1954). Science and human nature. *Advanc. Sci.* **11**, 121–8.

ALBRIGHT, L. E., BORRESON, C. R. and MARX, M. H. (1956). Reactive inhibition as a function of same hand and opposite hand inter-trial activity. *J. exp. Psychol.* **51**, 353–7.

ANDJUS, R. K., KNOPFELMACHER, F., RUSSELL, R. W. and SMITH, A. U. (1956). Some effects of severe hypothermia on learning and retention. *Quart. J. exp. Psychol.* **8**, 15–23.

ANGER, D. J. (1956). The dependence of inter-response times upon the relative reinforcement of different inter-response times. *J. exp. Psychol.* **52**, 145–61.

BAHRICK, H. P., NOBLE, M. and FITTS, P. M. (1954). Extra-task performance as a measure of learning a primary task. *J. exp. Psychol.* **48**, 298–302.

BAKAN, P. (1952). Preliminary tests of vigilance for verbal materials. *U.S.A.F. Human Resources Research Center Research Note* 52–7, Lackland Air Force Base.

BAKAN, P. (1955). Discrimination decrement as a function of time in a prolonged vigil. *J. exp. Psychol.* **50**, 387–90.

BAKER, C. H. (1956). Biassing attention to visual displays during a vigilance task: a summary report. *Royal Navy Personnel Research Committee Report* 56/876.

BAKER, K. E., WYLIE, R. C. and GAGNÉ, R. M. (1951). The effects of an interfering task on the learning of a complex motor skill. *J. exp. Psychol.* **44**, 428–33.

BARTLETT, F. C. (1932). *Remembering.* Cambridge University Press.

BARTLETT, F. C. (1943). Fatigue following highly skilled work. *Proc. roy. Soc. B* **131**, 247–57.

BARTLETT, F. C. (1948). The measurement of human skill. *Occup. Psychol.* **22**, 31–8.

BERLYNE, D. E. (1950). Novelty and curiosity as determinants of exploratory behaviour. *Brit. J. Psychol.* **41**, 68–80.

BERLYNE, D. E. (1951a). Attention to change. *Brit. J. Psychol.* **42**, 269–78.

BERLYNE, D. E. (1951b). Attention, perception and behaviour theory. *Psychol. Rev.* **58**, 137–46.

317

BERRIEN, F. K. (1946).    The effects of noise.    *Psychol. Bull.* **43,** 141–61.

BERTSCH, W. F., WEBSTER, J. C., KLUMPP, R. G. and THOMPSON, P. O. (1956).    Effects of two message storage schemes upon communications within a small problem-solving group.    *J. acoust. Soc. Amer.* **28,** 550–3.

BEXTON, W. H., HERON, W. and SCOTT, T. H. (1954).    Effects of decreased variation in the sensory environment.    *Canad. J. Psychol.* **8,** 70–6.

BILLS, A. G. (1931).    Blocking: a new principle in mental fatigue.    *Amer. J. Psychol.* **43,** 230–45.

BILLS, A. G. and SHAPIN, M. J. (1936) Mental fatigue under automatically controlled rates of work.    *J. gen. Psychol.* **15,** 335–46.

BINDRA, D., PATERSON, A. L. and STRZELECKI, J. (1955).    On the relation between anxiety and conditioning.    *Canad. J. Psychol.* **9,** 1–6.

BIRMINGHAM, H. P. and TAYLOR, F. V. (1954).    A design philosophy for man-machine control systems.    *Proc. I.R.E.* **42,** 1748–58.

BLUM, R. A. and BLUM, J. S. (1949).    Factual issues in the continuity controversy.    *Psychol. Rev.* **56,** 33–50.

BOURNE, L. E. (1955).    An evaluation of the effect of induced tension on performance.    *J. exp. Psychol.* **49,** 418–22.

BOWEN, H. M. (1956).    *The Appreciation of Serial Discrimination.* Doctoral thesis, University of Cambridge.

BRICKER, P. D. and CHAPANIS, A. (1953).    Do incorrectly perceived tachistoscopic stimuli convey some information ?    *Psychol. Rev.* **60,** 181–88.

BROADBENT, D. E. (1950).    The twenty dials test under quiet conditions. *Applied Psychol. Unit Report* No. 130.

BROADBENT, D. E. (1951).    The twenty dials and twenty lights tests under noise conditions.    *Applied Psychol. Unit Report* No. 160.

BROADBENT, D. E. (1952a).    Speaking and listening simultaneously. *J. exp. Psychol.* **43,** 267–73.

BROADBENT, D. E. (1952b).    Listening to one of two synchronous messages.    *J. exp. Psychol.* **44,** 51–5.

BROADBENT, D. E. (1952c).    Failures of attention in selective listening. *J. exp. Psychol.* **44,** 428–33.

BROADBENT, D. E. (1953a).    Noise, paced performance, and vigilance tasks.    *Brit. J. Psychol.* **44,** 295–303.

BROADBENT, D. E. (1953b).    Economizing VHF channels: synthetic trials of a technique.    *Flying Personnel Research Committee Report* No. 831.

BROADBENT, D. E. (1953c).    Classical conditioning and human watchkeeping.    *Psychol. Rev.* **60,** 331–9.

BROADBENT, D. E. (1954a).    Some effects of noise on visual performance. *Quart. J. exp. Psychol.* **6,** 1–5.

BROADBENT, D. E. (1954b).    The role of auditory localization in attention and memory span.    *J. exp. Psychol.* **47,** 191–6.

BROADBENT, D. E. (1955). The bass-cutting of frequency transposed speech. *Applied Psychol. Unit Report* No. 223.

BROADBENT, D. E. (1956a). Listening between and during practised auditory distractions. *Brit. J. Psychol.* **47,** 51–60.

BROADBENT, D. E. (1956b). In *Information Theory.* (Edited by E. C. CHERRY.) Butterworth.

BROADBENT, D. E. (1956c). Successive responses to simultaneous stimuli. *Quart. J. exp. Psychol.* **8,** 145–52.

BROADBENT, D. E. (1957a). In *Handbook of Noise Control.* (Edited by C. M. HARRIS.) McGraw-Hill.

BROADBENT, D. E. (1957b). Effects of noises of high and low frequency on behaviour. *Ergonomics* **1,** 21–9.

BROADBENT, D. E. (1957c). Immediate memory and simultaneous stimuli. *Quart. J. exp. Psychol.* **9,** 1–11.

BROADBENT, D. E. (1957d). A mechanical model for human attention and immediate memory. *Psychol. Rev.* **64,** 205–15.

BROADBENT, D. E. (1957e). An effect of noise on an ' intellectual ' task. *R.N. Personnel Research Committee Report* No. 57/892.

BROADBENT, D. E. (1959). Human perception and animal learning. To appear in a volume edited by O. L. ZANGWILL and W. H. THORPE.

BROADBENT, D. E. and FORD, H. K. (1955). Two channel listening in the aircraft situation. *Flying Personnel Research Committee Report* No. 945.

BROGDEN, W. J. (1939). Sensory preconditioning. *J. exp. Psychol.* **25,** 323–32.

BROUSSARD, I. G., WALKER, R. Y. and ROBERTS, E. (1952). The influence of noise on the visual contrast threshold. *U.S. Army Medical Research Lab. Report* No. 101, Fort Knox.

BROWN, J. (1954). The nature of set-to-learn and of intra-material interference in immediate memory. *Quart. J. exp. Psychol.* **6,** 141–8.

BROWN, J. (1955). *Immediate Memory.* Doctoral thesis, University of Cambridge. See also *Quart. J. exp. Psychol.* **10,** 12–21.

BROWN, J. S. (1942). The generalization of approach responses as a function of stimulus intensity and strength of motivation. *J. comp. Psychol.* **33,** 209–26.

BRYAN, W. L. and HARTER, W. (1899). Studies in the telegraphic language. *Psychol. Rev.* **6,** 345–75.

BURNISTON BROWN, G. (1950). *Science, its Method and its Philosophy.* Norton.

BUXTON, C. E. and BAKAN, M. B. (1949). Correction vs. non-correction learning techniques as related to reminiscence in serial anticipation learning. *J. exp. Psychol.* **39,** 338–41.

CHAPANIS, A., GARNER, W. R. and MORGAN, C. T. (1949). *Applied Experimental Psychology.* Wiley.

CHERNIKOFF, R., BIRMINGHAM, H. P. and TAYLOR, F. V. (1956). A comparison of pursuit and compensatory tracking in a simulated aircraft control loop. *J. appl. Psychol.* **40**, 47–52.

CHERRY, E. C. (1953). Some experiments on the recognition of speech, with one and with two ears. *J. acoust. Soc. Amer.* **25**, 975–9.

CHERRY, E. C. and TAYLOR, W. K. (1954). Some further experiments upon the recognition of speech, with one and with two ears. *J. acoust. Soc. Amer.* **26**, 554–9.

CHOCHOLLE, R. (1946). Variation des temps de reaction auditifs en fonction de l'intensite a diverses frequences. *Ann. Psychol.* 41–2, 65–124.

CONRAD, R. (1951). Speed and load stress in a sensorimotor skill. *Brit. J. industr. Med.* **8**, 1–7.

CONRAD, R. (1955a). Adaptation to time in a sensorimotor skill. *J. exp. Psychol.* **49**, 115–21.

CONRAD, R. (1955b). Some effects on performance of changes in perceptual load. *J. exp. Psychol.* **49**, 313–22.

CONRAD, R. (1957). Decay theory and immediate memory. *Nature* **179**, 831–2.

CONRAD, R. and HILLE, B. A. (1955). Comparison of paced and unpaced performance at a packing task. *Occup. Psychol.* **29**, 15–28.

CONRAD, R. and HILLE, B. A. (1957). Self-pacing performance as a function of perceptual load. *J. exp. Psychol.* **53**, 52–4.

COOPER, F. S., DELATTRE, P., LIBERMAN, A. M., BORST, J. M. and GERSTMAN, L. J. (1952). Some experiments on the perception of synthetic speech sounds. *J. acoust. Soc. Amer.* **24**, 597–606.

COTTON, J. W. (1955). On making predictions from Hull's theory. *Psychol. Rev.* **62**, 303–14.

COX, D. R. and SMITH, W. L. (1953). The superposition of several strictly periodic sequences of events. *Biometrika* **40**, 1–11.

CRAIK, K. J. W. (1948). Theory of the human operator in control systems: II. Man as an element in a control system. *Brit. J. Psychol.* **38**, 142–8.

CROSSMAN, E. R. F. W. (1953). Entropy and choice-time: the effect of frequency unbalance on choice response. *Quart. J. exp. Psychol.* **5**, 41–51.

CROSSMAN, E. R. F. W. (1955). The measurement of discriminability. *Quart. J. exp. Psychol.* **7**, 176–95.

CULPIN, M. and SMITH, M. (1930). The nervous temperament. *Industr. Hlth. Research Board Report* No. 61. H.M. Stationery Office.

DAVIS, D. R. (1948). *Pilot Error*. Air Publication 3139a, H.M. Stationery Office.

DAVIS, R. (1956a). The limits of the ' psychological refractory period '. *Quart. J. exp. Psychol.* **8**, 24–38.

DAVIS, R. (1956b). Comments on 'central inhibition: some refractory observations', by A. Elithorn and C. Lawrence. *Quart. J. exp. Psychol.* **8,** 39.

DAVIS, R. (1957). The human operator as a single-channel information system. *Quart. J. exp. Psychol.* **9,** 119–29.

DEESE, J. (1951). The extinction of a discrimination without performance of the choice response. *J. comp. physiol. Psychol.* **44,** 362–6.

DEESE, J. (1955). Some problems in the theory of vigilance. *Psychol. Rev.* **62,** 359–68.

DEESE, J., LAZARUS, R. S. and KEENAN, J. (1953). Anxiety, anxiety reduction, and stress in learning. *J. exp. Psychol.* **46,** 55–60.

DEUTSCH. J. A. (1951). A preliminary report on a new auditory after-effect. *Quart. J. exp. Psychol.* **3,** 43–6.

DEUTSCH, J. A. (1953). A new type of behaviour theory. *Brit. J. Psychol.* **44,** 304–17.

DEUTSCH. J. A. (1954). A machine with insight. *Quart. J. exp. Psychol.* **6,** 6–11.

DEUTSCH, J. A. (1956). A theory of insight, reasoning, and latent learning. *Brit. J. Psychol.* **47,** 115–25.

DREW, G. C. (1940). Mental fatigue. *Flying Personnel Research Committee Report* No. 227.

DREW, G. C. (1950). Variations in reflex blink rate during visual-motor tasks. *Quart. J. exp. Psychol.* **3,** 73–88.

DUNCAN, C. P. (1956). On the similarity between reactive inhibition and neural satiation. *Amer. J. Psychol.* **69,** 227–35.

DUNLAP, K. and WELLS, G. R. (1910). Some experiments with reactions to visual and auditory stimuli. *Psychol. Rev.* **17,** 319–35.

ECCLES, J. C. and McINTYRE, A. K. (1953). The effects of disuse and of activity on mammalian spinal reflexes. *J. Physiol.* **121,** 492–516.

EGAN, J. P., CARTERETTE, E. C. and THWING, E. J. (1954). Some factors affecting multi-channel listening. *J. acoust. Soc. Amer.* **26,** 774–82.

EHRENFREUND, D. (1948). An experimental test of the continuity theory of discrimination learning with pattern vision. *J. comp. physiol. Psychol.* **41,** 408–22.

ELITHORN, A. and LAWRENCE, C. (1956). Central inhibition: some refractory observations. *Quart. J. exp. Psychol.* **7,** 116–27.

ELLIOTT, E. (1957). Auditory vigilance tasks. *Advanc. Sci.* **14,** 393–9.

ESTES, W. K. (1950). Towards a statistical theory of learning. *Psychol. Rev.* **57,** 94–107.

EYSENCK, H. J. (1947). *Dimensions of Personality.* Kegan Paul.

EYSENCK, H. J. (1950). Cyclothymia and schizothymia as a dimension of personality: I. Historical review. *J. Pers.* **19,** 123–52.

EYSENCK, H. J. (1952). Schizothymia-cyclothymia as a dimension of personality: II. Experimental. *J. Pers.* **20,** 345–84.

EYSENCK, H. J. (1955a). A dynamic theory of anxiety and hysteria. *J. ment. Sci.* **101**, 28–51.

EYSENCK, H. J. (1955b). Cortical inhibition, figural after-effect, and theory of personality. *J. abn. soc. Psychol.* **51**, 94–106.

EYSENCK, H. J. (1956). Reminiscence, drive, and personality theory. *J. abn. soc. Psychol.* **53**, 328–33.

FANO, R. M. (1949). The transmission of information. *M.I.T. Research Lab. of Electronics Report* No. 65.

FARRELL, B. A. (1955). On the limits of experimental psychology. *Brit. J. Psychol.* **46**, 165–77.

FERSTER, C. B. and SKINNER, B. F. (1957). *Schedules of Reinforcement.* Appleton-Century.

FESSARD, A. and KUCHARSKI, P. (1935). Recherches sur le temps de réaction aux sons de hauteurs et d'intensités différentes. *Ann. Psychol.* **35**, 103–17.

FINKLE, A. L. and POPPEN, J. R. (1948). Clinical effects of noise and mechanical vibrations of a turbo-jet engine on man. *J. appl. Physiol.* **1**, 183–204.

FITTS, P. M. and SEEGER, C. M. (1953). S–R compatibility: spatial characteristics of stimulus and response codes. *J. exp. Psychol.* **46**, 199–210.

FLESCH, R. (1948). A new readability yardstick. *J. appl. Psychol.* **32**, 221–33.

FLETCHER, H. (1953). *Speech and Hearing in Communication.* Van Nostrand.

FLOYD, W. F. and WELFORD, A. T. (1953). *Ergonomics Symposium on Fatigue.* H. K. Lewis.

FORD, A. (1929). Attention-automatization: an investigation of the transitional nature of mind. *Amer. J. Psychol.* **41**, 1–32.

FOULDS, G. A. (1951). Temperamental differences in maze performance: I. Characteristic differences among psychoneurotics, *Brit. J. Psychol.* **42**, 209–17.

FOULDS, G. A. (1952). Temperamental differences in maze performance: II. The effects of distraction and of electroconvulsive therapy on psychomotor retardation. *Brit. J. Psychol.* **43**, 33–41.

FRANKS, C. M. (1956). Conditioning and personality: a study of normal and neurotic subjects. *J. abn. soc. Psychol.* **52**, 143–50.

FRANKS, C. M. and LAVERTY, S. G. (1955). Sodium amytal and eyelid conditioning. *J. ment. Sci.* **101**, 654–63.

FRASER, D. C. (1950). The relation between angle of display and performance in a prolonged visual task. *Quart. J. exp. Psychol.* **2**, 176–81.

FRASER, D. C. (1953a). The relation of an environmental variable to performance in a prolonged visual task. *Quart. J. exp. Psychol.* **5**, 31–2.

FRASER, D. C. (1953b). A study of fatigue in aircrew: I. Validation of techniques. *Applied Psychol. Unit Report* No. 185.

FRASER, D. C. (1957). *A Study of Vigilance and Fatigue.* Doctoral thesis, University of Edinburgh.

GAGNÉ, R. M. (1941). External inhibition and disinhibition in a conditioned operant response. *J. exp. Psychol.* **29,** 104–16.

GAGNÉ, R. M. (1953). In *Ergonomics Symposium on Fatigue.* (Edited by W. F. FLOYD and A. T. WELFORD.) H. K. Lewis.

GALAMBOS, R. and DAVIS, H. (1944). Inhibition of activity in single auditory nerve fibres by acoustic stimulation. *J. Neurophysiol.* **7,** 287–303.

GALAMBOS, R., ROSENBLITH, W. A. and ROSENZWEIG, M. R. (1950). Physiological evidence for a cochleo-cochlear pathway in the cat. *Experientia* **6,** 438–40.

GALAMBOS, R., SHEATZ, G. and VERNIER, V. G. (1956). Electrophysiological correlates of a conditioned response in cats. *Science* **123,** 376–7.

GARNER, W. R., HAKE, H. W. and ERIKSEN, C. W. (1956). Operationism and the concept of perception. *Psychol. Rev.* **63,** 149–59.

GARVEY, W. D. (1957). The effects of ' task-induced stress ' on man-machine system performance. *U.S. Naval Research Lab. Report* No. 5015.

GIBBS, C. B. (1951). Transfer of training and skill assumptions in tracking tasks. *Quart. J. exp. Psychol.* **3,** 99–111.

GIBBS, C. B. (1952). Car turning signals and delays in responding to visual information. *Applied Psychol. Unit Report* No. 176. Cambridge.

GIBBS, C. B. (1954). The continuous regulation of skilled responses by kinaesthetic feed-back. *Brit. J. Psychol.* **45,** 24–39.

GLANZER, M. (1953). Stimulus satiation: an explanation of spontaneous alternation and related phenomena. *Psychol. Rev.* **60,** 257–68.

GLEITMAN, H. (1950). Studies in motivation and learning: II. Thirsty rats trained in maze with food but not water, then run hungry. *J. exp. Psychol.* **40,** 169–74.

GLEITMAN, H. (1955). Place learning without prior performance. *J. comp. physiol. Psychol.* **48,** 77–9.

GOUGH, H. G. (1946). The relationship of socio-economic status to personality inventory and achievement. *J. educ. Psychol.* **37,** 527–40.

GOUGH, H. G. (1949). Factors relating to the academic achievement of high-school students. *J. educ. Psychol.* **40,** 65–78.

GREGORY, R. L. (1953). On physical model explanations in psychology. *Brit. J. Philos. Sci.* **4,** 192–7.

GREGORY, R. L. (1956). In *Information Theory.* (Edited by E. C. CHERRY.) Butterworth.

HAMILTON, J. A. and KRECHEVSKY, I. (1933). Studies in the effect of shock upon behaviour plasticity in the rat. *J. comp. Psychol.* **16,** 237–53.

HARMON, F. L. (1933). The effects of noise upon certain psychological and physiological processes. *Arch. Psychol.* No. 147.

HEAD, H. (1920). *Studies in Neurology.* Oxford University Press.

HEARNSHAW, L. S. (1956). Temporal integration and behaviour. *Bull. Brit. Psychol. Soc.* No. 30.

HEBB, D. O. (1949). *The Organization of Behavior.* Wiley.

HEBB, D. O. (1955). Drives and the C.N.S. (Conceptual Nervous System). *Psychol. Rev.* **62,** 243–54.

HELPER, M. M. (1957). The effects of noise on work output and physiological activation. *U.S. Army Med. Res. Lab. Report* No. 270.

HELSON, H. (1948). Adaptation level as a basis for a quantitative theory of frames of reference. *Psychol. Rev.* **55,** 297–313.

HENDERSON, D. K. and GILLESPIE, R. D. (1947). *A Text-book of Psychiatry.* (6th edition.) Oxford University Press.

HERNANDEZ-PEON, R., SCHERRER, H. and JOUVET, M. (1956). Modification of electrical activity in cochlear nucleus during ' attention ' in unanesthetized cats. *Science* **123,** 331–2.

HERON, A. (1956). A two-part personality measure for use as a research criterion. *Brit. J. Psychol.* **47,** 243–51.

HICK, W. E. (1952). On the rate of gain of information. *Quart. J. exp. Psychol.* **4,** 11–26.

HICK, W. E. and BATES, J. A. V. (1950). *The Human Operator of Control Mechanisms.* Ministry of Supply.

HICK, W. E. and WELFORD, A. T. (1956). Comments on ' central inhibition: some refractory observations ', by A. Elithorn and C. Lawrence. *Quart. J. exp. Psychol.* **8,** 39–41.

HILGARD, E. R. (1948). *Theories of Learning.* (1st edition.) Appleton-Century.

HILGARD, E. R. (1956). *Theories of Learning.* (2nd edition.) Appleton-Century.

HILGARD, E. R., JONES, L. V. and KAPLAN, S. J. (1951). Conditioned discrimination as related to anxiety. *J. exp. Psychol.* **42,** 94–9.

HILGARD, E. R. and MARQUIS, D. G. (1940). *Conditioning and Learning.* Appleton-Century.

HINDE, R. A. (1954). Changes in responsiveness to a constant stimulus. *Brit. J. anim. Behav.* **2,** 41–55.

HIRSH, I. J. (1948a). Binaural summation and interaural inhibition as a function of the level of masking noise. *Amer. J. Psychol.* **61,** 205–13.

HIRSH, I. J. (1948b). The influence of interaural phase on interaural summation and inhibition. *J. acoust. Soc. Amer.* **20,** 536–44.

HIRSH, I. J. (1950). The relation between localization and intelligibility. *J. acoust. Soc. Amer.* **22,** 196–200.

HIRSH, I. J., DAVIS, H., SILVERMAN, S. R., REYNOLDS, E. G., ELDERT, E. and BENSON, R. W. (1952). Development of materials for speech audiometry. *J. Speech Dis.* **17,** 321–37.

HOFFMAN, A. C. and MEAD, L. C. (1943). The performance of trained subjects on a complex task of four hours duration. *U.S. O.S.R.D. Publ. Bd.* No. 20284.

HOLLAND, J. G. (1956). Vigilance and schedules of reinforcement. *Amer. Psychologist* **11**, 414.

HOLLAND, J. G. (1957). Technique for behavioural analysis of human observing. *Science* **125**, 348–50.

HOWES, D. H. and SOLOMON, R. L. (1950). A note on McGinnies' 'Emotionality and perceptual defense'. *Psychol. Rev.* **57**, 229–34.

HULL, C. L. (1920). Quantitative aspects of the evolution of concepts. *Psychol. Monog.* No. 123.

HULL, C. L. (1930). Knowledge and purpose as habit mechanisms. *Psychol. Rev.* **37**, 511–25.

HULL, C. L. (1935). The conflicting psychologies of learning—a way out. *Psychol. Rev.* **42**, 491–516.

HULL, C. L. (1937). Mind, mechanism, and adaptive behaviour. *Psychol. Rev.* **44**, 1–32.

HULL, C. L. (1943). *The Principles of Behavior.* Appleton-Century.

HULL, C. L. (1952). *A Behavior System.* Yale University Press.

HULL, C. L., HOVLAND, C. I., ROSS, R. T., HALL, M., PERKINS, D. T. and FITCH, F. B. (1940). *Mathematico-deductive Theory of Rote Learning.* Yale University Press.

HUNTER, W. S. (1920). The temporal maze and kinesthetic sensory processes in the white rat. *Psychobiol.* **2**, 1–17.

HURWITZ, H. M. B. (1954). Response-duration of lever pressing in the white rat. *Quart. J. exp. Psychol.* **6**, 62–71.

HURWITZ, H. M. B. (1955). Response elimination without performance. *Quart. J. exp. Psychol.* **7**, 1–7.

HURWITZ, H. M. B. (1957). Periodicity of response in operant extinction. *Quart. J. exp. Psychol.* **9**, 177–84.

HUSBAND, R. W. (1929). A note on maze learning with the time factor held constant. *J. gen. Psychol.* **2**, 366–9.

HYMAN, R. (1953). Stimulus information as a determinant of reaction time. *J. exp. Psychol.* **45**, 188–96.

IRVINE, D. H. (1957). Visual inspection as a vigilance task. *Advanc. Sci.* **14**, 402–8.

JACKSON, W. (Editor) (1953). *Communication Theory.* Butterworth.

JAMES, W. (1890). *Principles of Psychology.* Holt.

JENKINS, W. O. and STANLEY, J. C. (1950). Partial reinforcement: a review and a critique. *Psychol. Bull.* **47**, 193–234.

JERISON, H. J. (1954). Paced performance on a complex counting task under noise and fatigue conditions. *Amer. Psychologist*, **9**, 399.

JERISON, H. J. (1956). Differential effects of noise and fatigue on a complex counting task. *Wright Air Development Center Tech. Report* 55–359.

JERISON, H. J. (1957). Performance on a simple vigilance task in noise and quiet. *J. acoust. Soc. Amer.* **29**, 1163–5.

JERISON, H. J. and WING, S. (1957). Effects of noise and fatigue on a complex vigilance task. *Wright Air Development Center Tech. Report* 57–14.

KAPPAUF, W. E., PAYNE, M. C. and POWE, W. (1955). Performance decrement in relation to task difficulty. *University of Illinois Memorandum Report* H-6; *U.S.A.F. Contract* No. A.F. 33(038)-25726.

KAY, H. (1956). What do we learn? *Proc. roy. Soc. Med.* **49**, 1021–3.

KAY, H. and POULTON, E. C. (1951). Anticipation in memorizing. *Brit. J. Psychol.* **42**, 34–41.

KENDLER, H. H. (1952). Some comments on Thistlethwaite's perception of latent learning. *Psychol. Bull.* **49**, 47–51.

KIMBLE, G. A. and KENDALL, J. W. (1953). A comparison of two methods of producing experimental extinction. *J. exp. Psychol.* **45**, 87–90.

KINNAMAN, A. J. (1902). Mental life of two macacus rhesus monkeys in captivity. *Amer. J. Psychol.* **13**, 98–148; 173–218.

KLEIN, G. S. and KRECH. D. (1952). Cortical conductivity in the brain-injured. *J. Pers.* **21**, 118–48.

KLEITMAN, N. (1939). *Sleep and Wakefulness.* University of Chicago Press.

KLEMMER, E. T. (1956). Time uncertainty in simple reaction time. *J. exp. Psychol.* **51**, 179–84.

KONORSKI, J. (1948). *Conditioned Reflexes and Neuron Organization.* Cambridge University Press.

KRECH, D., ROSENZWEIG, M. R., BENNETT, E. L. and KRUECKEL, B. (1954). Enzyme concentrations in the brain and adjustive behaviour patterns. *Science* **120**, 994–6.

KRECH, D., ROSENZWEIG, M. R. and BENNETT, E. L. (1956). Dimensions of discrimination and level of cholinesterase activity in the cerebral cortex of the rat. *J. comp. physiol. Psychol.* **49**, 261–8.

KRECHEVSKY, I. (1938). A study of the continuity of the problem-solving process. *Psychol. Rev.* **45**, 107–33.

KRUEGER, W. C. F. (1932). Learning during directed attention. *J. exp. Psychol.* **15**, 517–27.

KRYTER, K. D. (1950). The effects of noise on man. *J. Speech Dis. Monog. Suppl.* **1**.

KOCK, W. E. (1950). Binaural localization and masking. *J. acoust. Soc. Amer.* **22**, 801–4.

LANDIS, C. and HUNT, W. A. (1939). *The Startle Pattern.* Farrar.

LASHLEY, K. S. (1938). The mechanism of vision. XV Preliminary studies of the rat's capacity for detail vision. *J. gen. Psychol.* **18**, 123–93.

LAWRENCE, D. H. and LABERGE, D. L. (1956). Relationship between recognition accuracy and order of reporting stimulus dimensions. *J. exp. Psychol.* **51**, 12–18.

LAWRENCE, D. H. and MASON, W. A. (1955). Systematic behaviour during discrimination reversal and change of dimensions. *J. comp. physiol. Psychol.* **48**, 1–7.

LAZARUS, R. S. and McCLEARY, R. A (1951). Autonomic discrimination without awareness. *Psychol. Rev.* **58**, 113–22.

LEE, B. S. (1950). Effects of delayed speech feed-back. *J. acoust. Soc. Amer.* **22**, 824–6.

LEONARD, J. A. (1953). Advance information in sensorimotor skills. *Quart. J. exp. Psychol.* **5**, 141–9.

LIBERMAN, A. M., DELATTRE, P. and COOPER, F. S. (1952). The role of selected stimulus variables in the perception of the unvoiced stop consonants. *Amer. J. Psychol.* **65**, 497–516.

LICKLIDER, J. C. R. (1948). The influence of interaural phase relations upon the masking of speech by white noise. *J. acoust. Soc. Amer.* **20**, 150–9.

LOEB, M., JEANTHEAU, G. and WEAVER, L. A. (1956). A field study of a vigilance task. *U.S. Army Medical Research Lab. Report* No. 230.

LYNN, R. (1955). Personality factors in reading achievement. *Proc. roy. Soc. Med.* **48**, 996 -7.

MACQUARRY, J. P. (1953). Some relationships between non-intellectual characteristics and academic achievement. *J. educ. Psychol.* **44**, 215–28.

MACKWORTH, N. H. (1950). Researches in the measurement of human performance. *Medical Research Council Special Report Series* No. 268. H.M. Stationery Office.

MACKWORTH, J. F. and MACKWORTH, N. H. (1956). The overlapping of signals for decisions. *Amer. J. Psychol.* **69**, 26–47.

MAIER, N. R. F. (1931). Reasoning in humans: the solution of a problem and its appearance in consciousness. *J. comp. Psychol.* **12**, 181–94.

McGINNIES, E. (1949). Emotionality and perceptual defence. *Psychol. Rev.* **56**, 244–51.

McNAMARA, H. J., LONG, J. B. and WIKE, E. L. (1956). Learning without response under two conditions of external cues. *J. comp. physiol. Psychol.* **49**, 477–80.

MELTON, A. W. and IRWIN, J. McQ. (1940). The influence of degree of interpolated learning on retroactive inhibition and the overt transfer of specific responses. *Amer. J. Psychol.* **53**, 173–203.

MELTON, A. W. and VON LACKUM, W. J. (1941). Retroactive and proactive inhibition in retention: evidence for a two-factor theory of retroactive inhibition. *Amer. J. Psychol.* **54**, 157–73.

MICHOTTE, A. (1946). *La perception de la causalite.* Louvain.

MILLER, G. A. (1951). *Language and Communication.* McGraw-Hill.

MILLER, G. A. (1956). The magical number seven, plus or minus two. *Psychol. Rev.* **63**, 81–97.

MILLER, G. A., HEISE, G. A. and LICHTEN, W. (1951). The intelligibility of speech as a function of the context of the test materials. *J. exp. Psychol.* **41**, 329–35.

MILLER, G. A. and LICKLIDER, J. C. R. (1950). The intelligibility of interrupted speech. *J. acoust. Soc. Amer.* **22**, 167–73.

MONTGOMERY, K. C. (1952). A test of two explanations of spontaneous alternation. *J. comp. physiol. Psychol.* **45**, 287–93.

MORGAN, J. J. B. (1916). The overcoming of distraction and other resistances. *Arch. Psychol.* No. 35.

MOWBRAY, G. H. (1952). Simultaneous vision and audition: the detection of elements missing from overlearned sequences. *J. exp. Psychol.* **44**, 292–300.

MOWBRAY, G. H. (1953). Simultaneous vision and audition: the comprehension of prose passages with varying levels of difficulty. *J. exp. Psychol.* **46**, 365–72.

MOWBRAY, G. H. (1954). The perception of short phrases presented simultaneously for visual and auditory reception. *Quart. J. exp. Psychol.* **6**, 86–92.

MOWRER, O. H. (1940). Preparatory set—some methods of measurement. *Psychol. Monog.* No. 52.

MOWRER, O. H. (1950). *Learning Theory and Personality Dynamics.* Ronald Press.

NOBLE, M., FITTS, P. M. and WARREN, C. E. (1955). The frequency response of skilled subjects in a pursuit tracking task. *J. exp. Psychol.* **49**, 249–56.

NORTH, J. D. (1954). *The Rational Behaviour of Mechanically Extended Man.* Boulton Paul Aircraft Co.

OLDFIELD, R. C. and ZANGWILL, O. L. (1942). Head's concept of schema and its application in contemporary British psychology. *Brit. J. Psychol.* **32**, 267–86; **33**, 58–64; **33**, 113–29; **33**, 143–9.

PARE, C. B. M. (1956). Acetyl choline as a therapeutic agent in mild psychiatric disorders. *J. Ment. Sci.* **102**, 847–50.

PAVLOV, I. P. (1927). *Conditioned Reflexes.* Oxford University Press.

PETERS, R. W. (1954a). Competing messages: the effect of interfering messages upon the reception of primary messages. *U.S. N. School of Aviat. Med. Project* NM00106401 *Report* No. 27.

PETERS, R. W. (1954b). Message reception as a function of the time of occurrence of extraneous messages. *U.S. N. School of Aviat. Med. Project* NM00106401 *Report* No. 33.

PETRIE, A. (1952). *Personality and the Frontal Lobes.* Routledge & Kegan Paul.

PIÉRON, H. (1952). *The Sensations.* Miller.

POLLACK, I. (1952). The loudness of bands of noise. *J. acoust. Soc. Amer.* **24**, 533–8.

POLLACK, I. (1953). Assimilation of sequentially encoded information. *Amer. J. Psychol.* **66**, 421–35.

POLLOCK, K. G. and BARTLETT, F. C. (1932). Psychological experiments on the effects of noise. *Industrial Hlth. Research Board Report* No. 65, Part I. H.M. Stationery Office.

POULTON, E. C. (1950). Perceptual anticipation and reaction time. *Quart. J. exp. Psychol.* **2**, 99–112.

POULTON, E. C. (1952a). Perceptual anticipation in tracking, with two pointer and one pointer displays. *Brit. J. Psychol.* **43**, 222–9.

POULTON, E. C. (1952b). The basis of perceptual anticipation in tracking. *Brit. J. Psychol.* **43**, 295–302.

POULTON, E. C. (1953a). Two-channel listening. *J. exp. Psychol.* **46**, 91–6.

POULTON, E. C. (1953b). Memorization during recall. *Brit. J. Psychol.* **44**, 173–6.

POULTON, E. C. (1954). The eye-hand span in simple serial tasks. *J. exp. Psychol.* **47**, 403–10.

POULTON, E. C. (1956). Listening to overlapping calls. *J. exp. Psychol.* **52**, 334–9.

POULTON, E. C. (1957). On prediction in skilled movements. *Psychol. Bull.* **54**, 467–78.

POULTON, E. C. and GREGORY, R. L. (1952). Blinking during visual tracking. *Quart. J. exp. Psychol.* **4**, 57–65.

QUASTLER, H. (1956). In *Information Theory*. (Edited by E. C. CHERRY.) Butterworth.

RAZRAN, G. (1956). Extinction examined and re-analysed: a new theory. *Psychol. Rev.* **63**, 39–52.

REID, R. L. (1952). A test of sensory preconditioning in pigeons. *Quart. J. exp. Psychol.* **4**, 49–56.

ROBINSON, E. S. and BROWN, M. A. (1926). Effects of serial position upon memorization. *Amer. J. Psychol.* **37**, 538–52.

ROSENBLITH, W. A. (1950). Auditory masking and fatigue. *J. acoust. Soc. Amer.* **22**, 792–800.

ROSENZWEIG, M. R., KRECH, D. and BENNETT, E. L. (1956). Effects of pentobarbital sodium on adaptive behaviour patterns in the rat. *Science* **123**, 371–2.

SALDANHA, E. (1955). An investigation into the effects of prolonged and exacting visual work. *Applied Psychol. Unit Report* No. 243. Cambridge.

SALDANHA, E. (1957). Alternating an exacting visual task with either rest or similar work. *Applied Psychol. Unit Report* No. 289. Cambridge.

SCHUBERT, E. D. and PARKER, C. D. (1955). Addition to Cherry's findings on switching speech between the two ears. *J. acoust. Soc. Amer.* **27**, 792–4.

SEWARD, J. P. (1948). The sign of a symbol: a reply to Professor Allport. *Psychol. Rev.* **55**, 277–96.

SHEFFIELD, F. D. and ROBY, T. B. (1950). Reward value of a non-nutritive sweet taste. *J. comp. physiol. Psychol.* **43**, 471–81.

SHEFFIELD, F. D., WOLFF, J. J. and BACKER, J. (1951). Reward value of copulation without sex drive reduction. *J. comp. physiol. Psychol.* **44**, 3–8.

SHELDON, W. H. and STEVENS, S. S. (1942). *The Varieties of Temperament*. Harper Bros.

SHERIF, M. (1936).   *The Psychology of Social Norms.*   Harper Bros.

SHERRINGTON, C. S. (1906).   *The Integrative Action of the Nervous System.*   Scribner.

SIDDALL, G. J. and ANDERSON, D. M. (1955).   Fatigue during prolonged performance on a simple compensatory tracking task. *Quart. J. exp. Psychol.* **7,** 159–65.

SINGER, B. R. (1956).   An experimental inquiry into the concept of perceptual defence.   *Brit. J. Psychol.* **47,** 298–311.

SKINNER, B. F. (1938).   *The Behavior of Organisms.*   Appleton-Century.

SOLOMONS, L. M. (1899).   Automatic reactions.   *Psychol. Rev.* **6,** 376–94.

SPENCE, K. W. (1940).   Continuous versus non-continuous interpretations of discrimination learning.   *Psychol. Rev.* **47,** 271–88.

SPENCE, K. W. and TAYLOR, J. A. (1951).   Anxiety and strength of the UCS as determiners of the amount of eyelid conditioning.   *J. exp. Psychol.* **42,** 183–8.

SPIETH, W., CURTIS, J. F. and WEBSTER, J. C. (1954).   Responding to one of two simultaneous messages.   *J. acoust. Soc. Amer.* **26,** 391–6.

SPIETH, W. and WEBSTER, J. C. (1955).   Listening to differentially filtered competing voice messages.   *J. acoust. Soc. Amer.* **27,** 866–71.

STEVENS, S. S. *et al.* (1941).   The effects of noise on psychomotor efficiency.   *U.S. O.S.R.D. Report* No. 274.   Harvard University.

STEVENS, S. S. and DAVIS, H. (1938).   *Hearing.*   Wiley.

STONE, C. P. (1954).   *Annual Review of Psychology.*   Vol. 5.   Stanford.

STRANGE, J. R. (1950).   Latent learning under conditions of high motivation.   *J. comp. physiol. Psychol.* **43,** 194–7.

SUTCLIFF, J. P. (1955).   Task variability and the level of aspiration. *Aust. J. Psychol. Monog. Suppl.* No. 2.   (Seen in abstract only.)

TAYLOR, J. A. (1951).   The relationship of anxiety to the conditioned eyelid response.   *J. exp. Psychol.* **41,** 81–92.

TAYLOR, J. A. and SPENCE, K. W. (1952).   The relationship of anxiety to performance in serial learning.   *J. exp. Psychol.* **44,** 61–4.

TAYLOR, F. V. and BIRMINGHAM, H. P. (1956).   Simplifying the pilot's task through display quickening.   *J. Aviat. Med.* **27,** 27–31.

TELFORD, C. N. (1931).   Refractory phase of voluntary and associative responses.   *J. exp. Psychol.* **14,** 1–35.

THISTLETHWAITE, D. L. (1951).   A critical review of latent learning and related experiments.   *Psychol. Bull.* **48,** 97–129.

THISTLETHWAITE, D. L. (1952).   Reply to Kendler and Maltzman. *Psychol. Bull.* **49,** 61–71.

TINBERGEN, N. (1951).   *The Study of Instinct.*   Oxford University Press.

TOLHURST, G. C. and PETERS, R. W. (1956).   Effect of attenuating one channel of a dichotic circuit upon the word reception of dual messages.   *J. acoust. Soc. Amer.* **28,** 602–5.

TROTTER, J. R. (1956). The physical properties of bar-pressing behaviour and the problem of reactive inhibition. *Quart. J. exp. Psychol.* **8,** 97–106.

TUFTS COLLEGE (1942). The effects of loud sounds on the accuracy of azimuth tracking and of stereoscopic range-finding. *U.S. National Defense Research Council Report* No. 37.

UNDERWOOD, B. J. (1952). Studies of distributed practice: VI. The influence of rest-interval activity in learning. *J. exp. Psychol.* **43,** 329–40.

UNDERWOOD, B. J. (1953). Studies of distributed practice: XI. An attempt to resolve conflicting facts on the retention of serial nonsense lists. *J. exp. Psychol.* **45,** 355–9.

UNDERWOOD, B. J. and RICHARDSON, J. (1955). Studies of distributed practice: XIII. Interlist interference and the retention of serial nonsense lists. *J. exp. Psychol.* **50,** 39–48.

UTTLEY, A. M. (1955). The conditional probability of signals in the nervous system. *Radar Research Establishment Memo.* No. 1109.

VENABLES, P. H. (1955). Changes in motor response with increase and decrease in task difficulty in normal industrial and psychiatric patient subjects. *Brit. J. Psychol.* **46,** 101–10.

VENABLES, P. H. and TIZARD, J. (1956a). The effect of stimulus light intensity on reaction time of schizophrenics. *Brit. J. Psychol.* **47,** 144–6.

VENABLES, P. H. and TIZARD, J. (1956b). Performance of functional psychotics on a repetitive task. *J. abn. soc. Psychol.* **53,** 23–6.

VERNON, M. D. (1931). *The Experimental Study of Reading.* Cambridge University Press.

VERNON, M. D. (1952). *A Further Study of Visual Perception.* Cambridge University Press.

VERNON, P. E. (1939). Educational abilities of training course students. *Brit. J. educ. Psychol.* **23,** 89–91.

VINCE, M. A. (1948). The intermittency of control movements and the psychological refractory period. *Brit. J. Psychol.* **38,** 149–57.

VINCE, M. A. (1950). Learning and retention of an 'unexpected' control-display relation under stress conditions. *Applied Psychol. Unit Report* No. 125. Cambridge.

VITELES, M. S. and SMITH, K. R. (1946). An experimental investigation of the effect of change in atmospheric conditions and noise upon performance. *Trans. Amer. Soc. Heat. Vent. Engrs.* **52** (1291), 167–82.

VON FOERSTER, H. (1952). *Cybernetics.* Josiah Macy.

WALKER, E. L., DEMBER, W. N., EARL, R. W., FLIEGE, S. E. and KAROLY, A. J. (1955). Choice alternation: II. Exposure to stimulus or stimulus and place, without choice. *J. comp. physiol. Psychol.* **48,** 24–8.

WATSON, R. H. J. (1955). Environmental conditions and behaviour: effects of drugs. *Bull. Brit. Psychol. Soc.* No. 26.

WEBSTER, J. C. and THOMPSON, P. O. (1953). Some audio considerations in air control towers. *J. audio. Engng. Soc.* **1**, 171–5.

WEBSTER, J. C. and THOMPSON, P. O. (1954). Responding to both of two overlapping messages. *J. acoust. Soc. Amer.* **26**, 396–402.

WEBSTER, J. C. and SHARPE, L. (1955). Improvement in message reception resulting from sequencing competing messages. *J. acoust. Soc. Amer.* **27**, 1194–8.

WEBSTER, J. C. and SOLOMON, L. N. (1955). Effects of response complexity upon listening to competing messages. *J. acoust. Soc. Amer.* **27**, 1199–203.

WELCH, L. and KUBIS, J. (1947a). The effect of anxiety on the conditioning rate and stability of PGR. *J. Psychol.* **23**, 83–91.

WELCH, L. and KUBIS, J. (1947b). Conditioned PGR (psychogalvanic response) in states of pathological anxiety. *J. nerv. ment. Dis.* **105**, 372–81.

WELFORD, A. T. (1951). *Skill and Age.* Oxford University Press.

WELFORD, A. T. (1952). The 'psychological refractory period' and the timing of high-speed performance—a review and a theory. *Brit. J. Psychol.* **43**, 2–19.

WELFORD, A. T., BROWN, R. and GABB, J. E. (1950). Two experiments on fatigue as affecting skilled performance in civilian aircrew. *Brit. J. Psychol.* **40**, 195–211.

WESTON, H. C. and ADAMS, S. (1932). The effect of noise on the performance of weavers. *Industrial Hlth. Research Board Report* No. 65, Part II. H.M. Stationery Office.

WESTON, H. C. and ADAMS, S. (1935). The performance of weavers under varying conditions of noise. *Industrial Hlth. Research Board Report* No. 70. H.M. Stationery Office.

WEVER, E. G. (1949). *Theory of Hearing.* Wiley.

WHITTENBURG, J. A., ROSS, S. and ANDREWS, T. G. (1956). Sustained perceptual efficiency as measured by the Mackworth Clock Test. *Percep. and Motor Skills.* **6**, 109–16.

WILKINSON, R. T. (1957). *The Effects of Lack of Sleep.* Doctoral Thesis, University of Cambridge. See also *Applied Psychol. Unit Report* No. 323.

WOODHEAD, M. M. (1956). Effects of bursts of loud noise on a visual task. *Royal Navy Personnel Research Committee Report* No. 56/875.

WOODWORTH, R. S. (1938). *Experimental Psychology.* Holt.

WYATT, S. and LANGDON, J. N. (1932). Inspection processes in industry. *Industrial Hlth. Research Board Report* No. 63. H.M. Stationery Office.

# NAME INDEX

ABORN, M., 229, 317
ADAMS, J. A., 112, 138, 190, 317
ADAMS, S., 81, 82, 103, 332
ADRIAN, E. D., 7, 317
ALBRIGHT, L. E., 138, 317
ANDERSON, D. M., 137, 330
ANDJUS, R. K., 207, 311, 317
ANDREWS, T. G., 113, 127, 132, 136, 332
ANGER, D. J., 203, 317

BACKER, J., 10, 329
BAHRICK, H. P., 56, 286, 317
BAKAN, M. B., 238, 319
BAKAN, P., 113, 114, 233, 317
BAKER, C. H., 116, 123, 148, 317
BAKER, K. E., 56, 317
BARTLETT, F. C., 7, 8, 53, 61, 64, 65, 67, 83, 101, 136, 317, 328
BATES, J. A. V., 51, 324
BENNETT, E. L., 162, 163, 164, 326, 329
BENSON, R. W., 70, 324
BERLYNE, D. E., 85, 174, 245, 246, 266, 307, 317
BERRIEN, F. K., 81, 82, 318
BERTSCH, W. F., 29, 318
BEXTON, W. H., 125, 318
BILLS, A. G., 128, 129, 288, 318
BINDRA, D., 151, 318
BIRMINGHAM, H. P., 277, 292, 318, 320, 330
BLUM, J. S., 249, 250, 251, 318
BLUM, R. A., 249, 250, 251, 318
BORRESON, C. R., 138, 317
BORST, J. M., 279, 320
BOURNE, L. E., 128, 318
BOWEN, H. M., 115, 121, 122, 131, 318
BRICKER, P. D., 52, 318
BROADBENT, D. E., 11, 14, 21, 25, 28, 29, 30, 32, 44, 45, 56, 72, 75, 76, 81, 92, 94, 96, 98, 100, 104, 114, 129, 133, 144, 145, 147, 160, 176, 177, 196, 197, 210, 212, 213, 221, 227, 230, 249, 251, 267, 286, 307, 318, 319
BROGDEN, W. J., 244, 319
BROUSSARD, I. G., 94, 319
BROWN, J., 218, 225, 226, 234, 319
BROWN, J. S., 175, 319
BROWN, M. A., 218, 329
BROWN, R., 101, 160, 332
BRYAN, W. L., 282, 319
BURNISTON BROWN, G., 303, 312, 319
BUXTON, C. E., 238, 319

CARTERETTE, E. C., 20, 21, 22, 321
CHAPANIS, A., 52, 294, 318, 319
CHERNIKOFF, R., 277, 320
CHERRY, E. C., 14, 22, 23, 44, 213, 214, 228, 279, 280, 320
CHOCHOLLE, R., 100, 320
CONRAD, R., 29, 136, 236, 288, 289, 290, 320
COOPER, F. S., 279, 320, 327
COTTON, J. W., 310, 320
COX, D. R., 290, 320
CRAIK, K. J. W., 268, 277, 320
CROSSMAN, E. R. F. W., 78, 118, 320
CULPIN, M., 103, 320
CURTIS, J. F., 22, 24, 26, 27, 28, 42, 330

DAVIS, D. R., 156, 320
DAVIS, H., 1, 12, 70, 323, 324, 330
DAVIS, R., 268, 270, 272, 273, 274, 275, 278, 281, 320, 321
DEESE, J., 112, 116, 117, 118, 121, 122, 131, 160, 189, 321
DELATTRE, P., 279, 320, 327
DEMBER, W. N., 176, 199, 331
DEUTSCH, J. A., 1, 10, 180, 257, 260, 261, 262, 263, 264, 265, 267, 321
DREW, G. C., 96, 136, 321
DUNCAN, C. P., 154, 321
DUNLAP, K., 293, 321

EARL, R. W., 176, 199, 331
ECCLES, J. C., 126, 321
EGAN, J. P., 20, 21, 22, 321
EHRENFREUND, D., 251, 321
ELDERT, E., 70, 324
ELITHORN, A., 272, 273, 274, 276, 321
ELLIOTT, E., 115, 119, 233, 321
ERIKSEN, C. W., 304, 323
ESTES, W. K., 183, 321
EYSENCK, H. J., 73, 140, 142, 144, 150, 152, 153, 154, 155, 157, 159, 161, 162, 165, 167, 321, 322

FANO, R. M., 293, 322
FARRELL, B. A., 305, 322
FERSTER, C. B., 203, 322
FESSARD, A., 100, 322
FINKLE, A. L., 83, 322
FITCH, F. B., 236, 237, 308, 310, 325
FITTS, P. M., 56, 278, 286, 294, 317, 322, 328
FLESCH, R., 33, 322
FLETCHER, H., 1, 13, 69, 322
FLIEGE, S. E., 176, 199, 331

333

FLOYD, W. F., 6, 322
FORD, A., 83, 322
FORD, H. K., 76, 319
FOULDS, G. A., 157, 160, 165, 322
FRANKS, C. M., 150, 152, 161, 322
FRASER, D. C., 111, 112, 114, 119, 322

GABB, J. E., 101, 160, 332
GAGNE, R. M., 56, 138, 204, 317, 323
GALAMBOS, R., 12, 18, 305, 323
GARNER, W. R., 294, 304, 319, 323
GARVEY, W. D., 295, 323
GERSTMAN, L. J., 279, 320
GIBBS, C. B., 30, 293, 294, 323
GILLESPIE, R. D., 153, 324
GLANZER, M., 176, 323
GLEITMAN, H., 260, 262, 323
GOUGH, H. G., 153, 323
GREGORY, R. L., 5, 96, 279, 280, 323, 329
GUTHRIE, E. R., 59

HAKE, H. W., 304, 323
HALL, M., 236, 237, 308, 310, 325
HAMILTON, J. A., 206, 323
HARMON, F. L., 83, 323
HARTER, W., 282, 319
HEAD, H., 63, 324
HEARNSHAW, L. S., 168, 324
HEBB, D. O., 126, 127, 211, 306, 324
HEISE, G. A., 13, 327
HELPER, M. M., 127, 324
HELSON, H., 173, 275, 324
HENDERSON, D. K., 153, 324
HERNADEZ-PEON, R., 305, 324
HERON, A., 147, 160, 324
HERON, W., 125, 318
HICK, W. E., 51, 78, 85, 118, 269, 271, 273, 280, 324
HILGARD, E. R., 9, 151, 180, 266, 307, 310, 313, 324
HILLE, B. A., 29, 136, 289, 290, 320
HINDE, R. A., 167, 324
HIRSH, I. J., 19, 25, 70, 324
HOFFMAN, A. C., 137, 324
HOLLAND, J. G., 124, 131, 205, 325
HOVLAND, C. I., 236, 237, 308, 310, 325
HOWES, D. H., 53, 325
HULL, C. L., 3, 6, 8, 9, 49, 55, 56, 59, 151, 175, 236, 237, 241, 245, 307, 308, 310, 312, 313, 314, 325
HUNT, W. A., 84, 326
HUNTER, W. S., 46, 325
HURWITZ, H. M. B., 132, 176, 177, 178, 199, 203, 325
HUSBAND, R. W., 240, 325
HYMAN, R., 78, 85, 118, 325

IRVINE, D. M., 143, 325
IRWIN, J. McQ., 241, 327

JACKSON, W., 69, 325
JAMES, W., 55, 56, 58, 301, 325
JEANTHEAU, G., 92, 327
JENKINS, W. O., 122, 194, 256, 325
JERISON, H. J., 93, 94, 96, 102, 103, 104, 325
JONES, L. V., 151, 324
JOUVET, M., 305, 324

KAPLAN, S. J., 151, 324
KAPPAUF, W. E., 114, 326
KAROLY, A. J., 176, 199, 331
KAY, H., 57, 218, 219, 220, 222, 237, 326
KEENAN, J., 160, 321
KENDALL, J. W., 176, 199, 326
KENDLER, H. H., 255, 326
KIMBLE, G. A., 176, 199, 326
KINNAMAN, A. J., 47, 326
KLEIN, G. S., 161, 326
KLEITMAN, N., 119, 326
KLEMMER, E. T., 275, 326
KLUMPP, R. G., 29, 318
KNOPFELMACHER, F., 207, 311, 317
KOCK, W. E., 20, 326
KONORSKI, J., 4, 183, 184, 185, 186, 187, 195, 201, 205, 326
KRECH, D., 161, 162, 163, 164, 326, 329
KRECHEVSKY, I., 163, 206, 323, 326
KRUECKEL, B., 162, 326
KRUEGER, W. C. F., 237, 326
KRYTER, K. D., 81, 82, 101, 326
KUBIS, J., 150, 332
KUCHARSKI, P., 100, 322

LABERGE, D. L., 219, 221, 222, 223, 224, 225, 326
LANDIS, C., 84, 326
LANGDON, J. N., 125, 332
LASHLEY, K. S., 249, 326
LAVERTY, S. G., 161, 322
LAWRENCE, C., 272, 273, 274, 275, 321
LAWRENCE, D. H., 219, 221, 222, 223, 224, 225, 250, 326
LAZARUS, R. S., 52, 53, 160, 321, 327
LEE, B. S., 23, 327
LEONARD, J. A., 94, 282, 327
LIBERMAN, A. M., 279, 320, 327
LICHTEN, W., 13, 327
LICKLIDER, J. C. R., 19, 214, 327
LOEB, M., 92, 324
LONG, J. R., 260, 327
LYNN, R., 153, 327

MACKWORTH, J. F., 290, 327
MACKWORTH, N. H., 110, 111, 117, 143, 232, 233, 290, 327
MAIER, N. R. F., 49, 327
MARQUIS, D. G., 180, 324
MARX, M. H., 138, 317
MASON, W. A., 250, 326
MEAD, L. C., 137, 324
MELTON, A. W., 241, 327
MICHOTTE, A., 2, 327
MILLER, G. A., 1, 13, 214, 228, 229, 327
MONTGOMERY, K. C., 245, 328
MORGAN, C. T., 294, 319
MORGAN, J. J. B., 83, 294, 328
MOWBRAY, G. H., 33, 34, 41, 231, 328
MOWRER, O. H., 157, 274, 328
MACQUARRY, J. P., 153, 327
McINTYRE, A. K., 126, 321
McGINNIES, E., 53, 327
McLEARY, R. A., 52, 53, 327
McNAMARA, H. J., 260, 327

NOBLE, M., 56, 277, 286, 317, 328
NORTH, J. D., 278, 328

OLDFIELD, R. C., 62, 63, 64, 328

PARE, C. M. B., 162, 328
PARKER, C. D., 214, 329
PATERSON, A. L., 151, 318
PAVLOV, I. P., 8, 140, 144, 175, 182, 183, 185, 186, 187, 192, 193, 194, 195, 196, 201, 204, 206, 208, 247, 248, 328
PAYNE, M. C., 114, 326
PERKINS, D. T., 236, 237, 308, 310, 325
PETERS, R. W., 18, 20, 328, 330
PETRIE, A., 161, 328
PIERON, H., 100, 328
POLLACK, I., 103, 228, 328
POLLOCK, K. G., 83, 328
POPPEN, J. R., 83, 322
POULTON, E. C., 14, 15, 16, 17, 24, 26, 27, 28, 30, 32, 41, 55, 84, 96, 218, 219, 220, 222, 235, 237, 269, 272, 277, 283, 284, 285, 287, 326, 328, 329
POWE, W., 114, 326

QUASTLER, H., 270, 293, 329

RAZRAN, G., 187, 197, 198, 329
REID, R. L., 253, 329
REYNOLDS, E. G., 70, 324

RICHARDSON, J., 238, 331
ROBERTS, E., 94, 318
ROBINSON, E. S., 218, 329
ROBY, T. B., 10, 329
ROSENBLITH, W. A., 12, 18, 323, 329
ROSENZWEIG, M. R., 18, 162, 163, 164, 323, 326, 329
ROSS, R. T., 236, 237, 308, 310, 325
ROSS, S., 113, 127, 132, 136, 332
RUBENSTEIN, H., 229, 317
RUSSELL, R. W., 162, 207, 311, 317

SALDANHA, E., 137, 329
SCHERRER, H., 305, 324
SCHUBERT, E. D., 214, 329
SCOTT, T. H., 125, 318
SEEGER, C. M., 294, 322
SEWARD, J. P., 3, 46, 329
SHAPIN, M. J., 288, 318
SHARPE, L., 29, 332
SHEATZ, G., 305, 323
SHEFFIELD, F. D., 10, 329
SHELDON, W. H., 159, 329
SHERIF, M., 7, 329
SHERRINGTON, C. S., 2, 4, 330
SIDDALL, G. J., 137, 330
SILVERMAN, S. R., 70, 324
SINGER, B. R., 53, 330
SKINNER, B. F., 59, 124, 201, 203, 204, 322, 330
SMITH, A. N., 207, 311, 317
SMITH, K. R., 89, 331
SMITH, M., 103, 320
SMITH, W. L., 290, 320
SOLOMON, L. N., 25, 27, 31, 332
SOLOMON, R. L., 53, 325
SOLOMONS, L. M., 55, 330
SPENCE, K. W., 150, 151, 152, 153, 156, 164, 266, 316, 330
SPIETH, W., 22, 24, 26, 27, 28, 42, 330
STANLEY, J. C., 194, 256, 325
STEVENS, S. S., 1, 83, 87, 159, 329, 330
STONE, C. P., 10, 330
STRANGE, J. R., 262, 330
STRZELECKI, J., 151, 318
SUTCLIFF, J. P., 170, 330

TAYLOR, F. V., 277, 292, 318, 320, 330
TAYLOR, J. A., 150, 164, 330
TAYLOR, W. K., 213, 214, 279, 280, 320
TELFORD, C. N., 269, 330
THISTLETHWAITE, D. L., 255, 330
THOMPSON, P. O., 15, 17, 24, 28, 29, 41, 318, 332
THWING, E. J., 20, 21, 22, 321
TINBERGEN, N., 2, 37, 330
TIZARD, J., 159, 196, 331

TOLHURST, G. C., 18, 330
TROTTER, J. R., 177, 331

UNDERWOOD, B. J., 238, 331
UTTLEY, A. M., 179, 180, 182, 183, 184, 185, 186, 187, 189, 193, 195, 197, 198, 200, 201, 209, 244, 256, 262, 263, 267, 331

VENABLES, P. H., 158, 159, 162, 171, 196, 331
VERNIER, V. G., 305, 323
VERNON, M. D., 1, 153, 282, 332
VERNON, P. E., 153, 331
VINCE, M. A., 268, 295, 331
VITELES, M. S., 89, 331
VON FOERSTER, H., 3, 5, 331
VON LACKUM, W. J., 24, 327

WALKER, R. Y., 94, 176, 199, 319
WARREN, C. E., 278, 328
WATSON, R. H. J., 162, 331

WEAVER, L. A., 92, 327
WEBSTER, J. C., 15, 17, 22, 24, 25, 26, 27, 28, 29, 31, 41, 42, 318, 330, 332
WELCH, L., 150, 332
WELFORD, A. T., 6, 101, 160, 268, 269, 270, 271, 272, 273, 275, 276, 278, 280, 281, 322, 324, 332
WELLS, G. R., 293, 321
WESTON, H. C., 81, 82, 103, 332
WEVER, E. G., 1, 332
WHITTENBURG, J. A., 113, 127, 132, 136, 332
WIKE, E. L., 260, 327
WILKINSON, R. T., 104, 121, 122, 123, 127, 136, 148, 149, 166, 332
WING, S., 93, 325
WOLFF, J. J., 10, 329
WOODHEAD, M. M., 87, 332
WOODWORTH, R. S., 241, 332
WYATT, S., 125, 332
WYLIE, R. C., 56, 317

ZANGWILL, O. L., 62, 63, 64, 328

# SUBJECT INDEX

Activation, 119, 125–128, 289
Analyser–link theory, 257–265
Anticipation, 32, 96, 282–287
Anxiety, 151–154
Attention,
  division and alternation of, 34, 47, 58, 108
  time taken to shift, 212–215, 299
Automatization,
  see Practice
Behaviour theory,
  see S–R theory
Blinking, 96
Blocking of performance, 128–132, 177, 232, 239
Capacity, 5, 6, 35, 40, 48, 60, 85, 120, 263, 271, 291, 297
Cholinesterase, 162–164
Coding, 40, 44, 292–295
Communication theory, 5, 15, 29, 31, 33, 36, 39, 56, 78, 85, 118, 187, 304, 311
Compatibility of stimulus and response, 294
Conditional probabilities, 179–187, 198, 199, 204, 244, 252, 253, 262, 298
Conditioning,
  classical, 140, 171–187
  instrumental, 124–125, 177, 201–205
  see also S–R theory
Consciousness, 65
Continuity controversy,
  see Hypothesis behaviour
Control–display relations, 292–295
Counter-conditioning, 178–187, 197, 200
Decaying trace theory, 225–231
Disinhibition, 117, 175, 180, 182, 193, 199, 201, 203, 204, 205–209
Expectancy, 118, 119, 122–125, 272–277
External inhibition, 180, 182, 194, 196, 200
Extraversion,
  and conditioning, 150–153, 172
  and figural after-effects, 154, 155, 172
  and prolonged work, 152–157
  and reactive inhibition, 140, 143, 161, 165–167, 181–182
  and stress, 157–161
  and vigilance tasks, 143–150

Fatigue, perceptual versus motor, 135–138
Filtering of sensory information, 41, 47, 53, 61, 85, 120, 128, 132–134, 138, 174, 190–196, 198, 231, 251–256, 297
Gestalt, 5, 60
Hypothesis behaviour, 162, 163, 249–251
Immediate memory, 103, 104, 207–209, 210–243
Induction (in conditioning), 184–186, 194
Information,
  see Communication theory
Inhibition,
  as a theory of extinction, 175–178, 184, 187–190, 197, 200
  as a theory of vigilance, 116–118, 121, 122
Introspection, 48, 55, 58
Latent learning, 244, 254, 255, 261–264
Level of aspiration, 169–171
Localization of loudspeakers,
  see Multi-channel listening
Motivation, 7, 59, 111, 298
Multi-channel listening,
  as affected by information presented, 14, 15, 16, 17, 23, 27, 29, 30, 33, 41
  as affected by localization, 15, 17, 18, 22, 24–26, 75–77, 210
  as affected by spectral filtering, 15, 20, 21, 22, 26, 213
  as showing effects other than masking, 11–14, 41
Noise,
  high and low pitch, 98–102
  industrial studies, 81–83
  long-term studies, 86–96
  practical conclusions, 104, 105
  short-term studies, 83–86
  theory, 96–98
Novelty of stimuli, 84, 85, 246, 298
Overlearning, 241
Pacing, 288–290
Perceptual defence, 53
Practice, 31–33, 35, 55–57, 83, 286
Psychological refractory period, 268–282
Radar, 108, 109, 112, 116
Reflexes and attention, 4, 6
Rehearsal,
  see Decaying trace theory

337

Reinforcement, 9, 10, 175, 193, 244–247, 251–256, 301

S–R theory, 8, 31, 35, 59, 61, 66, 256, 260, 265, 266, 292, 304, 305, 307, 314, 315

Sampling time in information handling, 168–173, 214, 278–282, 299

Schema theory, 62–67

Scientific method, 7, 167, 237, 255, 302–316

Serial order in memory, 217–221, 234–237

Set, 218, 219, 221–223, 237

Speech,
  and bodily response, 49–57

Speech,
  as peculiar to man, 3, 45
  intelligibility and other qualities, 68
  transposition of frequency, 70–75

Speed and load, 287–291

Spontaneous recovery, 175, 181, 193, 198

Stimulus dynamisms, 247–251.

Stimulus satiation, 176

Tracking, 32, 73–77, 87, 88, 137, 268, 269, 277, 278, 281, 285

Vigilance tasks,
  auditory, 110, 114, 115
  clock test type, 109–113
  non-clock test type, 113–116

Vision and hearing, 2, 33, 70–77, 215